DREAMWEAVER 3
for PC/MAC

DREAMWEAVER 3

Dreamweaver is a registered trademark of Macromedia.

Windows is a registered trademark of Microsoft Corporation. Macintosh is a registered trademark of Apple Computer, inc. All other trademarks quoted are the property of their respective editors.

All rights reserved. No part of this publication may be reproduced, stored in a retrieval system, or transmitted, in any form, or by any means, electronic, mechanical, photocopying, recording or otherwise, without the prior permission of the publishers.

Copyright - Editions ENI - July 2000
ISBN: 2-7460-1077-1
Original edition: 2-7460-1026-7

ENI Publishing LTD

500 Chiswick High Road
London W4 5RG

Tel: 020 8956 2320
Fax: 020 8956 2321

e-mail: publishing@ediENI.com
http://www.eni-publishing.com

Editions ENI

BP 32125
44021 NANTES Cedex 1

Tel: (33) 2.51.80.15.15
Fax: (33) 2.51.80.15.16

e-mail: editions@ediENI.com
http://www.editions-eni.com

Studio Factory collection directed by Corinne HERVO
Author: Christophe AUBRY
Translated from the French by Elisabeth BLAMIRE

Foreword

This book is for anyone who uses the Dreamweaver 3 Web site creation application, on a PC or Macintosh. It has been designed so that you can look up the task you want to perform and find a clear description of how to go about it. Throughout the book, screen shots showing relevant examples or dialog boxes are used to illustrate the explanations.

In each chapter you will find detailed explanations of Dreamweaver functions associated with particular topics, from the basic functions (such as creating pages, lists, images, tables and links) to the more advanced functions (including cascading style sheets, behaviors, and optimising the HTML code).

At the end of the book you will find a glossary and index.

Typographic conventions

To help you find the information you need quickly and easily, the following conventions have been adopted:

bold indicates the option to take in a menu or dialog box.

italics is used for introductory and explanatory comments.

[Ctrl] represents a key from the keyboard. When two keys appear side by side, they should be pressed simultaneously.

The following symbols indicate:

the action to be carried out (such as activating a button or clicking with the mouse).

a general comment about the command in question.

Table of contents

Introduction
Internet, HTML and W3C 1

The Dreamweaver interface
The system environment 3
The windows 3
The status bar 9
Browsers 11
Saving documents 12
The History 12
Customising the interface 15
Context menus 16
Shortcut keys 17

Your first page
Defining the site 18
Page properties 20
The page title 21
The page background 21
Defining the default colours 22
Margins 22
Character encoding 23
Using a design template 24

Inserting/presenting text
Text or inserting text: principle 25
Creating paragraphs 25
Special characters 27
Managing the lines in a paragraph 28
Formatting paragraphs 28
Defining divisions 31
Preformatted text 31
Finding and replacing text 32
Spelling 36

©Editions ENI - All rights reserved

Table of contents

Lists
Principle. 38
Bulleted lists 38
Numbered lists. 40
Creating nested lists 42
Changing the list type. 43
Creating a definition list 43

Formatting text
General principles. 45
Applying character formatting. 45
Choosing the character font 47
Choosing the character size 51
Applying colour to characters 53
Saving formatting in a style 54
Defining the default display characters 57

Horizontal rules
Principle. 58
Inserting a horizontal rule. 58
Formatting a horizontal rule 58

Images
Principle. 60
Image formats 60
Image file paths 60
Inserting an image 62
Defining the image's properties. 63
Formatting an image. 64
Using an external image editor 68
Using Macromedia® Fireworks 69
Defining image behaviors. 71

Tables
Principles for using tables. 74
Inserting a table. 75
Formatting a table 79
Changing the structure of a table 86

Table of contents

Forms
Principle 91
Creating a form. 92
Adding objects to a form 93
Verifying a form's validity 102

Inserting objects
Principle 107
Inserting the date 108
Inserting a Flash movie 109
Inserting a Shockwave movie 110
Inserting Generator objects 110
Inserting a Fireworks object. 111
Inserting a Java applet 111
Inserting an ActiveX control. 113
Inserting plugin content. 114
Inserting scripts 117
Inserting SSI files 120
Behaviors linked to objects. 122

Layers
Principle 124
Inserting a layer 125
Formatting a layer. 127
Selecting a layer 130
Changing a layer's attributes 131
Creating nested layers. 132
Managing layers 133
Transforming layers into tables and vice-versa. 136
Tracing images 140
Timelines. 142
Behaviors associated with layers 152

Style sheets
Principle 160
CSS-1 in the page. 160
Creating an external style sheet 172
Defining preferences for CSS styles 176
Converting styles. 176

Table of contents

Links
Different types of link 178
Formatting text links 178
Creating links in the same page. 179
Creating page to page links. 181
Jump menus 185
Creating external links 188
Creating links on images. 189
Managing your site's structure. 197
Managing links 201
Checking links. 204

Frame sets
Principle. 208
Creating a frameset 209
Formatting a frameset 213
Formatting frames 215
Construction strategy for framesets. 217
Defining links in a frameset. 218
Defining the frameset-free content 219
Defining behaviors linked to framesets. 220

Libraries and templates
Principles. 224
Using a library 224
Using templates. 231
Exporting data in XML format 240

Behaviors
Principles. 245
Managing behaviors 248
Using a JavaScript. 249
Changing an object's properties 251
Opening a browser window 254
Displaying a message 256
Changing the text in a form field 257
Placing text on the status bar 258
Checking plugins. 259
Checking the browser. 261

Table of contents

Other behaviors. 262
Downloading more behaviors. 263

Optimising HTML code
Why optimise code?. 264
Setting HTML code parameters 264
Visualising code in the page 268
Changing the source code 269
Finding and replacing HTML 276
Cleaning up HTML source code. 282
Showing comments 287
Validating code for browsers 288

Publishing a site
Make yourself known 290
Inserting meta-information. 291
Information about links. 295
Managing the site 297
Publication 302
Teamwork 308

Customising Dreamweaver
The Objects palette. 318
Changing the Commands menu. 320
Customising dialog boxes 323
Customising the menus 325
Customising file types 331
Customising markup tags. 332
Customising the source code format 333
Extending Dreamweaver's functions 335

Glossary. 336

Index. 338

Introduction

Internet, HTML and W3C

The Internet as we know it today is still very young, not even 10 years old! The first Web server appeared in October 1991 in CERN's (European Nuclear Research Council) laboratories on a NeXT computer. The scientists working at CERN and their colleagues in other laboratories around the world wanted to be able to share and consult data rapidly using their computers. What was needed was a language that would be simple to implement, compatible with any platform, and transportable via HTTP. Under the leadership of Tim Berners-Lee and Robert Cailliau the first server and HTML were devised. For users, the green light came from the NCSA (National Center for Supercomputing Applications), where, thanks to Marc Andersen (future founder of Netscape) and Eric Bina, the first commercial browser was created: Mosaic.

HyperText Markup Language is based on computing norms that allow the creation of markup languages: SGML (System Generalized Markup Language). Today, HTML has been completely standardised, and the latest version, 4.01, was released in August 1999 (the first version dates from 1992). Following the Internet's success, the main Internet players have formed a consortium with the aim of proposing standards for Internet languages: the World Wide Web Consortium (W3C) was created in 1995, and has undertaken to recommend the standards for Internet languages such as HTML, CSS, XML, XSL and SMIL.

The W3C site is possibly the most comprehensive site for anyone who wants to create a Web site: http://www.w3.org.

Web site creation software

The first site-builders needed only a text editor, as basic as possible, and knowledge of HTML. Times have changed since then: web site creation programs have become WYSIWYG (What You See Is What You Get). You work in a graphic interface and the software creates the HTML code.

Dreamweaver 3
Introduction

Macromedia Dreamweaver is one of these programs. In addition to HTML code, Dreamweaver can generate DHTML, support style sheets (CSS-1 and CSS-P), and allow you to create dynamic pages using ready-made JavaScripts through the intermediary of Behaviors. Furthermore, you can easily insert your pages into server scripts created using other languages (ASP, PHP and Perl, for instance). Finally, Dreamweaver integrates an FTP (File Transfer Protocol) client so that you can upload your sites to a Web server. To resume, Dreamweaver is software that generates HTML code that is very close to the W3C standard. It is amongst the latest Internet technology and is very complete.

Developing Web sites today is also (to say the least) about creating "visuals", images, animations and programming. For the creation of "visuals", in other words buttons that let you browse a site, logos, banners and other headers, applications such as Macromedia Fireworks and Adobe Illustrator are ideal. Adobe Photoshop and Adobe ImageReady can produce marvels in image retouching, photo editing and optimisation. As for interactive, vector-based movies, Macromedia Flash has become a "must". For programmers who want to create interactivity, dynamically change the appearance of pages, create forms that can ask questions or supply data to databases, they will find what they need to create client and server scripts using JavaScript, Java, ASP, ActiveX, PHP and Perl.

©Editions ENI - All rights reserved

The Dreamweaver interface

The system environment

This book was written using a Windows platform. However, it is also suitable for Macintosh users. Dreamweaver has the same interface on both these operating systems, but the way in which windows are managed differs. In Windows, each document is in a different window with its own menu bar, accessible via the taskbar. The same is true for the site window. In Macintosh, all the documents share the same menu bar. The differences between the two platforms concern mostly the management of the site window, in which case access to both Windows and Macintosh commands will be indicated.

The windows

The main screen

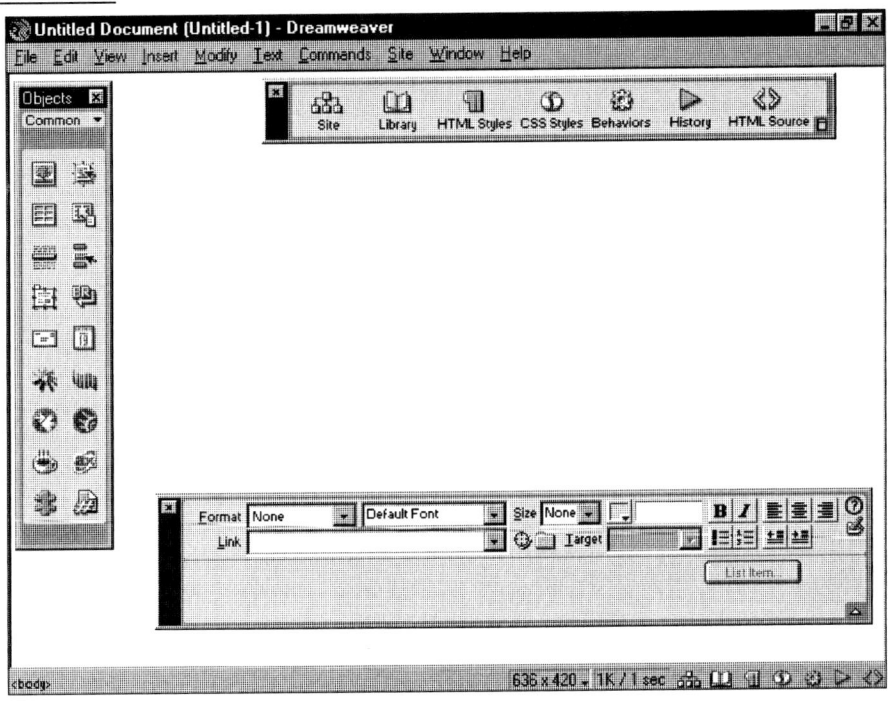

When you start Dreamweaver for the first time, you can see the **Document** window with 3 floating palettes: the **Objects** palette on the left, the **Property inspector** at the bottom and the **Launcher** at the top. At the bottom of the screen you can see the status bar.

©Editions ENI - All rights reserved

Dreamweaver 3
The Dreamweaver interface

The floating palettes

*The floating palettes are all accessible through the **Window** menu. They enable you to access Dreamweaver's essential features rapidly.*

- By default, all the floating palettes are placed on top of the document window. If you want to change this so that the document window can hide a palette, change the settings:

  Edit - Preferences - Floating Palettes category

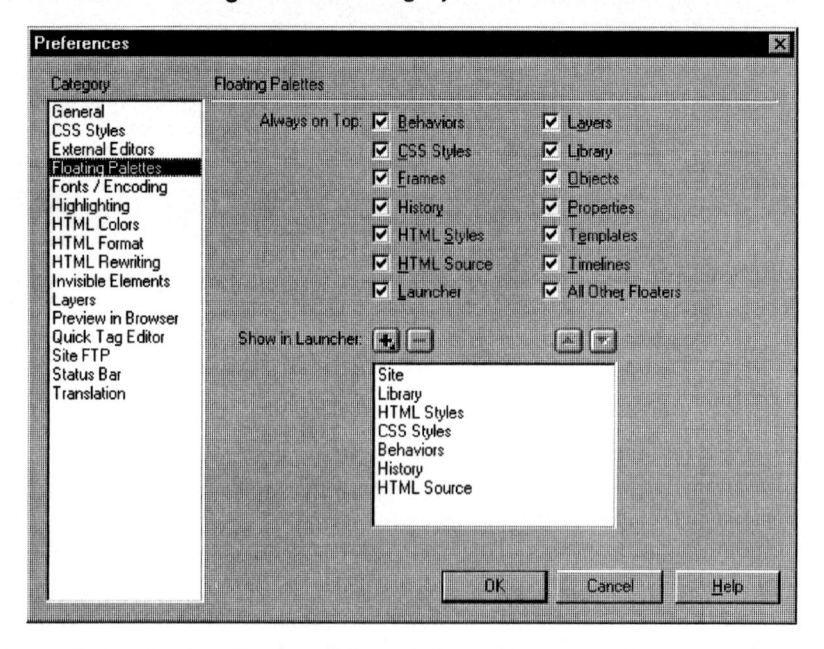

*The **Always on Top** option is active for all the palettes.*

- If you deactivate the **Always on Top** option for the **Objects** palette, for example, as soon as you click in the document window it will come in front of the **Objects** palette. To access the palette, you will need to use the **Window** menu.

  All the palettes can be moved by dragging their title bars. They can also be docked (combined) with other palettes to create one tabbed palette, which can be very useful if you do not have a very big screen.

- To dock palettes together, open several palettes by activating the corresponding options in the **Window** menu.

©Editions ENI - All rights reserved

The Dreamweaver interface

☐ Drag one of the palettes' tabs so that it is placed next to another: the palettes are now combined. Do the same thing for any other palettes on the screen.

These three palettes are independent:

The palettes have been docked together to create one tabbed palette:

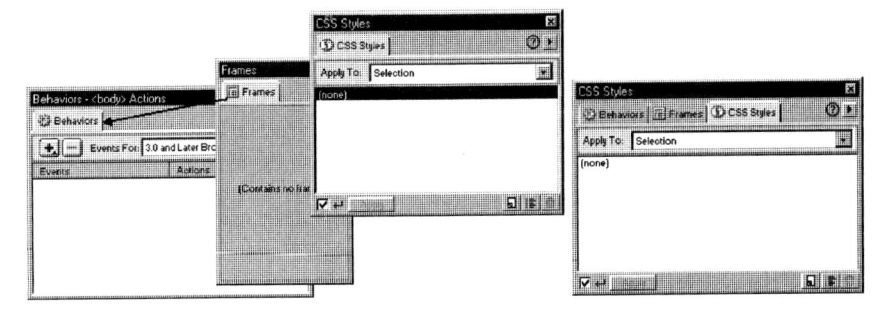

☐ To remove a palette from a tabbed palette, drag its tab out of the window.

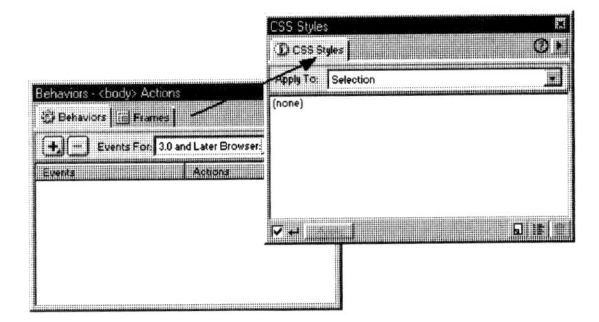

Using palettes

You can access all the palettes using the **Window** menu, but also via the **Launcher** palette.

☐ To show the Launcher: **Window - Launcher**

The Launcher with its default buttons:

©Editions ENI - All rights reserved

Dreamweaver 3
The Dreamweaver interface

- You can show or hide a palette simply by clicking the corresponding button.
- To switch the Launcher's orientation between vertical and horizontal, click the orientation icon .

  You can find all these buttons on the status bar, at the bottom right of the screen, in the Mini-Launcher.

- Make sure the Mini-Launcher is active: **Edit - Preferences - Status Bar** category.
- Activate the **Launcher** option: **Show Mini-Launcher in Status Bar**.
- Make sure that the status bar is displayed: **View - Status Bar**.

  In the right of the status bar you can see the Mini-Launcher, which works in the same way as the Launcher:

  You can customise the Launcher palette and, at the same time, the Mini-Launcher, by adding, deleting and moving buttons on the palette.

- **Edit - Preferences - Floating Palettes category**

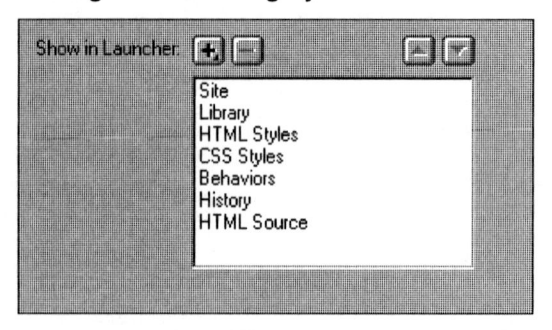

- To add a palette, click the add button then choose the palette.
- To remove a palette, select it then click .
- To move a palette, select it then click either or .

In this book you will always be directed to access the palettes using the **Windows** menu. Of course, you can also use the Launcher or Mini-Launcher. The choice is yours!

The Dreamweaver interface

The Objects palette

The **Objects** palette allows you to insert a whole series of objects into a page, such as images, tables, rollover images, movies, special characters, and forms. At the top of the palette is a pop-up menu that you can use to go to any of the six panels in the palette: **Characters**, **Common** (shown by default), **Forms**, **Frames**, **Head** and **Invisibles**.

*Using the pop-up menu in the **Objects** palette:*

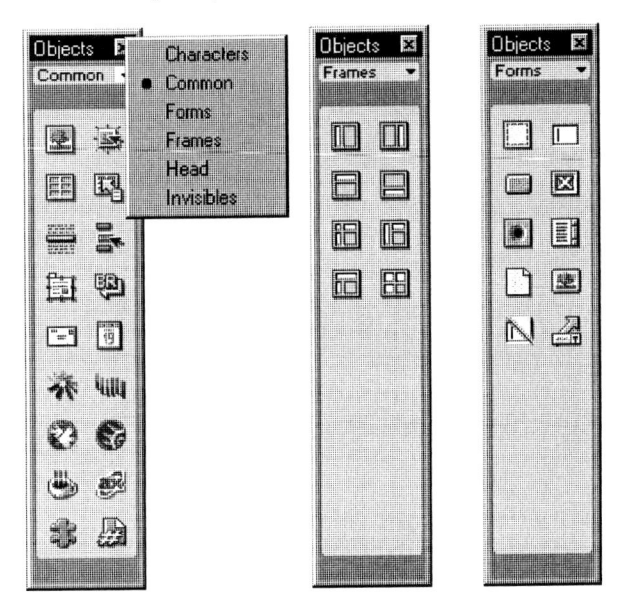

*You can customise the appearance of the **Objects** palette. You can choose to show buttons with only icons or text, or both.*

Edit - Preferences - General category

Choose an option in the **Object Palette** pop-up menu: **Icons Only** (default option), **Icons and Text** or **Text Only**.

©Editions ENI - All rights reserved

The Property inspector

→ The Property inspector allows you to see and edit the properties of an item in a page (such as text, a table or an image). It cannot access all the item's properties, but you can parameter the most commonly used properties.

The Property inspector:

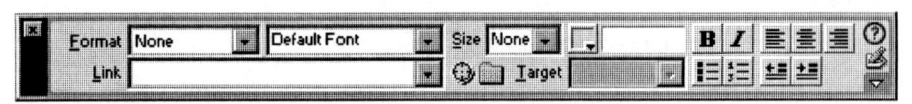

→ To see more properties, click the expander arrow in the bottom right of the Property inspector.

The Property inspector fully expanded:

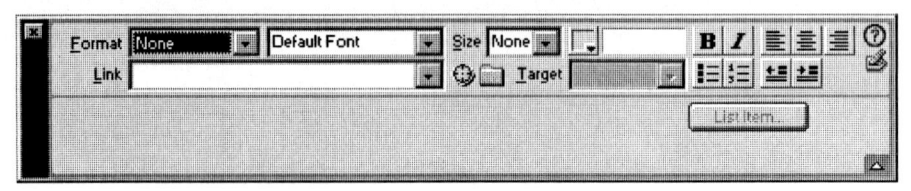

You are advised to leave the Property inspector expanded.

→ The formatting settings in the Property inspector change according to the object that is selected in the page.

The Property inspector for tables:

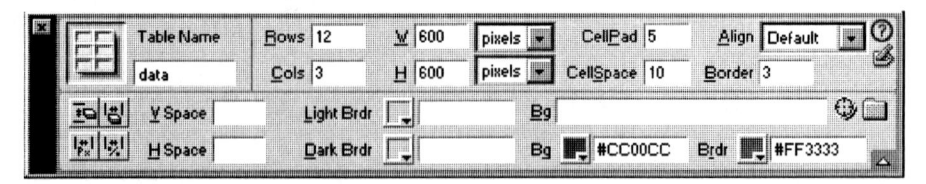

The Property inspector for images:

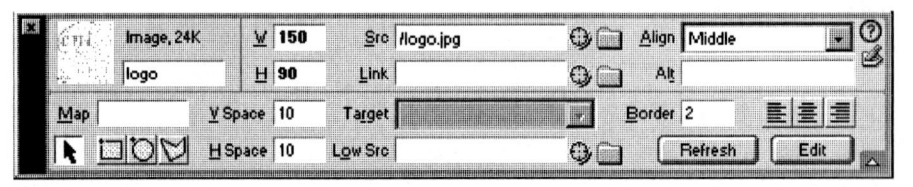

©Editions ENI - All rights reserved

The Dreamweaver interface

The status bar

Showing the status bar

The status bar displays a certain number of parameters: HTML code, the size of the window and the document, the download time and the Mini-Launcher.

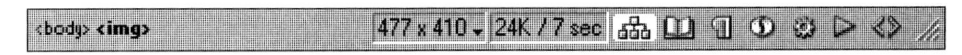

- First make sure that the bar is open: **View - Status Bar**.

The Tag selector

The Tag selector tells you where you are in the HTML code (of course, this means that you need to know HTML code). It is associated with the Quick Tag Editor, which you can use to edit HTML code rapidly in order to optimise your page.

- Dreamweaver shows the HTML code of the item that is selected in bold in the Tag selector.

Example:

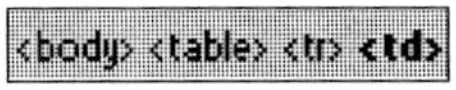

When the insertion point is in the body of the page the `<body>` tag is in bold, when a table is selected, the `<table>` tag is bold, when a row is selected, the `<tr>` tag is bold, and the `<td>` tag is bold when the insertion point is in a cell.

The size of the window

This part of the status bar enables you to change the size of the window rapidly so that you can optimise your page according to the screen sizes of browsers.

- Click this area to open the pop-up menu: 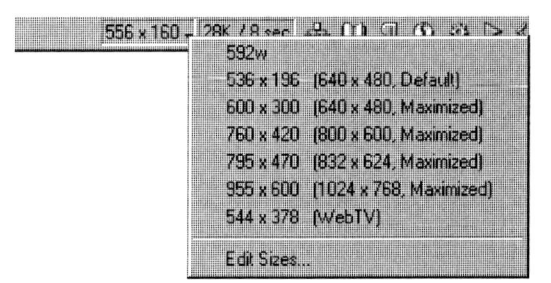

The first pair of values indicates the actual size that is visible in a browser window with no borders, and the second pair indicates the total size of the screen.

- To change these values or create your own screen sizes, click **Edit Sizes** in the screen sizes pop-up menu.

©Editions ENI - All rights reserved

Dreamweaver 3
The Dreamweaver interface

or **Edit - Preferences - Status Bar** category

Window Sizes:	Width	Height	Description
	600	300	(640 x 480, Max...
	760	420	(800 x 600, Max...
	795	470	(832 x 624, Max...
	955	600	(1024 x 768, M...
	544	378	(WebTV)

- Enter the values you want in the **Width** and **Height** text boxes.
- Type any extra information in the **Description** text box.

Document size and download time

When you create a Web site, you must always remember that the longer the text and the more images and movies you include, the longer the download time of a page will be. Do not forget that many surfers are not very patient! Make sure that your pages do not go over 50 K. However, the time it takes for a page to download will vary depending on the connection used, such as RTC, digital, DSL or cable.

- Dreamweaver helps you by telling you how long a page will take to download at modem speed, on the status bar.

    Example:

    24K / 7 sec

    This page's size is 24 K and it will take 7 seconds to download.

- To set the connection speed:

    Edit - Preferences - Status Bar category

- In the **Connection Speed** pop-up menu, choose a connection speed in **Kilobits per Second**.

©Editions ENI - All rights reserved

The Dreamweaver interface

Browsers

It is essential that you check your work in one or more browsers. In fact, each Web browser editor interprets HTML code in its own way. Of course, they must do so according to the W3C recommendations, but browsers do not recognise all HTML items and they sometimes have quite different interpretations! This makes your job as a Web designer much more complicated. In Dreamweaver, you can indicate the browsers in which you want to display and check your pages.

→ **Edit - Preferences - Preview in Browser** category

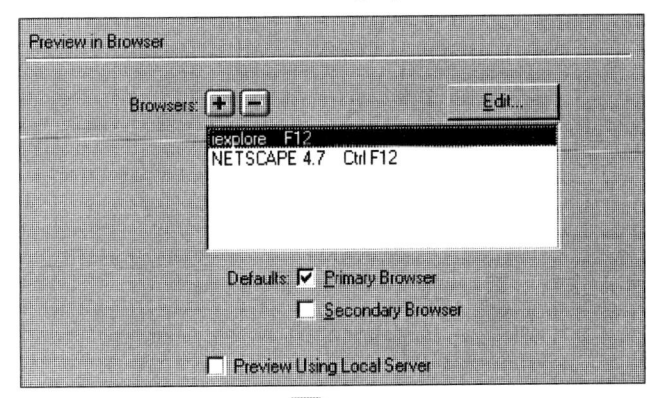

→ To add a browser click the add button [+].

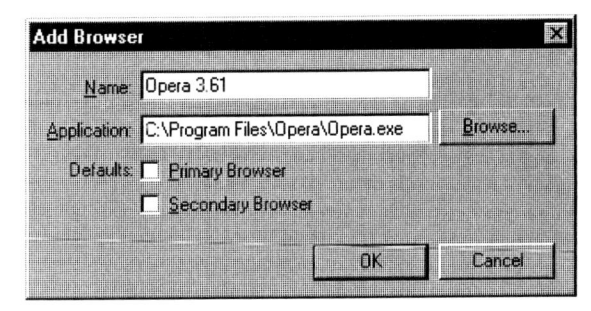

→ Type the name of the browser in the **Name** box, or leave it empty and the name of the program will appear automatically.

→ Type the application's path in the **Application** box, or click the **Browse** button to select the program on your computer.

→ Activate one of the **Defaults** check boxes if the selected browser is to be one of two accessible via keyboard shortcuts. The **Primary Browser** will be accessible via F12 and the **Secondary Browser** via ⌘ F12 (Macintosh) or Ctrl F12 (Windows).

©Editions ENI - All rights reserved

- To see your pages:
  File - Preview in Browser - choose the browser

Saving documents

As with all current applications, there are several ways to save your documents.

- To save: **File - Save**.
- To save a copy: **File - Save As**.
- To save all the open documents: **File - Save All**.
- To return to the document as it was when you last saved it: **File - Revert**.

The History

Principle

- Like all software, Dreamweaver includes the undo command:

  Edit - Undo

  *However, in addition to this function, Dreamweaver uses a history: all your actions are saved in the **History** palette. This means that you can undo several actions at once and return to the previous steps.*

- To set the number of actions saved in the history:

  Edit - Preferences - General category

- Indicate the number of actions to be stored in the history in the **Maximum Number of History Steps** text box (between 2 and 99 999!).

- To see the **History** palette: **Window - History**.

The Dreamweaver interface

Using the History palette

⇨ To undo actions, drag the slider ▷ upwards.

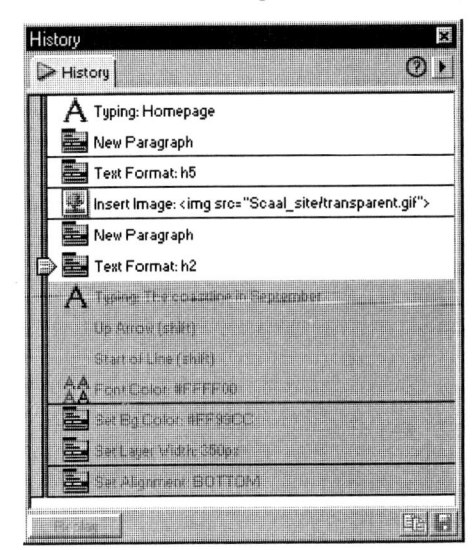

In this example, text and an image have been inserted and formatting applied. Each type of action has its own icon. The steps that have been undone have a grey background.

⇨ You can change your mind and restore the steps you have undone by dragging the slider downward as far as the appropriate step.

Be careful! As soon as you carry out a new action, the greyed steps are permanently deleted!

Automating actions

You can do something once then, just afterwards, do the same thing to other items in your page. For example, if you want to format several headings in the same way, type all the text, format the first heading and then reproduce this formatting on all the headings.

⇨ Type some text then apply some simple formatting.

©Editions ENI - All rights reserved

➭ In the **History** palette, select the steps you want to repeat (the formatting) by dragging:

Some actions cannot be reproduced (such as dragging an item on the page or inserting a frame). When you do these actions, their icon appears in the **History** palette with a red cross:

➭ Select another heading in the document and click the **Replay** button in the **History** palette.

Be careful! You cannot replay steps that are separated by a horizontal line in the **History** palette. A warning message will appear if you try to do so.

➭ To reproduce a series of actions in another document, select, in the first document, the steps you want to reproduce, then click the **Copy selected steps** button in the **History** palette. Go to the second document, select the item to which you want to apply the steps and use **Edit - Paste**.

Recording actions temporarily

You can record repetitive actions that you want to re-use immediately for a short time. This means that you do not have to select these steps in the **History** palette before replaying them, but you can record only one series of actions at a time.

➭ **Commands - Start Recording**

The mouse pointer takes this shape: .

➭ Make the insertions and formatting you want.

©Editions ENI - All rights reserved

The Dreamweaver interface

During recording, there are some things you cannot do with the mouse. Dreamweaver displays a message to tell you this.

- When you have finished your actions: **Commands - Stop Recording**.
- To replay a series of recorded steps:

   Commands - Play Recorded Command

Customising the interface

The palettes

You can change the appearance of the palettes only in Windows.

- **Edit - Preferences - General** category
- In the **Color Scheme** pop-up menu, select the colour of the palettes: **Dreamweaver Two-Tone**, **Desktop Two-Tone** or **Desktop Standard**.

Extension for saving documents

All pages created for the Web should have either .htm or .html as their file extension. Traditionally, the .html extension is for Macintosh and Unix servers, and the .htm extension for Windows servers. The .htm extension is also supported by Unix and Macintosh servers.

- To choose the file extension you want to use when you save documents:

   Edit - Preferences - General category

- To apply one or other extension automatically when you save, activate the **Add Extension when Saving** option and, in the text box, type the appropriate extension.

Opening documents

In Windows, each document is opened in a separate window. You can change this setting.

- **Edit - Preferences - General** category
- If you want only one window for all the documents you open, deactivate the **Open Files in New Window** option.

View at startup

When you start Dreamweaver, you can choose to have the site window open by itself or with a new, empty document.

- **Edit - Preferences - General** category
- If you want both the windows to open when you start Dreamweaver, leave the **Show Only Site Window on Startup** option inactive.

©Editions ENI - All rights reserved

Warning when you open locked files

When a file is locked, in read-only, Dreamweaver can warn you.

- **Edit - Preferences - General** category
- Activate the **Warn when Opening Read-Only Files** option.

This message will appear when you open a locked file:

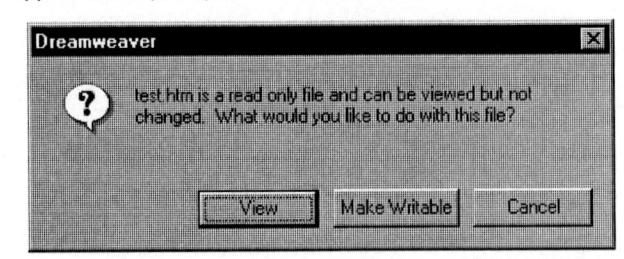

- Click the **View** button to open the document without being able to save any changes you make. Click **Make Writable** to unlock the document when you are publishing it on a server (see the chapter that deals with publishing a Web site).

Context menus

Whether under Windows or Macintosh, context menus are used in many different applications. Dreamweaver offers context menus that give you access to the most frequently used commands, all of which are relative to the selected object.

- In Macintosh, hold down the Ctrl key and click the object.
- In Windows, right-click the object.

In this book you will not necessarily be directed to use context menus, but feel free to use them all the same!

The Dreamweaver interface

Shortcut keys

As is the case for any recent software, Dreamweaver offers numerous shortcut keys. It is useful to learn some of them as soon as you start to use the software because they are essential (and will be indicated systematically throughout this book).

Ctrl F3	shows/hides the Property inspector.
F4	shows/hides all the floating palettes.
F10	shows the HTML Source inspector. This inspector allows you to see the source code of your page so that you can verify the code that is generated, and edit or add to it.
F5	shows all the files in your site. When you create a site that contains several files, you really must organise them properly: create folders in which you can place your HTML files, images, movies, script and so on.
F12	previews your page in the default browser. You should preview your page in a browser frequently. While Dreamweaver is WYSIWYG software, the HTML code will be interpreted differently by different browsers.
Ctrl F12 (Windows) ⇧ ⌘ F12 (Macintosh)	previews your page in the secondary browser. It is always useful to check the appearance of your pages in a second browser.

© Editions ENI - All rights reserved

Defining the site

Principle

When you want to create a Web site, you should start by creating a local site on your machine. You will publish the site only when it is completely finished, when you will make a copy of it on a Web server (see the Publishing a site chapter).

All of the documents that constitute your site should be stored in a folder called a **Local site folder**. These documents might be html pages, images, scripts or movies, for example.

Creating the site

When you open Dreamweaver for the first time, two windows open: a blank, unsaved document and a window for the site map.

- In the empty document window: **Site - New Site**.

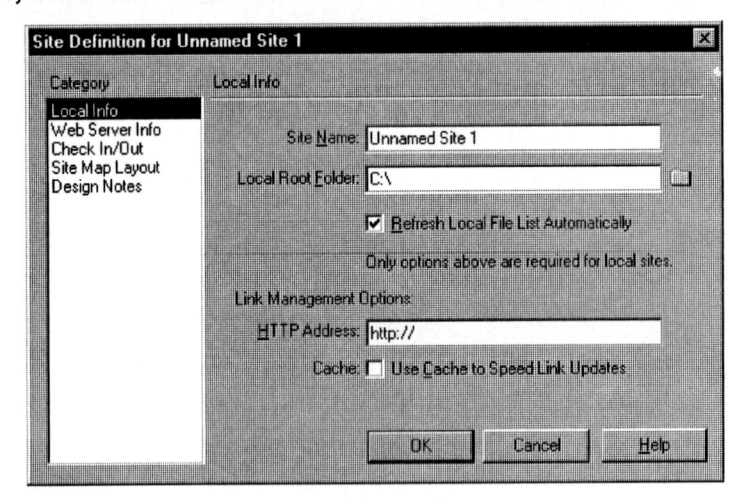

For the moment you need look only at the **Local Info** category.

- Type the name of your site in the **Site Name** text box. This name is for you and Dreamweaver, and has no relation with the publication name on the server.

- In the **Local Root Folder** text box, type the access path or click the folder icon to select a folder on your hard drive in which you will save all the files from your site. If this folder is to be published on the server, it must have the publication name. If only the contents of the folder and not the folder itself are to be published, you can call it what you like.

Your first page

For example, if your domain name is jsbach.org, the local root folder should be jsbach.

- The **Refresh Local File List Automatically** option enables automatic updating of the files in your local folder as soon as you copy files in this local folder.
- The **HTTP Address** text box allows you to give the publication address of your site if you are creating absolute paths (see the chapter about hyperlinks), so that Dreamweaver can check them.
- The **Cache** option enables Dreamweaver to create a cache file which will speed up the creation of hyperlinks in your site. You are advised to use this option.

Saving files

- You should save all the files in your Web site (images, HTML pages, etc) in the local folder in order to avoid creating absolute paths, and to facilitate the management and publication of the site (as all the files are in the same folder).
- Each time you save a document, make sure that you save it in the local folder. If you want to incorporate a file that is not in the root folder of your site, Dreamweaver displays a message to tell you that:

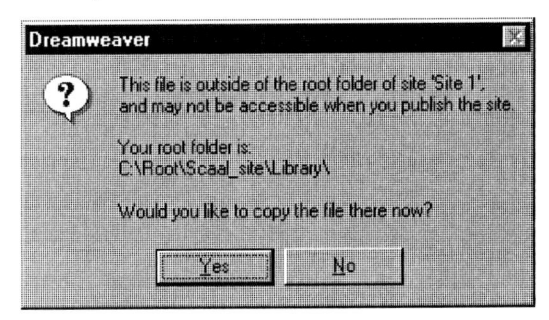

![Dreamweaver dialog: This file is outside of the root folder of site 'Site 1', and may not be accessible when you publish the site. Your root folder is: C:\Root\Scaal_site\Library\ Would you like to copy the file there now? Yes / No]

- In this case, make a copy of the file in the root folder of your site by clicking **Yes**.

Changing the site parameters

You can change the parameters of a site whenever you want.

- **Site - Define Sites**

©Editions ENI - All rights reserved

Dreamweaver 3
Your first page

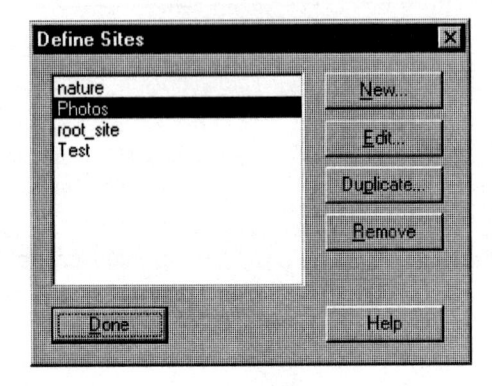

- Select the site concerned from the list of sites.
- Click the **Edit** button to change certain settings.
- Click the **Duplicate** button to make a copy of the selected site. You are making a copy of the site parameters, not the files.
- Click **Remove** to delete the site settings, but not the files.
- Once you have made any necessary changes, click **Done**.

Accessing a site

When you create several sites, you can access each of these sites.

- In the document window: **Site - Open Site** then choose the name of the site in the menu that appears.
- In the site window, use the site drop-down menu:

Page properties

When you want to create a page, start by editing its properties. In these properties you can define the page title, a background colour or image, different default colours, etc.

Next, save your page. If you do this, Dreamweaver does not have to remind you that the active document has not been saved, making it impossible to define file paths, when you want to insert images and create links.

For each of the page settings shown below, you can click the **OK** button in the page properties window, then save your page and preview it in the browser.

Your first page

The page title

You can give your page a title, which will appear in the title bar of the browser, and the words of which can be indexed in some search engines.

- **Modify - Page Properties**
- In the **Title** box, type the appropriate text.

This text appears in the browser's title bar:

You cannot change the formatting of this text.

The page background

Principle

In the background of your page you can choose to have a uniform colour, or an image, which will be tiled in the background so that it covers the entire browser window. You need to choose either a colour or an image. If you use both, the image will be displayed.

Inserting a background item

- **Modify - Page Properties**
- In the **Background Image** box, click the **Browse** button to choose a background image from your local site folder.
- In the **Background** text box, choose a colour from the palette, or type in the hexadecimal code of the colour you want (if you know it):

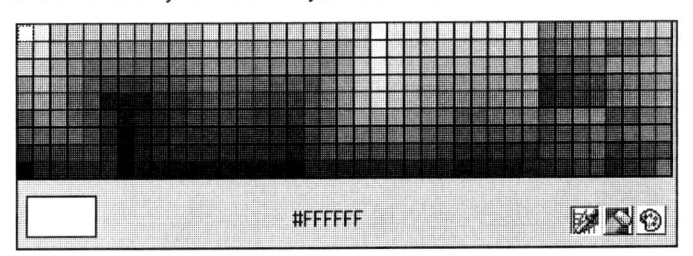

© Editions ENI - All rights reserved

or type the name of the colour (such as gold, teal or lightyellow) in the text box:

Defining the default colours

Principle

You can edit the default colours for text and hyperlinks in your page. Changing the default text colour does not mean that you cannot further change the colour of selected words in your document. As for hyperlinks, those that have not been visited are generally shown on the Internet underlined and coloured blue, and visited links are shown underlined and in purple. It is your choice whether to change the colour of your links, at the risk of upsetting the habits of Web users.

Choosing the colours

- **Modify - Page Properties**
- In the **Text**, **Links** (unvisited), **Visited Links** and **Active Links** (colour of the link when you click it) boxes, choose the colour you want to use in the palette, or type its hexadecimal code (if you know it) or its name in the text box.

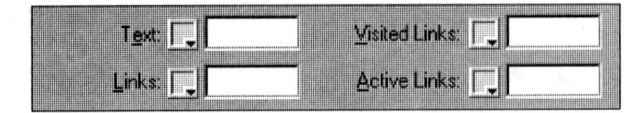

Margins

Principle

You can indicate the position of the page in the browser window using the **Left Margin** and **Top Margin** settings (supported only by Microsoft Internet Explorer) and **Margin Width** and **Margin Height** (supported only by Netscape Navigator).

The values given here will indent the page to the right or downward in the browser window, by as many pixels as you choose.

These items are not defined in the W3C guidelines.

Your first page

Creating margins

- **Modify - Page Properties**
- In the **Left Margin**, **Top Margin**, **Margin Width** and **Margin Height** boxes, type the values you want.

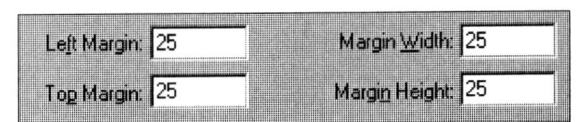

> Left Margin: 25   Margin Width: 25
> Top Margin: 25   Margin Height: 25

Type the same value in the **Left Margin** and **Top Margin** boxes and the **Margin Width** and **Margin Height** boxes if you want to achieve the same effect in both Microsoft Internet Explorer and Netscape Navigator.

If you enter 0 as the value, the page will be completely in the top left corner of the browser window.

Character encoding

Principle

This feature allows you to tell the browser the character encoding you have used in a page. In the **HTML 4** guidelines, W3C wanted there to be the possibility to insert several languages in the same page. This is why it is important to be able to indicate which characters are used in a page, or in a specific paragraph. Not all browsers in use today are capable of showing several types of characters in the same page.

Setting the page encoding

- **Modify - Page Properties**
- In the **Document Encoding** pop-up menu choose the encoding you want:

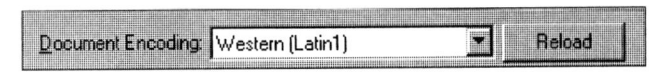

> Document Encoding: Western (Latin1)   Reload

For Western European languages the type is **Western (Latin1)** and the norm iso-8859 1.

©Editions ENI - All rights reserved

Setting the default encoding

This enables you to indicate the encoding that will be used by default for all new documents.

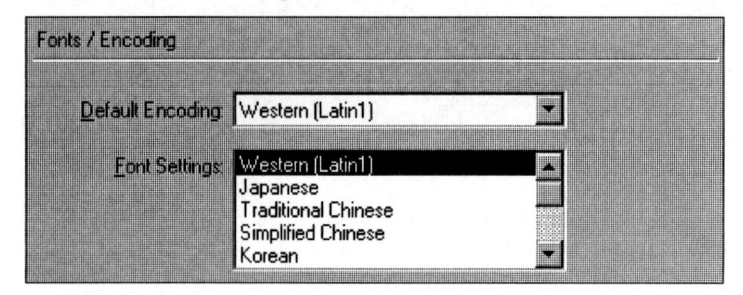

⇨ **Edit - Preferences - Fonts/Encoding** category

⇨ Choose the encoding you want from the **Default Encoding** pop-up menu.

⇨ Choose the encoding type from the **Font Settings** list then, using the pop-up menus below, define the font that is to be used for the chosen encoding. If you choose a specific encoding and font (such as Japanese or Cyrillic), the relevant character set must be installed on your computer.

This is not the same as formatting text. It is simply the choice of font used in the display when you have not used any formatted text.

Using a design template

Principle

In order to create your homepage (or any other page), you can ask a graphic designer to create a "model" (or you can do this yourself), which can be produced in "paper" format. You will need to scan this image (in .gif, .jpg or .png format) and use it as the document background in order to make the best use of it.

Using tables or layers, work with this design template. This is what is called a **tracing image** in Dreamweaver. A tracing image appears only in your Dreamweaver document, and not in a browser.

Use

Refer to the use of images, tables and layers later in this book for a precise idea of the application of graphic design techniques.

The precise use of a tracing image is explained in the chapter about layers.

Inserting/presenting text

Text or inserting text: principle

The notion of paragraphs

In **HTML** everything is a container or content! When you want to insert text into a Web page, you need a "container", of which there are two main types: paragraphs and headings. The content is the text you type.

In Dreamweaver you will mostly use paragraphs. The <p> element defines a paragraph in HTML. Each time you press the ⏎ key on the keyboard, you create a new paragraph. The spacing between paragraphs is the equivalent of an empty line.

The notion of whitespace

You will naturally space your words using one space in your text. In HTML there is only one whitespace element between words: the space between two words. Extra spaces, those before the first word in a paragraph, several spaces between words, spaces after words at the end of paragraphs, and tab stops are not managed by HTML or Dream-weaver, and will not be interpreted by a browser.

Creating paragraphs

Entering text

- Click in an open document where you want to start.
- Type the text of the first paragraph.
- Press ⏎ on the keyboard.

    A new paragraph is created.

- Type the text of the second paragraph.

    The paragraphs are spaced by a whitespace that is equivalent to a line:

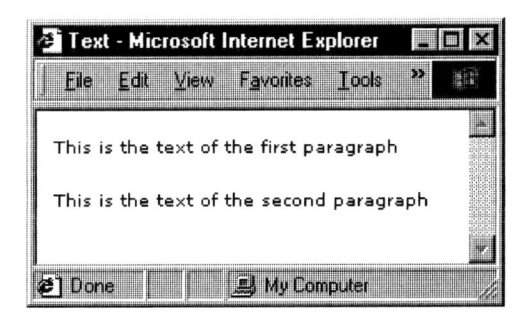

©Editions ENI - All rights reserved

Dreamweaver 3
Inserting/presenting text

Copying/pasting text

You can copy and paste from another program to insert text into your document.

- Select the text in the other application and copy it.
- In Dreamweaver use **Edit - Paste as Text**.

The pasted text loses its original formatting. You can use this method to copy text (which may be formatted) and paste it as plain text in the same document or in another document in Dreamweaver:

- Select some formatted text.
- **Edit - Copy Text Only**
- Click the place where you want to paste the text.
- **Edit - Paste as Text**

In some cases, such as the creation of an HTML manual, you can copy formatted text and paste it as HTML code:

- Select some formatted text.

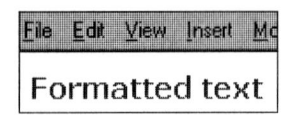

```
File  Edit  View  Insert  Mo
Formatted text
```

- **Edit - Copy**
- Click where you want to paste the code.
- **Edit - Paste as Text**

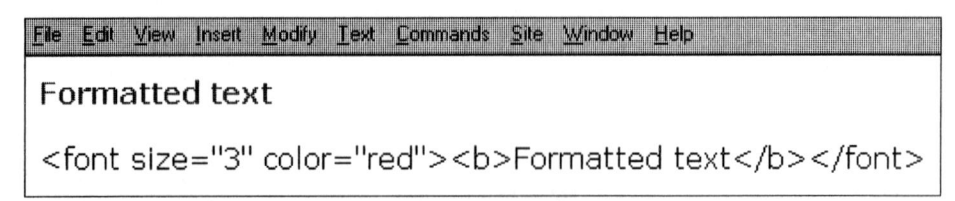

```
File  Edit  View  Insert  Modify  Text  Commands  Site  Window  Help
Formatted text
<font size="3" color="red"><b>Formatted text</b></font>
```

You can see the formatting on the page:
`<b>` *for bold.*
`<font size="3" color="red">` *for size 3 and the colour red.*

©Editions ENI - All rights reserved

Inserting/presenting text

Special characters

Principle

In Dreamweaver, special characters are what are called character entities in HTML. Character entities are accented characters, national characters (like Å and ñ), special symbols (such as © and ®) and mathematical symbols (α or π). In HTML, all these entities begin with the & (ampersand) character and end with a ; (semi-colon).

Examples:
the © characters is coded as `&copy;`
the α characters is coded as `&alpha;`
the à character is coded as `&agrave;`
the £ character is coded as `&pound;`

Inserting special characters

*National characters and special symbols can be found in the **Objects** palette.*

→ In an open document, click where you want to insert the text then use **Insert - Characters**. Choose the character you want or click **Other**.

or open the **Objects** palette: **Window - Objects** then choose **Characters** from the panels pop-up menu.

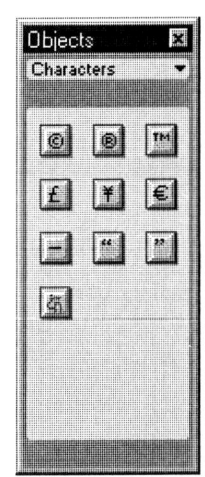

→ Click one of the buttons or click the **Insert Other Character** button. In the dialog box, click the character you want then click **OK**.

©Editions ENI - All rights reserved

Managing the lines in a paragraph

Paragraph spacing

If you want to increase the spacing between two paragraphs, you can do so only by creating "empty" paragraphs (unless you are using CSS cascading style sheets, which enable you to manage the paragraph spacing precisely). In fact the paragraphs are not empty, but contain a non-breaking space: the `&nbps;` *entity, which you can see by showing the source code (press* F10*).*

- Type the first paragraph text, press ⏎ several times then type the second paragraph.

Creating a line break

You can insert a new line inside a paragraph without creating a new paragraph. The `<br>` *HTML element is inserted in this case.*

- Type the text of the paragraph, if you need to, then click where you want to insert the line break.

- **Insert - Line Break**

    or, in the **Objects** palette, click the **Insert Line Break** tool from the **Common** panel.

    The insertion point goes to the start of the following line but it remains in the same paragraph.

    To see any line breaks on your page better, you need first to make sure that **Line Breaks** *are among the invisible elements which can be shown, and then activate the option which displays the invisible elements.*

- **Edit - Preferences - Invisible Elements** category
- Activate the **Line Breaks** option then click **OK**.
- Show invisible elements using **View - Invisible Elements**.

    The line break invisible element appears in the page:

    > This is the text of the
    > first paragraph
    >
    > This is the text of the second paragraph

Formatting paragraphs

Changing paragraph alignment

- To change the alignment of a paragraph, click inside it.

Inserting/presenting text

- **Text - Alignment - Left**, **Center** or **Right**

    or, in the Property inspector, click the button that corresponds to the alignment you want: .

    There is no menu command or tool for a justified alignment in Dreamweaver, despite the fact that it is a standard paragraph attribute, defined in the W3C guidelines.

- To apply a justified alignment, click in the appropriate paragraph and apply a left alignment so that you do not have to type all of the code then show the source code by pressing F10.

- Type justify as the align value in place of left:

    ```
    <p align="justify">Paragraph containing a lot of text...</p>
    ```

Applying indents

In HTML, except if you are using CSS-1 cascading style sheets, you cannot define left, right or first-line indents in a paragraph. Using indents in Dreamweaver allows you to create only equally sized left and right indents for a paragraph.

- Click in the paragraph in question.

- **Text - Indent**

    or click the button in the Property inspector.

    An example of different indent levels applied to justified paragraphs:

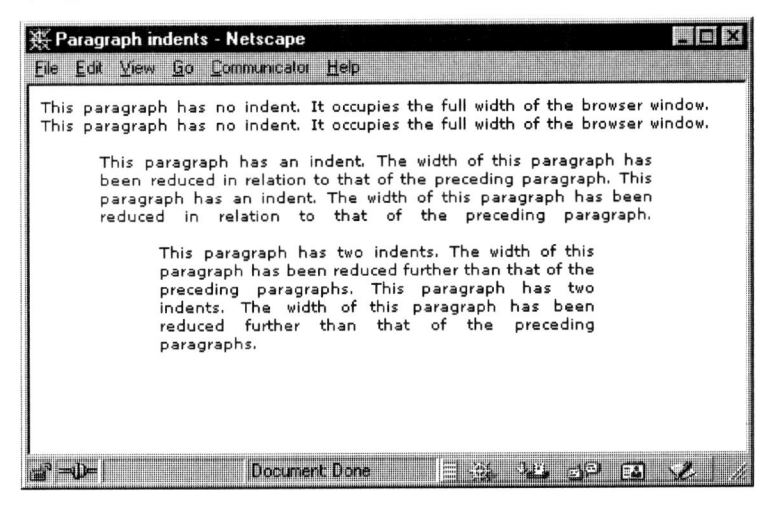

© Editions ENI - All rights reserved

Dreamweaver 3
Inserting/presenting text

Each time you apply a new indent, the width of the paragraph is reduced.

- To remove a paragraph indent, click in the paragraph concerned then

    Text - Outdent

    or click the [≛] button on the Property inspector.

When you apply indents, Dreamweaver uses the `blockquote` HTML element, which was intended by the W3C to indicate quoted text.

Defining headings

In HTML, headings were created to indicate visually headings of greater or lesser importance in long documents. This should mean that you can create a table of contents using the different levels, but current browsers do not know how to do this!

When you apply a heading, the text appears in bold, and the size varies according to the importance of the heading. Heading 1 is the biggest, and Heading 6 the smallest.

- Click in the text that is to become a heading.

- **Text - Format - Heading 1** to **Heading 6**

    or use the **Format** pop-up menu in the Property inspector to choose the level of heading you want: [Format Heading 4].

Examples of heading levels:

Headings - Netscape
File Edit View Go Communicator Help

Level 1 heading

Level 2 heading

Level 3 heading

Level 4 heading

Level 5 heading

Level 6 heading

© Editions ENI - All rights reserved

Inserting/presenting text

You can apply left, centred, right and justified alignments to headings in the same way as you do for paragraphs. Justified alignment is, however, not often used for headings, as they are mostly used as titles and not body text.

Defining divisions

When text contains several elements that are to be, for example, centred (such as paragraphs, headings or images), you can use the `<div>` element to optimise your code. This element creates a logical division in the document. The `<div>` element can be given the `align` attribute.

- Type and insert all the necessary elements.
- Show the source code by pressing F10.
- Type the opening tag `<div align="center">` before all the elements you want to centre.
- Type the closing tag `</div>` after all these elements.

```
<div align="center">
<p>A paragraph</p>
<h3>Level 3 heading</h3>
<p>Another paragraph</p>
<p>The last paragraph</p>
<h6>Level 6 heading</h6>
</div>
```

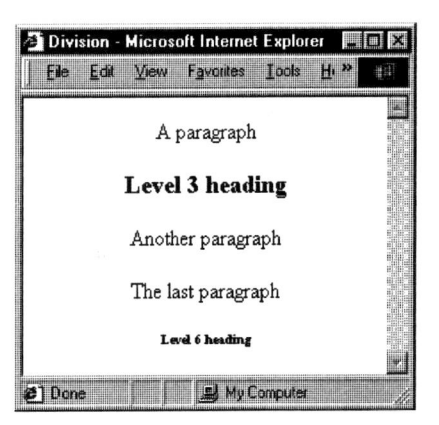

A paragraph

Level 3 heading

Another paragraph

The last paragraph

Level 6 heading

Preformatted text

Principle

In the first versions of HTML the notion of a table did not exist. To simulate the appearance of columns, Web page architects used the `<pre>` element (for PREformatted text).

All the spaces in the `<pre>` element are conserved: tab stops, extra spaces between words and so on. This made it possible to simulate columns. By default, a fixed-space font is used, and this font is defined by the browser.

©Editions ENI - All rights reserved

As browsers now support tables, the use of the `<pre>` element is not widespread.

Inserting preformatted text

- In your document, click where you want to insert the text.
- **Text - Format - Preformatted Text**

  or use the Property inspector: Format Preformatted.
- Type your text with the extra spacing and tab stops you want, using line breaks to insert new lines.
- When you have finished, insert a paragraph break by pressing the ↵ key.
- **Text - Format - Paragraph**

  or use the Property inspector: Format Paragraph.

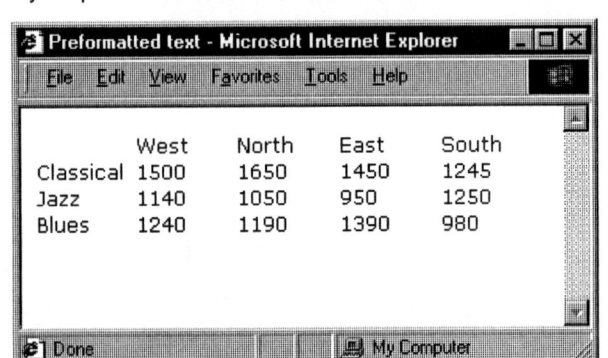

```
            West     North    East     South
Classical   1500     1650     1450     1245
Jazz        1140     1050     950      1250
Blues       1240     1190     1390     980
```

Finding and replacing text

You can search for text in the active document, in the site, or in a particular folder, and replace it, if necessary.

Carrying out a simple search for text

- Open a document.
- **Edit - Find**

Inserting/presenting text

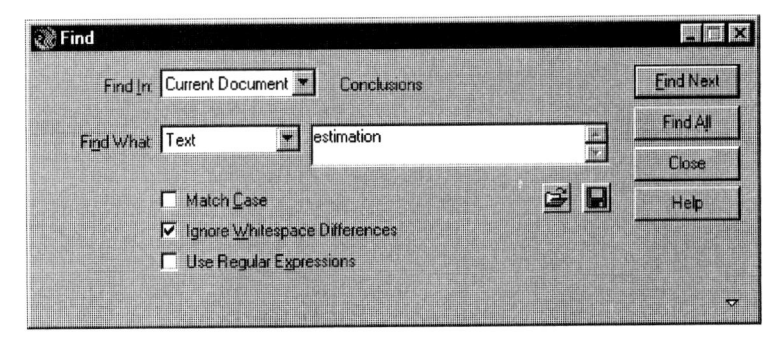

- In the **Find In** pop-up menu choose:

    Current Document   to search only the open document

    Current Site   to search all the files in the site

    Folder   to select the folder in which you want to carry out the search.

- Choose **Text** in the **Find What** pop-up menu, and, in the text box to the right, type the text you want to find.

- The **Match Case** option allows you to distinguish between upper and lower case in the document text.

- The **Ignore Whitespace Differences** option means that any extra spaces will be ignored.

- The **Use Regular Expressions** option enables you to use "wildcard" characters when you are searching for unknown characters in a word, or to look for the start of a word (use Dreamweaver's help to see all the "wildcard" characters).

- The **Save** and **Open** buttons allow you to save and open searches in .dwq files that are stored in the **Queries** folder in the Dreamweaver folder.

- Start the search by clicking:

    - the **Find Next** button to find each occurrence one after the other, with each occurrence selected in the document.

    - the **Find All** button to find all the occurrences at once. You will see the result in the lower part of the **Find** window.

Dreamweaver 3
3-4 Inserting/presenting text

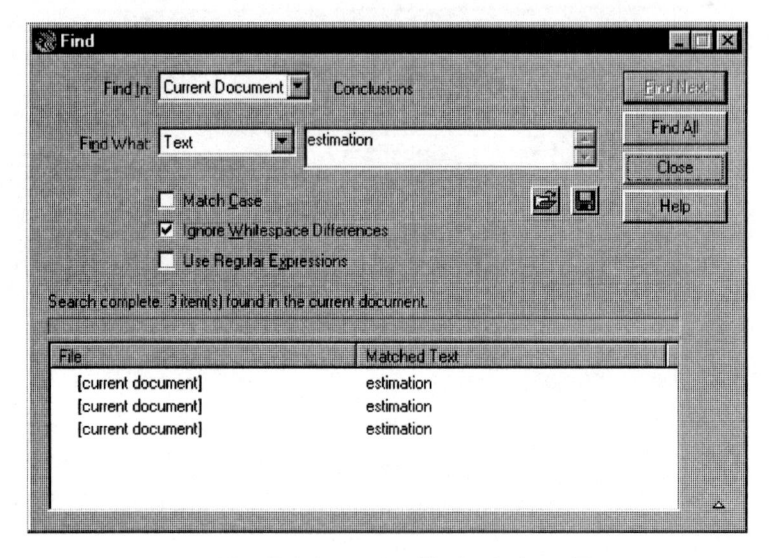

[Screenshot of Find dialog window showing Find In: Current Document, Find What: Text "estimation", with search results showing 3 items found in current document]

- To go to an occurrence, double-click it in the **Find** window. The occurrence is selected in the document. If the search was carried out for the whole site and the document in question is closed, Dreamweaver will open it.
- Click the **Close** button to close the search window without erasing the search details.
- Use **Edit - Find Next** to restart the same search.

Making an advanced search for text

- Open a document.
- **Edit - Find**

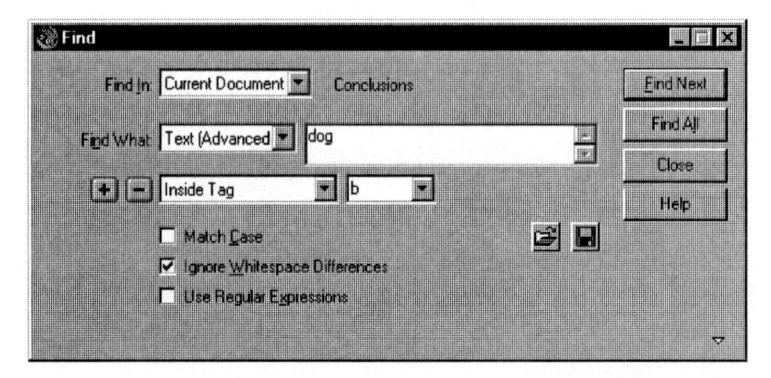

[Screenshot of Find dialog window showing Find In: Current Document, Find What: Text (Advanced) "dog", Inside Tag: b]

©Editions ENI - All rights reserved

Inserting/presenting text

- In the **Find In** pop-up menu choose where you want to make the search.
- In **Find What** choose **Text (Advanced)** and, in the text box to the right, type the text you want to find.
- In the pop-up menu just below, choose: **Inside Tag** if the text is formatted or **Not Inside Tag** if the text does not have any formatting defined by its HTML code (see the text formatting elements later in this book).
- Choose the formatting element that should or should not be associated with the text in the pop-up menu to the right.

    Example 1:

    Find: **dog** with **Inside Tag b** (HTML element <b> for bold)

    This will search for and find only the text "dog" in bold type, but not the text "dog" without formatting or in bold and italic.

    Example 2:

    Find: **dog** with **Not Inside Tag b**

    This will search for and find the text "dog" without bold formatting and the text "dog" in italic, but not the text "dog" in bold and italic.

- To add or remove search criteria, use the ⊟ and ⊞ buttons.

    The **Find Next** and **Find All** buttons are used in the same way as for a simple search.

Replacing text

You can find and replace text in your document, in a folder, or in the entire site. The principles of the search and replacement techniques are the same as those explained above.

- **Edit - Replace**
- Use the **Find What** box to indicate whether you want to make a simple **Text** search or a **Text (Advanced)** search.
- Indicate the replacement word in the **Replace With** box.

Dreamweaver 3
3.6 Inserting/presenting text

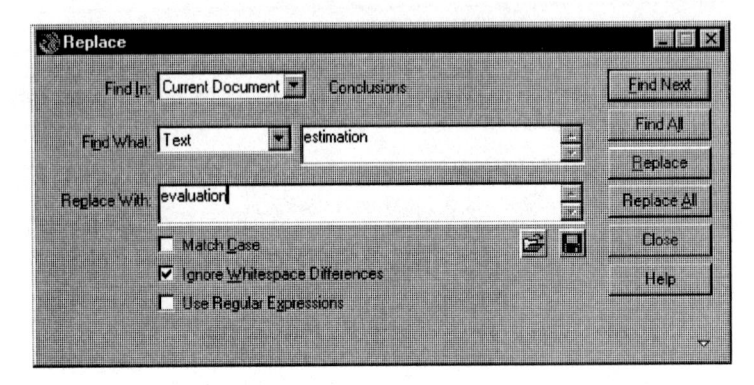

The options are the same as for a text search.

Spelling

Dreamweaver provides you with a spelling checker which you can use to check the text in your document, and you can also save any words that you use regularly but that Dreamweaver does not recognise.

Choosing the language

You can check spelling in different languages

- **Edit - Preferences - General** category
- Choose the language that is to be used during a spelling check in the **Dictionary** pop-up menu.

If you are checking the spelling of a multilingual document (in English and French for example), you should first choose one of the languages in the preferences then run the spelling check. Change language then run the spelling check a second time.

Checking the spelling

- To check the spelling in a document in order to find any mistakes: **Text - Check Spelling**

Inserting/presenting text

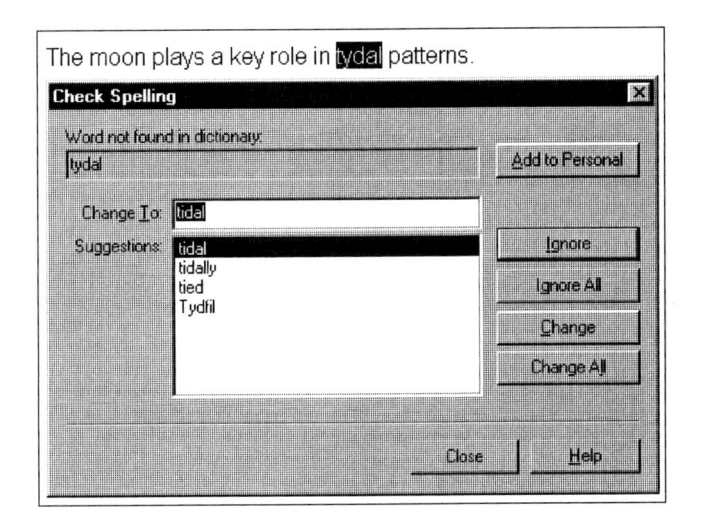

Dreamweaver detects and selects the first spelling mistake.

→ In the **Suggestions** list, select the correct spelling of the word.

The word you choose appears in the Change To box.

→ If the spelling checker does not know the correct spelling, type it yourself in the **Change To** box.

→ Click:

Change	to change only this occurrence.
Change All	to change all the occurrences of the word.
Ignore	to choose not to correct the word.
Ignore All	to leave the word uncorrected throughout the document.
Add to Personal	to add the word to your personal dictionary.

The personal dictionary

→ All the words that you add to your personal dictionary are stored in the **Personal.dat** file in the **Macromedia\Dreamweaver 3\Configuration\Dictionaries**.

→ To make changes to your personal dictionary, open the **Personal.dat** file with a simple text editor (SimpleText in Macintosh or Notepad in Windows).

©Editions ENI - All rights reserved

Principle

Lists enable you to enumerate items. You can create bulleted lists, numbered lists, and definition lists. You can also nest a list inside another.

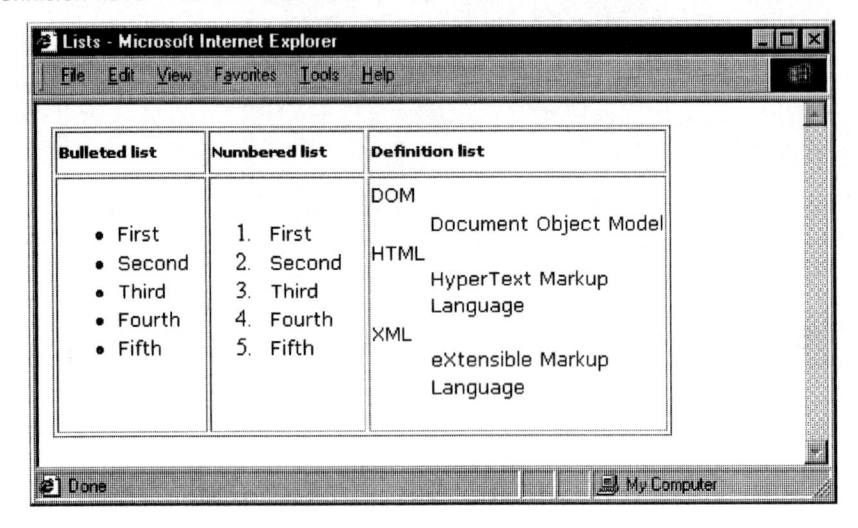

Bulleted list	Numbered list	Definition list

• First
• Second
• Third
• Fourth
• Fifth
	1. First
	2. Second
	3. Third
	4. Fourth
	5. Fifth
		DOM
		    Document Object Model
		HTML
		    HyperText Markup Language
		XML
		    eXtensible Markup Language

Bulleted lists

Creating the list

- Click in the document where you want to start the list.
- **Text - List - Unordered List**

    or click the [icon] button in the Property inspector.
- Type the contents of the list, pressing [Enter] after each one.
- When you have finished the list, press [Enter] twice.

You can also type the list then select all the paragraphs and use **Text - List - Unordered List** or click the [icon] button on the Property inspector.

Lists

Formatting the list items

You can change the appearance of the bullets of one or all the list items.

- Click in the list item you want to format. If all the items are concerned, click any item.
- **Text - List - Properties**

    or click the **List Item...** button on the Property inspector.

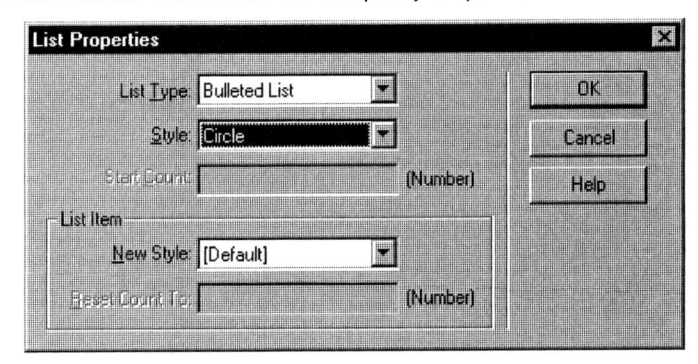

- In the **List Type** pop-up menu, leave the **Bulleted List** option.
- If all the items are to be changed, choose the bullet you want to use from the **Style** pop-up menu. If only the active item is to be changed, choose the new bullet (**Bullet** (default option), **Circle** or **Square**) from the **New Style** pop-up menu.
- Click **OK**.

    Examples of lists with different bullet styles:

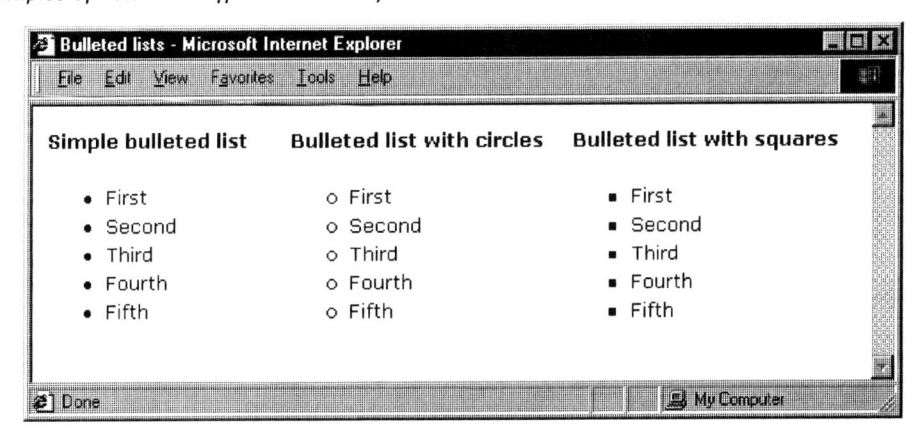

©Editions ENI - All rights reserved

Dreamweaver 3
Lists

> Take care: if you modify a single item, Microsoft Internet Explorer 5 changes the appearance of the item in question only. However, Microsoft Internet Explorer 4 and Netscape Navigator 4 change the appearance of the item and the following elements.

Numbered lists

Creating a numbered list

- Click the appropriate place.
- **Text - List - Ordered List**

    or click the button on the Property inspector.
- Type the list, pressing ↵ after each item.
- When you have finished the list, press ↵ twice.

> You can also type the list then select all the paragraphs and use **Text - List - Ordered List** or click the button on the Property inspector.

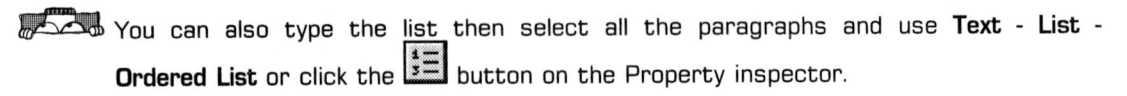

Formatting the list items

You can change the appearance of the numbers of one or all the list items.

- Click in the list item you want to format. If all the items are concerned, click any item.
- **Text - List - Properties**

    or click the **List Item...** button on the Property inspector.

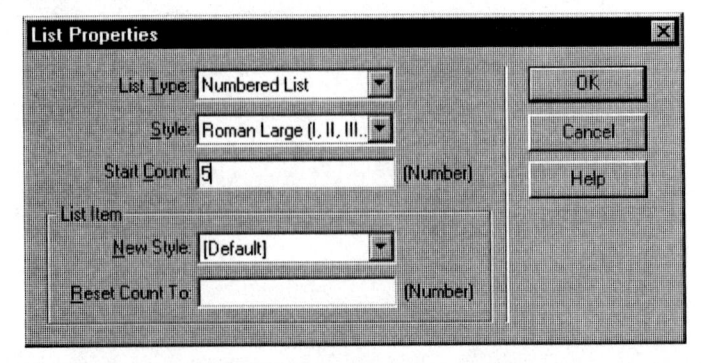

    List Properties
    - List Type: Numbered List
    - Style: Roman Large (I, II, III...)
    - Start Count: 5 (Number)
    - List Item
        - New Style: [Default]
        - Reset Count To: (Number)

- In the **List Type** pop-up menu, leave **Numbered List**.

©Editions ENI - All rights reserved

Lists

- If you want to change all the items, choose the new numbering style in the **Style** pop-up menu. If only the selected item is to be changed, choose its new appearance in the **New Style** list:
  Number (1, 2, 3...) (default option),
  Roman Small (i, ii, iii...),
  Roman Large (I, II, III...),
  Alphabet Small (a, b, c...) or
  Alphabet Large (A, B, C...).

- Enter the value (always a numerical value whatever the number style) from which the numbering of the list should begin in the **Start Count** text box (if all the items are concerned), or the **Reset Count To** box (if only the active item is concerned).

- Click **OK**.

  Examples of formatting:

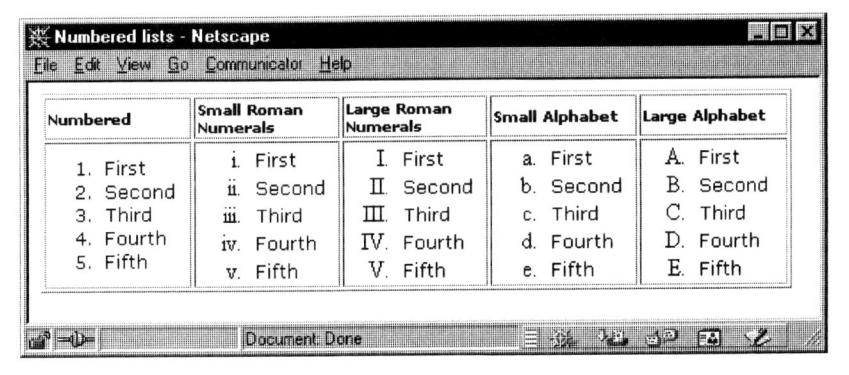

Numbered	Small Roman Numerals	Large Roman Numerals	Small Alphabet	Large Alphabet
1. First	i. First	I. First	a. First	A. First
2. Second	ii. Second	II. Second	b. Second	B. Second
3. Third	iii. Third	III. Third	c. Third	C. Third
4. Fourth	iv. Fourth	IV. Fourth	d. Fourth	D. Fourth
5. Fifth	v. Fifth	V. Fifth	e. Fifth	E. Fifth

Be careful: if you modify a single item, Microsoft Internet Explorer 5 changes the appearance of the item in question only. However, Microsoft Internet Explorer 4 and Netscape Navigator 4 change the appearance of the item and the following items.

4.2 Dreamweaver 3
Lists

Creating nested lists

You can nest lists inside each other in order to show several hierarchical levels, indented in the nested list:

```
1. Language
      o HTML
      o XML
      o XHTML
2. Style Sheets
      1. CSS-1
      2. CSS-P
      3. XSL
```

- Click the appropriate place.
- Click the **Ordered List** button on the Property inspector.
- Type the text of the first element in the numbered list and press ⏎ to create the next element.
- Click the **Text Indent** button on the Property inspector.
- Click the **Unordered List** button on the Property inspector.
- Type the contents of the nested, bulleted list.
- Press ⏎ at the end of the line.
- Click the **Text Outdent** button on the Property inspector.
- Click the **Ordered List** button on the Property inspector.
- Type the text of the second element in the numbered list.
- Repeat these steps for each level.
- When you have finished the list, press ⏎ twice.

©Editions ENI - All rights reserved

Lists

Changing the list type

You can change the list type whenever you want: go from an unordered list to an ordered list, or the inverse.

- Select the whole list.
- **Text - List - Ordered List** or **Unordered List**

  or click the ▭ or ▭ buttons on the Property inspector.

Creating a definition list

A definition list contains a defined term and, on the next line, its definition.

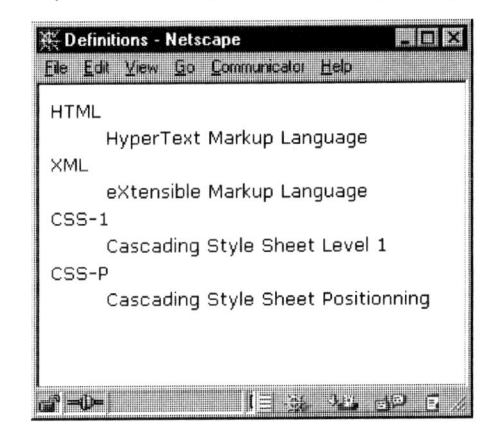

```
HTML
        HyperText Markup Language
XML
        eXtensible Markup Language
CSS-1
        Cascading Style Sheet Level 1
CSS-P
        Cascading Style Sheet Positionning
```

Creating the list

- Click in the appropriate place.
- **Text - List - Definition List**
- Type the text of the first term.
- Press ⏎ to go to the next line.
- Type the definition of the term.
- Press ⏎ to go to the next line.
- Type the second term.
- Press ⏎ to go to the next line.
- Type the definition of the term.

Dreamweaver 3
Lists

- Do this for all the terms and definitions.
- When you have finished the list, press ⏎ twice.

Identifying the elements

- Keep a close eye on the document window status bar so that you know which level of the list you are in. There you will see the HTML element in which you are working:

  `<dl>`   is the declaration of the **definition list**.
  `<dt>`   is the **defined term**.
  `<dd>`   is the **definition description**.

  Example of the status bar when the insertion point is in the defined term: `<body> <dl> <dt>`.
  You are in the body of the page `<body>`, *in a definition list* `<dl>` *and in the defined term* `<dt>`.

©Editions ENI - All rights reserved

Formatting text

General principles

As for paragraph formatting, the W3C guidelines strongly recommend that you do not use traditional HTML formatting (such as `<font>`, `<basefont>` and `<u>` elements). These elements have been declared obsolete. The W3C also recommends the use of style sheets (CSS-1). However, considering that browsers do not recognise CSS-1 recommendations in the same way, "traditional" formatting has not yet breathed its last!

This character formatting can be applied to all the text elements mentioned previously: paragraphs, headings and lists.

Applying character formatting

HTML distinguishes two different types of text formatting: "traditional" formatting elements that are applied using a style: bold or italic, for example, and locution elements that give semantic information about the contents.

Applying traditional formatting

The "traditional" formatting elements are: Bold, Italic, Underline, Strikethrough and Teletype. Larger and Smaller are not available in Dreamweaver, but are included in the HTML 4 recommendations.

Bold Style ~~Strikethrough Style~~
Italic Stye   `Teletype Style`
Underline Style

- Select the text.
- **Text - Style - Bold, Italic, Underline, Strikethrough or Teletype**

  or use the Property inspector to apply **Bold** or **Italic**: **B** *I*.

Applying superscript and subscript formatting

*The W3C conceived two elements that would enable you to put text in superscript and subscript, but they are not accessible in Dreamweaver. This means that you need to type them in the source code (you can also use the **Quick Tag Editor** to make occasional changes to the source code: see the Optimising HTML code chapter).*

- The element for superscript formatting is: `<sup>text</sup>`.
- The element for subscript formatting is: `<sub>text</sub>`.

©Editions ENI - All rights reserved

Dreamweaver 3
4.6 Formatting text

- For example, type the following text in your document:

    A 10m3 container holds water (H2O)

- Press F10 to show the source code and add these elements:

    ```
    <p>A 10m<sup>3</sup> container holds water (H<sub>2</sub>0).</p>
    ```

- Return to the page by pressing F10.

⚠ Be careful! Because Dreamweaver does not contain these formats, you will not see them in your document, only in a browser!

- Save the page and preview it in a browser.

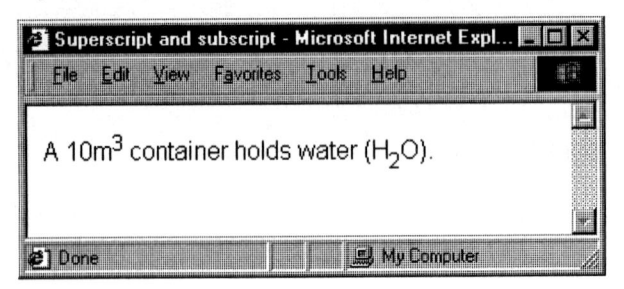

Superscript and subscript - Microsoft Internet Explorer window showing:
A 10m^3 container holds water (H$_2$O).

Applying locution elements

*These formatting elements are used to indicate the type of the formatted items: a sample of programming code is formatted with the **Code** style, the definition of a term is formatted with **Definition**, for a vocal browser the **Emphasis** style tells the vocal synthesiser to change the intensity of the voice, and so on.*

- The locution elements are: Emphasis, Strong, Code, Variable, Sample, Keyboard, Citation, Definition and Acronym, which is not accessible in Dreamweaver.

- Select the text you want to format.

- **Text - Style - Emphasis, Strong, Code, Variable, Sample, Keyboard, Citation** or **Definition**

    The on-screen formatting is left to the browsers to define.

©Editions ENI - All rights reserved

Formatting text

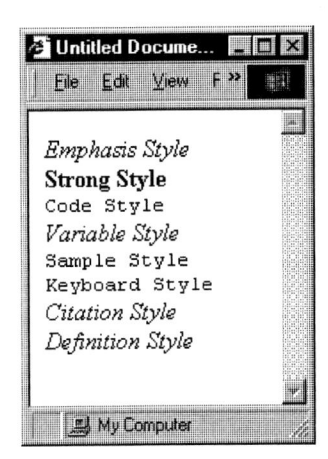

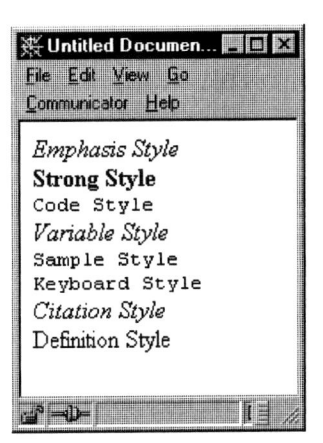

Browsers use a default fixed width font to format the Teletype, Code, Sample and Keyboard styles.

To change this default fixed width font in the browsers:

- In Microsoft Internet Explorer 5, select it in the **Plain text font** list in the **Fonts** dialog box (**Tools - Internet Options - General** tab - **Fonts** button).

The default setting is Courier New.

- In Netscape Navigator 4.7, select it in the **Fixed Width Font** list in the **Fonts** dialog box (**Edit - Preferences - Appearance** category - **Fonts** option).

The default setting is Courier New, size 10.

Choosing the character font

"Owned" fonts

When you create a Web page or site you should avoid using "owned" fonts. To understand the problem, take this example: you are developing a site in Windows and you decide to use the font Tahoma in your formatting. The problem is that Tahoma is a Windows-only font, and so does not exist in Macintosh or Unix. In this case, browsers will display the formatted text in their default font, because the font you had chosen does not exist on the user's system. This will mean that the on-screen appearance of the page will not be the same in Windows as it is on a Macintosh or in Unix.

Substitute fonts

You can avoid this sort of problem by working with substitute fonts. This allows browsers to display one of a list of similar fonts.

Dreamweaver offers these character groups, whose fonts are almost identical on all computer platforms (PC, Mac and Unix).

There are three families with different styles:

- The sans-serif group: Arial, Helvetica and sans-serif.
- The serif group: Times New Roman, Times and serif.
- The fixed width group: Courier New, Courier and mono.

If you use these font groups, when a browser interprets an HTML page it analyses the font list in ascending order and uses the first font that is installed on the operating system.

If none of the fonts are installed, the browser's default font is used.

Applying a font

- Select the text concerned.
- **Text - Font** then choose one of the font groups offered

or use the Property inspector: `Verdana, Arial, Helveti`

or, if you want to use a specific font whose name you know, type it in the font box: `Garamond`

Example of the code for text formatted with the serif font group:

```
<font face="Times New Roman, Times, serif">text</font>
```

If the user's machine is a Macintosh, the browser will not find Times New Roman in the system folder, but the second font, Times, is present and can be used.

Furthermore, Dreamweaver offers two more groups in the sans-serif and serif families. These two groups have, at the start of their lists, two fonts that have been specifically designed to make the screen easier to read: Verdana and Georgia, which were created by Matthew Carter at Microsoft's request, and are freely available.

Example of code:

```
<font face="Georgia, Times New Roman, Times, serif">text</font>
<font face="Verdana, Arial, Helvetica, sans-serif">text</font>
```

Formatting text

Example of text formatted using the different character groups:

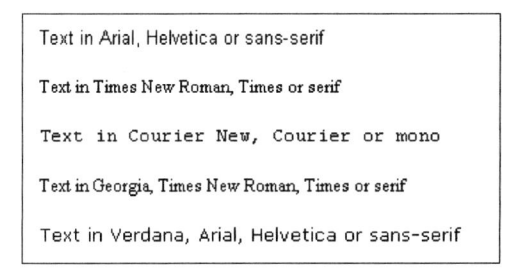

> Text in Arial, Helvetica or sans-serif
>
> Text in Times New Roman, Times or serif
>
> Text in Courier New, Courier or mono
>
> Text in Georgia, Times New Roman, Times or serif
>
> Text in Verdana, Arial, Helvetica or sans-serif

If you do not specify a font for your document, the browser's default font will be used. This means that your page setup will differ from one browser to another. It is always a good idea to define fonts for your Web pages.

Creating your own character groups

→ **Text - Font - Edit Font List**

or use the font list menu in the Property inspector and choose **Edit Font List**.

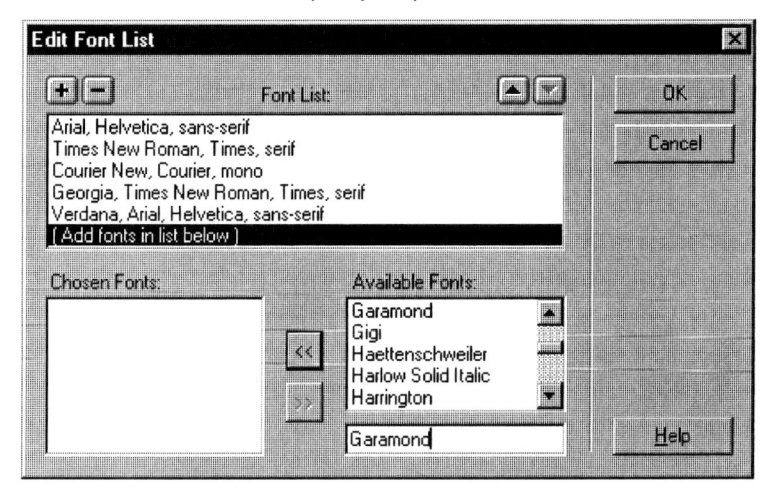

The **Font List** box contains a list of the font groups that are already installed in Dreamweaver. A list of **Available Fonts** indicates the fonts that are installed on your system.

©Editions ENI - All rights reserved

Dreamweaver 3
Formatting text

- In the **Font List** box make sure the **(Add fonts in list below)** option is selected so that you can start creating your own group.
- Select the first font you want to add to your group in the **Available Fonts** list.
- Click the **Add** button ⟪.

  The font appears in the Chosen Fonts list.

- Do this for every font you want to add to this group.
- If you want to remove one of the fonts you have chosen, select it and click the **Remove** button ⟫.
- To add a new font group, click ➕.
- To delete one of the font groups you have created, click ➖.
- To change the order in which the groups appear in the menu, select a group and click ▲ to move it up in the list or ▼ to move it down.

Setting the browser's default font

*If, in Dreamweaver, you do not indicate the character font precisely (the **Default Font** choice in the font list), the browser's default font is used.*

- In Microsoft Internet Explorer 5:

  Tools - Internet Options - General tab - **Fonts** button - **Web page font** drop-down menu

  *The default font is **Times New Roman**.*

- In Netscape Navigator 4.7:

  Edit - Preferences - Appearance category - **Fonts** option - **Variable Width Font** menu

  *The default font is **Times New Roman**.*

- Leave the **Use document-specified fonts, including Dynamic Fonts** option active.

©Editions ENI - All rights reserved

Formatting text

Choosing the character size

Using absolute sizes

HTML offers only seven character sizes: from 1 to 7. These are fixed (absolute) sizes. Be careful: it is indicated in the W3C specifications that the "real" size shown on the screen is left up to the browser to decide. Due to this, there might be some slight differences in the same document shown in different browsers and platforms.

- Select the text you want to format.
- **Text - Size - 1** to **7**

    or use the Property inspector: [Size 4]

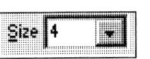

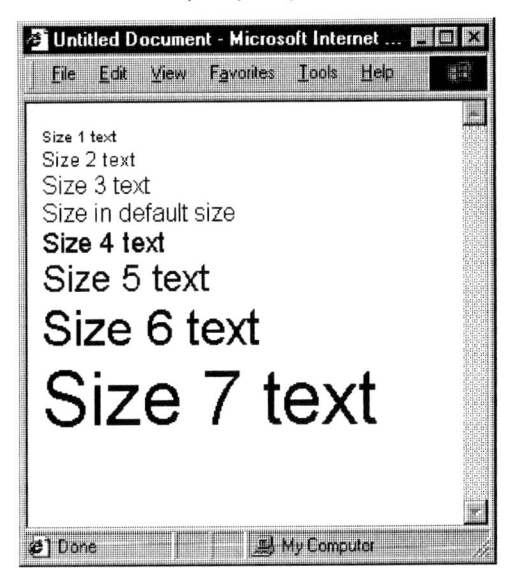

These fixed sizes correspond approximately to typographic sizes:
1 to 8 pts
2 to 10 pts
3 or default to 12 pts
4 to 14 pts
5 to 18 pts
6 to 14 pts
7 to 36 pts

If the character size has not been indicated (size **None**), size 3 is used by Dreamweaver. The size used in the browser will be the default font size. As with the character fonts, you should always try to define the character size of the text in your Web pages.

© Editions ENI - All rights reserved

Dreamweaver 3
Formatting text

Using relative sizes

You can choose to indicate a relative character size which is calculated in relation to the default size (which is size 3 if no size has been specified). The relative sizes go from -7 to +7, but the size you obtain is never less than 1 or more than 7.

→ To apply a size that is relative to the default size, select the text concerned and use **Text - Size Increase** then choose **+1** to **+7**

or **Text - Size Decrease** then choose **-1** to **-7**

or use the **Size** pop-up menu in the Property inspector: Size +3

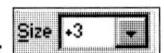

Example of a document with different relative sizes:

Size None = size 3

Size -7
Size -6
Size -5
Size -4
Size -3
Size -2
Size -1

Size +7
Size +6
Size +5
Size +4
Size +3
Size +2
Size +1

No size has been applied to the text "Size None = size 3", and so it is in size 3. All the other sizes are calculated in relation to size 3.

The first column shows the relative negative sizes:
Size -1: 3-1=2, the text is thus size 2
Size -2: 3-2=1, the text is thus size 1
Size -3: 3-3=1, the size cannot be less than 1.

The second column shows the relative positive sizes:
Size +1: 3+1=4, the text is thus size 4
Size +2: 3+2=5, the text is thus size 5
Size +3: 3+3=6, the text is thus size 6
Size +4: 3+4=7, the text is thus size 7
Size +5: 3+5=7, the size cannot be more than 7
Size +6: 3+6=7, the size cannot be more than 7
Size +7: 3+7=7, the size cannot be more than 7

©Editions ENI - All rights reserved

Formatting text

Setting the default size in the browser

The character size used by browsers changes the sizes specified in the HTML page. This means that browsers with different character size settings will display the same page differently.

- In Microsoft Internet Explorer 5:

    View - Text Size - Largest, Larger, Medium, Smaller, Smallest

    *The default setting is **Medium**.*

- In Netscape Navigator 4.7:

    Edit - Preferences - Appearance category - **Fonts** option - choose the **Size** for the **Variable Width Font**

    *The default size is **12**.*

Applying colour to characters

Applying a standard colour

In Dreamweaver there are several methods for choosing the text colour. You can choose a "Websafe" colour (recognised by different browsers on different platforms), a custom colour, or type the name of the colour you want.

- Select the text concerned then **Text - Color**.

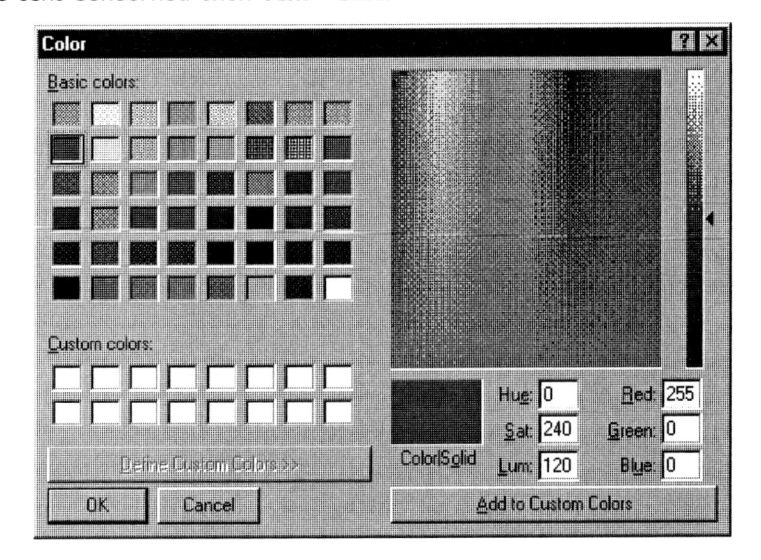

©Editions ENI - All rights reserved

Choose Websafe colour from the **Basic colors**, or create a custom colour in the palette on the right, but this colour will not necessarily be Websafe.

- You can also use the Property inspector: click the menu to choose a Websafe colour:

    The colour's hexadecimal code appears.

- If you know the name of the colour you want to use, you can type it directly in the colour text box:

Defining the default colour

- To define a colour as the default text colour, use **Modify - Page Properties** and choose a Websafe colour in the **Text** box.
Defining a default colour does not prevent you from changing the colour of selected text.

Saving formatting in a style

Principle

In a document, or an entire Web site, you will format text very often. For example, you will need to apply a bold, blue, size 4 serif font to your headings; for photograph legends you will want to apply a dark green, italic, size 1 serif font and so on. If you have to do this often, you will lose a lot of time re-applying the same formatting, and there is the risk of mistakes being made!

You can save the formatting for characters and paragraphs (without necessarily creating CSS-1 style sheets) using **HTML Styles**. You can create these in your site and apply them when you wish: thus saving time and ensuring the homogeneity of your pages.

Formatting text

Applying predefined HTML styles

- Select the word or click in the paragraph concerned.
- **Text - HTML Styles** or **Window - HTML Styles**

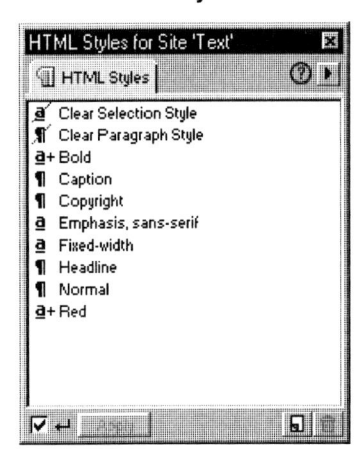

*The HTML styles that are applicable to characters are preceded by the **a** or **a+** symbols. Those that are destined for paragraphs are preceded by a ¶ symbol.*

- Choose a predefined style from the list.

  *The **a** symbol indicates that the style will override any existing formatting. The **a+** symbol indicates that when you apply the style it will be added to the existing formatting. If the **Apply** checkbox is ticked, the style is applied directly when you click it.*

- If this option is not ticked, click the **Apply** button to apply the selected style.
- To clear a character style, use the **Clear Selection Style** style. If you want to clear a paragraph style, choose **Clear Paragraph Style**.

Creating HTML styles

You can create your own styles that will be available to you for all the pages in your site.

- **Text - HTML Styles - New Style**

  or click the ▣ button on the **HTML Styles** palette

©Editions ENI - All rights reserved

Dreamweaver 3
5.6 Formatting text

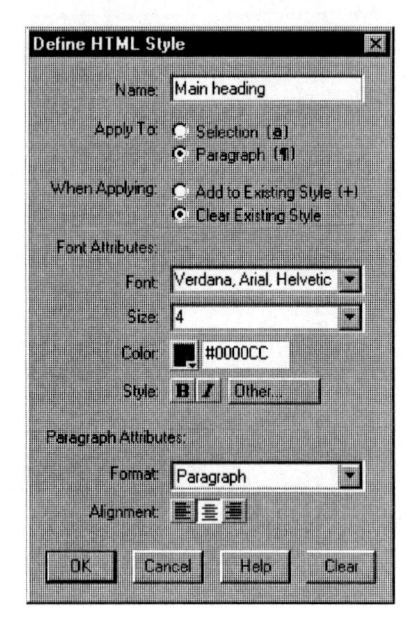

- In the **Name** box, type the style's name.
- For the **Apply To** option, choose:

  Selection (a)   to create a style that is for characters.

  Paragraph (¶)   to create a style that is for paragraphs.

- For the **When Applying** option, choose:

  Add to Existing Style (+)   so that when you apply the style it does not clear any existing formatting.

  Clear Existing Style   to delete all existing formatting elements when you apply the style.

- In the **Font Attributes** section, choose the character **Font**, **Size**, **Color** and **Style**.
- In the **Paragraph Attributes** section (only available for paragraph styles), choose a **Format** (**Paragraph**, **Heading x** or **Preformatted**) and an **Alignment** (**Left**, **Center** or **Right**).
- Click **OK**.

©Editions ENI - All rights reserved

Formatting text

Managing HTML styles

You can edit, copy and delete existing styles.

- **Window - HTML Styles**
- Select an existing style.
- Open the window's pop-up menu by clicking the ▶ button then choose **Edit**, **Duplicate** or **Delete**.

    You can also delete a style by clicking the trash can icon 🗑 that is visible at the bottom of the window.

> When you delete or edit a style this does not affect any text to which the style is applied: the changes to a style are not automatically updated in the text.

Sharing HTML styles

- All HTML styles are stored in a file called **styles.xml** in your site's **Library** folder. You can copy this file to another site or another computer.
- Press [F5] to show your site files.

```
└─ 📁 Library
     └─ 📄 styles.xml
```

Defining the default display characters

You can choose the characteristics of the font that will be used by default in documents when you do not apply a font or size.

- **Edit - Preferences - Fonts/Encoding** category
- Choose the characteristics for the display font of normal text in the current document in the **Proportional Font** and **Size** menus.
- Choose the characteristics of the display font of text for which the browser will use a fixed width font in the **Fixed Font** and **Size** menus.

> This feature is applied only to the appearance of the text in Dreamweaver, and has no influence on the formatting of the document or its appearance in a browser.

©Editions ENI - All rights reserved

Dreamweaver 3
5.8 Horizontal rules

Principle

You can insert a horizontal rule to separate different sections of your documents. This horizontal line can be placed in text or in a cell in a table.

The formatting options for this line are very restricted. You can change its width, thickness and alignment. You cannot change its colour (except with Microsoft Internet Explorer, where it will be an owned attribute, and outside W3C guidelines) or its style (no dashed lines with hyphens or dots).

Inserting a horizontal rule

- Click the appropriate place in the text.
- **Insert - Horizontal Rule**

or click the **Insert Horizontal Rule** button from the **Common** panel in the **Objects** palette.

By default, the horizontal rule separates the entire width of the window.

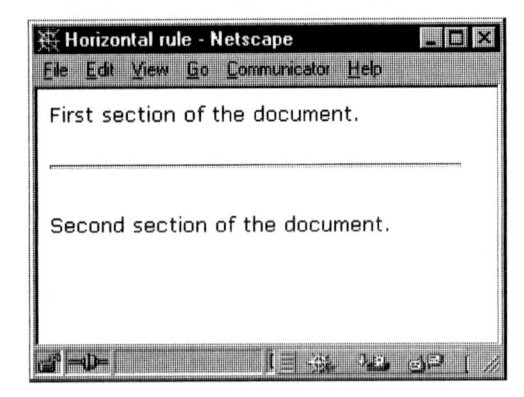

Formatting a horizontal rule

- Select the horizontal line by clicking it.

©Editions ENI - All rights reserved

Horizontal rules

- In the **Horizontal Rule** text box in the Property inspector, you can give the line a name, in case you are using it in a script.
- Define the width of the line in the **W** text box.

    You can choose a fixed value, in pixels.
    Example 1: 450 pixels. Whatever the size of the browser screen, the horizontal rule will always be 450 pixels wide. If a user resizes the browser window so that it is narrower than the rule, they will need to use the scroll bars in the browser window to see the whole bar.

    You can choose a relative value, given as a percentage:

    Example 2: 50%. The width of the rule is proportional to the width of the window. In this example, the rule is half as wide as the browser window. If a user resizes the browser window, the width of the rule is recalculated so that it remains 50% as wide as the window.

- Give the height of the rule in the **H** text box.

    The height is always given in pixels.

- Use the **Align** pop-up menu to choose the rule's alignment in the page: **Default** (centred), **Left**, **Center** or **Right**.
- Tick the **Shading** checkbox to give the rule a shadow aspect. Deactivate this option if you want the rule to look "filled".

    Examples of formatting:

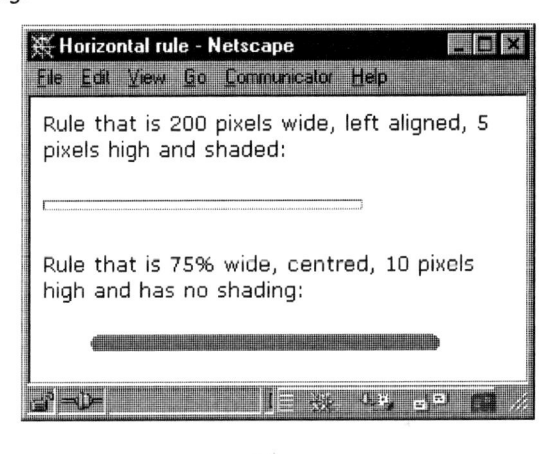

Principle

The first version of HTML did not support images: the aim was not to make "pretty" pages, but to transfer information rapidly. Today, the Web has very strong graphic connotations, to say the least. Images, videos and sounds are legion on the Internet.

Images that are inserted into your pages can have several roles: visual information, images that act as hyperlinks (buttons, rollovers and image-maps).

Image formats

There are two steps in the process of inserting an image into a Web page. The first step is the traditional work of correcting the colours: retouching and editing. The second step involves optimising the photo for Web publication. The aim is "simple": obtain a reasonable quality with the smallest possible file size! The skills of a Web graphic designer will produce a good-quality image without increasing the file size so much that the page takes too long to download in a browser. Do not forget that many Internet users are short on patience!

Three image formats are recognised by browsers:

.gif (Graphics Interchange Format)	this is a Unisys owned format and is ideal for vector-based images that do not use many colours (256 at the most) and use flat tints.
.jpeg (Joint Photographic Expert Group)	is ideal for photographic images that contain a high number of colours (thousands of colours), gradients or subtle shading (see the W3C site: http://www.w3.org/Graphics/JPEG/).
.png (Portable Network Graphics)	this format is perfect for images that are complex in terms of colour and transparency (see the W3C site: http://www.w3.org/Graphics/PNG/).

Image file paths

Principle

When you want to insert an image, you should define the file path for the image (as is the case for other resources that you might want to insert and for hyperlinks between documents).

You can define absolute paths and paths relative to the document or relative to the site root.

Images

Absolute paths

→ An absolute path gives the complete URL path to the resource:

```
<img src="http://www.mysite.org/general/images/chart.jpg">
```

`<img>` is the HTML element for an image.

`src="..."` is the attribute which indicates the image's path.

The chart.jpg image is in the images subfolder of the mysite Web site on the www machine, accessible using the http protocol.

→ Absolute paths are used when you are referring to a resource which is not in your site folder.

Document-relative paths

→ A document-relative path indicates a file path that is relative to the document.

Example 1:

```
<img src="chart.jpg">
```

C:\Sites\mysite
  chart.jpg
  page.htm

The chart.jpg image is in the same folder (the site folder here) as the page that contains it.

Example 2:

```
<img src="images/chart.jpg">
```

C:\Sites\mysite
  images
    chart.jpg
  page.htm

The document that contains the image is at the site root. The chart.jpg image is in the images folder, which is at the site root. The `images/` *code indicates that the images can be found lower down in the images folder branch.*

Example 3:

```
<img src="../images/chart.jpg">
```

©Editions ENI - All rights reserved

Dreamweaver 3
Images

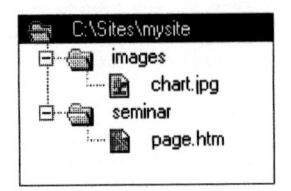

The document that contains the image is in a folder (seminar) that is at the site root. The chart.jpg image is in another folder, also at the site root. The .../code directs you to go up one level in the site structure in order to access the images folder. The images/ *code indicates that you need to go down the images branch of the structure.*

- Document-relative paths are used most of the time, because it is not necessary to indicate the URL elements about the site's protocol. If you move one of the site's folders on the server, all the links will be conserved.

Root-relative paths

- Root-relative paths give the path in relation to the site's root.

    Example:

    ```
    <img src="/images/chart.jpg">
    ```

    The chart.jpg image is in the images folder at the site root.
    In the image's path, the code / indicates the site root.

- If you move HTML documents that contain images inserted with a root-relative path, the image's path remains unchanged.

- Root-relative paths are used when you need to move files around your site on a regular basis.

Servers or browsers do not interpret root-relative paths. If you use this type of path, you should change the Dreamweaver settings so that you can use images and hyperlinks when you check your site in your browser on your computer. Use **Edit - Preferences - Preview in Browser** category and select **Preview Using Local Server**.

Inserting an image

You can insert an image into a document, table, layer, etc.

- Click in the appropriate place.

- **Insert - Image**

    or click the **Insert Image** button on the **Common** panel of the **Objects** palette.

©Editions ENI - All rights reserved

Images 6-3

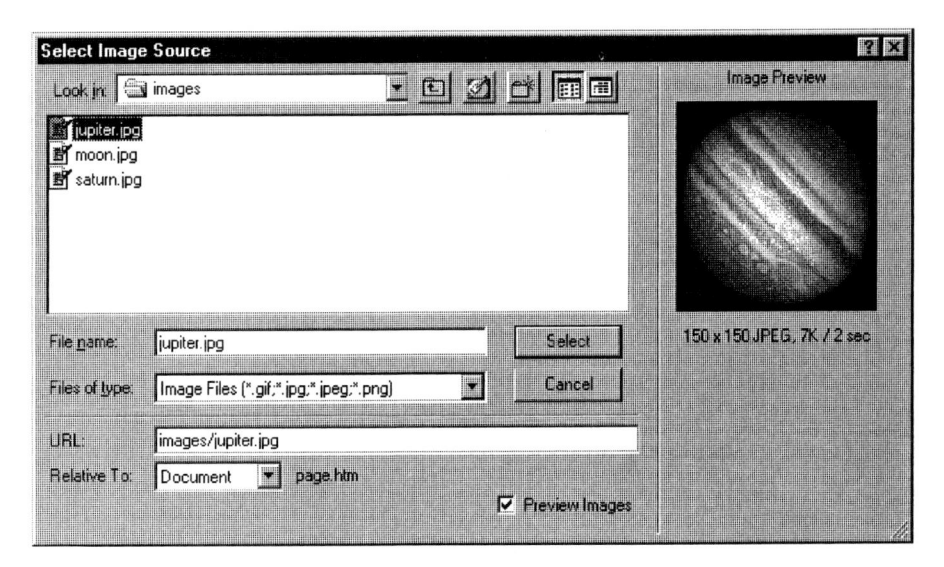

- Go to the folder in your site that contains the image you want to insert.
- In the **Relative To** pop-up menu, indicate the path: **Document** or **Site Root**.
- Click the **Select** button.

Defining the image's properties

- Select the inserted image.

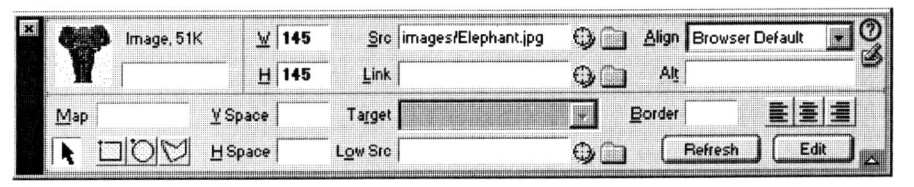

*The image's settings appear in the Property inspector. In the object type box **Image**, Dreamweaver tells you the size of the picture: here, it is 51K.*

- In the **Image** text box, type the name of the image in case you need to use it in a script.
- In the **W** and **H** boxes the image's height and width in pixels are shown automatically. If you change these details you will lose picture quality (you can also resize the image by dragging the black handles that appear around the selected image).

©Editions ENI - All rights reserved

If you do this, the new values are shown in bold.

- To reset the image's original dimensions, click **Refresh**.

- The image's file path is shown in the **Src** text box. You can change this by clicking the 📁 icon or by dragging the 🎯 icon towards the appropriate image in the **Site** window (see the chapter about Links for more information on how to use this icon).

- The **Link** text box can be used to define a hyperlink to another HTML page (you can use the **Target** pop-up menu to define the frame or page in which the linked page should load). The **Map** box can also be used to create hyperlinks (see the chapter about Links).

- The **Alt** text box (the `alt="..."` attribute of the `<img>` element) enables you to indicate an alternative text that will appear:
    - in place of the image in text-only browsers.
    - temporarily while the image is loaded.
    - when the link with the image is broken.
    - or to enable browsers that use speech synthesisers to describe the picture.

    Example of text that appears in place of an image when the file path is broken:

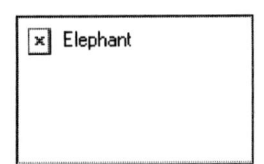

    ⌧ Elephant

Formatting an image

Adding a title

The **Alt** text box, which enables you to enter an alternative text, is used by Microsoft Internet Explorer and Netscape Navigator to show a "screen tip" when the mouse pointer is on the image. This does somewhat "hi-jack" the `alt` attribute. You should in fact use the `title="..."` attribute for the `img` element, according to the W3C guidelines.

- Select the image.
- Press [F10] to show the source code.

Images

You can see the code that inserts your image:

```
<img src="Elephant.jpg" width="546" height="594">
```

⊟ Add the attribute `"title="..."`.

```
<img src="Elephant.jpg" width="546" height="594" title="male
African elephant">
```

⊟ Return to the document by pressing F10.

⊟ Save your document and preview it in a browser, then place the mouse pointer over the image (without moving it!):

This standard W3C attribute is recognised by Microsoft Internet Explorer but not by Netscape Navigator: if you want your screen tip to appear in both browsers, use the `alt` attribute.

Aligning an image horizontally in relation to the page

⊟ Select the image.
⊟ In the Property inspector, click one of these buttons according to the alignment you want: **Left**, **Center** or **Right**.

Aligning an image vertically in relation to text

⊟ Select the image.
⊟ In the Property inspector, use the **Align** pop-up menu:

Browser Default	to use the default setting in the browser,
Baseline	to place the text baseline at the bottom of the image.
Top	aligns the top of the characters along the top of the image.

©Editions ENI - All rights reserved

Dreamweaver 3
Images

Middle	aligns the text baseline with the middle of the image.
Bottom	aligns the text baseline along the bottom of the image.
TextTop	aligns the tallest character with the top of the image.
Absolute Middle	aligns the middle of the text with the middle of the image.
Absolute Bottom	aligns the lowest characters (descenders such as the letters p, j and g) with the bottom of the image.

An example of alignments:

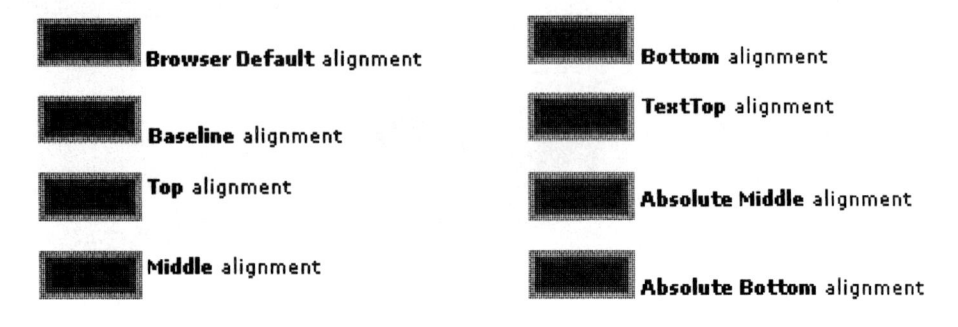

Browser Default alignment

Baseline alignment

Top alignment

Middle alignment

Bottom alignment

TextTop alignment

Absolute Middle alignment

Absolute Bottom alignment

Wrapping text around an image

You can insert an image into text and wrap this text around the image. The image (a floating image) is placed either in the paragraph of the text or to the left.

- Insert an image into a paragraph then select it.
- In the Property inspector, open the **Align** pop-up menu and choose **Left** or **Right**.
- You can move the image by dragging it (or by dragging the **Anchor Point**) in the paragraph.

Examples of wrapping:

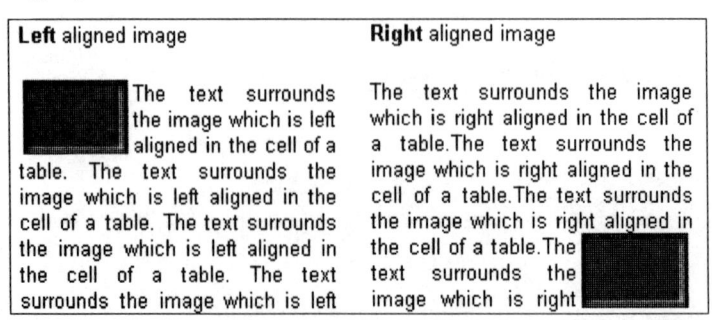

Left aligned image	**Right** aligned image
The text surrounds the image which is left aligned in the cell of a table. The text surrounds the image which is left aligned in the cell of a table. The text surrounds the image which is left aligned in the cell of a table. The text surrounds the image which is left	The text surrounds the image which is right aligned in the cell of a table. The text surrounds the image which is right aligned in the cell of a table. The text surrounds the image which is right aligned in the cell of a table. The text surrounds the image which is right

©Editions ENI - All rights reserved

Images

Changing the spacing between the image and text

You can increase the spacing between the image and the text so that the page does not look too "squashed". The spacing is given in pixels. The vertical spacing inserts x pixels above and below the image, and the horizontal spacing inserts x pixels to the left and right of the image.

- Insert a floating image (left or right) into a paragraph then select it.
- In the Property inspector, type the appropriate values, in pixels, in the **V Space** and **H Space** text boxes.

Example:

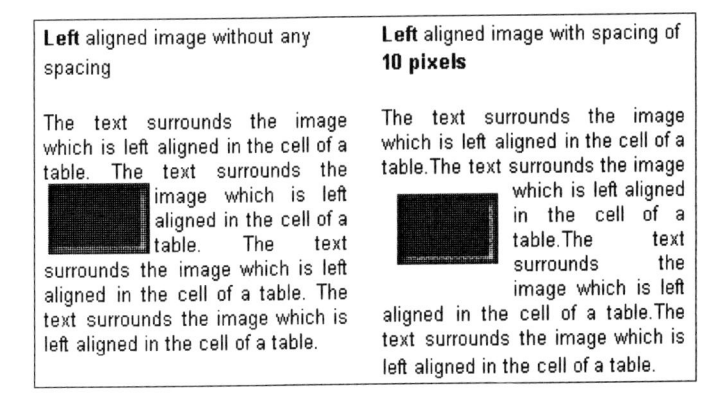

Left aligned image without any spacing	**Left** aligned image with spacing of **10 pixels**
The text surrounds the image which is left aligned in the cell of a table. The text surrounds the image which is left aligned in the cell of a table. The text surrounds the image which is left aligned in the cell of a table. The text surrounds the image which is left aligned in the cell of a table.	The text surrounds the image which is left aligned in the cell of a table. The text surrounds the image which is left aligned in the cell of a table. The text surrounds the image which is left aligned in the cell of a table. The text surrounds the image which is left aligned in the cell of a table.

Adding a border

You can frame an image with a black outline.

- Select the image.
- In the Property inspector, enter a value, in pixels, in the **Border** text box.

The border surrounds the image. This means that the image is not cut, and that it uses more space in the page.

Loading a low-resolution image temporarily

You can define a low-resolution image that will be loaded before the main, higher-resolution image. This will mean that a preview of the image will appear without having an adverse effect on the download time.

- Select the main image.
- In the **Low Src** text box in the Property inspector, browse your site folder and choose the low-resolution image.

©Editions ENI - All rights reserved

Dreamweaver 3
Images

This attribute (`lowsrc`) is not a W3C standard.

Using an external image editor

You can open an image that is placed in a Dreamweaver document using an external graphics application in order to edit it.

Defining the external editor

- **Edit - Preferences - External Editors** category

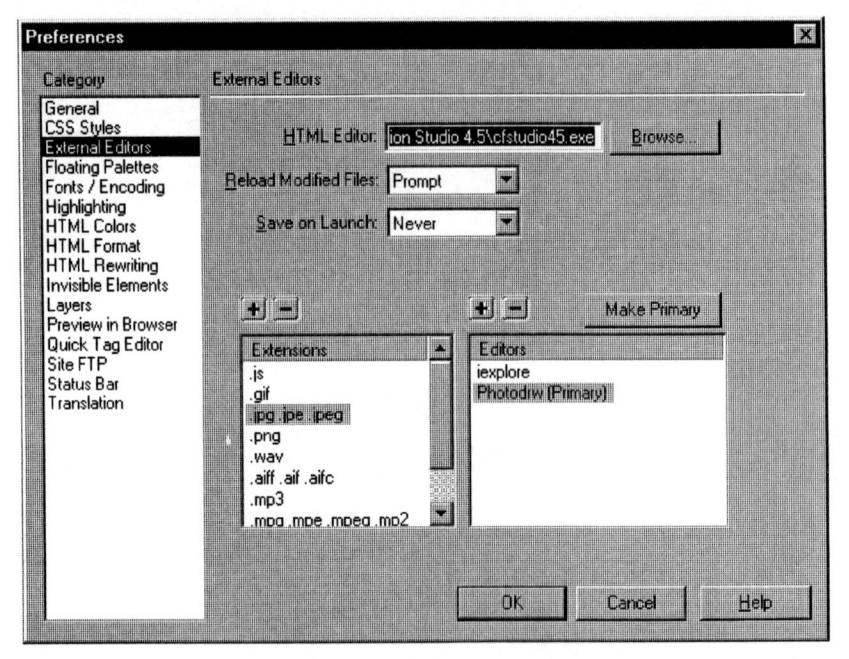

- In the **Extensions** list, choose or insert (using the ➕ symbol) the extension that corresponds to the file formats that will be managed by an external editor.

- In the **Editors** list choose or insert (using the ➕ symbol) the software you want to use to edit files with the selected extension.

    *The **Primary** application will be started by default.*

Images

Opening the external editor

- Select the image.
- Click the **Edit** button on the Property inspector. You can also right-click the image and choose **Edit With Software X**.

Using Macromedia® Fireworks

If you use Macromedia® Fireworks version 2 or 3 you can open the source file (not an optimised image) directly in order to edit it.

Editing images

- Select your image.
- **Commands - Optimize Image in Fireworks**

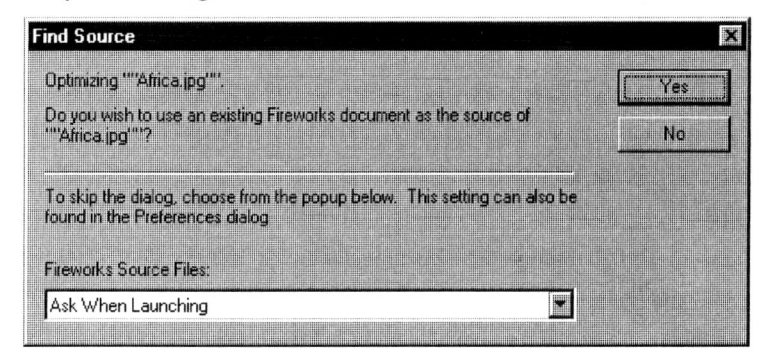

Dreamweaver asks you if you want to use an existing document for the changes.

- Click **Yes** to choose the .png format source file created in Fireworks.
  Click **No** to open the file in the Fireworks optimisation window.
- Make the necessary changes.
- Click **Update**.

Creating a photo album

Using Fireworks and automatically generated JavaScript you can create a page that contains low-resolution thumbnails in the form of an album in columns and with links to pages that contain larger, higher-definition versions of the images.

- **Commands - Create Web Photo Album**

Dreamweaver 3
Images

- In the **Photo Album Title, Subheading Info**, and **Other Info** text boxes, enter the details of the photo album.
- Give the folder that contains the originals in the **Source Images Folder** text box.
- Define the folder in which the optimised images will be stored in the **Destination Folder** text box.
- Indicate the size of the low-resolution images in the **Thumbnail Size** pop-up menu.
- Activate the **Show Filenames** option if you want to add the name of the original files under the thumbnails.
- In the **Thumbnail Format** pop-up menu, choose the optimisation format for the low-resolution images, and that of the high-resolution images in the **Photo Format** pop-up menu.
- Use the **Scale** text box to indicate by how much the images should be increased or reduced.
- Activate the **Create Navigation Page for Each Photo** option if you want to insert one high-resolution photo per HTML page.
- Click **OK**.

Dreamweaver generates hyperlinks in each of the thumbnails automatically. To see a high-resolution image in a page, simply click the appropriate thumbnail.

In the high-resolution image pages, there are links that return to the photo album home page and two other links: **Back** and **Next**.

- In the new page you will find links that enable you to browse the photo album:

    Home to return to the page that contains all the thumbnails.

    Back to go to the page that contains the previous (high-resolution) image in the photo album.

    Next to go to the page that contains the next (high-resolution) image in the photo album.

    In your site folder, Dreamweaver has created three subfolders in the destination folder:
    - an **images** folder which contains the high-resolution images,
    - a **pages** folder which contains the HTML pages with the high-resolution images and the hyperlinks for browsing,
    - a **thumbnails** folder which contains the image thumbnails.

©Editions ENI - All rights reserved

Images

Defining image behaviors

Behaviors are a combination of a user action (such as clicking a button) and an action which is a JavaScript. These behaviors can make your pages more dynamic. Some of the behaviors supplied with Dreamweaver can be applied directly to images. For more details about behaviors, see the relevant chapter.

Swapping images

Swapping images is a simple action: when an event occurs, one image can be replaced by another (in which case the script changes "only" the `src` attribute of the `img` element). The two images should be the same size otherwise they will be deformed. You can change one or several images at the same time.

- Insert the "button" image that will trigger the action (in other words, the button which the user will click): **Insert - Image**.
- In your page, insert the image(s) that will be swapped.
- Name these images in the Property inspector.
- Select the button image.
- Display the **Behaviors** palette: **Window - Behaviors**.
- Choose the appropriate browser version in the **Events For** pop-up menu.
- Click the ⊕ button to add a behavior and choose **Swap Image**.

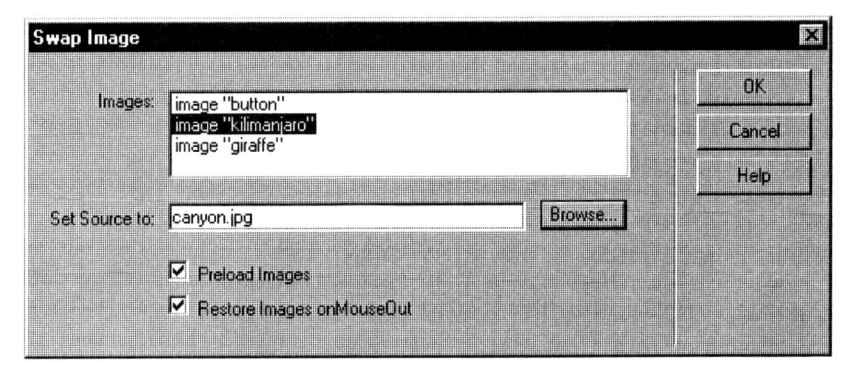

- In the **Images** list, select the first image you want to replace.
- In the **Set Source to** box, click the **Browse** button and select the replacement image.

©Editions ENI - All rights reserved

Dreamweaver 3
Images

- Activate these options:

    Preload Images to save time by downloading both images at the same time as the rest of the page. This will mean the replacement image will appear immediately.

    Restore Images onMouseOut to return to the original images when the mouse pointer is no longer over the trigger button.

- Select the next image you want to replace and repeat these steps.
- Click **OK**.

    In the **Behavior** palette you can see both the events:

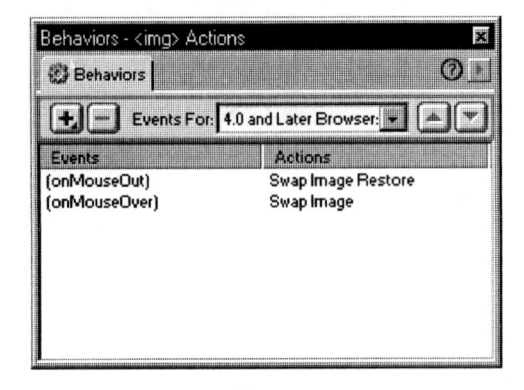

- To test the behaviour, save the document then preview the page in a browser.

    In this example, when the mouse pointer is over the button (onMouseOver), the images are swapped:

©Editions ENI - All rights reserved

Images

Preloading images

As you have just seen, some JavaScript functions use two images to make an image swap. If the replacement image has not been loaded, the user will have to wait until it has been loaded before he or she can see it, which can be time-consuming and irritating. You can use this action to load all the substitution images in your page, which can be done when the page loads (onLoad in the <body>).

- Select the <body> tag on the status bar <body>.
- Show the **Behaviors** palette: **Window - Behaviors**.
- Choose the browser version.
- Click the + button to add a behavior and choose **Preload Images**.

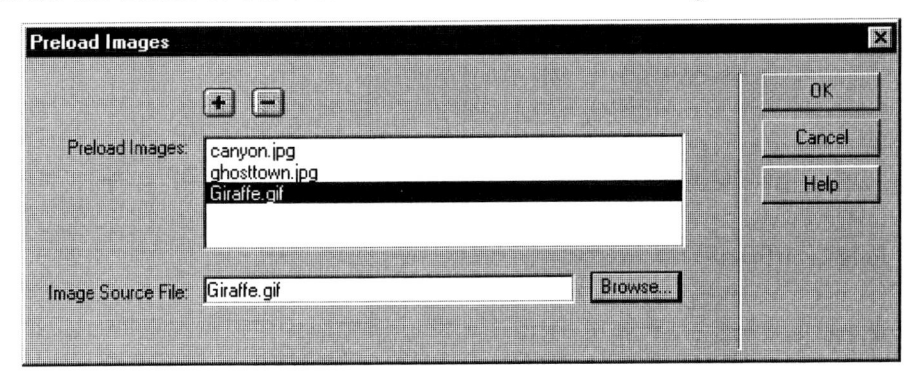

- Click the **Browse** button next to the **Image Source File** box and select the first image you want to preload.

   *Its name appears in the **Preload Images** list.*

- Click the + button to add another image to the list of images you want to preload.
- Click the **Browse** button again to select this second image. Do this for all the images you want to preload.
- Click **OK**.

©Editions ENI - All rights reserved

Principles for using tables

Tables play two important roles in Web pages: they can be used to create standard data tables and can produce an elaborate page setup.

Do not forget that the Internet, and thus HTML, was originally created for scientists for whom the use of data tables was extremely important for the presentation of results.

Example of a data table:

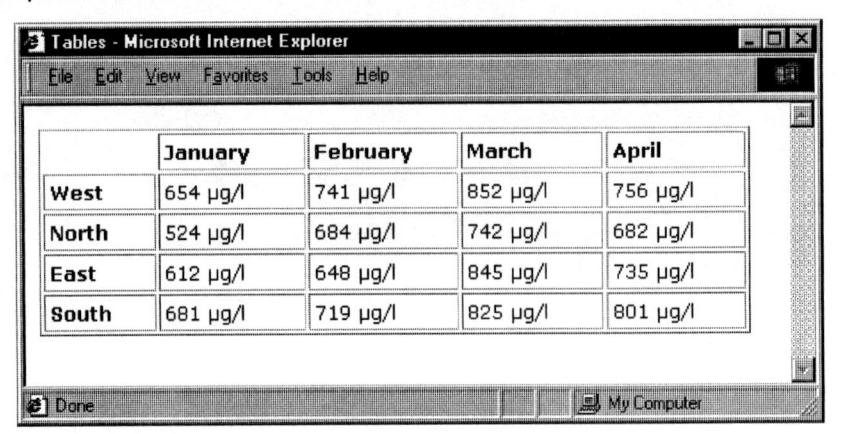

	January	February	March	April
West	654 µg/l	741 µg/l	852 µg/l	756 µg/l
North	524 µg/l	684 µg/l	742 µg/l	682 µg/l
East	612 µg/l	648 µg/l	845 µg/l	735 µg/l
South	681 µg/l	719 µg/l	825 µg/l	801 µg/l

These days, however, Web architects are no longer using tables in quite the same way. They use the cells of tables to position page setup elements by merging cells, if necessary, in order to centre text or images.

In fact, as long as browsers do not recognise positioning style sheets (CSS-P) (Dreamweaver layers) in the same way it will be necessary to use table cells in order to position elements such as images, text and multimedia objects where you want them in a page.

Tables

An example of page setup using tables:

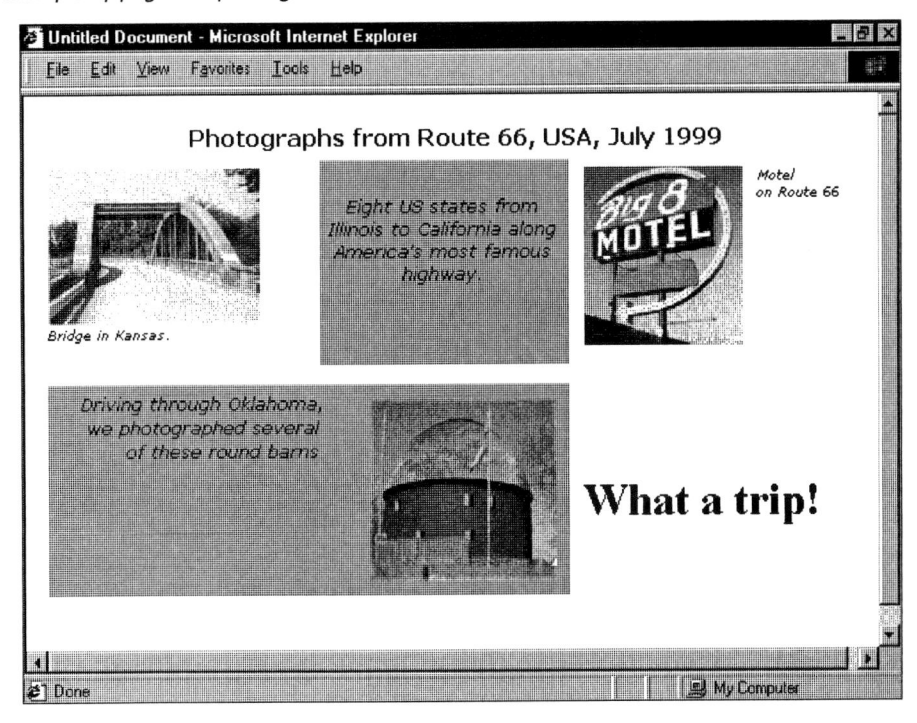

More and more Web visual creation applications (used for creating elements such as buttons, rollover images and image-maps) such as Macromedia Fireworks and Adobe ImageReady allow you to export complex compositions, which incorporate different image formats and scripts, in tables.
The use of tables is thus currently very important for the creation of Web pages.

Inserting a table

Creating a table

You can insert a table where you want in your document, including inside the cells of another table for complicated page setup.

- Click in the appropriate place.
- **Insert - Table**

  or click the **Insert Table** button on the **Common** panel of the **Objects** palette.

Dreamweaver 3
Tables

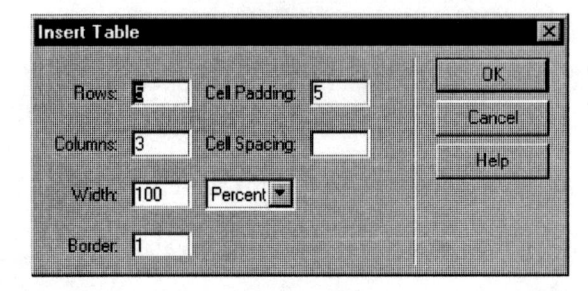

- Use the **Rows** and **Columns** text boxes to indicate the number of rows and columns you want in your table.
- Indicate the distance, in pixels, between the cell borders and their contents in the **Cell Padding** text box.

    This allows you to increase the spacing between the cell's border and the text or image it contains, giving a airier presentation.

- In the **Cell Spacing** box, indicate the space, in pixels, to be left between cells.

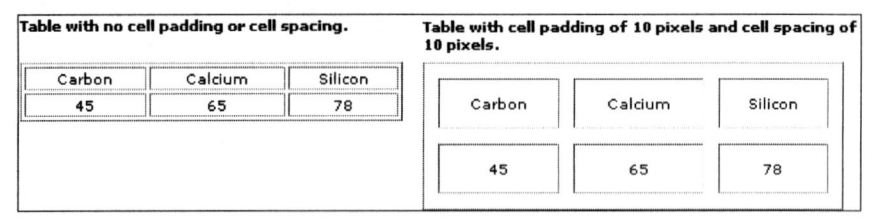

- The **Width** text box can be used to define the width of the table.

    *You can use **pixels** as the unit of measurement. If you choose pixels, the width of the table will be fixed, whatever the width of the browser window. If you resize the browser window by a considerable amount, you will need to use the horizontal scroll bar to see the right-hand part of the table:*

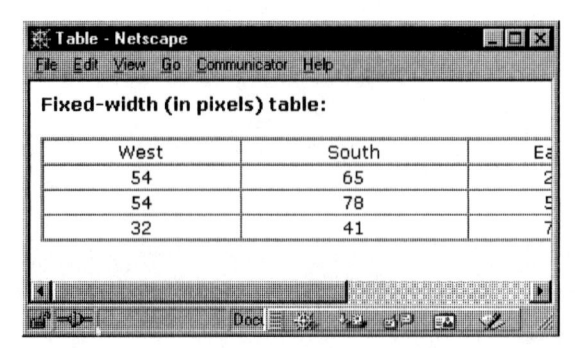

© Editions ENI - All rights reserved

Tables

You can use **Percent** as the unit of measurement. The width of the table will be proportional to that of the browser window. A table that is 75% wide will always be 3/4 as wide as the browser window, even if it has been resized (the only limit is the size required to show the cell contents!):

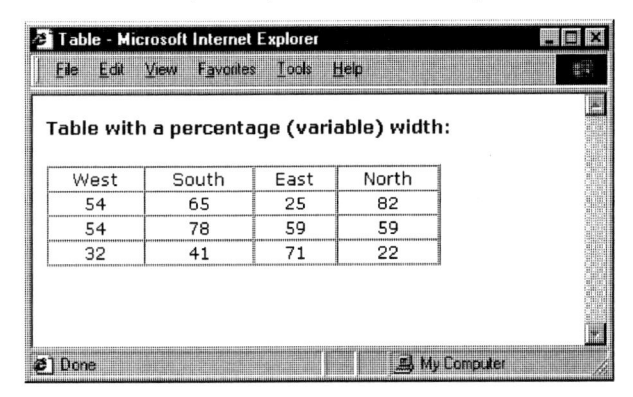

```
Table with a percentage (variable) width:

West    South   East    North
 54      65      25      82
 54      78      59      59
 32      41      71      22
```

If the contents are larger than the container (if, for example, you insert an image which is 200 pixels wide in a cell which is only 150 pixels wide) it will be perfectly visible because the table will grow to fit it.

- In the **Border** text box, enter the thickness of the table's external border, in pixels.

If you indicate a border of 8 pixels, this value will be applied to the external border of the table, but the internal grid will remain at 1 pixel.

```
Table with a border of 0 pixels          Table with a border of 8 pixels

Carbon    Calcium    Silicon
  45        65         78              Carbon    Calcium    Silicon
                                         45        65         78
Table with a border of 1 pixel

Carbon  | Calcium  | Silicon
  45    |   65     |   78
```

Setting the preferences

You can change the preferences so that you do not have to specify any values when you insert a table. Once the table is inserted, then you can format it.

- **Edit - Preferences - General** category
- Deactivate the **Show Dialog when Inserting Objects** option.

When you insert a table, it has the same characteristics as the last table inserted.

- You can speed up data entry in a table by deactivating the automatic update: **Edit - Preferences - General** category.

©Editions ENI - All rights reserved

🡢 Make sure the **Faster Table Editing (Deferred Update)** checkbox is ticked.

A table will be updated when you click outside the table. If you activate this option, you can also update the table using the following shortcut keys: ⌘ Space *(Macintosh) or* Ctrl Space *(Windows).*

Importing tabular data

You can import data from software which manages data in tables, such as a spreadsheet or database. Simply export the data in a format that uses a standard data separator (such as a tab stop or comma).

🡢 **File - Import - Import Table Data** or **Insert - Tabular Data**

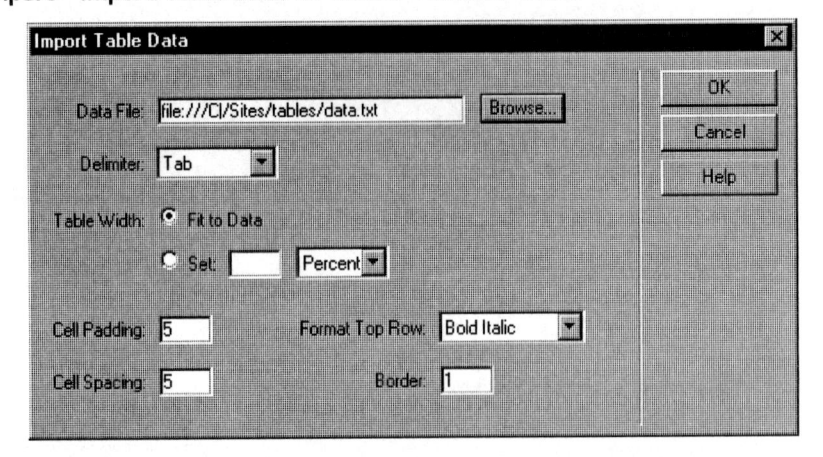

🡢 Type the name of the data file in the **Data File** box, or click **Browse** to find the file.

🡢 In the **Delimiter** pop-up menu, choose the data separator: **Tab**, **Comma**, **Semicolon**, **Colon** or **Other**.

🡢 Activate the **Fit to Data** option if you want the column widths to adjust to the widest data, or choose **Set** if you want to choose your own table width in the text box to the right (choose the unit of measurement from the pop-up menu: **Percent** or **Pixels**).

🡢 Use the **Format Top Row** menu to apply particular formatting to the data in the first row.

🡢 Define the standard formatting: **Cell Padding**, **Cell Spacing** and **Border**.

Tables

This document has been created with the Windows Notepad, and each item of data is separated by a tab stop:

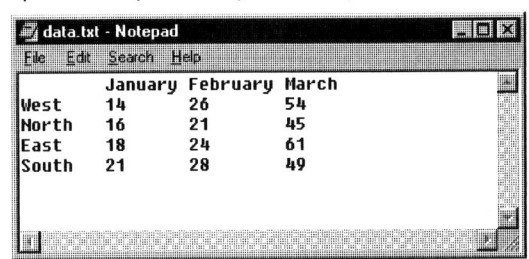

This is the result of the importation of the data into Dreamweaver:

Formatting a table

Selecting the table

- Point to one of the table's borders and click when the pointer becomes a four-headed arrow:

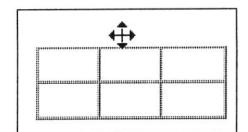

  or click once inside the table and use **Modify - Table - Select Table** or **Edit - Select All**.

Formatting the table

- Select the table.
- Use the Property inspector:

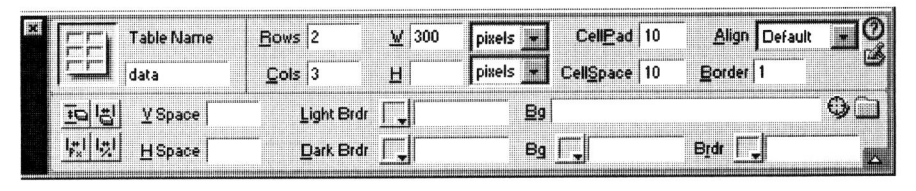

The top part of the Property inspector contains the settings you chose when you inserted the table.

©Editions ENI - All rights reserved

Dreamweaver 3
Tables

- In the **Table Name** text box, type the name of the table if you need to refer to it in a script.
- In the **Rows** and **Cols** text boxes, change the number of rows and columns in the table, if necessary.
- Use the **W** and **H** text boxes to change the width and height of the table, and choose **pixels** or **%** as the unit of measurement.
- Indicate the distance, in pixels, between the cell borders and their contents in the **CellPad** box.
- Indicate the spacing between each cell in the **CellSpace** box.
- In the **Border** box, enter the thickness of the table's external border. If you type 0, you will not be able to see the table in your Dreamweaver page unless you activate the command **View - Table Borders**.
- Choose the table's position on the page from the **Align** pop-up menu: **Left**, **Center** or **Right**.
- The buttons enable you to manage the width, height and unit of measurement of the table, which are explained in the next section of this topic.
- Use the **V Space** and **H Space** boxes to define the space, in pixels, above, below and on each side of the table so that you can move the table away from text elements in the page.

Take care, as this is not W3C standard HTML code.

- The **Light Brdr** and **Dark Brdr** colours enable you to choose light or dark colours in order to create a 3-D effect on the table's external border.

This is not W3C standard HTML code. The effect produced in this way is recognised only by Microsoft Internet Explorer.

- Use the **Bg** box to choose a background image for the table.

This is not W3C standard HTML code. However, this effect is recognised by Microsoft Internet Explorer and Netscape Navigator.

- The **Bg** pop-up menu is for choosing the table's background colour.
- You can choose the colour of the border in the **Brdr** colour box.

©Editions ENI - All rights reserved

Tables

Changing the width and height of a table

The width and height of a table can also be changed manually using the mouse.

- Select the table.

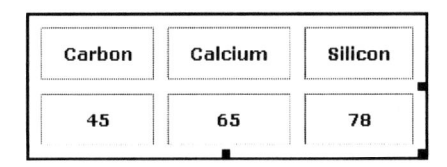

Carbon	Calcium	Silicon
45	65	78

- Drag the bottom handle to resize the table vertically, the right handle to resize it horizontally, or the corner handle to resize it in both directions.

Converting the table's width into pixels/percentage

Sometimes it is useful to switch the width of a table from pixels (fixed width) to percentage (relative width).

- Select the table.
- **Modify - Table - Convert Widths to Pixels** or **Convert Widths to Percent**

  or click the [icon] or [icon] buttons on the Property inspector.

Deleting the cells' heights/widths

When the dimensions indicated for the table are incorrect and this causes display problems, sometimes the simplest solution is to delete the dimensions and start again.

- Select the table.
- **Modify - Table - Clear Cell Heights** and **Clear Cell Widths**

  or click the [icon] and [icon] buttons on the Property inspector.

Selecting cells in a table

- To activate a cell, click in it once.

  The insertion point flashes in the cell and you can type text, select existing text, etc.

- To select a cell, [⌘]-click (Macintosh) or [Ctrl]-click (Windows) in the cell.

  The cell is selected as an object.

©Editions ENI - All rights reserved

Dreamweaver 3
8.2 Tables

- To select non-adjacent cells you can ⌘-click (Macintosh) or Ctrl-click (Windows) in the first cell, hold down the ⌘ or Ctrl keys then click in each of the other cells you want to select.
- If you select a cell by accident, click it again to deselect it.
- You can select several adjacent cells by dragging over them, or click in the first cell, hold the Shift key down and click in the last cell.
- Select a column by pointing to the top of the column and clicking when the pointer becomes a thick black arrow:

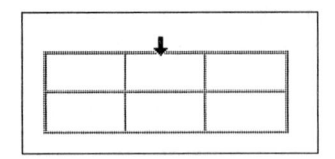

- To select a row, click to the left of the row, when the pointer takes the shape of a thick black arrow.

Formatting cells

You can format cells in your table in a particular way. This formatting takes priority over the overall table formatting. For example, a coloured cell will appear with its own colour, even if you have applied a background colour to the table.

- Select the cells concerned.
- Use the lower part of the Property inspector (the options at the top of the Property inspector enable you to define the formatting or the cell contents such as text or images):

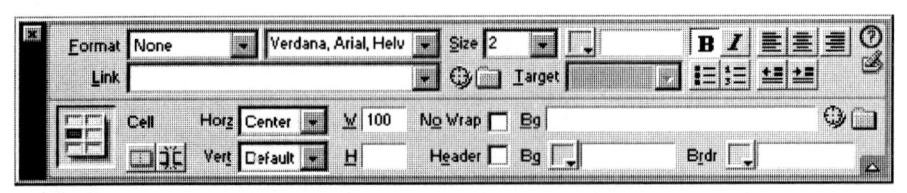

- Use the **Horz** pop-up menu to choose the cell contents' horizontal alignment: **Left**, **Center**, **Right** or **Default**. This last choice uses the browser's default settings, usually a left alignment.

©Editions ENI - All rights reserved

Tables

- Indicate the vertical alignment of the contents using the **Vert** pop-up menu:

  Default   uses the browser's default settings, usually a middle alignment.
  Top   the contents are placed at the top of the cell.
  Middle   the contents are placed in the middle of the cell.
  Bottom   the contents are placed at the bottom of the cell.
  Baseline all first lines of text in each cell with this attribute will be aligned.

  In order to see the effect of these alignments, the contents of one cell needs to be much bigger (a big image, a lot of text, or a fixed height) than that of the other cells:

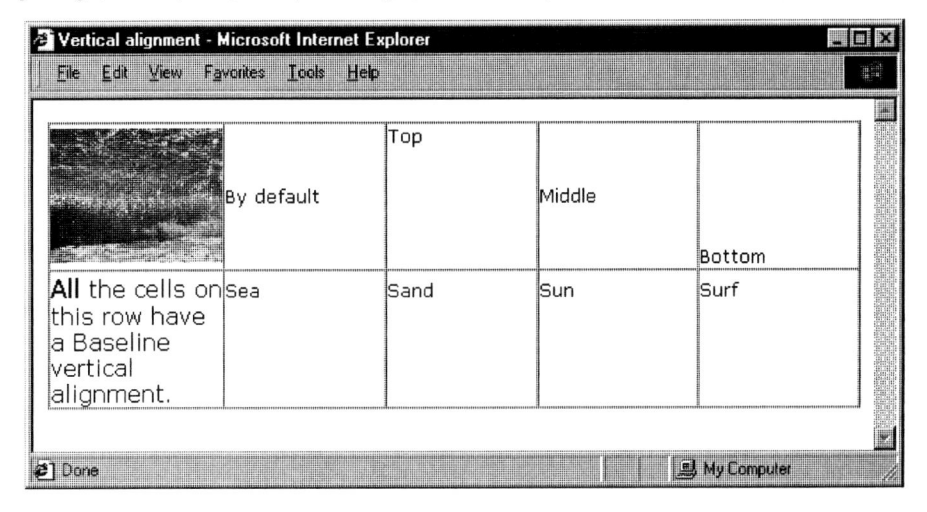

	Top		
By default		Middle	
			Bottom
All the cells on this row have a Baseline vertical alignment. Sea	Sand	Sun	Surf

- You can indicate the width and height of the table in pixels or percentage (type %) in the **W** and **H** text boxes.

- Be careful! To avoid any strange results when you display the page, make sure that the sum of the cell widths is equal to that of the table, and the same for the height. If you do not check this, you may end up with cells that are not placed in the table properly and the result will not be what you were expecting. Also, try to avoid mixing pixel measurements with those expressed as percentages, as this too can lead to surprising results!

- When the **No Wrap** option is active, no automatic line breaks are inserted into the text in the cell. The size of cell increases as you type text.

©Editions ENI - All rights reserved

Dreamweaver 3
Tables

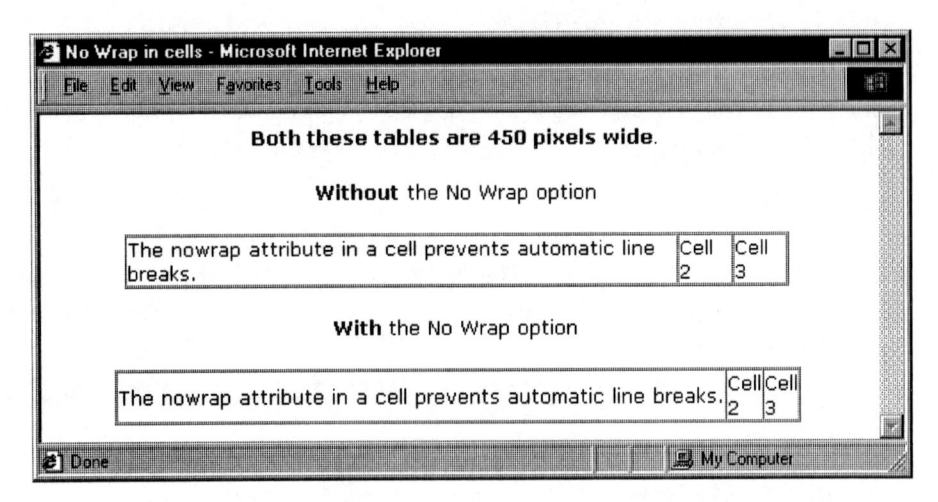

> *Screenshot: No Wrap in cells - Microsoft Internet Explorer*
>
> Both these tables are 450 pixels wide.
>
> **Without** the No Wrap option
>
> | The nowrap attribute in a cell prevents automatic line breaks. | Cell 2 | Cell 3 |
>
> **With** the No Wrap option
>
> | The nowrap attribute in a cell prevents automatic line breaks. | Cell 2 | Cell 3 |

- Activate the **Header** option if the text in the selected cells should be automatically formatted in bold type and centred.

- Use the **Bg** pop-up menu to choose a background colour for the selected cells `Bg  #CCCCFF`.

- You can use the **Bg** text box to apply a background image to the selected cells using the **Point to File** and **Browse to File** icons `Bg blue.gif`.

> 📖 This is not W3C standard HTML code. However, Microsoft Internet Explorer and Netscape Navigator support this formatting.

- The colour you choose in the **Brdr** box will be applied to the borders of the selected cells `Brdr  #FF0033`.

> 📖 This is not W3C standard HTML code. However, this formatting is recognised by Microsoft Internet Explorer and Netscape Navigator.

Formatting tables using templates

You can format your tables using different predefined templates.

- Select the table.
- **Commands - Format Table**

©Editions ENI - All rights reserved

Tables

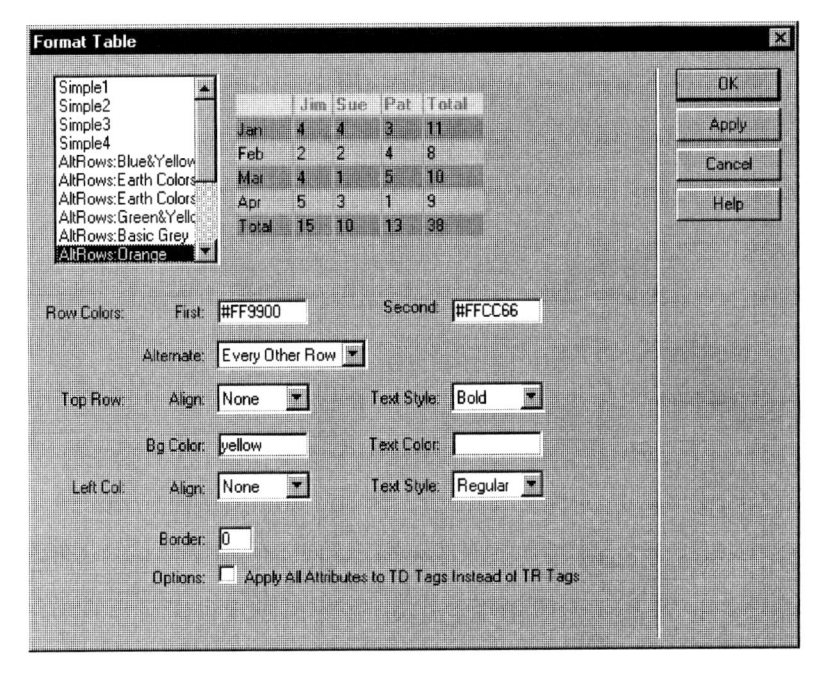

- Select the format you want from the list on the left.
- Under **Row Colors**, choose the **First** and **Second** colours by typing the colour code or its name in the text boxes.
- Use the **Alternate** menu to choose how you want to apply the colours to the table's rows: if you choose <do not alternate> the first colour will be applied to every row, **Every Other Row**, **Every Two**, **Three** or **Four Rows**.

*The **Top Row** options enable you to customise the appearance of the first row in the table.*

- Choose the text alignment for the cells in the first row in the **Align** pop-up menu: **None**, **Left**, **Center** or **Right**.
- Choose the text format for the cells in the first row in the **Text Style** pop-up menu: **Regular**, **Bold**, **Italic** or **Bold Italic**.
- You can choose a background colour for the cells in the first row using the **Bg Color** text box.
- In the **Text Color** box you can choose a specific colour for the text in the cells of the first row.

*Use the **Left Col** options to define the format of the first column in the table.*

- Choose the alignment for text in all the cells in the first column from the **Align** menu: **None**, **Left**, **Center** and **Right**.
- Use the **Text Style** pop-up menu to define the text format for the cells in the first column: **Regular**, **Bold**, **Italic** or **Bold Italic**.
- You can enter the thickness of the table's external border, in pixels, in the **Border** text box.
- Activate the **Apply All Attributes to TD Tags Instead of TR Tags** if you want to apply all the formatting attributes (text, alignment, colour etc) to the cell HTML elements `<td>` and not to the rows in the table `<tr>`.

Formatting cell contents

- A cell can contain text, lists, and images. All these contents can be formatted using traditional formatting, as seen previously.
- If you select an image or text in the cell of a table, the Property inspector displays formatting elements relevant to the selected contents.

Changing the structure of a table

Adding rows and columns

You can add rows and columns to a table whenever you choose. There are several ways to do this.

- Click in the last cell in your table then press [icon]: a new row is inserted.

    You can also use the Property inspector.

- Select the table. In the Property inspector, increase the value in the **Rows** and/or **Cols** text box(es).

    New rows appear at the bottom of the table and new columns at the right. The third technique uses the **Modify** menu.

- Click in the cell above which you want to insert a new row and use **Modify - Table - Insert Row**.
- Click in the cell to the left of which you want to insert a new column and use **Modify - Table - Insert Column**.
- Click in the cell next to which you want to insert rows or columns and use **Modify - Table - Insert Rows or Columns**.

Tables 8-7

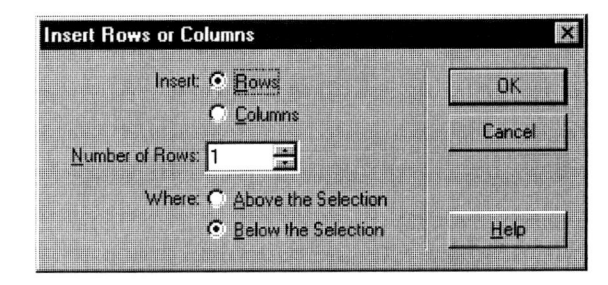

- Choose to **Insert Rows** or **Columns**.
  Indicate the **Number of Rows** or **Columns** you want to insert.
  In the **Where** options, choose **Above** or **Below the Selection** for rows; **Before** or **After current Column** for columns.

Deleting rows and columns

There are several techniques for deleting rows and columns.

- Click in the cell, row or column you want to delete.

  Modify - Table - Delete Row or **Delete Column**

  You can also use the Property inspector:

- Select your table. In the Property inspector, reduce the value in the **Rows** and/or **Cols** text box(es).

  Rows are deleted from the bottom of the table and columns from the right.

  You can also use the keyboard:

- Select the row or column you want to delete and press the ⌫ key.

Merging cells in a table

You can improve the format of a table by merging cells horizontally or vertically, if, for example, you want to insert a title. Only adjacent cells can be merged. Merging cells in tables is a key tool for a good page setup.

- Select the adjacent cells that you want to merge.

- **Modify - Table - Merge Cells**

  or click the ▫ tool on the Property inspector.

©Editions ENI - All rights reserved

Dreamweaver 3
Tables

Orginal table:	Table with merged cells:

- You can increase the size of a merged cell by clicking in it then:

  Modify - Table - Increase Row Span or **Increase Column Span**

- To reduce the size of a merged cell, click in it then:

  Modify - Table - Decrease Row Span or **Decrease Column Span**

Splitting cells

You can choose to split cells that you have merged to return to the original presentation, or simply split any selected cell.

- Click in the cell concerned.
- **Modify - Table - Split Cell**

  or click the [ ] button on the Property inspector.

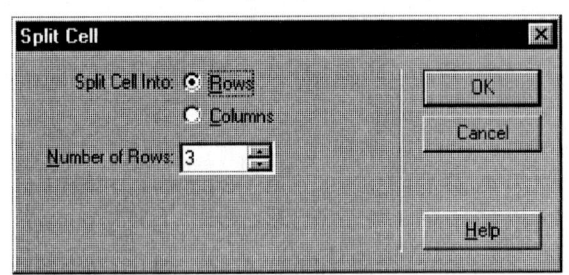

- You can choose to **Split Cell Into Rows** or **Columns** then indicate the **Number of Rows** or **Columns**.

©Editions ENI - All rights reserved

Tables

Inserting a table into another table

You can achieve complicated formatting, or non-uniform frames by inserting a table into the cell of another table.

☐ Click in the table's cell and create another table.

In this example, the first table has 3 columns and 4 rows. The cells in the first and last rows have been merged. In the first and last cells of the third row, two tables with their own formatting have been inserted.

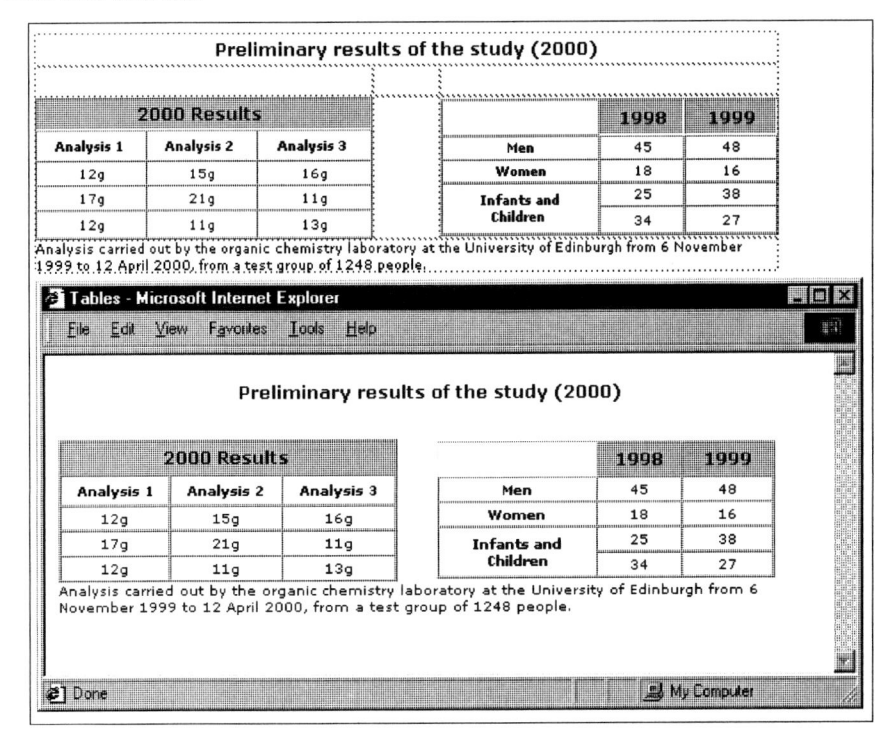

Preliminary results of the study (2000)						
2000 Results					**1998**	**1999**
Analysis 1	Analysis 2	Analysis 3		Men	45	48
12g	15g	16g		Women	18	16
17g	21g	11g		Infants and Children	25	38
12g	11g	13g			34	27
Analysis carried out by the organic chemistry laboratory at the University of Edinburgh from 6 November 1999 to 12 April 2000, from a test group of 1248 people.						

Tables - Microsoft Internet Explorer

File Edit View Favorites Tools Help

Preliminary results of the study (2000)						
2000 Results					**1998**	**1999**
Analysis 1	Analysis 2	Analysis 3		Men	45	48
12g	15g	16g		Women	18	16
17g	21g	11g		Infants and Children	25	38
12g	11g	13g			34	27
Analysis carried out by the organic chemistry laboratory at the University of Edinburgh from 6 November 1999 to 12 April 2000, from a test group of 1248 people.						

Done — My Computer

Sorting a table

You can sort the data in a table according to up to two criteria.

☐ Click in the table.

☐ **Commands - Sort Table**

©Editions ENI - All rights reserved

Dreamweaver 3
Tables

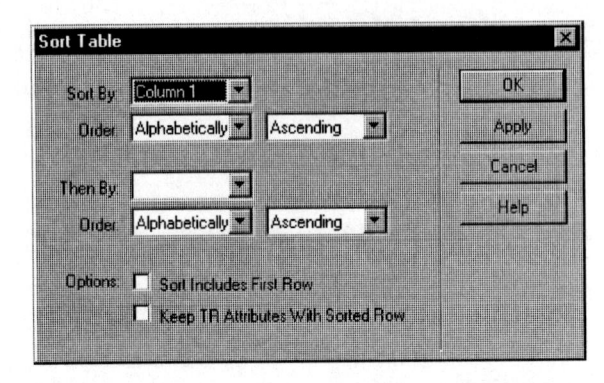

- Choose which column should be sorted in the **Sort By** pop-up menu: **Column 1**, **Column 2**, etc.
- Use the **Order** pop-up menus to choose how you want to sort: **Alphabetically** or **Numerically**, then **Ascending** or **Descending**.
- In the **Then By** pop-up menu, choose the second column to be sorted in case of identical values in the first column and indicate the sort order in the same way as you did for the first column.
- Activate the **Sort Includes First Row** option if the first row in the table is to be sorted. If it is included, it may well be moved.
- Activate the **Keep TR Attributes With Sorted Row** option to make sure that any formatting on the first row is moved with the row.

Exporting a table

If you need to, you can export a table you have created in Dreamweaver. You need to choose the export format.

- Click in the table.
- **File - Export - Export Table**
- Choose the **Delimiter** from the pop-up menu: **Tab**, **Space**, **Comma**, **Semicolon** or **Colon**.
- Choose the type of **Line Breaks**: **Windows**, **Mac** or **UNIX**.

Forms

Principle

Forms enable you to create a certain amount of interactivity between a surfer and the Web site developer. Users can enter data, make choices from lists, select choices using check boxes and radio buttons, etc.

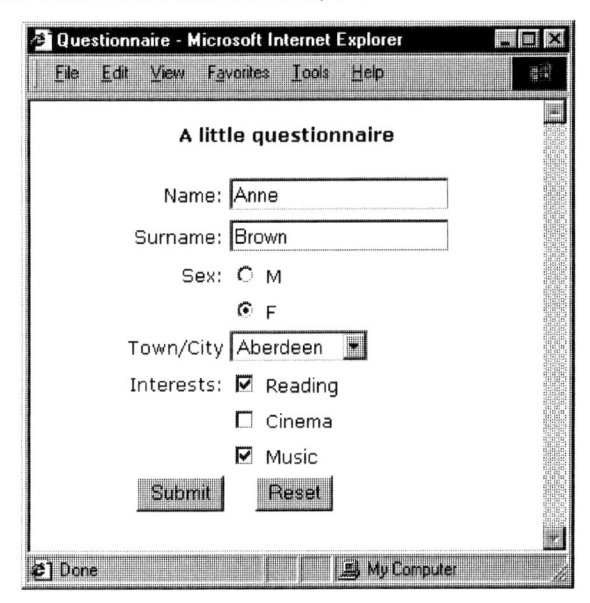

Two elements are essential if you want to use forms: the form and all its objects (text boxes, lists, menus, checkboxes and so on) and a script that will manage the data. You can create the form in Dreamweaver, but you will need to create the script with another tool using a programming language (such as Perl, php or Java).

In a form, only the objects (text boxes, lists etc) are used in the script, which recovers the name of these objects and their values; these are name/value couples. To avoid any ambiguity between different form objects, each object must have only one name. The script ignores all the other elements in the form: text, tables, any formatting etc.

To improve the page setup of a form, the different elements (form objects and text) are generally placed in cells in a table.

Creating a form

⇨ You must first insert the form, which will appear as a rectangle drawn with a dashed red line. Make sure that this invisible element can be seen:

Edit - Preferences - Invisible Elements category

Make sure the **Form Delimiter** check box is ticked.

⇨ Check that the invisible elements are visible: **View - Invisible Elements**.

⇨ Click in the page where you want to insert the form and use **Insert - Form** or open the **Forms** panel in the **Objects** palette and click the **Insert Form** button.

One of the essential parameters for a form is the path to the script that will manage the data. You can define it in the Property inspector:

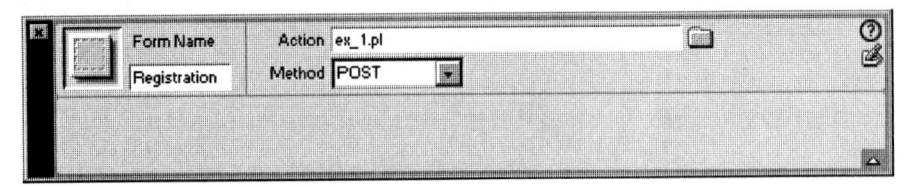

⇨ Give the form's name in the **Form Name** text box.

⇨ In the **Action** text box, enter the path to the script that will manage the form. Click the folder icon to select the path on your disk.

⇨ Use the **Method** pop-up menu to choose the way in which the data should be handled:

- The **GET** method sends the data to the server on a URL using a GET request.
- The **POST** method sends the form values to the server as the body of a message using a POST request.

You should ask your developer (unless you are the developer!) which method has been chosen for the script.

©Editions ENI - All rights reserved

Forms

Adding objects to a form

Inserting a simple text box

You can insert a simple text box in which a user can type short texts (such as their name, surname, the town where they live, etc).

- Click the appropriate place in the form.
- If necessary, type the text that will indicate what sort of data is required in the text field.
- **Insert - Form Object - Text Field**

    or click the **Insert Text Field** button from the **Forms** panel on the **Objects** palette.

    The Property inspector enables you to choose the settings for the text field:

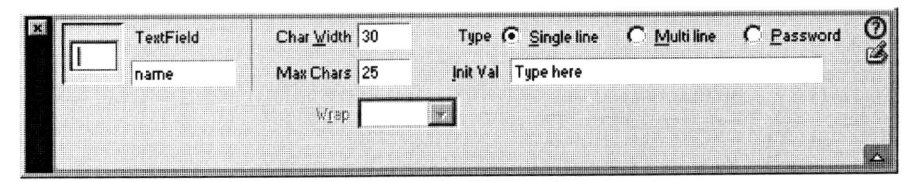

- In the **TextField** box give the field a name in place of **textfield**.
- Choose **Single line** as the **Type**.
- In the **Char Width** box, enter the graphic width of the text field, using characters as the unit of measurement.
- Indicate the maximum number of characters that the user can enter in the **Max Chars** text box.
- If necessary, type the text that will appear by default in the text field (which users will replace with their data) in the **Init Val** box.

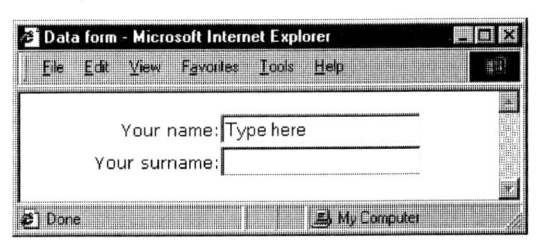

*An example of single line text fields: The Your name and Your surname text fields are **Single line** text fields.*

©Editions ENI - All rights reserved

Inserting a multi line text field

Users can type more text in larger text fields.

- As in the previous case, insert the text field.
- In the **TextField** box, replace **textfield** with the field's name.
- Choose **Multi line** as the **Type**.
- In the **Char Width** box, enter the graphic width of the text field, using characters as the unit of measurement.
- Indicate the height of the field in the **Num Lines** text box.
- In the **Wrap** pop-up menu, choose how the text should behave in the text box:

Default	uses the browser's default settings.
Off	lines that are too long will not be cut at the right, and the text will continue along the same line. This will activate the horizontal scroll bar.
Virtual	lines that are too long will be cut at the right and the text will continue on the next line in the text box. However, no line break is inserted into the form.
Physical	lines that are too long will be cut at the right and the text will continue on the next line. In the form, line breaks will be inserted where they are in the text.

This attribute (wrap) is not a W3C standard, but is supported by Microsoft Internet Explorer and Netscape Navigator.

- In the **Init Val** type any text that should appear by default before the user types his or her data.

Inserting a password text field

In this type of text field, users will not see the characters they type, but will see "bullets".

- Insert the text field as before.
- Define the text field as being a **Password** field under **Type**.

Examples of different text fields: the Your Password field, **Password** type; the Your Comments field **Multi line** type.

©Editions ENI - All rights reserved

Forms

Inserting check boxes

In most graphic interfaces, check boxes are synonymous with multiple choices, which means that users can select several options.

- Click in the appropriate place in your form.
- If you need to, type some text to indicate the nature of the check box.
- **Insert - Form Object - Check Box**

    or click the **Insert Checkbox** button from the **Forms** panel on the **Objects** palette.

    You can choose the settings for this object in the Property inspector:

    | CheckBox interests | Checked Value music | Initial State ○ Checked ● Unchecked |

- Give the field a name in place of **checkbox** in the **CheckBox** text box.
- Use the **Checked Value** text box to indicate the value that will be used in the script.
- Under **Initial State** choose the default appearance of the check box, before any intervention by the user:

    Checked the check box will be ticked. Use this option if you are sure that most users will choose this check box.

    Unchecked choose this option if you do not want the check box to be ticked.

- Insert any more check boxes that you may need, and define their characteristics.

Inserting radio buttons

In most graphic interfaces, radio buttons are synonymous with single choices, which means that users can select only one option from those available.

- Follow the same procedure as for a check box; only, insert a **Radio Button**.

If you want to ensure that only one choice is possible in a group of radio buttons, make sure that **all** the buttons have the **same name**. This way, if a user makes a choice then changes his or her mind and clicks another button, the first will be deselected.

Examples of option fields: the Title field use single choice radio buttons, and the Interests field uses multiple-choice check boxes.

© Editions ENI - All rights reserved

Dreamweaver 3
Forms

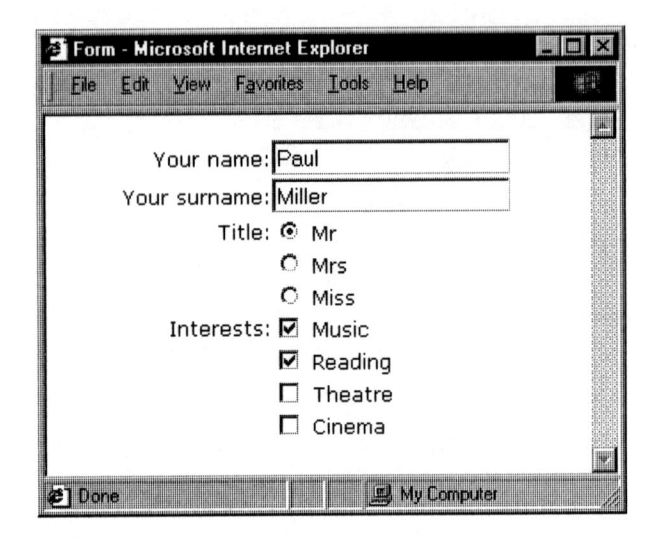

Inserting a pop-up menu

You can use pop-up menus to offer several choices, from which the user can choose one.

- Click the appropriate place in your form.
- If necessary, type some explanatory text for the pop-up menu.
- **Insert - Form Object - List/Menu**

  or click the **Insert List/Menu** button from the **Forms** panel on the **Objects** palette.

  Use the Property inspector to define the object's settings:

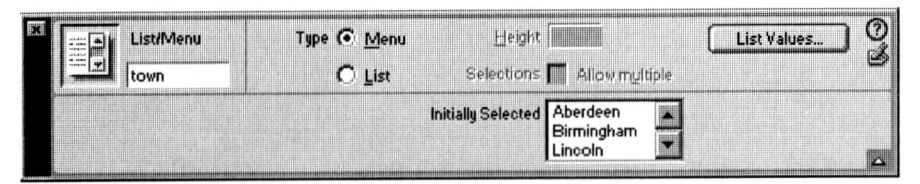

- Type the field's name in the **List/Menu** box in place of **select**.
- Choose **Menu** as the **Type**.
- Click the **List Values** button to enter the different list items.

©Editions ENI - All rights reserved

Forms

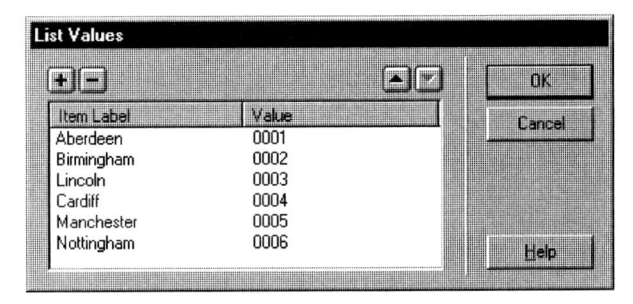

*The text entered in the **Item Label** column will be shown in the menu. The data entered in the **Value** column is the text that will be used in the script. These values can be the same, but they do not have to be.*

- Move from one text box to another rapidly by pressing [Tab].
  Add or remove items by clicking the [+] [−] buttons.
  You can move items in the list by selecting them then clicking the [▲] [▼] buttons.
- Click **OK**.
- In the **Initially Selected** list, click the item that is to be selected by default when the form loads.

Inserting a scrolling list

With a scrolling list you can offer a number of choices to users. If you want, you can authorise users to choose several of these options (using [Shift] and [Ctrl]-clicks).

- Insert the same form object as for a pop-up menu.

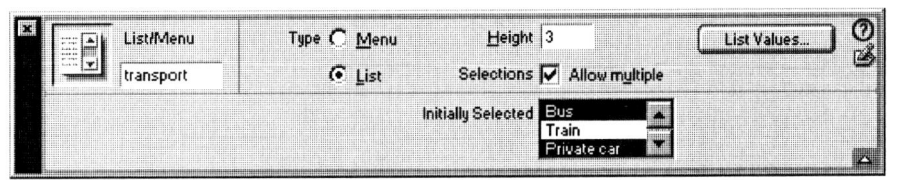

- Choose **List** as the **Type**.
- Indicate how many items will be visible in the list using the **Height** text box. The other items will not be visible but you can scroll down the list using the vertical scroll bar. For example, you can choose to have 3 out of 5 items visible.
- Activate the **Allow multiple** check box under **Selections** if you want users to be able to choose several elements from the list.

Dreamweaver 3
Forms

- In the **Initially Selected** list, click the item that is to be selected by default when the form is loaded. Use the `Shift` or `Ctrl` keys to make a multiple default selection.

    Examples of form fields: the Town/City field is a pop-up menu, and the Transport field is a multiple-choice scrolling list.

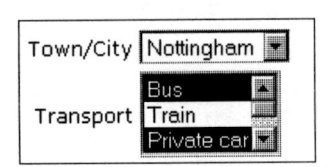

Inserting a file field

In addition to enabling users to enter data and choose from a list of options, you can also ask them to send files from their computers. The files will be sent to the server as attachments.

If you insert this sort of field into your form, the **Method** in the form settings must be **POST**. Furthermore, if you display the source code you will notice that the encoding is `enctype="multipart/form-data"`, which enables users to send attachments to the server.

- Click in the appropriate place.
- **Insert - Form Object - File Field**
    or click the **Insert File Field** button from the **Forms** panel on the **Objects** palette.

    Use the Property inspector to define the object's settings:

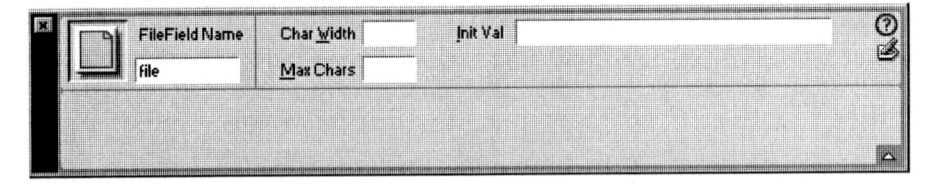

- In the **FileField Name** box, enter the object's name in place of **file**.
- In the **Char Width** box enter the graphic width of the object, using characters as the unit.
- Indicate the maximum number of characters a user can enter in this field in the **Max Chars** box. You are advised not to place a limit on the number of characters for obvious reasons of selection and verification.
- If necessary, type the text that will appear in the field by default in the **Init Val**.

©Editions ENI - All rights reserved

Example of a file field:

Inserting a hidden field

A hidden field is not visible in the browser window when a user is consulting the site, but is visible only for the developer in Dreamweaver, or in the source code.

A hidden field can be very useful in, for example, a site that sells merchandise (you can see the total sales per category) or for the automatic construction of an e-mail address by concatenating the name and surname of the person using the form.

- Click in the appropriate place.
- **Insert - Form Object - Hidden Field**

  or click the **Insert Hidden Field** button from the **Forms** panel on the **Objects** palette.

  Use the Property inspector to define the object's settings:

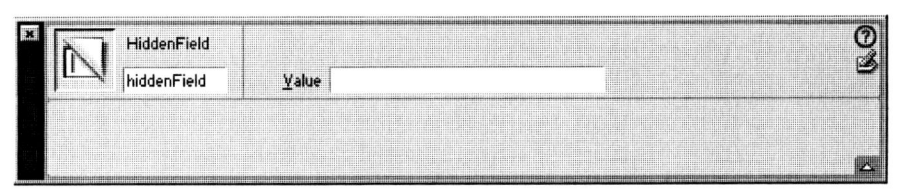

- Type the name of the field in the **HiddenField** box in place of **hiddenField**.
- Indicate the value that will be used by the script in the **Value** box, or enter this value using a script.
- The hidden field is shown in the page as an invisible element. If you want to see it, make sure that it is selected in the invisible elements:

  Edit - Preferences - Invisible Elements category
  The **Hidden Form Fields** option should be active.

- You should also make sure that the invisible elements are displayed (**View - Invisible Elements**).

  The invisible element for a hidden field is . When you select it, its settings appear in the Property inspector.

Creating a concatenation script

To give you a precise example of the use of a hidden field in a form, here is a simple script which will create an e-mail address by combining the name and surname entered by a user.

- Use the following fields:
    - The form is called `registration`.
    - The name field is called `firstname`.
    - The surname field is called `surname`.
    - The hidden field is called `email`.
- Press F10 to show the source code.
- Type the script in the `<head>`:

```
<head>
...
<script language="JavaScript">
function createmail(){
var thefirstname=document.registration.firstname.value
var thesurname=document.registration.surname.value
document.registration.email.value=thefirstname+"."+thesurname+"@jsbach.org"
}
</script>
...
</head>
```

You have declared a function called createmail: `function createmail ()`

You have declared the first value as `thefirstname`.

This variable takes the value of the name field in the registration form in the document: `var thefirstname=document.registration.firstname.value`.

You have declared the second value as `thesurname`.

This variable takes the value of the surname field in the registration form in the document: `var thesurname=document.registration.surname.value`.

The email value in the registration form has been assigned the combination of the `thefirstname` variable, the text ".", the `thesurname` variable and the text `@jsbach.org`.

Forms

Now you need an event to trigger the function. A good event to use would be the moment when the user, having entered his or her name and surname, leaves the field. Thus the event will be "leaves the surname field". You need to place the `onBlur` event in the surname field. As the script is simple, it does not detect when data has been entered in the firstname and surname fields.

⊡ In the surname field, add this code:

```
<input type="text" name="surname"
onBlur="createmail()">
```

When the user leaves this field, the `createmail()` function will be triggered and the concatenation will be made.

Inserting submit and reset buttons

For a form to be of any use, you will need to insert two buttons. The first sends the form (submit). This button will look for a script to start. The second button gives the user the possibility to cancel and start again (reset).

⊡ Click in the appropriate place.

⊡ **Insert - Form Object - Button**

or click the **Insert Button** button from the **Forms** panel on the **Objects** palette.

Use the Property inspector to define the object's settings:

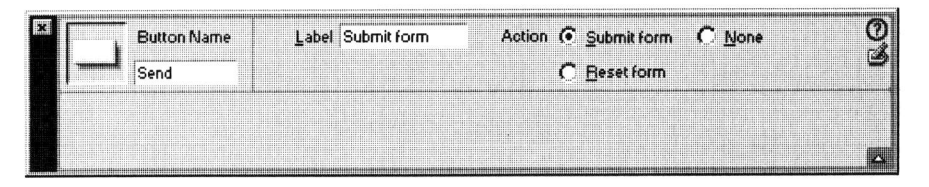

⊡ In the **Button Name** box, replace the word **Submit** with the object's name, if you wish.

⊡ Type the text that will appear on the button in the **Label** text box.

⊡ Under **Action**, choose to **Submit form** (submit) for the first button and **Reset form** (reset) for the second.

*You can replace the **Submit form** button by an image that behaves like a* submit *button.*

⊡ Click in the appropriate place.

⊡ **Insert - Form Object - Image Field**

or click the **Insert Image Field** button from the **Forms** panel on the **Objects** palette.

©Editions ENI - All rights reserved

Dreamweaver 3
Forms

- Define the image as you would any image in the Property inspector.

Verifying a form's validity

Inserting behaviors

It is sometimes useful to verify some of the text fields in a form, such as required fields, and fields which should contain an e-mail address. To do this, Dreamweaver offers you the possibility of adding a validation script to your form.

These are Dreamweaver **Behaviors**. A behavior associates an event (such as a mouse event from the user: selecting of a field, leaving a field etc) with an action, which is the script.

You can verify the form when the user fills in the fields in the field one after the other (onBlur event) or when they click the submit button (onSubmit event).

Validating when the form is submitted

In the first instance, you can create a behavior that will check the fields in the form all at once when it is submitted.

- Select your form by clicking the `<form>` element on the status bar `<body> <form> <p>`.
- Display the **Behaviors** palette: **Window - Behavoirs**.
- Choose the browser compatibility you want from the **Events For** pop-up menu in the **Behaviors** palette.
- Click the button to add a behavior.
- Choose **Validate Form**.
- Choose the settings for the validation of each of the form fields:

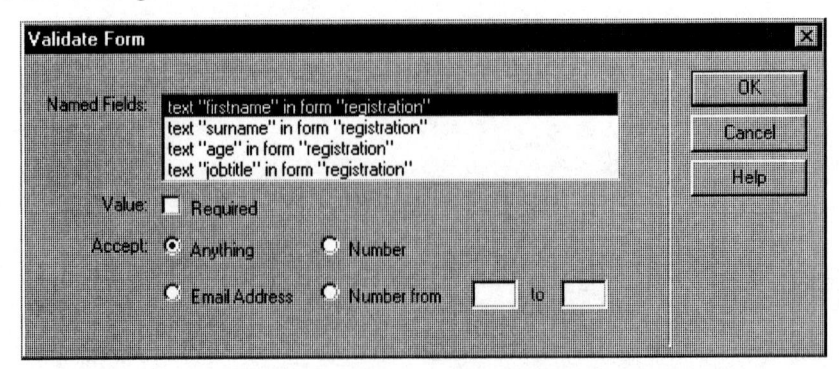

©Editions ENI - All rights reserved

Forms

- In the **Named Fields** list, select the field to be validated.
- Under **Value**, tick the **Required** check box if the selected field cannot be left empty.
- Under **Accept** choose from:

Anything	if you do not want to define a particular type of data (in which case it is logical to have ticked the **Required** option).
Number	to authorise numerical values only.
Email Address	if the @ character should be present.
Number from X to Y	for a numerical value from the specified interval.

- Once you have set the parameters for the first field, select the second and parameter it in the same way, then do the same thing for all the other fields. They will all be checked together at the moment when the form is submitted.
- Click **OK**.

In the **Behaviors** palette, you can see the **onSubmit** event:

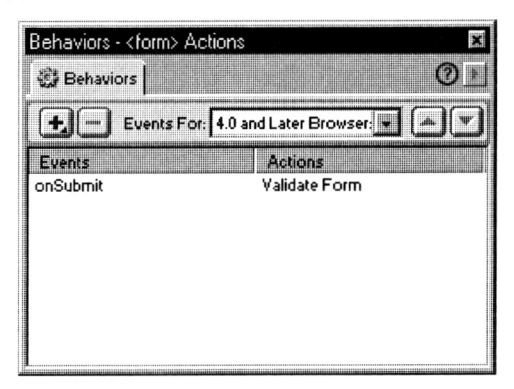

Field by field verification

In this case, the form is validated field by field, each time the user leaves a field.

- In the form, select the first text field that is to be validated.
- **Window - Behaviors**
- Click the button to add a new action and choose **Validate Form**.
- Choose the parameters as shown previously.

©Editions ENI - All rights reserved

- Click **OK**.

    You can see the **onBlur** event in the **Behaviors** palette:

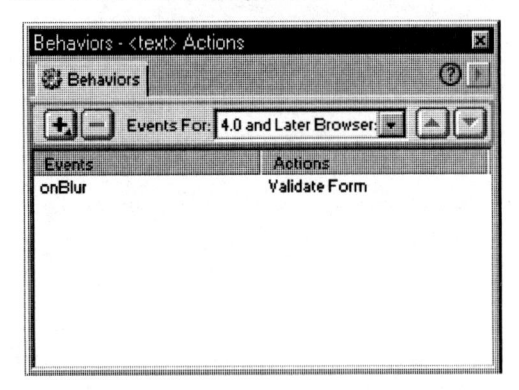

- Do the same for all the text fields that are to be validated.

Customising messages

    Example of an error message:

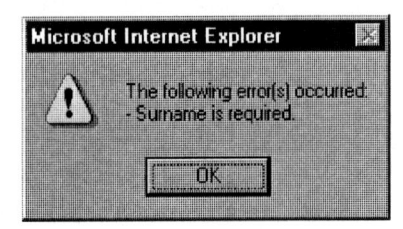

    You can change the messages by changing the words in the source code.

- Press F10 to display the source code.
- Find the character string for the title of the error message.

    ```
    alert('The following error(s) occurred:\n'+errors)
    ```

    Change only the words **The following error(s) occurred:**. Do not delete the quotes '.

    \n   this is a line break in the message box.

    +errors   this is where the type of error that has occurred is added.

Forms

- For example, you could change this text to:

  ```
  alert('This form contains errors:\n'+errors)
  ```

  For the second line of the message, each case is specific.

- For data which is necessary, the JavaScript code is:

  ```
  errors += '- '+nm+' is required.\n'
  ```

  You can change some of the parameters:

  - replace - by the field or by some other text.
    nm represents the name of the field so leave it.

  - replace **is required** by **must be given** (for example, but you can use any message you choose):

  ```
  errors += 'The '+nm+' must be given.\n'
  ```

- Save your document and preview it in a browser.
- Leave the validated field blank:

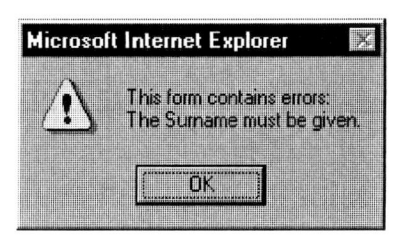

  > Microsoft Internet Explorer
  >
  > ⚠ This form contains errors:
  > The Surname must be given.
  >
  > [OK]

- This is the JavaScript code for the validation of an e-mail field:

  ```
  errors+='- '+nm+' must contain an e-mail address.'
  ```

  Change the text in the same way as the previous texts:

  ```
  errors+='An e-mail address is required in the '+nm+' field.'
  ```

©Editions ENI - All rights reserved

Dreamweaver 3
Forms

- This is the JavaScript code for the validation of a numerical field:

  ```
  errors+='- '+nm+' must contain a number.'
  ```

  Change the text in the same way as the previous texts:

  ```
  errors+='Enter a number in the '+nm+' field.'
  ```

- This is the JavaScript code for the validation of a numerical field with a specific interval:

  ```
  errors+='- '+nm+' must contain a number between '+min+' and '+max+'.'
  ```

  Change the text in the same way as the previous texts:

  ```
  errors+='- '+nm+' should contain a number from '+min+' to '+max+'.'
  ```

©Editions ENI - All rights reserved

Inserting objects

Principle

Objects

This is a very general chapter that will explain how to insert objects such as Flash movies, Java applets, scripts and videos.

Whenever you want to insert a multimedia object (such as a movie, sound or Shockwave movie), remember that users of your site will need the appropriate plugin on their computer if they are to be able to use this object. Do not forget that browsers can interpret only HTML and client script, and nothing else. This is why plugins are necessary.

Editing objects

When you have inserted a media object into your page you can open it directly if you have defined a relationship between the file extension and an external editor:

Edit - Preferences - External Editors category

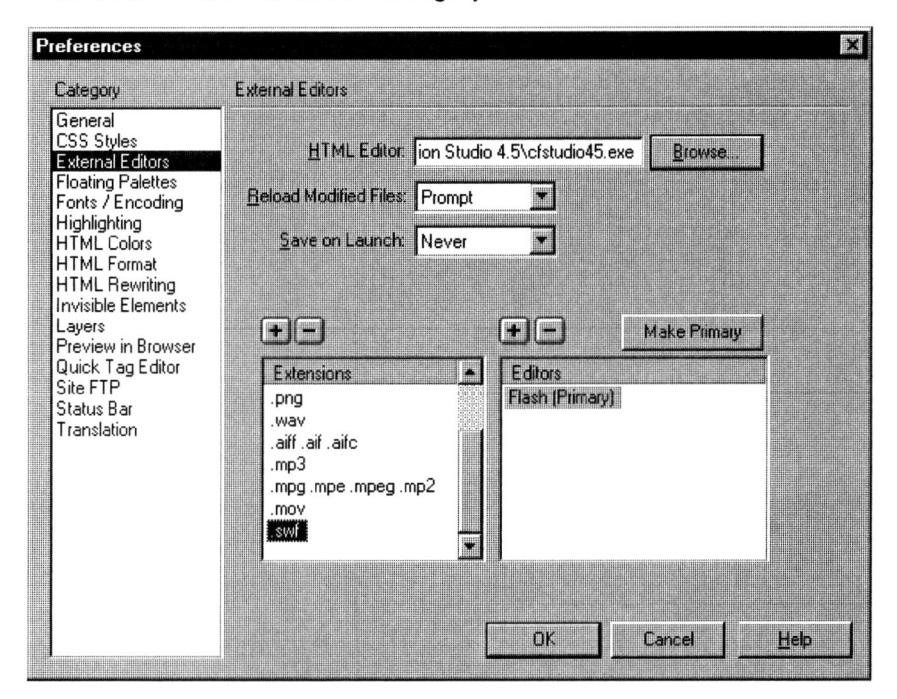

You can see all the file extensions that are already set in the **Extensions** list.

©Editions ENI - All rights reserved

Dreamweaver 3
Inserting objects

- To add an extension, click the ⊞ button and type the extension.
- Click the ⊞ button in the **Editors** list to select an editor from your computer which will be associated with the selected extension.

    The **Make Primary** button enables you to define the program that should be opened first if you have chosen several editors for the same extension.

- Click **OK**.
- To open an image (only) in a Dreamweaver document, select the image and open its context menu then choose **Edit With application_name**.
- Open a multimedia object from your Dreamweaver site by opening the site window (press [F5]) and double-clicking the object.

Inserting the date

You can insert the date in your Web page using different formats, with the possibility of an automatic update.

- Click the appropriate place in your document.
- **Insert - Date**

    or click the **Insert Date** button 📅 from the **Common** panel on the **Objects** palette.

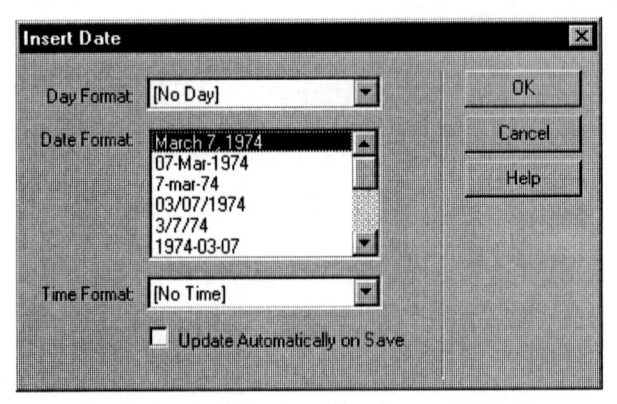

- Choose the format for the **Day**, **Date** and/or **Time** from each of the menus.
- Tick the **Update Automatically on Save** checkbox if you want the date to be updated each time you save the document. If you have not activated this option, the date is inserted as text.

©Editions ENI - All rights reserved

Inserting objects

Inserting a Flash movie

Macromedia Flash can be used to create very stylish vector-based movies. You need the Flash Player plug-in for Netscape Navigator or the ActiveX control for Microsoft Internet Explorer in order to play Flash movies. These plug-ins are supplied with the latest versions of these browsers.

- Click in your page at the place where you want to insert the Flash movie.
- **Insert - Media - Flash**
  or click the **Insert Flash** button from the **Common** panel on the **Objects** palette.
- Select the .swf file in your site.
  The movie appears as an icon in the document:
  Use the Property inspector to define the movie's parameters:

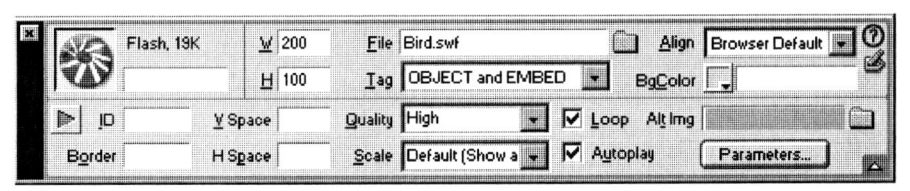

- Use the **Flash** text box to define the movie's name if you need to refer to it in a script.
- Change the width and height of the movie in the **W** and **H** boxes. The **File** box contains the .swf source file.
- Choose the tag(s) you want to use for the movie from the **Tag** pop-up menu. By default, Dreamweaver uses `<object>` for Microsoft Internet Explorer and `<embed>` for Netscape Navigator. Leave this choice for the best compatibility.
- Use the **Align** pop-up menu to choose the movie's alignment in the page. The alignments are the same as those for an image.
- Choose the background colour for movies without a background (or for when the movie is not playing) from the **BgColor** pop-up menu.
- Click the play button to see the movie in your page.
- You can define an identifier for information exchanges between ActiveX controllers in the **ID** box.
- The **Borders** box indicates the width of the movie's border (which will not appear in either Microsoft Internet Explorer or Netscape Navigator!).
  The **V Space** and **H Space** boxes enable you to define the spacing, in pixels, between the movie and any text, for example, that surrounds it.

©Editions ENI - All rights reserved

Dreamweaver 3
Inserting objects

- The **Quality**, **Scale**, **Loop** and **Autoplay** settings are linked to the settings defined in Flash.
- Click the **Parameters** button to define specific parameters for the movie that can be used in scripts.
- The **Alt Img** box allows you to define the source of an image that is to be used if Microsoft Internet Explorer does not have the appropriate ActiveX controls.

Inserting a Shockwave movie

Shockwave is the Macromedia®-owned format for Web-destined interactive movies created in Director. As with Flash, you need the appropriate plugin in Netscape Navigator and/or ActiveX for Microsoft Internet Explorer in order to read these files.

- Click the place where you want to insert the Shockwave movie.
- **Insert - Media - Shockwave**

  or click the **Insert Shockwave** button from the **Common** panel on the **Objects** palette.

Define the parameters for this movie using the **Property** inspector in the same way as for a Flash movie.

Inserting Generator objects

Generator is a Macromedia® application which can be used to create dynamic Web content. This content is created using Flash and exploited on the server with Generator. The use of this application is widespread for the creation of adverts and banners that change regularly in a Web page.

- Click in your page at the place where you want to insert the Generator object.
- **Insert - Media - Generator**

  or click the **Insert Generator** button from the **Common** panel of the **Objects** palette.

- Give the .swt file you want to use in the **Template File** box, or click **Browse** to select it in your site.
- Select the format used in the **Type** pop-up menu (Flash, GIF, JPEG, MOV or PNG).
- Use the **Parameters** box to add parameters to your Generator object.

©Editions ENI - All rights reserved

Inserting objects

Inserting a Fireworks object

You can use Macromedia® Fireworks to create visual objects for Web sites such as interactive buttons, image-maps and rollover buttons very rapidly by generating the necessary JavaScript and HTML code. You can incorporate these elements into Dreamweaver by opening the HTML file generated by Fireworks, selecting the necessary code and doing a Copy/Paste. However, you can use the more failsafe method of importing the file directly into your Dreamweaver page.

- Click in your page at the place where you want to import the Fireworks objects.
- **Insert - Media - Fireworks HTML**
  or click the **Insert Fireworks HTML** button from the **Common** panel on the **Objects** palette.

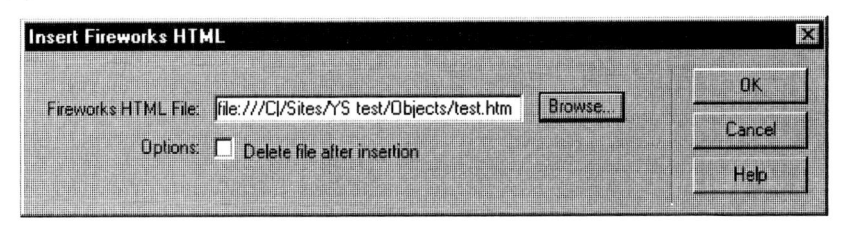

- Type the name of the file you want to incorporate in the **Fireworks HTML File** box, or click **Browse** to select the file in your site.
- Activate the **Delete file after insertion** option if you want to delete the file that Fireworks has generated after it has been inserted into Dreamweaver.

Inserting a Java applet

The Java language, defined by Sun, can be used to create applications (applets) which can be inserted into Web pages. The applet is then interpreted by the Java Virtual Machine which is installed on almost all computer platforms.

- Click in your page where you want to insert the Java applet.
- **Insert - Media - Applet**
  or click the **Insert Applet** button from the **Common** panel of the **Objects** palette.
- Select the .class file you want to insert.

©Editions ENI - All rights reserved

Dreamweaver 3
1-1-2 Inserting objects

The applet is represented by this icon in your document: ☕.
Use the Property inspector to define the applet's parameters:

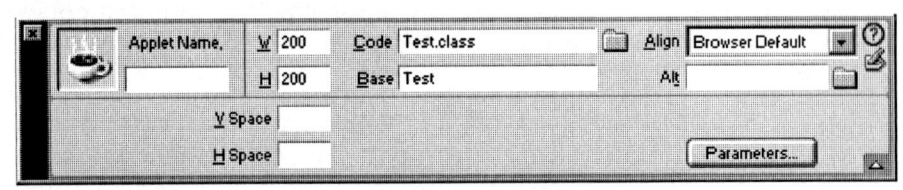

	Applet Name.	W 200	Code Test.class		Align Browser Default	
		H 200	Base Test		Alt	
		V Space				
		H Space			Parameters...	

- You can give the applet a name in the **Applet Name** box if you want to refer to it in a script.
- Use the **W** and **H** boxes to indicate the width and height of the applet in pixels.

    The **Code** box shows the name of the source file. The **Base** box shows the folder that contains the applet.

- Use the **Align** pop-up menu to choose the alignment of the applet, in the same way as for images.
- The **Alt** text box can indicate an alternative image to be used if the browser does not support Java.
- The **V Space** and **H Space** text boxes can be used to define the spacing, in pixels, around the applet.

    Example: this applet can calculate and draw segments of a circle:

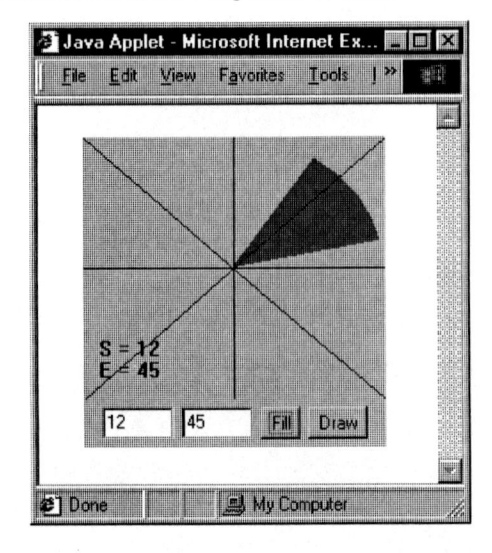

Inserting objects

Inserting an ActiveX control

ActvieX controls are components, like miniature applications, that run under Windows and that, to all intents and purposes, can be used only with Microsoft Internet Explorer. Their use on the Internet is random and even discouraged by Microsoft for security reasons, but ActiveX controls are quite at home when used on an intranet.

- Place the insertion point where you want to insert the ActiveX control.
- **Insert - Media - ActiveX**
  or click the **Insert ActiveX** button from the **Common** panel on the **Objects** palette.
  This icon represents the ActiveX control in your document: .
  Use the Property inspector to define the settings for the control:

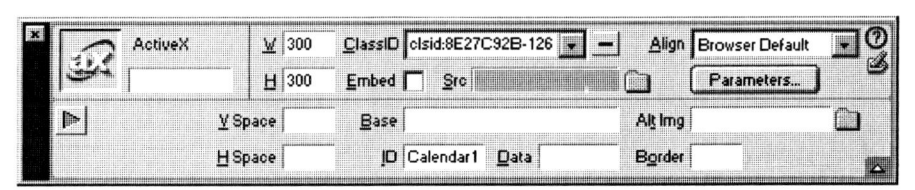

- In the **ActiveX** text box, type the control's name if you want to refer to it in a script.
- The **W** and **H** text boxes indicate the control's width and height (in pixels, by default).
- Specify the ActiveX control for the browser in the **ClassID** text box. Use the pop-up menu or type the value yourself. The browser will use this value to find the ActiveX control. If the browser cannot find the ActiveX control, it will use the URL indicated in the **Base** text box to download it.
- Activate the **Embed** option if you want to add a tag so that the control will be visible with Netscape Navigator, provided the control has a plugin equivalent.
  The **Src** text box is for indicating the path for Netscape plugins.
- The **ID** text box enables you to define an identifier for the control, which is for passing information between ActiveX controls.
  The **Data** box specifies the data file that the control can load.
- In the **Align** pop-up menu, align the control as you would an image.
- The **V Space** and **H Space** boxes can be used to define the spacing, in pixels, around the ActiveX control.
- Use the **Border** option to specify the width of the border around the control.
- In **Alt Img**, give the image to be shown if the browser does not support ActiveX controls.

©Editions ENI - All rights reserved

Dreamweaver 3
Inserting objects

This is an example of an ActiveX control that displays a calendar. A programmer can link scripts to the action of dates being clicked by a user:

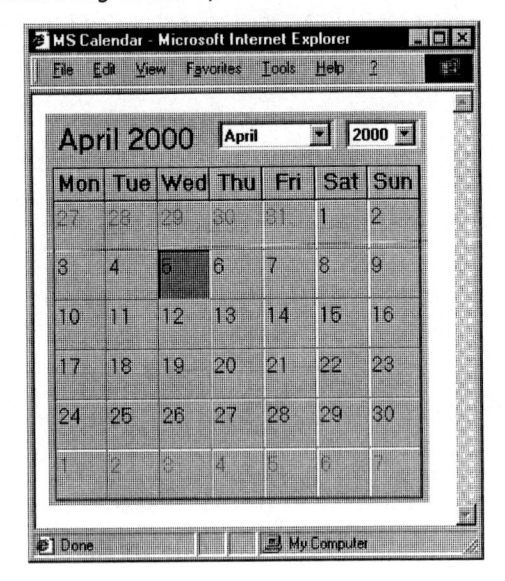

Inserting plugin content

Inserting a sound

Currently, there are several different audio formats available (such as RealAudio, QuickTime and MP3). A user absolutely must have the necessary plugin to be able to listen to a sound file. If is thus prudent to test for the presence of this plugin on the user's machine (see the chapter about behaviors to learn how to do this).

To insert a sound or piece of music into your page you can simply insert an image button with a hyperlink to an audio file. The user can then click the button to hear the audio sequence. You can also insert the audio file directly into your page and it will be interpreted - played - when the browser gets to its line in the HTML code.

- If you want to insert a sound file that is linked to an image button which will trigger a sound, create a link to the audio file in the Property inspector in the **Link** field.
  Save the page and preview it in a browser.
  Click the button and listen!

- To insert the audio file directly into the page, place the insertion point in the appropriate place then:

  Insert - Media - Plugin

©Editions ENI - All rights reserved

Inserting objects

or click the **Insert Plugin** button from the **Common** panel on the **Objects** palette.

→ In the window that appears, select the audio file you want to insert.

Use the Property inspector to choose the file's parameters:

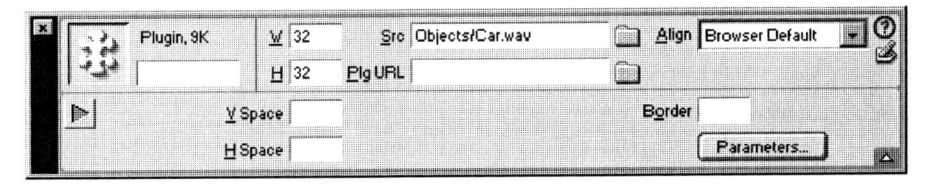

→ Give the file a name in the **Plugin** text box if you want to refer to it in a script.

→ Use the **W** and **H** text boxes to indicate the width and height of the object. In this case, it will be the size of the plugin interface necessary to play the sound.

*The **Src** text box indicates the file path.*

→ In the **Plg URL** box you can indicate the Web site from which users can download the necessary plugins if they do not have them.

→ Use the **Align**, **V Space**, **H Space** and **Border** parameters to place the object in the page.

Inserting a movie

As with sounds, there are many movie formats (such as QuickTime and RealVideo). Again, users need to have the appropriate plugins to use the files. With Dreamweaver you can insert movies, but the parameters are rather basic.

→ Place the insertion point where you want to insert the movie.

→ **Insert - Media - Plugin**

→ Select the file you want to insert.

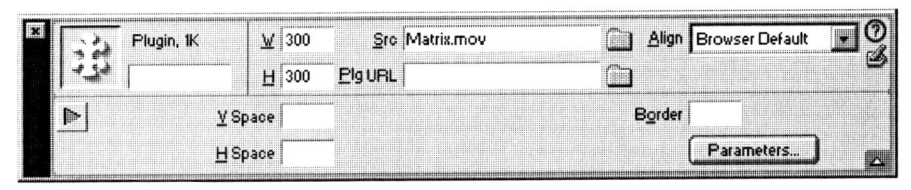

You will see the same attributes as for sounds.

©Editions ENI - All rights reserved

Dreamweaver 3
Inserting objects

When you insert a movie, you should download the QuickTime or RealVideo insertion plugin from the Macromedia site:

- Go to http://www.macromedia.com/software/dreamweaver/download/extensions/.
- After you have downloaded the extensions, install them on your computer.
- Place the insertion point at the appropriate place in your page and, for example, insert a .mov format QuickTime movie.
- On the **Objects** palette, in the **Common** category, click the **Insert Quicktime Movie** button.
- Use the QuickTime assistant to insert the movie.

In the **Property** inspector you can see the characteristics of the QuickTime movie:

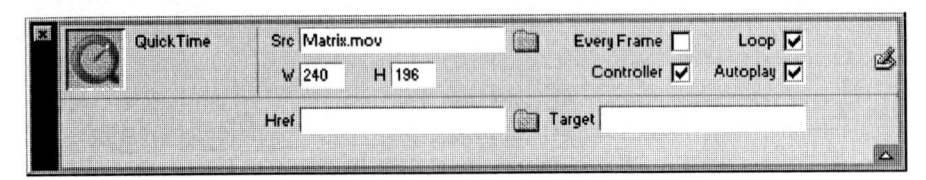

- Save the page then preview it in your browser to watch the movie.

Playing files that require a plugin

You can choose to play the files that use Netscape Navigator plugins (the <embed> tag) directly in the document window. You will need to have the necessary plugins installed on your computer, and Dreamweaver will look for them on your machine (in the Configuration/Plugins folder then in the folders of the installed browsers).

- To play a file that uses a plugin, select the item in the page.
- **View - Plugins - Play**

   or click the ▶ button on the Property inspector.

- When you have finished, select the item and use **View - Plugins - Stop**

   or click ■ on the Property inspector.

- If you want to play then stop all the movies in the page:

   View - Plugins - Play All and **Stop All**

©Editions ENI - All rights reserved

Inserting objects

Inserting scripts

You can insert scripts into your Web page which will trigger different actions. You need to use a programming language to create a script. Currently, the most popular and effective client script language is JavaScript.

In this example you can create a simple script which will test whether the value in a form field is greater than 100.

- Create a form and call it **test**.
- Insert a text field and call it **value**.
- Insert a button but do not assign any actions to it.
- To insert the script, click in your page where you want to insert it. You need to insert the script **before the form**, because it needs to be loaded before it is used.
- **Insert - Script**

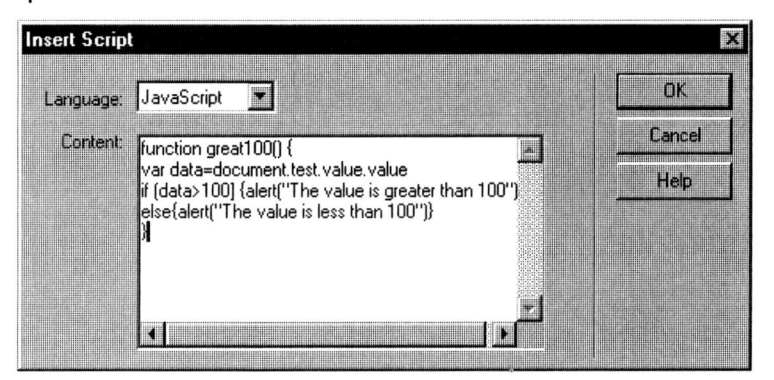

- Select the language you want from the **Language** pop-up menu: **JavaScript** (and the version) or **VBScript**.
- Type the code in the **Content** text box.

  This is the script:

  ```
  function great100() {
  var data=document.test.value.value
  if (data>100] {alert("The value is greater than 100")}
  else{alert("The value is less than 100")}
  }
  ```

  You have declared the creation of a function called: `function great100()`.
  You have declared a variable `(var)` called `data`.

©Editions ENI - All rights reserved

Dreamweaver 3
Inserting objects

This variable takes the contents `value` of the `value` field in the `test` form of the document.
You are using the `if` conditional function to test the `data` variable.
If the `data` variable is greater than 100: `if (data>100)`,
the message: `alert("The value is greater than 100")` will appear.
If the value is less than or equal to 100, another message will be shown: `else{alert("The value is less than 100")}`.

- To see the script item in the page, make sure the invisible element **Script** is active: **Edit - Preferences - Invisible Elements** category.
  The **Scripts** check box should be ticked.

- Ensure that the invisible elements are displayed: **View - Invisible Elements**.

  The script is represented by this symbol:
  You can change the script's parameters in the Property inspector:

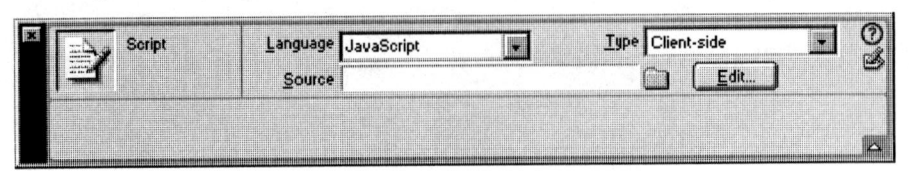

- The **Language** pop-up menu can be used to change the language of the script.

- Choose between a **Client-side** or **Server-side** script in the **Type** pop-up menu.

- The **Source** box is for indicating the script's path.
  You can open the script in the editor window by clicking **Edit**.

The editor window: *The document obtained:*

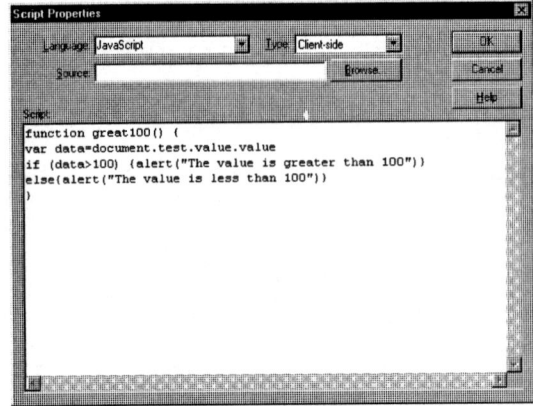

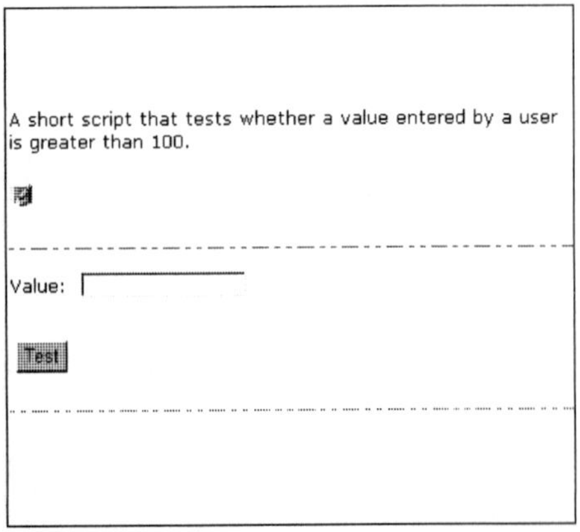

©Editions ENI - All rights reserved

Inserting objects

- You can associate the button with script. Select the button and press F10 to show the source code then add this action to the button:

```
<input type="button" name="Button" value="Test"
onClick="great100()">
```

A mouse click (onClick) *will invoke the* great100() *function.*
You can make the script more interactive by adding the value entered by the user to the alert message.

- Press F10 to show the source code then add the code that will insert the variable data into the alert messages:

```
if (data>100) {alert("The value "+data+" is greater than 100")}
else{alert("The value "+data+" is less than 100")}
```

The + symbols concatenate the character strings between the quotation marks.

- To test the script, first save the document then preview it in a browser. Type a value and click the **Test** button:

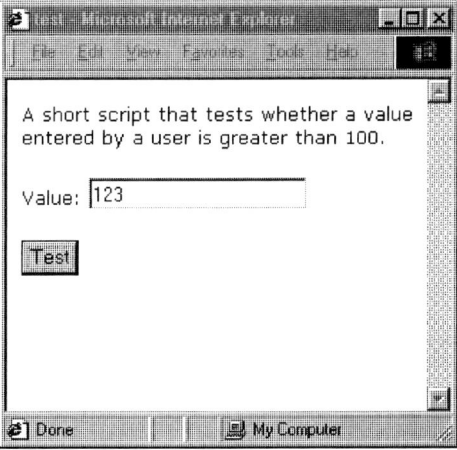

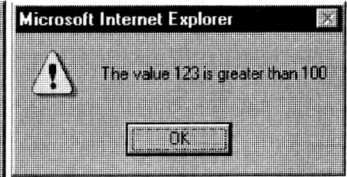

©Editions ENI - All rights reserved

Inserting SSI files

Principle

SSI stands for server-side include. If certain elements are to be present in nearly all the pages in your site, such as a header, address, telephone number or e-mail address, it would be very tedious to have to insert them into every page. SSI is the solution! Create an HTML document that contains all the necessary information. In each of your pages in your site you then make a "link" to the HTML file so that it is inserted into the page. This is the code you should use to invoke an SSI:

```
<!--#include virtual="/common/header.htm" -->
```

The header.htm file is in the common folder at the site root.

Another advantage is updating. Simply edit the included file and all the pages that invoke it will be updated. All these SSI files are stored and managed by the server. If, for example, you change the telephone number in your header.htm file, all the pages that include this file will include this modification.

Creating and inserting an SSI file

- You can use any HTML editor to create an SSI file. If you use Dreamweaver, make sure to "tidy up" the file, because SSI files must not contain the elements `<head>`, `<title>`, `<frameset>` and `<body>`. Save the SSI file.

- Open the document that is to include the SSI file and place the insertion point in the appropriate place.

- **Insert - Server-Side Include**

    or click the **Insert Server-Side Include** button in the **Common** panel of the **Objects** palette.

- Select the file you want to include.

- As a general rule, you should use a root-relative path when you insert an SSI file: choose **Site Root** in the **Relative To** pop-up menu.

©Editions ENI - All rights reserved

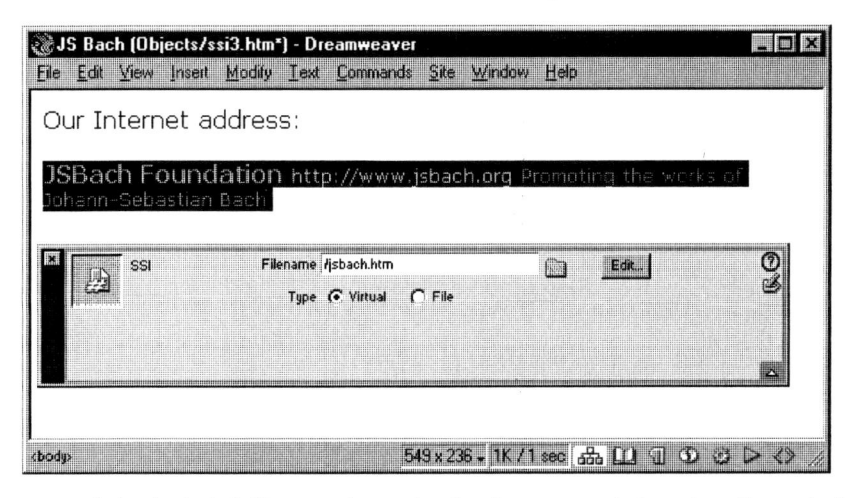

Inserting objects

The contents of the included file are shown in the document window, but if you look at the source code (press F10), you will see only the inclusion:

```
<!--#include virtual="/jsbach.htm" -->
```

In the Property inspector the **Filename** text box contains the SSI file path and the **Edit** button opens the SSI file so that you can make changes to it.

Showing an SSI file in a page

Generally, all SSI files are shown in Dreamweaver. You can specify a particular display if need be.

⇥ **Edit - Preferences - Translation** category

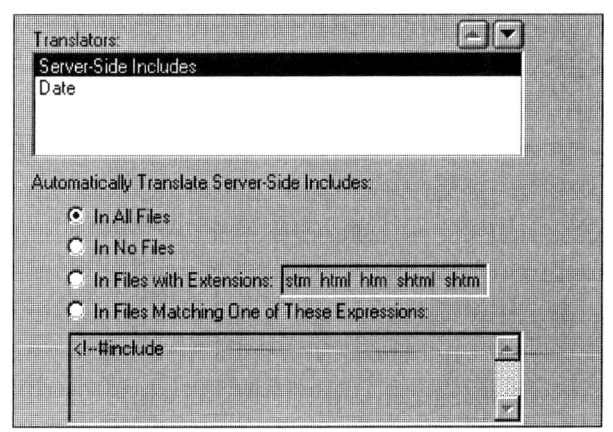

©Editions ENI - All rights reserved

Dreamweaver 3
Inserting objects

- Select **Server-Side Includes** from the **Translators** list.
- Under **Automatically Translate Server-Side Includes**, choose:

    In All Files: Dreamweaver will show the contents of all SSI files.

    In No Files: SSI file contents will not be shown.

    In Files With Extensions: only the contents of SSI files with an extension from the text box to the right will be shown.

    In Files Matching One of These Expressions: the contents of SSI files which conform to the code specified below will be shown.

Editing an SSI file

- To edit the contents of an included file, open the SSI file from your site's folder list,

    or select an inclusion of the file in a document and click **Edit** on the Property inspector.

- As was mentioned previously, all the files that include the SSI file will be updated as a matter of course.

Behaviors linked to objects

Behaviors are a combination of a user action (such as clicking on a button) and a JavaScript action. They add dynamism to your pages. Some of the behaviors supplied with Dreamweaver can be applied directly to objects. For more details, see the chapter about behaviors.

Playing a sound

You can insert a sound into your Web page which a user can then play by clicking a button or by pointing the mouse to this button or a link.

- Insert an image button to act as the trigger using **Insert - Image**. Choose an image for the button.
- Associate the button and the behavior by selecting the button then **Window - Behaviors**.
- Choose the browser version from the **Events For** pop-up menu.
- Click the button to add a behavior.
- Choose **Play Sound**.
- Click the **Browse** button in the **Play Sound** text box to select the sound you want to play.

©Editions ENI - All rights reserved

Inserting objects

- Click **OK**.
- Test the behavior by saving the document and opening it in a browser. Click the button and listen!

Controlling a Flash or Shockwave movie

You can use a behavior to control a Flash or Shockwave movie: pause and stop it, rewind it or go to a specific frame.

- After having inserted in the movie, name it in the Property inspector.
- Insert two image buttons that will play and stop the movie.
- Select the Play button.
- Open the **Behaviors** palette: **Window - Behaviors**.
- Choose the browser version.
- Click the ⊞ button and choose **Control Shockwave or Flash** from the pop-up menu.

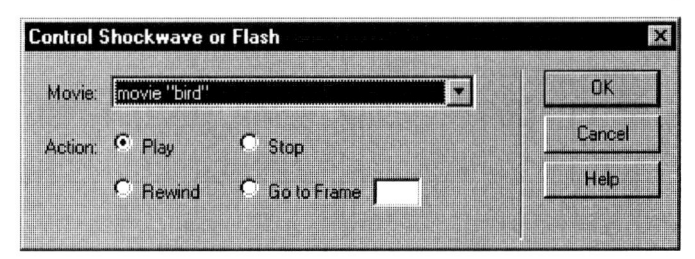

- If you need to, select the movie you inserted in the **Movie** box.
- Under **Action** choose the appropriate control, **Play**, in this case.
- Click **OK**.
- Do the same for the Stop button, choosing the **Stop** option.

*If you want, you can create buttons for the **Rewind** (to the beginning of the movie) and **Go to Frame** actions.*

- Save your document and open it in a browser to test the behaviors.

©Editions ENI - All rights reserved

Dreamweaver 3
Layers

Principle

Cascading style sheets

Layers are part of a large family of cascading style sheets. They are positioning style sheets: CSS-P for W3C (but they are now integrated into CSS-2),

The introduction of positioning style sheets by the W3C was in response to the need to place "containers" anywhere in a page, in a very precise manner. In Dreamweaver you use layers to do this. A layer can contain text, images, movies, or any other element that can be inserted into an HTML document.

Using these layers gives you the possibility to work on your pages in the same way as a DTP model-maker. Your page need no longer be linear in its presentation, with elements placed one under the other; you can create a page that can be read in many directions by stacking images and text and other elements on top of each other. Reading your page becomes a dynamic experience!

Positioning

The position of layers is indicated in three dimensions:

- the horizontal position from the left of the layer: x
- the vertical position from the top of the layer: y
- and the stacking order in relation to other layers: z.

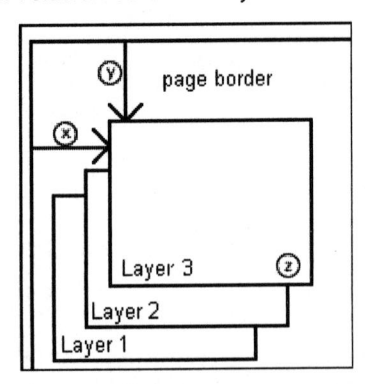

Layers are positioned absolutely in Dreamweaver: a layer is placed in relation to the borders of the page and is positioned over the contents of the page.

Layers

Example: this page contains text that has been typed as usual, and a layer has been placed over it containing an image of a giraffe. Another layer has been placed over that layer, containing the text "The giraffe".

Making your pages dynamic

- You can record the movements of your layers (thus creating "movies") or allow users to move the layers. To increase the interactivity of your page, you can insert action buttons for these movies (stop, pause etc). All this will make your page more dynamic and your site will become more interactive.

Inserting a layer

Inserting the right HTML element

You can use two types of HTML element to position your layers: divisions, `<div>` *element, which are recognised by all browsers and are the W3C standard, or* `<layer>` *elements, which are specific to Netscape Navigator and are recognised only by this browser.*

- Use **Edit - Preferences - Layers** category to choose the HTML element.

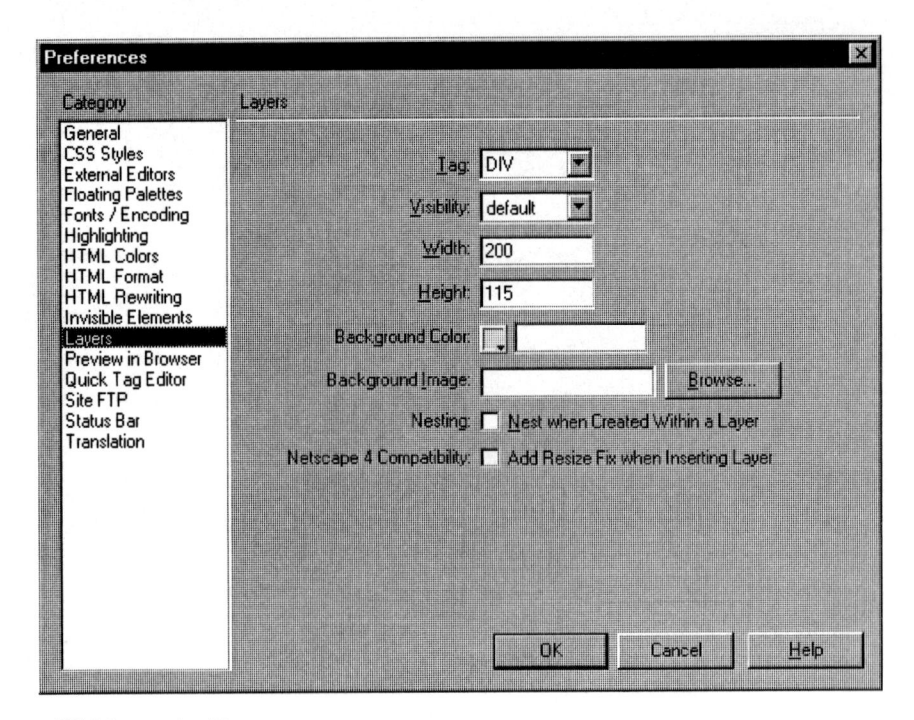

Dreamweaver 3
Layers

- Choose **DIV** from the **Tag** menu.

    The **Visibility, Width, Height, Background Color** and **Background Image** choices can be used to define the default parameters for the creation of layers. These different settings will be examined below.

- The **Nesting** option enables you to nest a layer inside another (see Creating nested layers).

- The **Netscape 4 Compatibility** option corrects a bug in Netscape Navigator which means that layer-containing pages that are resized by the user are redisplayed badly. You should tick this checkbox to optimise your pages that contain layers.

Creating a layer

There are several ways to proceed

- Place the insertion point where you want to insert the layer.
- **Insert - Layer**
    or click the **Draw Layer** button from the **Common** panel on the **Objects** palette.

Layers

⇨ Drag the mouse over your page, from the top left corner to the bottom right corner.

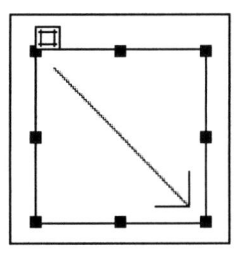

⇨ If you want to create several layers in succession, click the **Draw Layer** button and hold the [Shift] key down. Without releasing the key, draw all the layers you want.

Formatting a layer

⇨ To format layers show the **Layers** palette (**Window - Layers**) and the **Property** inspector.

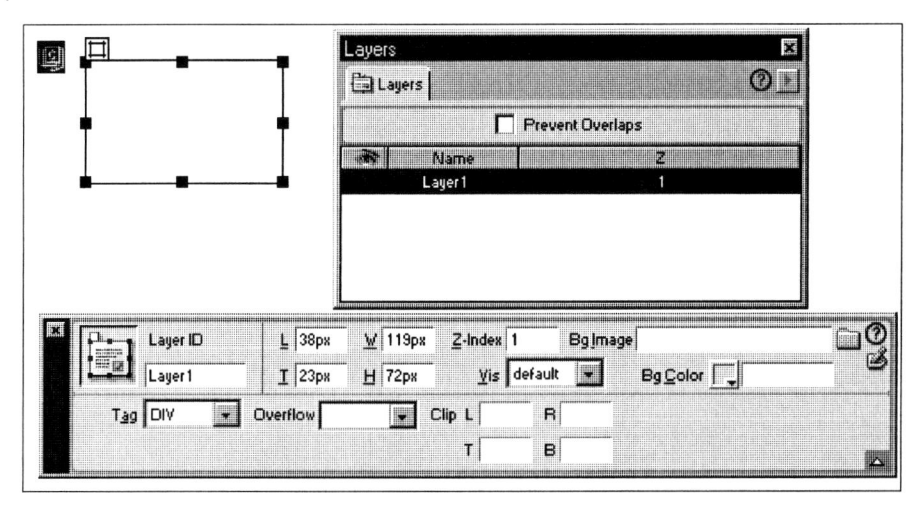

You can use the Property inspector to choose the layer's parameters.

⇨ Use the **Layer ID** text box to name the layer, making it easier to select and so that you can use it for timelines and behaviors.

⇨ The **L** text box is for indicating the distance, in pixels, between the left border of the page and the left border of the layer.

©Editions ENI - All rights reserved

Dreamweaver 3
Layers

- The **T** text box is for indicating the distance of the top layer, in pixels, from the top border of the page.
- In the **W** text box you can define the width of the layer and its height in the **H** text box.
- The **Z-Index** option is for defining the stacking order of layers. The lowest z-index (1) indicates that the layer is underneath all the others, and is the lowest in the stack of layers.

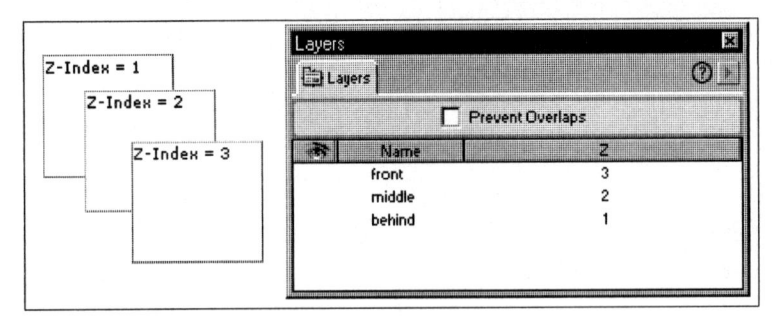

- The **Vis** pop-up menu is for defining the layer's visibility:

    default: this attribute has not been defined. Browsers will generally display the layer.

    inherit: the layer inherits this attribute from the parent layer, which is the layer that contains it, when you are using nested layers.

    visible: the layer is immediately visible in the page. In the **Layers** palette an open eye is shown next to the layer.

    hidden: this layer will be hidden. It will only appear when, for example, triggered by a user action linked to a behavior. A closed eye is shown next to this layer in the **Layers** palette.

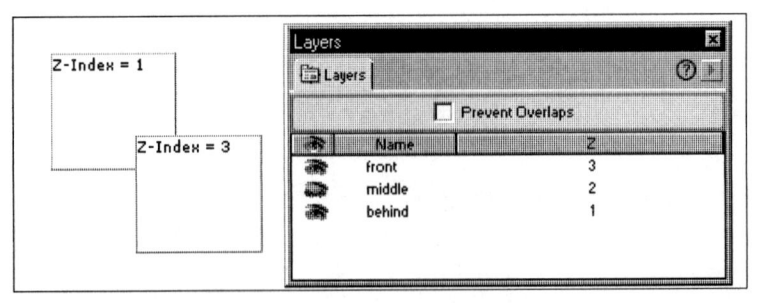

- In the **Bg Image** you can specify a background image for the layer. Click the folder icon to select an image from your site.

©Editions ENI - All rights reserved

Layers

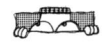

- Do not confuse placing an image in the layer's background with inserting an image in a layer. When the image is in the background, you cannot move it around in the layer.

- The **Bg Color** text box is where you can choose a background colour for the layer. Choose a colour from the palette, type its code, or type its name.

- Select the tag you want to use for the layer from the **Tag** pop-up menu:

    DIV or **SPAN**   these are W3C standard tags, or

    LAYER or **ILAYER**   tags specific to Netscape Navigator.

- The **Overflow** pop-up menu can be used to indicate what the browser should do when the contents of the layer are too large in relation to the specified dimensions:

    empty of **default** indicates that no attribute is specified. Browsers will increase the size of layer so that all the contents can be seen.

    visible: the layer can be resized to see all its contents.

    hidden: the overflowing contents will be hidden.

    scroll: the scroll bars will always be visible, even if the contents are smaller than the layer.

    auto: the scroll bars will only appear when necessary.

Example: these 5 layers show the possibilities listed above:

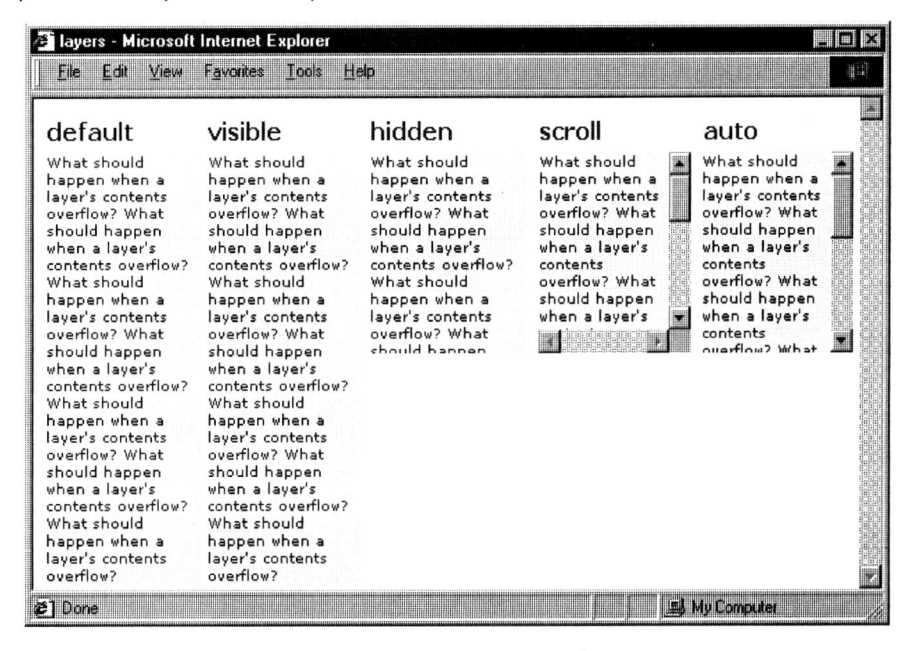

©Editions ENI - All rights reserved

Dreamweaver 3
Layers

- The **Clip** text boxes are for cutting the contents of the layer: you indicate the area in which the layer's contents are visible.

  L: indicates the start of the area visible on the left from the left of the layer.

  R: indicates the end of the area visible on the right from the left of the layer.

  T: indicates the start of the area visible at the top from the top of the layer.

  B: indicates the end of the area visible at the bottom from the top of the layer.

  Example:

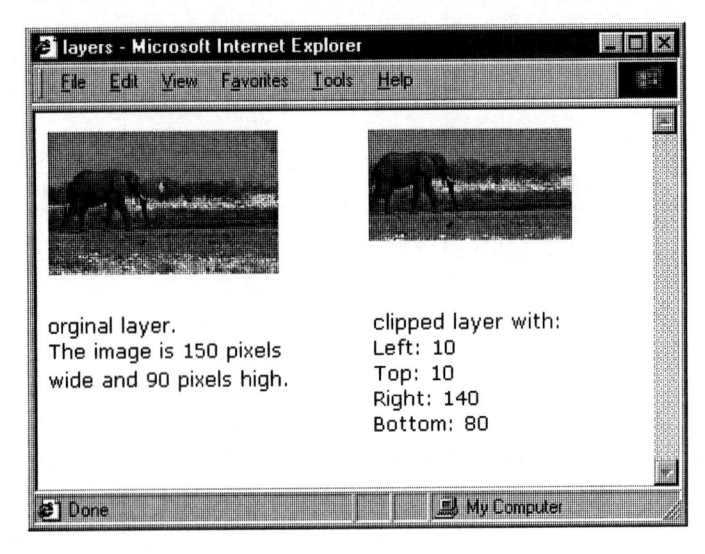

  orginal layer.
  The image is 150 pixels wide and 90 pixels high.

  clipped layer with:
  Left: 10
  Top: 10
  Right: 140
  Bottom: 80

Selecting a layer

- First make sure that the layers' invisible elements are active:

  Edit - Preferences - Invisible Elements category
  The **Anchor Points for Layers checkbox** should be ticked.

- In the document window the invisible elements and layer borders should be visible (**View - Invisible Elements** and **Layer Borders**).

- Select a layer by clicking its invisible element

  or click its name in the **Layers** palette

©Editions ENI - All rights reserved

Layers

or, when the insertion point is in the layer, click its selection handle (the square on the top left corner of the layer):

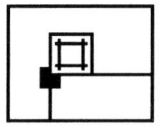

or, if no layer is active (when the insertion point is not flashing in a layer), hold down the Shift key and click anywhere in the layer you want to select.

➢ You can select several layers by holding the Shift key down and clicking the invisible elements, the layers' names, their selection handles, or in the layers themselves.

Changing a layer's attributes

➢ You can use the Property inspector to edit a layer's properties using the different text boxes and pop-up menus. Use the parameters explained previously:

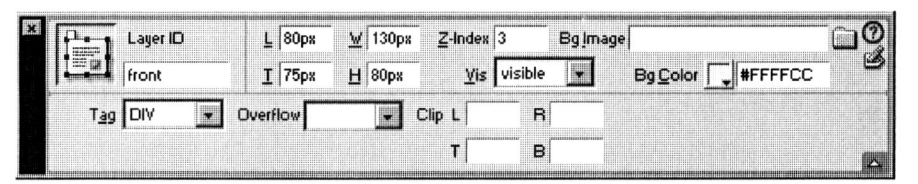

➢ You can also change some settings in the Layers palette (open it with **Window - Layers**).

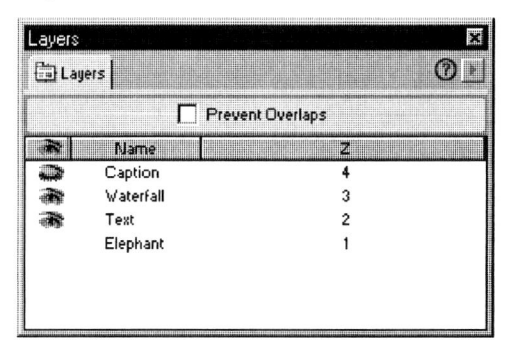

In this example, the Elephant layer has the default attribute (no eye is shown), the Text and Waterfall layers are visible and the Caption layer is hidden.

➢ Check the visibility of layers in the eye-icon column.

Click the column header to show/hide all the layers at once, and click on individual eyes to toggle between the **default hidden**, and **visible** attributes.

©Editions ENI - All rights reserved

- You can see the layers' names in the **Name** column. Double-click a name to change it. Do not use any accented characters or spaces.
- The stacking order of the layers is shown in the **Z** column.
- To change a layer's place in the stacking order, double-click its number and type the new number. Higher numbers place the layer higher up in the stack, and lower numbers send it further down. Avoid identical values if you do not want to have any layer management problems.

You can also drag the layer's name upwards or downwards in the palette.

Creating nested layers

You can nest a layer inside another, in which case the "child" layer (the nested one) moves with the "parent" layer (which contains the child layer) and it inherits the parent layer's visibility. The child layer can be moved outside of the parent layer. A layer can contain several nested layers. If you delete the parent layer you will delete all the child layers too.

First method

You can create nested layers manually.

- Draw the first layer and call it **parent**.
- Keep the parent layer selected, and in the **Objects** palette, **Common** panel, click the **Draw Layer** button.
- Hold the ⌘ key (Macintosh) or Ctrl key (Windows) down.
- Draw the second layer inside the **parent** layer and call it **child**.

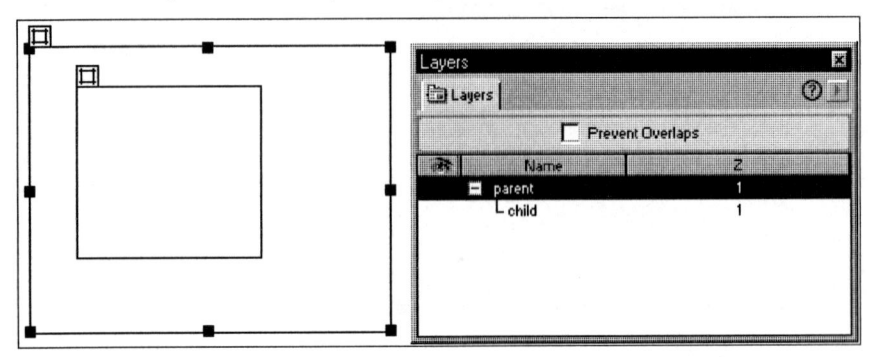

Layers

*In the **Layers** palette you can identify the nested layer thanks to the indentation of the child layer in the parent layer and the ⊟ symbol in front of the parent layer. You can click on this sign to collapse the list of nested layers. The symbol changes to ⊞, which you can click to expand the list of nested layers.*

Second method

You can create nested layers automatically by changing the preferences.

- **Edit - Preferences - Layers** category

    Tick the **Nest when Created Within a Layer** check box.

- Click **OK**.
- Draw the first layer and call it **parent**.
- Inside the first layer, draw a second layer and call it **child**. It is automatically nested in the **parent** layer.

In this case, any new layer which is drawn within the limits of an existing layer will be nested into that layer. Do not forget to deactivate this option unless you want your layers to be nested systematically!

Managing layers

Moving layers

You can move layers (and any nested layers) around in your page.

- If necessary, select the layers concerned.
- Change the values in the **L** and **T** text boxes. If you have selected several layers, these options are under **Multiple Layers**,

    or select the layer and move it by dragging it in the page

- or select a layer and use the arrow keys on the keyboard to move the layer one pixel at a time. If you hold down the [Shift] key, you will move the layer on a grid (see below).

If the **Prevent Overlaps** option is active (in the **Edit** menu or the **Layers** palette) you cannot stack the layers. This option can come in very useful if you want to transform your layers into a table.

©Editions ENI - All rights reserved

Resizing layers

- Select the layer(s) concerned.
- Type new values in the **W** and **H** text boxes in the Property inspector or drag one of the black sizing handles:

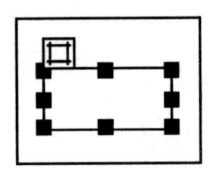

- Do the same thing to resize a layer and align it on the grid, but hold the [Shift] key down as you do.
- To apply the width and height of the last layer you selected to your other layers, use:

    Modify - Layers and Hotspots - Make Same Width or **Make Same Height**

Aligning layers in relation to each other

- Select the layers concerned.

    The layers are aligned in relation to the last layer selected.

- **Modify - Layers and Hotspots - Align Left, Align Right, Align Top** or **Align Bottom**

    Example: the last layer selected here was the middle layer (its sizing handles are black). The top alignment is in relation to this layer; the other layers move upwards:

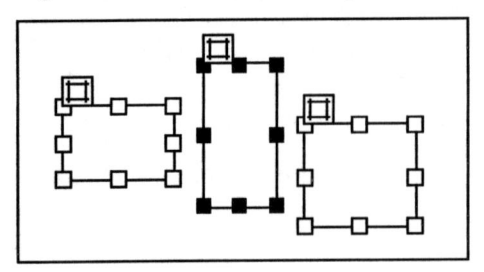

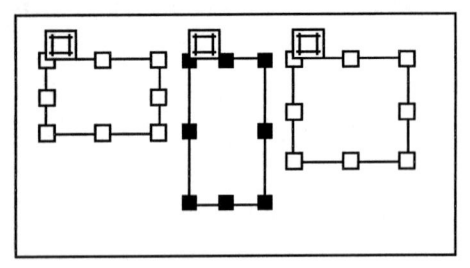

Layers

Using the ruler and the snap feature

You can also use the rulers and the snap to grid feature to help you.

- Show the ruler using **View - Rulers - Show**.

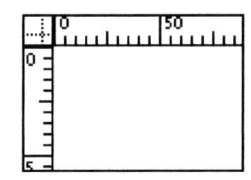

- You can move the origin of the rulers by dragging the intersection (in the top left corner of the screen) then releasing the mouse button when you reach the place in the page where you want the new origin to be.

- To restore the origin to its original location, double-click the intersection of the rulers or **View - Rulers - Reset Origin**

- You can choose the unit used on the ruler by activating the appropriate option in the **View - Rulers** menu (**Pixels, Inches** or **Centimeters**).

- To show the grid use **View - Grid - Show**.

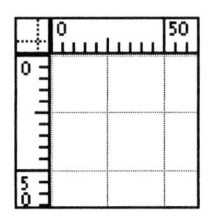

- If you want the grid to "fit" into the top left corner of the screen, you need to specify margins of 0 in the page properties: **Modify - Page Properties**.
Type 0 in the **Left Margin, Top Margin, Margin Width** and **Margin Height** text boxes:

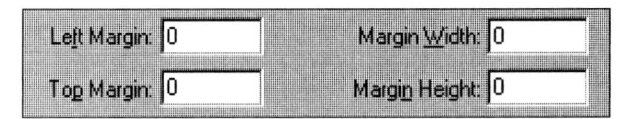

- To activate the snap feature, so that the layers are attracted to the grid when you draw and move them, activate the **Snap To** option in the **View - Grid** menu.

- You can choose the grid settings in **View - Grid - Settings**.

©Editions ENI - All rights reserved

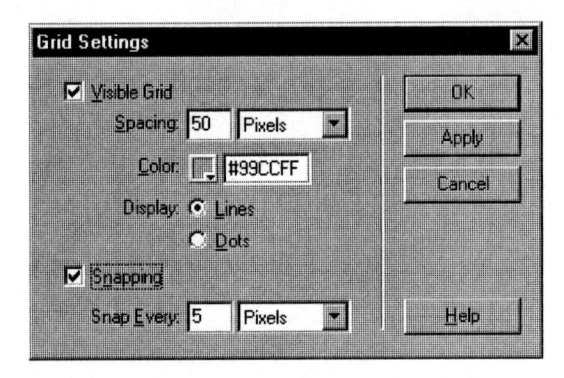

- The **Visible Grid** checkbox must be ticked for the grid to appear in the window.
- Indicate the value of the line spacing in the **Spacing** text box. Choose a unit from the pop-up menu: **Pixels**, **Inches** or **Centimeters**.
- Choose the **Color** of the gridlines.
- You can **Display** the grid as **Lines** or **Dots**.
- Activate the **Snapping** option to turn on the snap to grid feature.
  Use **Pixels**, **Inches** or **Centimeters** to indicate the snapping unit in the **Snap Every** text box.
- Click **OK**.

In order for the snap to grid feature to be active, the unit of the grid and the snapping must be the same.

Transforming layers into tables and vice-versa

Using layers is clearly the easiest way to place elements where you want them in your page. They are ideal for creating complex page setups. However, because the use of layers requires HTML 4 features, users will need browsers which are version 4 (or later), which is not yet the case for all Internet users. Dreamweaver offers you the possibility of changing your layers into a table, or converting your page to make it compatible with version 3 browsers.

Transforming layers into a table

- You should first make sure that the layers do not overlap, otherwise you will not be able to create table cells using the layers. Activate the **Prevent Overlaps** option in the **Layers** palette

  or activate **Prevent Layer Overlaps** in the **View** menu.

Layers

⊡ Draw your layers and insert text, images, whatever you want.

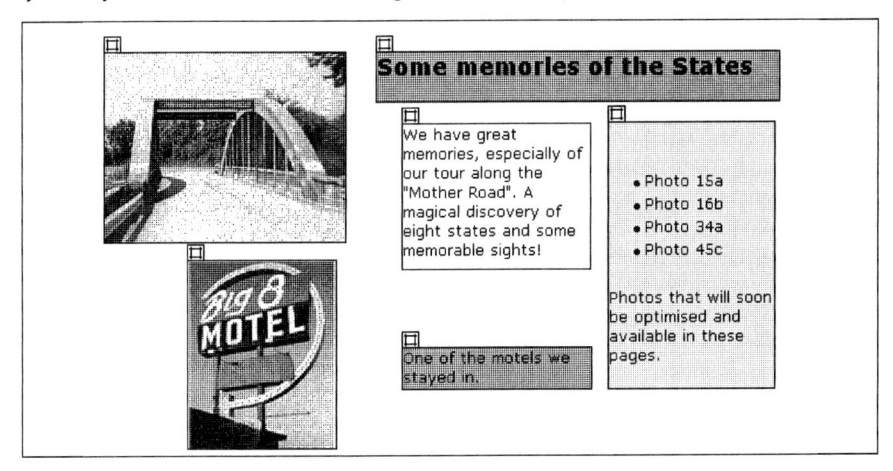

⊡ Select all your layers.
⊡ **Modify - Layout Mode - Convert Layers to Table**

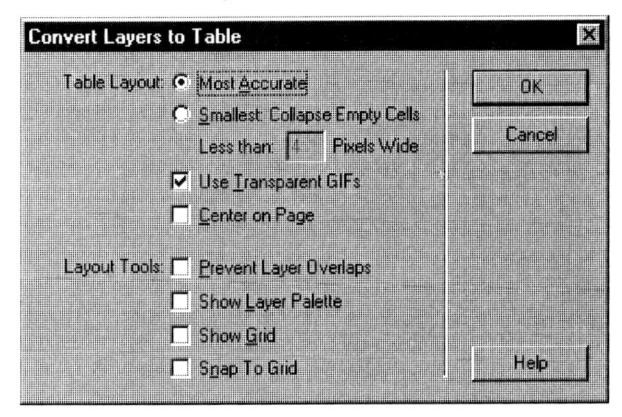

⊡ In the **Table Layout** options:

Most Accurate: to create one cell per layer and keep the spacing between layers by creating as many cells as are necessary.

Smallest: Collapse Empty Cells: if the layers are **Less than X Pixels Wide**, align them one after the other. This will reduce the number of cells in the table.

Use Transparent GIFs: to insert transparent GIFs into the cells of the last row in the table so that the page will be displayed in the same way in all browsers.

©Editions ENI - All rights reserved

Center on Page: centre the table you will create in the page.

⇨ Under **Layout Tools**:

Prevent Layer Overlaps: you will be alerted when layers overlap. You cannot create a table with layers that overlap. Ticking this checkbox activates the **Prevent Layer Overlaps** option.

Show Layer Palette: opens the **Layers** palette window.

Show Grid: to show the grid in the page.

Snap To Grid: so that cells will be aligned on the grid, whenever possible.

⇨ Click **OK**.

This is the result obtained from the example shown above:

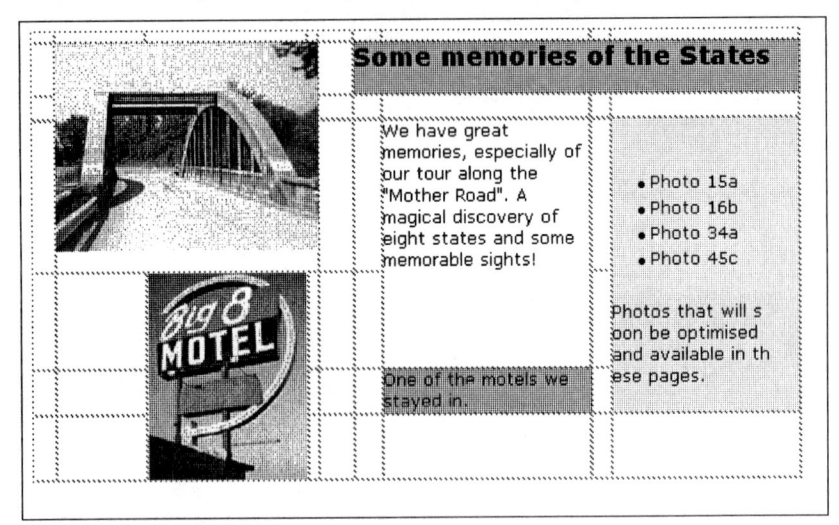

Creating a document that is compatible with version 3 browsers

The other way to make your layers page accessible is to convert it so that it is compatible with version 3 browsers. In this case, Dreamweaver makes a copy of the original page so that the layers page is conserved.

⇨ Open the page that uses layers.

⇨ **File - Convert - 3.0 Browser Compatible**

Layers

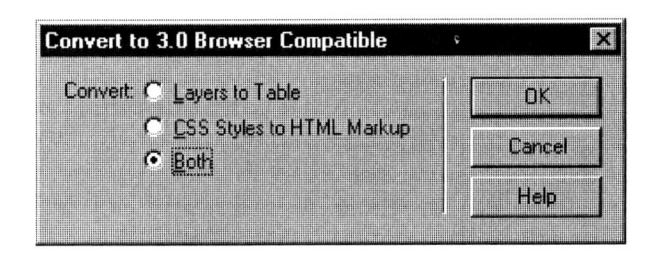

- You can **Convert**:

    Layers to Table, meaning you convert the CSS-P into tables.

    CSS Styles to HTML Markup (see the chapter about CSS-1 cascading style sheets).

    Both, which is both CSS-P and CSS-1.

- Click **OK**.
- A new document is created, which you should save.

Transforming a table into layers

You can also convert a table into layers in order to make the page setup easier to create.

- Create your table.
- Select it.
- **Modify - Layout Mode - Convert Tables to Layers**

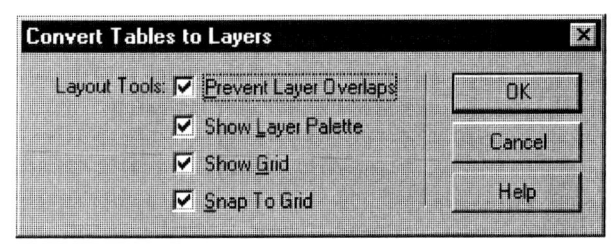

    Prevent Layer Overlaps: activates this option once the conversion is complete. This will put limits on how you can move and resize the layers.

    Show Layer Palette: to open the **Layers** palette window.

    Show Grid: shows the grid in the window.

    Snap To Grid: to align the layers along the gridlines.

- Click **OK**.

Tracing images

Principle

You can ask a graphic designer to create the page layout for your homepage (for example). The designer will give you the document in paper format, which you can then scan (as a .gif, .jpg or .png file). Place the image in the background of your page to use it as a template. This is the **Tracing Image** concept in Dreamweaver.

You can use layers to reproduce the paper design better. Here again you will find that layers are incredibly useful and well adapted for creating a good page setup.

This image will appear only to help you create your page; it will not be visible in a browser.

Placing the image

- Create a new document then use **Modify - Page Properties**

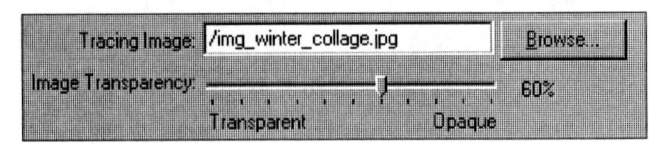

- Type the name of the file you want to use in the **Tracing Image** text box, or click the **Browse** button to select it.

- Use the **Image Transparency** slider to increase or decrease the transparency of the image, so that it does not interfere too much as you work with the layers.

- Click **OK**

    You can hide the tracing image whenever you want to.

- To hide the tracing image temporarily, deactivate the **Show** option in the **View - Tracing Image** menu. Reactivate this option to see the image again.

- Change the tracing image using **View - Tracing Image - Load**.

Layers

Working with layers

Now that you have inserted your tracing image, you need to create some layers to position your images and headings in the template. Below is an example of the use of layers over a tracing image:

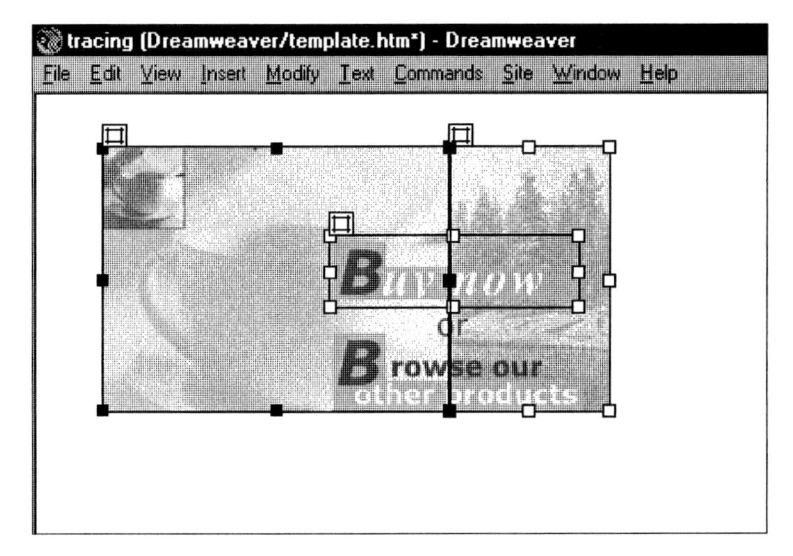

You can fit the tracing image to the layers by aligning the image with a layer.

- Select a layer that contains a graphic element (text or image).
- **View - Tracing Image - Align with Selection**

  The tracing image moves to align with the top left corner of the layer.

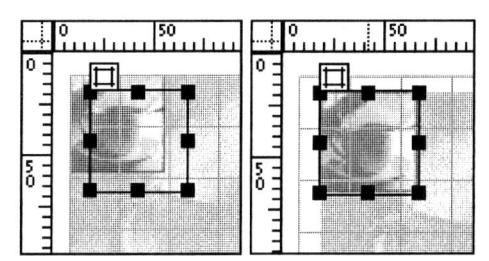

- Move the tracing image in the background of the page using **View - Tracing Image - Adjust Position**.

©Editions ENI - All rights reserved

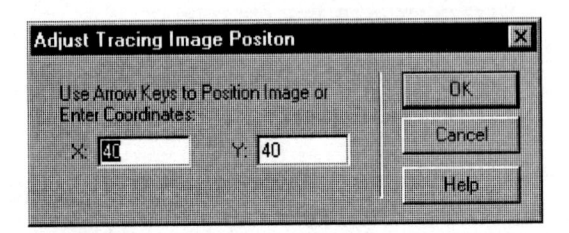

- You can move the tracing image manually, using the arrow keys on the keyboard.
  You can also type the X and Y co-ordinates of the image in relation to the top left corner of the page.
- To place the tracing image in the top left corner (0,0 co-ordinates) use **View - Tracing Image - Reset Position**.

Timelines

Principle

You can use layers to make your page more dynamic by recording the movement of layers and changing certain parameters (such as the size and visibility). This movement (a movie) will be activated automatically or after an action made by a user.

This technique uses what is called DHTML (Dynamic HTML), which is, in fact, an association of CSS-P style sheets and JavaScript. A version 4 or later browser is required to exploit this feature.

Setup

- To manage your timelines, show the Timeline inspector: **Window - Timelines**.

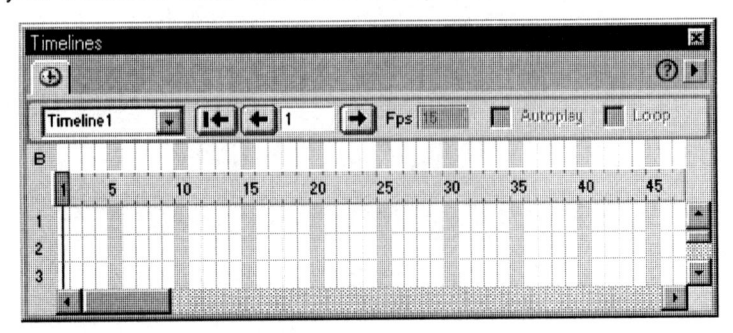

The timeline's name appears in the **Timeline1** pop-up menu.

Layers

The **B** area (**Behavior channel**) indicates where the behaviours should be executed in the timeline.

The red rectangle and associated vertical line represent the **Playhead**. Use the playhead to visualise the movement of the layer in the page. The graduation marks show the **Frame numbers**. The default frame speed is 15 frames per image, which is the standard speed for the Web.

Several **Animation channels** are available: the bars 1, 2, 3, etc, which can each contain an animation. This means you can have several animations in the same timeline. When you record the movement of a layer, the key positions will be indicated by **keyframes** in the animation channel.

Creating an animation

- Create a layer, name it, and insert an image inside it (for example).
- Select the layer.
- **Modify - Timeline - Record Path of Layer**
- Drag the layer's selection handle across the page.

    The layer's path is visible as a dotted line on the page:

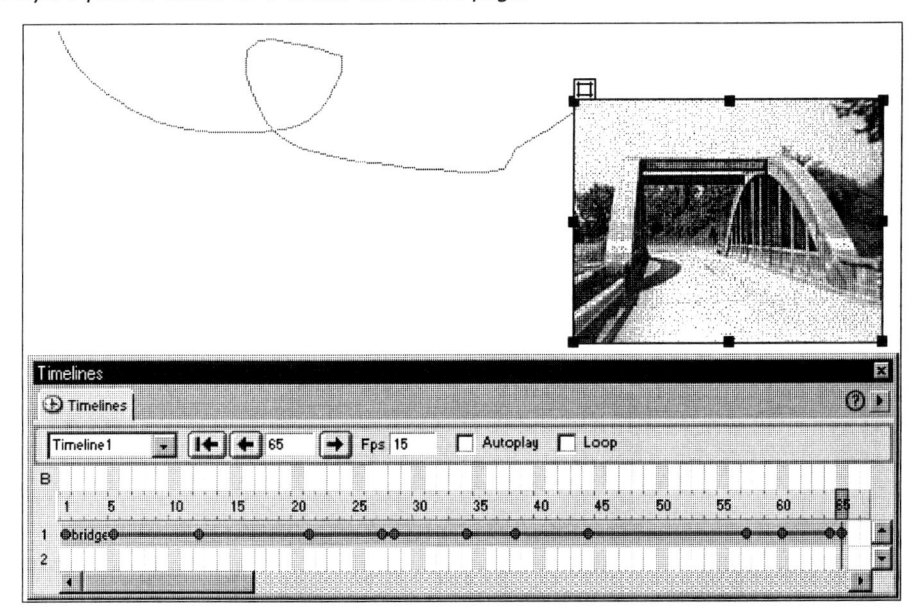

When you have drawn the path, Dreamweaver tells you that the Timeline inspector can animate only certain layer attributes (dimensions, visibility and stacking).

©Editions ENI - All rights reserved

In animation channel 1 you can see the name of the layer (bridge in this example) and each key position is indicated by a keyframe (small circle).

- To change the timeline's name, open the Timeline inspector's context menu by clicking the ▶ button and choose **Rename Timeline** or double-click the name of the timeline.

Watching the animation in the page

- Hold down the **Play** button ➡ and the **Back** button ⬅ in the Timeline inspector or drag the **Playhead**.

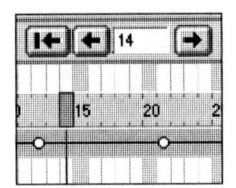

- Use the **Rewind** button ⏮ to return to the start of the animation.

Previewing the animation in a browser

- Before you can see your animation in a browser you will need to define its parameters in the Timeline inspector so that the animation will run when the page loads. Activate the **Autoplay** option in the Timeline inspector if you want the animation to play when the page loads.

    Dreamweaver tells you that an `onLoad` event is used to do this.

- If you want to see the JavaScript event, click the `<body>` tag on the status bar.

- **Window - Behaviors**

    You can see that when the page is loaded (`onLoad`) the **Play Timeline** action will be launched.

- If you want the animation to run on a loop, activate the **Loop** option. The animation will rewind and play itself again and again.

©Editions ENI - All rights reserved

Layers

Dreamweaver tells you that a behavior has been added after the last keyframe of your animation which will cause it to restart. This addition can be seen in the Timeline inspector, after the last keyframe, in the Behavior channel (B):

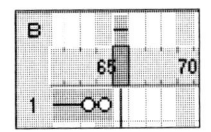

- Open the **Behaviors** palette to see this JavaScript event.

    The **Go To Timeline Frame** *action runs at the end of the animation, in frame 66 (in this example), that is,* **onFrame66**.

- Double-click this action:

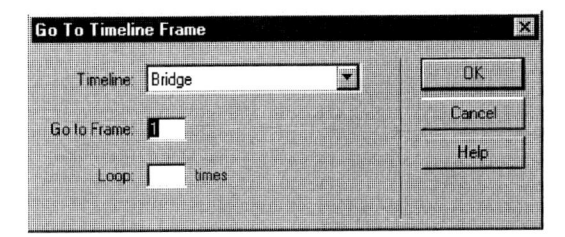

    The **Timeline** *is called Bridge. The action will* **Go to Frame 1**.

- Save your page and preview it in a browser.

Editing an animation

You can change (move, add or delete) the keyframes in your animation, which will change the movement of your layer. If you change the frames in the animation (add or remove them) you can increase or reduce the length of the animation.

Use the keyframe symbol for all of these changes: the white circle in the animation channel.

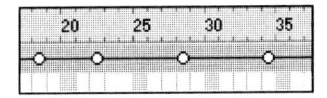

- To move a keyframe, drag it along the animation channel.
- You can increase the duration of the animation by dragging the last keyframe towards the right in the time scale.

    The other keyframes are moved in relation to this.

- If you do not want the other keyframes to be moved, hold the ⌘ (Macintosh) or Ctrl (Windows) key down while you are moving the last keyframe.

©Editions ENI - All rights reserved

- To move the layer to a specific keyframe, click the keyframe. In the page, move the layer to its new position.
- You can change the moment at which the animation starts by dragging the first keyframe.

    The other keyframes are moved in relation to this.

- Move the entire animation by dragging it in its animation channel (the blue bar).
- To add a keyframe, click in the animation channel at the appropriate place in the time scale. Open the context menu by clicking ▶ and choose **Add Keyframe**.

    or ⌘-click (Macintosh) or Ctrl-click (Windows) in the animation channel at the appropriate place.

    Now you can move the layer for this keyframe.

- Delete the selected keyframe by opening the context menu ▶ and choosing **Remove Keyframe**.
- You can add a frame by clicking in the animation channel where you want to insert the frame and opening the context menu ▶, and then choose **Add Frame**.

    When you add frames, the time interval between two keyframes is increased, and the length of the animation is increased.

- You can delete a frame by selecting the frame in question, opening the context menu ▶ and choosing **Remove Frame**.

    When you delete frames, the time lapse between two keyframes is reduced, as is the total duration of the animation.

Changing the properties of a layer associated with an animation

During an animation, you can change some of the layer's attributes, such as its visibility, stacking order and size.

- To change the stacking order of the layer, select a keyframe in your animation. Select the layer. In the Property inspector, change the value in the **Z-Index** text box. Type a higher value if you want the layer to appear on top of the others. Type a lower value if you want the layer to be under the others.

    You will need to do this for several keyframes in a row, otherwise the change will be apparent only for one keyframe.

Layers

- To change the visibility, select a keyframe in the animation. Select the layer. In the Property inspector, change the option in the **Vis** pop-up menu by choosing **hidden** to hide the layer or **visible** to show it.
  Do the same thing for several keyframes in a row, otherwise the change will be apparent only for one keyframe.
- Change the size of the layer by first selecting a keyframe in the animation then selecting the layer. Change the **W** and **H** values in the Property inspector.
  Do this for several keyframes in a row, otherwise the change will be apparent only for one keyframe.

At the time this book went to press, only Microsoft Internet Explorer was capable of managing the change in size.

Adding an animation

The same timeline can contain several animations.

- Create a new layer and name it.
- Insert some text or an image into the new layer.
- In the Timeline inspector, place the playhead at the beginning of the animation, on the first frame, if necessary. If you do not do this, the new animation will start where the playhead is.
- Select the new layer.
- **Modify - Timeline - Record Path of Layer**
- Do the same thing for any other animations.

   All of the animation management information detailed above can be applied to any animation in the timeline.

Adding an object to an animation channel

You can also add an object - a layer - to an animation channel, which may already contain an animation.

- Create a new layer and name it.
- Insert an image or some text in this new layer.
- Select the new layer.
- **Modify - Timeline - Add Object to Timeline**

   or drag the layer's selection handle onto the animation channel.

©Editions ENI - All rights reserved

In this example, the text2 layer has been inserted:

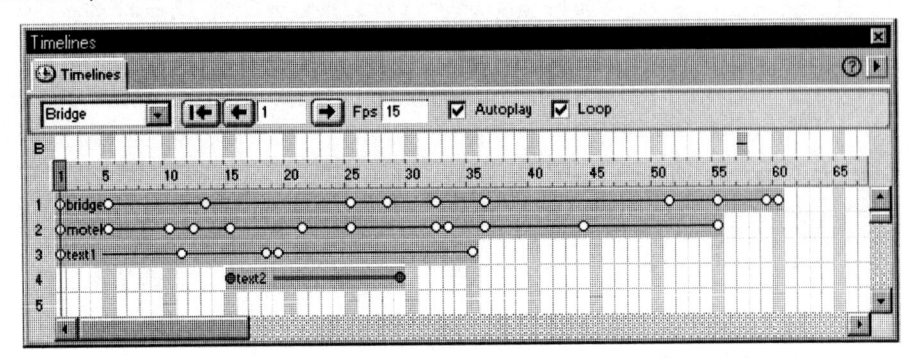

If you insert the object using the menu command, it is inserted in the frame where the playhead is. If you drag it into the timeline, you can place it wherever you want. The inserted object is always visible while the animation plays and will become animated only if you insert a keyframe in its animation channel. If you want to hide this new layer at the beginning of the animation, change the **Vis** attributes as shown previously.

Copying an animation

To save time, or create a more complicated presentation, you can duplicate an animation.

- Select an animation by clicking its blue bar in the Timeline inspector.
- Choose **Copy** from the context menu.
- Choose **Paste** from the context menu.

The animation appears at the end of the preceding animation. Both the animations use the same layer, and they cannot overlap in the time scale. You can move the pasted animation to another animation channel by dragging it.
Using a similar method, you can apply the path of one layer to another layer.

- In your page, create a new layer and name it.
- Select an animation by clicking its blue bar in the Timeline inspector.
- Choose **Copy** then **Paste** from the context menu.
- Choose **Change Object** from the context menu.
- Select the name of the layer you have just created from the **Object to Animate** pop-up menu.
- Click **OK**.

Layers

- Move the animation to a new channel.
- Make all the necessary changes to this new animation (if you do not make any changes, the new layer will follow exactly the same path as the original layer).

Deleting an animation

- Select an animation by clicking its blue bar in the Timeline inspector.
- Choose **Delete** from the context menu ▶.

Adding a timeline

If you are working on a very elaborate piece, it is often easier to manage several timelines. A page can contain several timelines, which each contain several animations!

- **Modify - Timeline - Add Timeline**
- You can rename the timeline by opening the context menu ▶ and choosing **Rename Timeline**, or by double-clicking its name.
- To delete a timeline, choose **Remove Timeline** from the context menu ▶.

You can copy animations from one timeline to another, and from one page to another.

Playing an animation with behaviors

*When you insert a timeline showing the movement of a layer in your page, you can choose to start it automatically when the page is loaded (**Autoplay** option) or you can use behaviors if you want to have more interactivity with the user. You can insert buttons to play and stop the animation, and also one to rewind the animation to the beginning (or to a particular keyframe in the scenario).*

Behaviors are associated with an event (such as mouse click by the user) and an action (a JavaScript) in Dreamweaver.

- To insert behaviors, create three buttons using a graphics application.
- Insert these three buttons for the Play, Stop and Rewind actions.
- Insert a layer, name it and place an image inside it.
- Record the layer's path, and make sure the **Autoplay** option is deactivated.
- Name the timeline.

©Editions ENI - All rights reserved

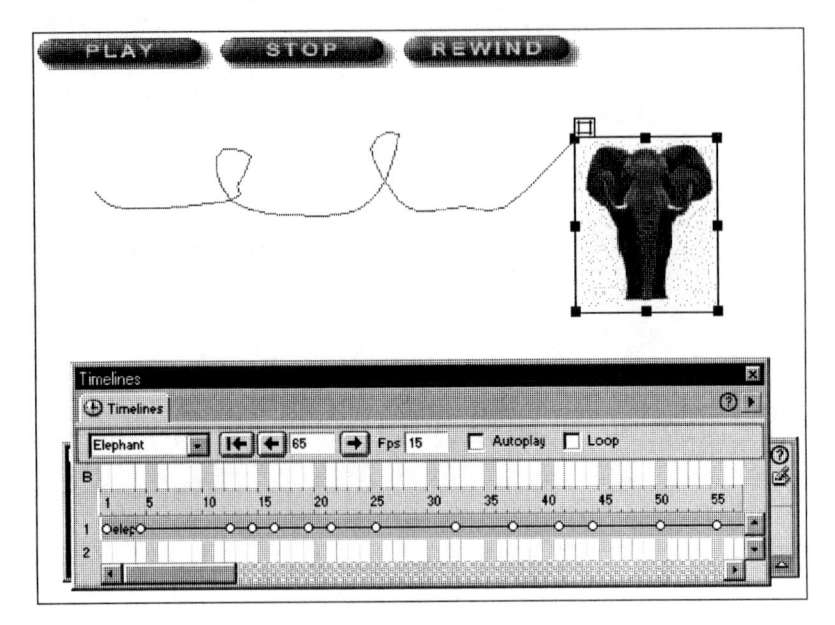

Dreamweaver 3
Layers

- Select the **PLAY** button.
- Open the **Behaviors** palette: **Window - Behaviors**.
- Choose the appropriate browser version.
- Click the button to add a behavior.
- Choose **Timeline - Play Timeline**.
- Select your timeline from the **Play Timeline** pop-up menu. 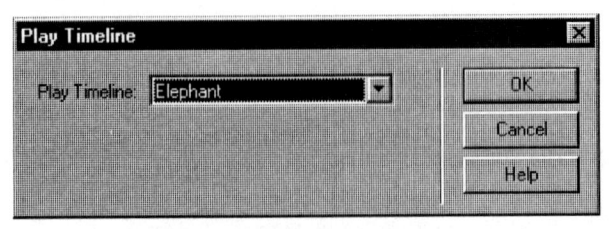
- Click **OK**.

Layers

- Use the same technique to associate the **Stop Timeline** behavior to the **STOP** button and the **Go To Timeline Frame** behavior to the **REWIND** button:

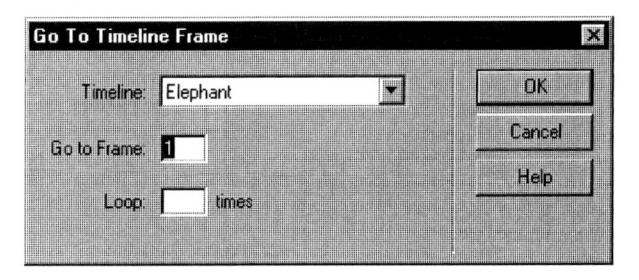

- Choose your timeline in the **Timeline** pop-up menu.
- Type the number of the frame you want to go to in the **Go to Frame** box (frame **1** to return to the start of the animation).
- If this action should be repeated several times in the animation channel (here called "elephant"), indicate the number of times in the **Loop** box. Leave this box empty if you do not want the action to be repeated.
- Click **OK**.
- In the **Behaviors** palette, choose the **Events** you want for each button (onClick, on MouseOver etc).
- Test the behaviors by saving your document then previewing it in a browser. Use the buttons to control the timeline.

Adding more behaviors

You can add numerous behaviors to your animation. These behaviors are applied only to one event, such as the arrival of the animation in a particular frame: the `onFrame25` *event indicates that the script will run when the animation reaches frame 25.*

- To add a behavior to a frame, in the time scale of the Timeline inspector, click in the frame in which the behavior is to be activated.
- Choose the appropriate browser version in the **Behaviors** palette.
- Click the [+] button to add a behavior and choose one of the appropriate behaviors, such as: **Show-Hide Layers, Call JavaScript, Go To URL, Swap Image**, or **Set Text**.

A line in the Behavior channel **B** *indicates the presence of a behavior in a timeline.*

©Editions ENI - All rights reserved

See the chapter about behaviors for more information about them and how to apply them to your timelines.

Behaviors associated with layers

Changing the contents of a layer

This behavior enables you to replace the contents and formatting of a specified layer by new contents and/or attributes, which you define. The contents can be HTML code.

- Choose an image that will start the action: **Insert - Image**.
- Select the image.
- Choose the appropriate browser version from the **Events For** pop-up menu in the **Behaviors** palette.
- Click the button to add a behavior and choose **Set Text - Set Text of Layer**.

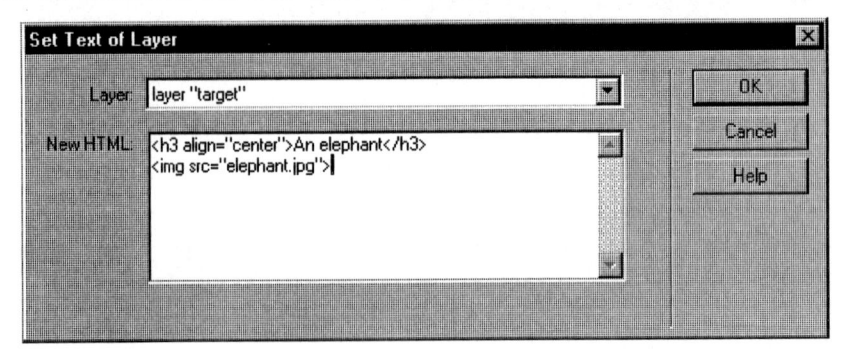

```
Set Text of Layer
    Layer:   layer "target"
    New HTML: <h3 align="center">An elephant</h3>
              <img src="elephant.jpg">
    OK
    Cancel
    Help
```

- Choose the target layer, the contents of which will be removed, from the **Layer** pop-up menu.
- In the **New HTML** text box, type the text which will appear in the layer, or the HTML code, as shown in the example.
- Click **OK**.
- Choose a mouse event: in the **Behaviors** palette, in the **Events** column, choose onClick, onMouseOver, etc.
- Save the page then open it in a browser to test the behavior.

©Editions ENI - All rights reserved

Layers

In this example, the layer initially contains an image, then its contents are replaced by text and a different image:

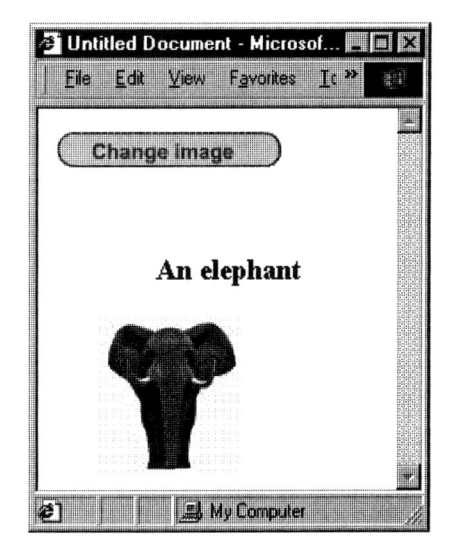

Showing and hiding layers

You can increase the interactivity with the user by showing hidden layers and hiding visible layers.

This technique enables you to create pop-up menus: in a visible layer, place the name of the menu, and in another layer, which is hidden, place the contents of the menu. Finally, in a last layer in the background, place another layer which will hide the contents of the menu when you "leave" it.

If you use Microsoft Internet Explorer 5 you can assign the behaviors to the layers directly. If you use Netscape Navigator 4 or Microsoft Internet Explorer 4, you must insert images in the background and menu layers and assign the behaviors to them.

- Create a background layer (Z-Index = 1). Name it **background**.
- Create a layer for the menu's name (Z-Index - 2). Name it **menu**.
- Create a layer that will contain the menu items (Z-Index = 3). Name it **items**. This layer's **Vis** attribute must be **hidden**. It should not be visible when you start to use the menu.
- Create links from the menu items to other pages in your site.

Dreamweaver 3
Layers

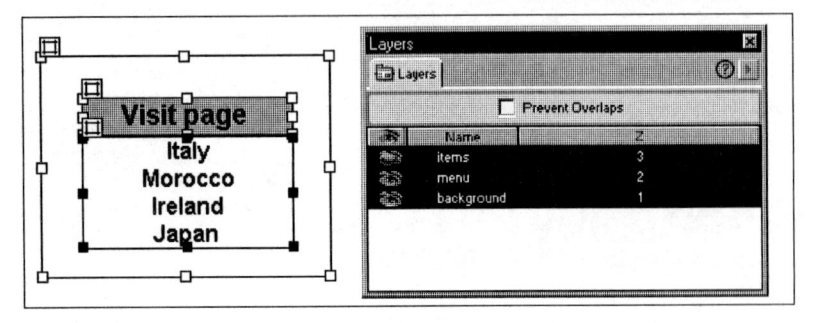

- Select the **menu** layer or the image it contains.
- In the **Behaviors** palette, choose the appropriate browser version.
- Click the ⊕ button to add a behavior and choose **Show-Hide Layers**.

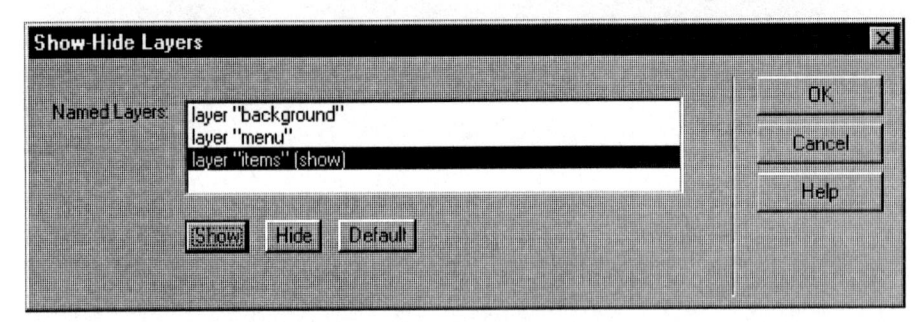

- Select the **layer "items"** in the **Named Layers** list and click the **Show** button.
- Click **OK**.
- Choose the **onMouseOver** event in the **Behaviors** palette.

©Editions ENI - All rights reserved

Layers

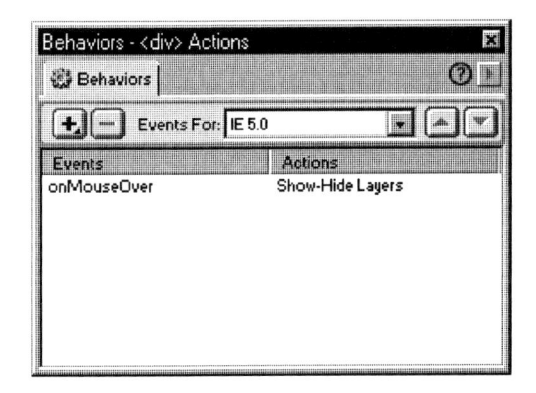

- Select the **background** layer.
- Click the [+] button in the **Behaviors** palette to add a behavior and choose **Show-Hide Layers**. Select **layer "items"** in the **Named Layers** list and click **Hide**.
- Click **OK**.
- Choose the **onMouseOver** event in the **Behaviors** palette.
- Test the behavior by saving the document and previewing it in your browser.

When the mouse is not on the menu, the items are not visible (`hidden` attribute):

When you place the mouse pointer over the menu (`onMouseOver`), the menu items appear:

Directly you move the mouse pointer back onto the background layer, the menu items disappear.

©Editions ENI - All rights reserved

Dreamweaver 3
Layers

Moving a layer

You can make your page even more interactive by allowing users to move a layer. They might be able to move the layer anywhere (to complete a puzzle, for example), or within constraints. Furthermore, you can define a "target" area for the move and tell the user when this area has been reached by means of a message.

- For an unrestricted move, insert a button image that will trigger the action.
- Insert a layer and name it. Insert an image into the layer.
- Select the button image.
- Choose the appropriate browser version in the **Behaviors** palette.
- Click the [+] button and choose **Drag Layer**. Activate the **Basic** tab.

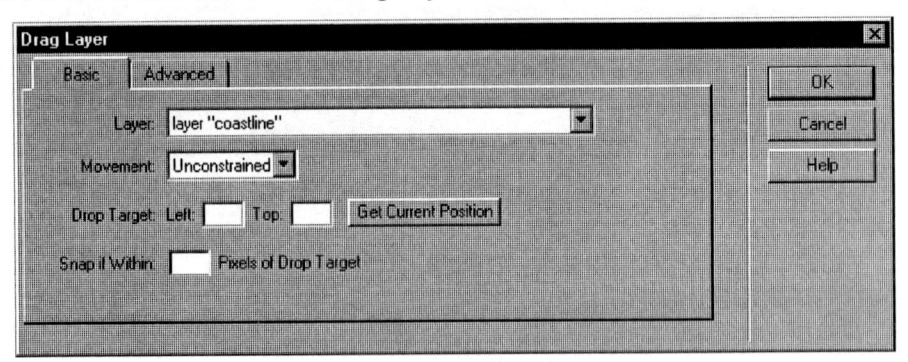

- Select the layer that is to be moved in the **Layer** pop-up menu.
- Leave **Unconstrained** selected in the **Movement** pop-up menu.
- Leave the other options inactive.
- Click **OK**.
- Choose the event you want from the **Behaviors** palette.
- Test the behavior by saving your page and previewing it in the browser. Activate the button to move the layer.
- To define a constrained movement, follow the steps above but, when you choose the **Behavior**, choose **Constrained** from the **Movement** pop-up menu.

©Editions ENI - All rights reserved

Layers

- Indicate how far the layer can be moved in relation to the top, bottom, left and right of the layer, in the **Up**, **Down**, **Left** and **Right** text boxes.

    In the example below you will see how to create a game, the aim of which is to move a layer onto a target (difficult stuff!).

- Insert a button image, called **PLAY** in this example.
- Insert a layer, called **canyon** in this example, which contains an image (of a canyon!). You can create a handle in the image with which to drag it. You can set parameters so that the user who wants to move the layer must drag the handle and not just any place on the layer's surface.
- Insert another layer to create a visible target.

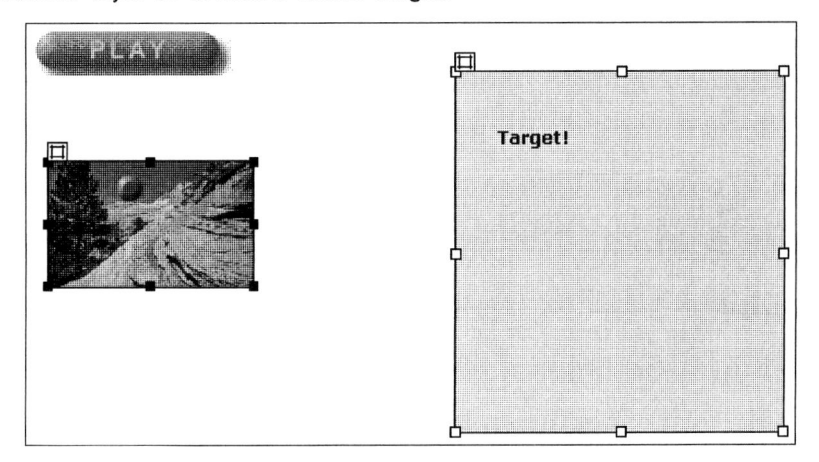

- Select the **PLAY** button.
- Add a behavior that allows you to move the layer, as shown previously.
- Activate the **Basic** tab.

©Editions ENI - All rights reserved

Dreamweaver 3
Layers

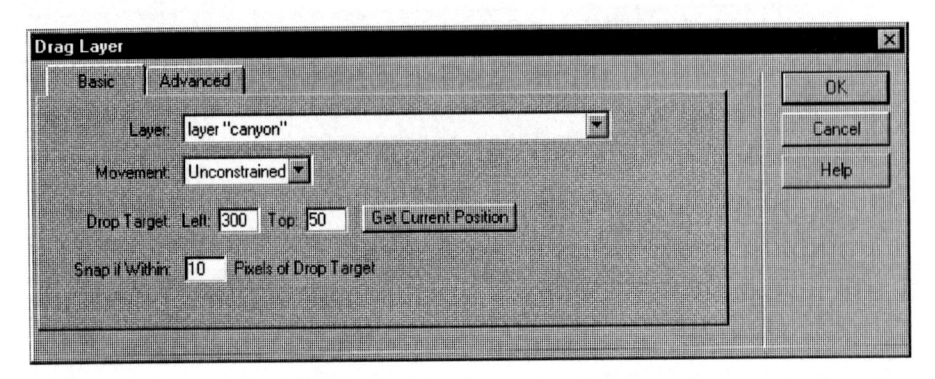

- In the **Layer** pop-up menu, select the layer you want to move (the **"canyon"** layer in this case).
- Leave **Unconstrained** as the choice in the **Movement** pop-up menu.
- Under **Drop Target** enter the **Left** and **Top** values which correspond to the target position. In this example, the target is the target layer, positioned 300 pixels from the left of the page and 50 pixels from the top.
- Click the **Get Current Position** button to find the position of the layer that is to be moved.
- In the **Snap if Within** box, enter a value in pixels, and if the layer is within this distance in **Pixels of Drop Target**, it will be snapped into place.
- Click the **Advanced** tab.

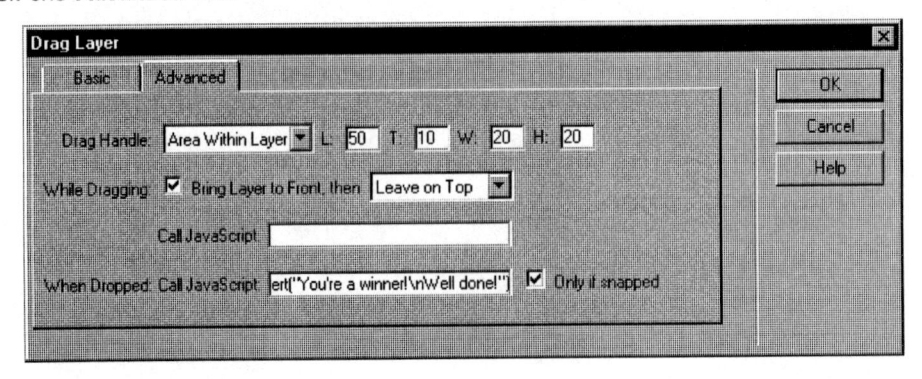

- In the **Drag Handle** options choose:

    Entire Layer if the user is to be able to "pick up" the layer by clicking anywhere on its surface.

Layers

Area Within Layer if you want to specify a handle in the layer by indicating its co-ordinates (in pixels) from the left of the layer **L**, and the top **T**, and the width **W** and the height **H** of the handle. The user must click in this area to be able to move the layer. In this example, the defined area corresponds to the button.

- The **While Dragging** options indicate how the layer should appear while the user is moving it. Activate the **Bring Layer to Front, then** check box if the layer is to be in the foreground while it is dragged. Use the following pop-up menu to indicate whether to **Leave on Top** or whether the preceding stacking order should be reapplied once the user releases the mouse button.

- The **Call JavaScript** box is for inserting or invoking a JavaScript during the movement of the layer.

- The **When Dropped: Call JavaScript** box is for inserting or invoking a JavaScript when the user drops the layer. Activate the **Only if snapped** option if the script is only to be run when the user drops the layer in the target area.

- Click **OK**.

- Choose the event you want in the **Behaviors** palette.

- Test the behavior by saving the document and previewing in the browser. Start playing and move the layer.

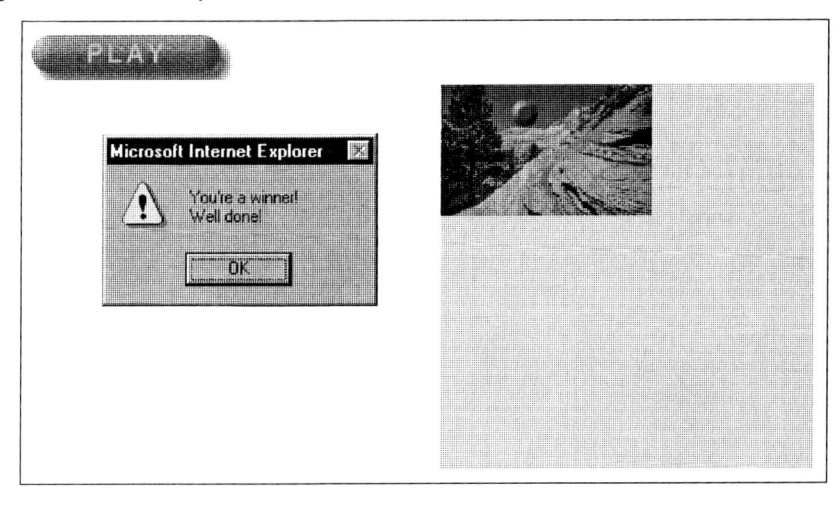

© Editions ENI - All rights reserved

Principle

In HTML 3.2, text was formatted "traditionally", using elements such as `<font>`, `<p>`, `<ol>` and `<ul>`. This posed two problems: the formatting was relatively limited; documents which were structured, for example, using headings that re-used the same formatting where time-consuming to create and update.

One of the great improvements in HTML 4 was the introduction of Cascading Style Sheet level 1, CSS-1. A style sheet is a group of formatting elements - styles - that control the formatting of a document. When the best use is made of them, a separate document contains all the styles that you might want to apply to any items in your pages. One single document stores all the formatting in your site, and you do not need to repeat the same formatting ad infinitum. Furthermore, if you want to change the formatting, you can simply edit the appropriate style in the style sheet and all the items throughout the site that use that style will be updated.

With cascading style sheets you can be sure that the presentation of your pages will be homogenous, and you will be able to work quickly and efficiently.

CSS-1 can be created at several levels. The least efficient way to create a CSS-1 is at the level of the item to which the style is applied. If you develop the styles at the level of the page, they will be available only for use in that page and all the items it contains. The best way to create a style sheet is to create an entirely separate document, which can be used by all the pages in the site which are linked to the style sheet. Its extension is .css.

Take care. CSS-1 can be used only with version 4 or later browsers. Earlier browsers cannot display formatting, only plain text (more or less). You need to be aware of the compatibility problems that can arise with older browsers.

CSS-1 in the page

The first method you can use to create a style sheet is to create it in the page in which it is to be used. The declaration of the style sheet is placed in the document header (`head` element). In this case, the style sheet can only be applied to the current document (unless you link it to another document).

Creating a style sheet

To create a style sheet in the open document:

Text - CSS Styles - Edit Style Sheet and click the **New** button

or open the **CSS Styles** palette using **Window - CSS Styles** and click the **New Style** button .

or open the context menu by clicking and choose **New**.

Style sheets

➡ Choose an option under **Type**:

Make Custom Style   if you want to create a custom style (class), to which you can apply a whole series of formatting elements. In the **Name** box, type the style's name. The name of a class should always begin with a . character (full stop). If you forget, Dreamweaver will add it for you.

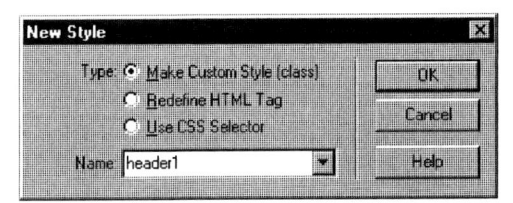

Redefine HTML Tag   if you want to redefine the formatting of an existing HTML element. For example, if you choose the h3 element from the **Tag** pop-up menu then specify some formatting, if you then use a level 3 heading (<h3>) in your document, this formatting will be applied.

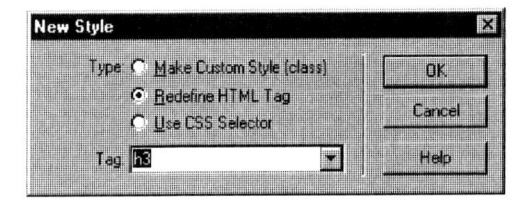

Use CSS Selector   this can be used firstly to define the appearance of links for four states:
a:link for the appearance of unvisited links.
a:hover for the appearance of links when the pointer is over them (without clicking).
a:active for the appearance of links when a user clicks them.
a:visited for the appearance of visited links.

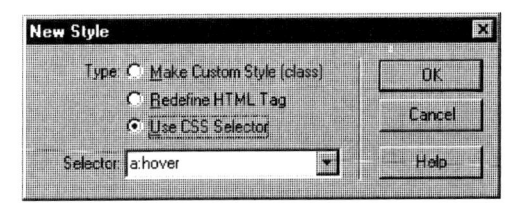

Dreamweaver 3
Style sheets

Use CSS Selector   can also be used to define the formatting of HTML elements, which are used in a particular context. For example, you can specify the formatting of words in italics used in a paragraph. In this case the **Selector** is **P I**. P for the paragraph element `<p>` and I for italics `<i>`.

- Once you have chosen what sort of style you want, click **OK**.

Defining the formatting

After having created a style, the **Style definition** dialog box opens.

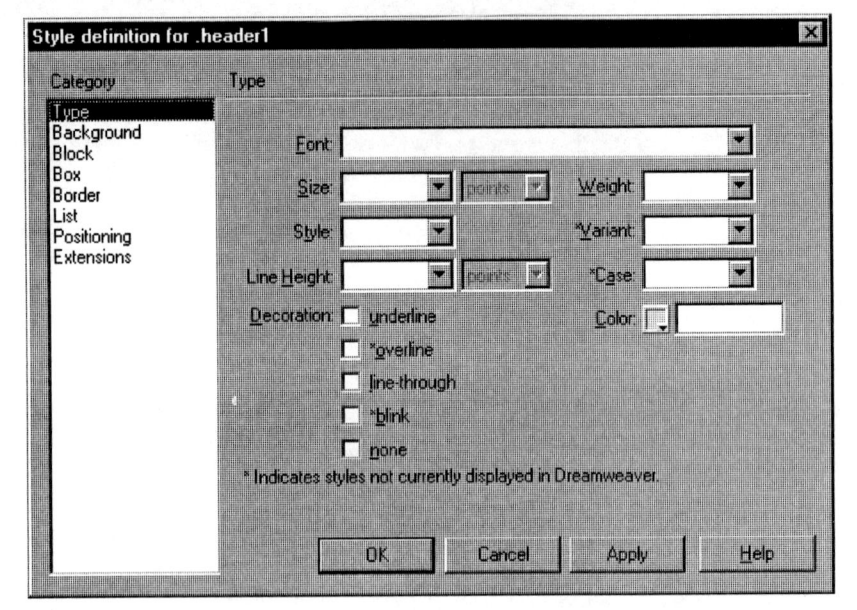

⛰ Caution! Dreamweaver shows an asterisk * next to some of the different formatting options. This signals that the formatting is not recognised by Microsoft Internet Explorer or Netscape Navigator, or that these browsers interpret it differently. Because of this, the formatting will not be visible in Dreamweaver, only in a browser.

Apply formatting using panels from each different **Category**. The **Type** category concerns the character formatting.

- Choose the character group from the **Font** pop-up menu.
- In the **Size** pop-up menu, define the character size and choose the unit from the pop-up menu to the right (choose **pixels**, **points**, **in**, **cm**, **mm**, etc).

©Editions ENI - All rights reserved

Style sheets

- In the **Weight** pop-up menu you can select the boldness of the characters (**normal, bold, bolder** and so on, or a preset boldness: **100, 200, 300** etc).
- Choose the character style from the **Style** pop-up menu: **normal, italic** or **oblique**.
- Use the **Variant** pop-up menu to choose whether you want the characters in **normal** or **small-caps**.
- Specify the line spacing of the text in the **Line Height** pop-up menu, and use the pop-up menu on the right to choose the unit (**pixels, points, in, cm, mm** and so forth).
- In the **Case** pop-up menu you can choose the characters' case: **capitalize, uppercase, lowercase** or **none**.
- The **Decoration** options apply different styles to the text.
- Choose the **Color** of the text either with the color picker, or by typing the name or hexadecimal code of the colour you want.

    The **Background** category is for applying a background to the selected element:

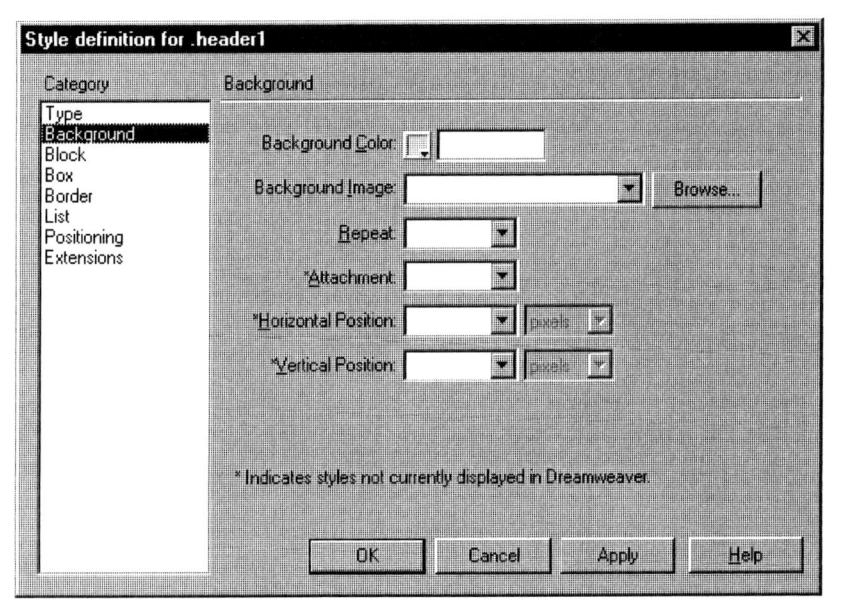

- Choose the **Background Color** either with the color picker, or by typing the colour's name or hexadecimal code in the text box.

©Editions ENI - All rights reserved

Dreamweaver 3
Style sheets

- Type the path of an image in the **Background Image** box, or click **Browse** to select the file.

- Choose how the image should be repeated in the element in the **Repeat** pop-up menu: **no-repeat** (the image will be displayed once), **repeat** (the image will be repeated as many times as necessary to cover the surface of the element), **repeat-x** (the image will be repeated x times horizontally) or **repeat-y** (the image will be repeated y times vertically).

- The **Attachment** pop-up menu is for indicating the behaviour of the background image when it is scrolled: choose **fixed** if the image is not to scroll with the contents or **scroll** if it is.

- In the **Horizontal Position** text box you can define the position of the top left corner of the image (using the unit chosen in the pop-up menu on the right) in relation to the left of the element that contains it.

- Use the **Vertical Position** text box to define the position of the top left corner of the image (using the unit chosen in the pop-up menu on the right) in relation to the top of the element that contains it.

    The **Block** category is for formatting the text.

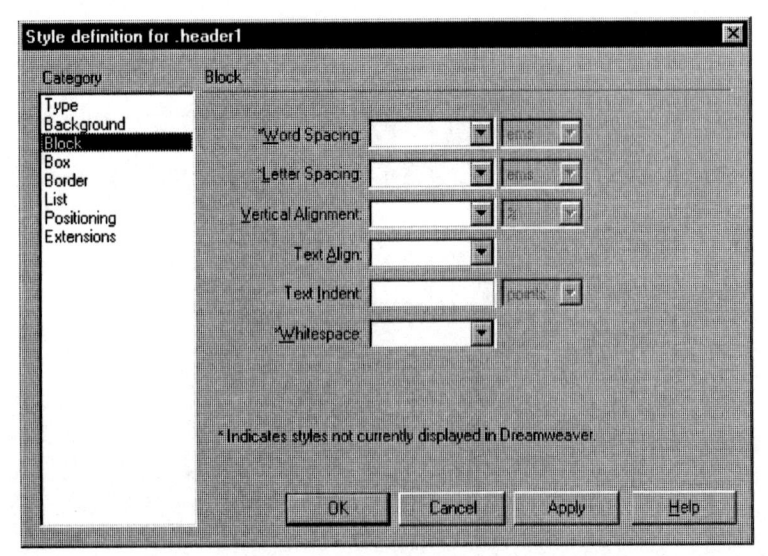

- Use the **Word Spacing** and **Letter Spacing** pop-up menus to indicate the spacing that you want between words and letters, using the unit selected in the pop-up menus to the right.

©Editions ENI - All rights reserved

Style sheets

- The **Vertical Alignment** pop-up menu is for choosing the vertical alignment of the element in relation to its parent element. For example, the vertical alignment of an image in relation to the text which contains it.
- Use the **Text Align** pop-up menu to define the alignment: **left**, **right**, **center** or **justify**.
- In **Text Indent** you can specify a first-line indent for the paragraph, using the unit chosen in the pop-up menu on the right.
- The **Whitespace** pop-up menu is for indicating how whitespaces between words should be managed: **normal** indicates that there is only one space between words, **pre** manages spaces as if the text is placed in the HTML element <pre>, and if you choose **nowrap**, only the element <br> will provoke a line break.

    The **Box** category is for formatting images, layers and blocks of text.

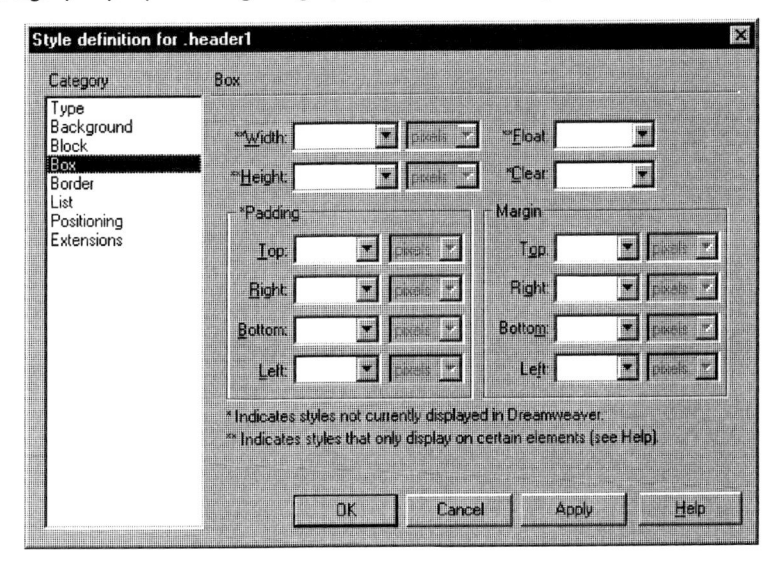

- The **Width** and **Height** pop-up menus are for indicating the height and width of images and layers, either by giving a value and a unit, or by leaving the original size by choosing **auto**.

©Editions ENI - All rights reserved

Dreamweaver 3
Style sheets

- The **Float** pop-up menu indicates how an image will behave in relation to text: choose **left** and the image will float to the left of the text, **right** and it will float to the right of the text, or **none** if the image is not to float.

- Use the options under **Padding** to indicate the distance between the contents of a block, which is principally text, and its border (even if there is no border). Indicate the value and unit for the **Top**, **Right**, **Bottom** and **Left**.

- The **Margin** options specify the distance between the block's border (even if there is no border) and other elements. Choose a value and unit for **Top**, **Right**, **Bottom** and **Left**.

    The **Border** category is for formatting the appearance of the block's border:

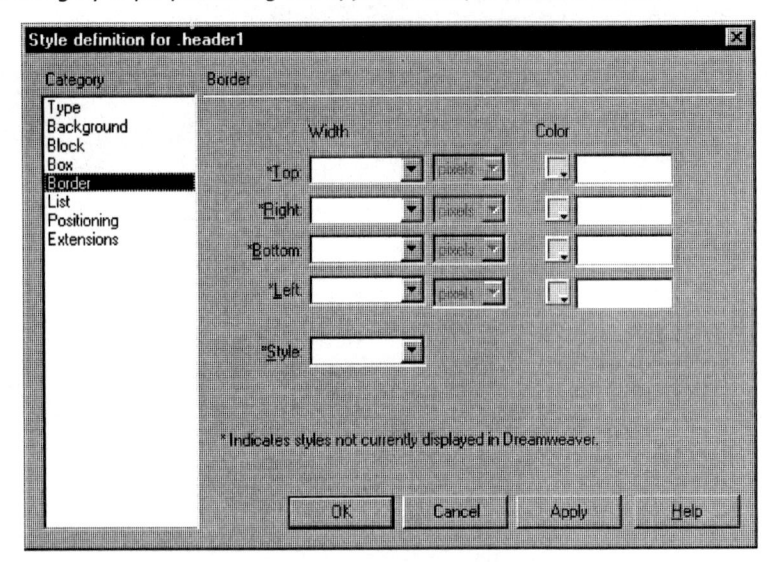

- Use the **Top**, **Right**, **Bottom** and **Left** pop-up menus under **Width** to choose a preset style (**thin**, **medium** or **thick**) or indicate a value and choose the unit, for each side of the frame. Use the **Color** pickers to choose the colour of each part of the border.

Style sheets

In the **List** category the options are for defining data lists:

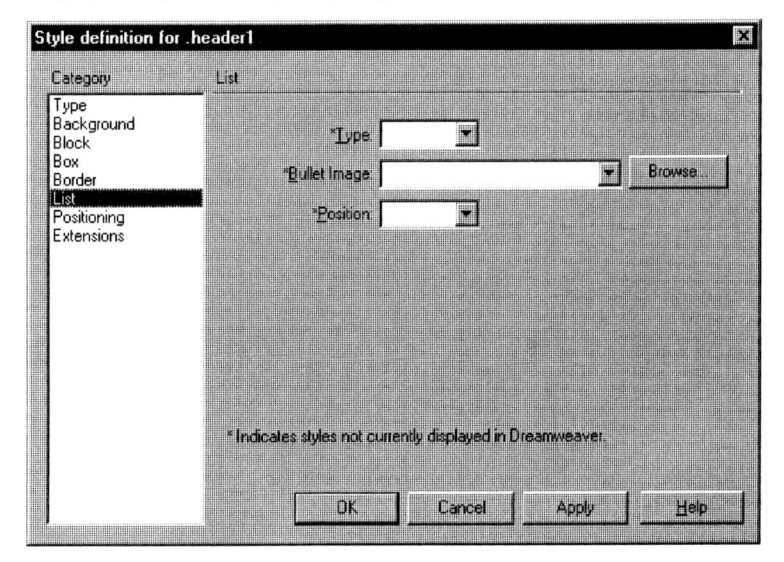

- Use the **Type** pop-up menu to choose the type of bullet or number: **disc**, **circle**, **square**, **decimal**, **lower-roman** and so forth.
- In the **Bullet Image** text box you can type the file path of the image that will serve as a bullet, or click the **Browse** button to select it.
- Use the **Position** pop-up menu to choose the position of the bullet or number: **inside** or **outside**.

©Editions ENI - All rights reserved

Dreamweaver 3
Style sheets

The **Positioning** category is for creating layers:

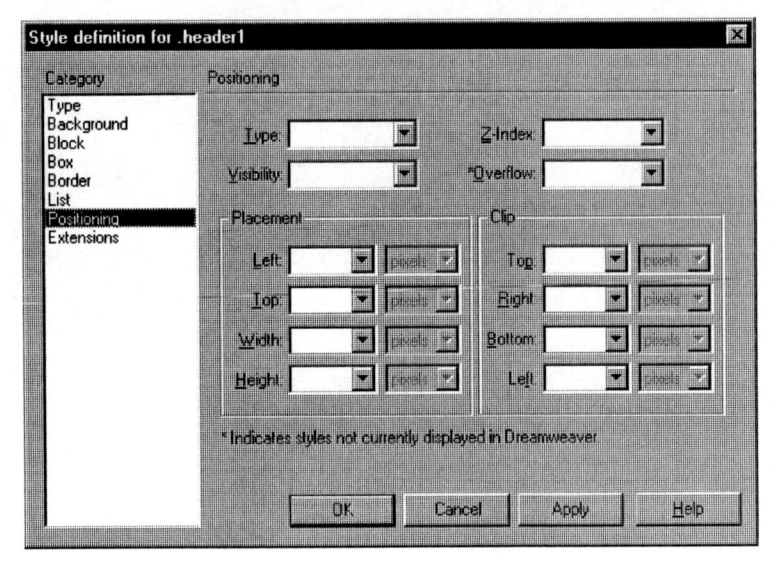

- In the **Type** pop-up menu, choose the type of layer you want:

    absolute   the layer will be positioned in the **Placement** you specify in relation to the parent element, usually the window.

    relative   if you want the layer to "move" with the flow of text in the page. If a paragraph is placed in front of the layer and you add a lot of text to this paragraph, your layer will "descend" in the page.

    static   the layer will be inserted inside an element in a position which is relative to 0.

- The other settings: **Z-Index, Visibility, Overflow, Placement** and **Clip** function as explained in the chapter about layers.

    The **Extensions** category is for choosing the settings of other extensions which are hardly recognised by browsers.

©Editions ENI - All rights reserved

Style sheets

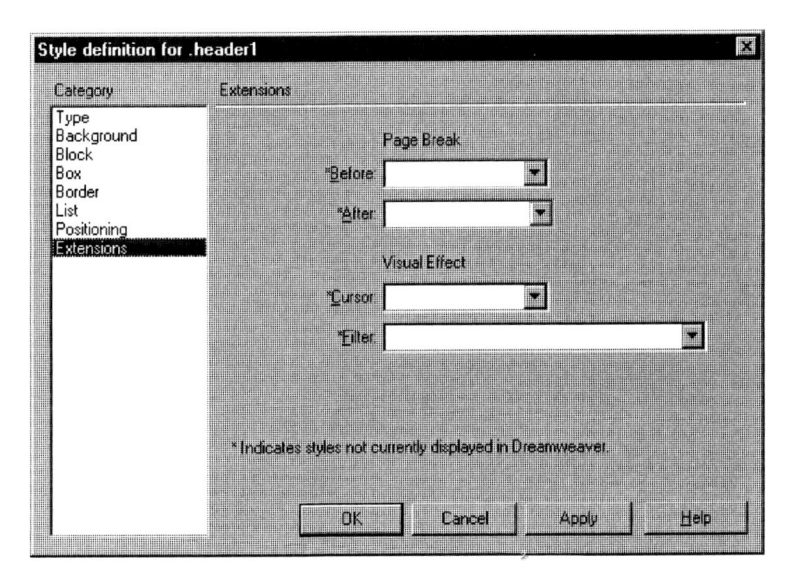

- Use the **Page Break** options to indicate a page break **Before** or **After** the element which uses the current style.
- The **Cursor** pop-up menu is for choosing a **Visual Effect** to be produced when the pointer passes over an element which uses the current style.
- In the **Filter** pop-up menu you can choose special effects to be applied to the element which uses the current style.

Applying styles

- Once you have created your styles, you can see a list of them in the **Text - CSS Styles** menu, or in the **CSS Styles** palette (**Window - CSS Styles**).

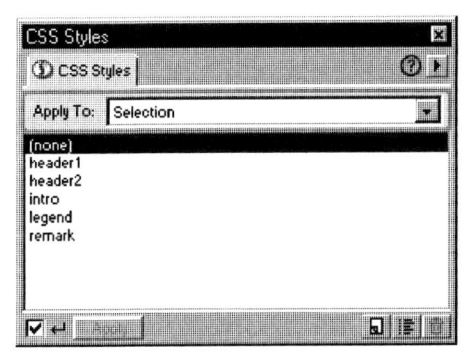

©Editions ENI - All rights reserved

Dreamweaver 3
Style sheets

- If you want styles to be applied as soon as you click them, make sure the **Apply** option is ticked in the **CSS Styles** palette. If you deactivate this option, you will need to click the **Apply** button to apply the style to text.
- To apply a style to text, first click in the appropriate paragraph or select the text in question. For images, select the image by clicking it.
- **Text - CSS Styles - Style_name**
  or click the appropriate style in the **CSS Styles** palette.

  When you apply a style to an entire element, such as a paragraph, the **CSS Styles** paragraph indicates the element to which you have applied the style. In this example, the **Apply To** pop-up menu shows that the paragraph that contains the insertion point carries the style intro: **<p> (intro)**.

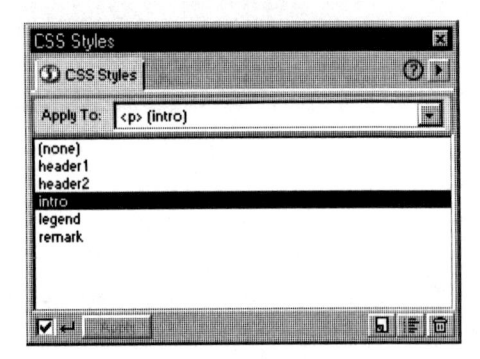

  A style in a paragraph is called using the `class` attribute in the HTML code, and its value is its name:

  ```
  <p class="intro">...</p>
  ```

  A style applied to a selection is called using the `span` attribute, which contains the `class` attribute, and the value is the name of the style:

  ```
  <p>...<span class="legend"> ... </span>...</p>
  ```

©Editions ENI - All rights reserved

Style sheets

Removing a style

- In the page, select the element which uses the style.
- **Text - CSS Styles - None**
    or click the **(none)** style in the **CSS Styles** palette.

Editing a style

As soon as you edit a style, all the elements in the page that carry the style are updated.

- **Text - CSS Styles - Edit Style Sheet**
    Select the name of the style in question then click **Edit**
    or click in an element that uses the style and open the context menu ▶ in the **CSS Styles** palette and choose **Edit**.
- Make the necessary changes.
- Click **OK**.

Copying a style

When you want to create two similar styles, the easiest way to proceed is to copy the first then make changes to this second style, rather than create the second from nothing.

- **Text - CSS Styles - Edit Style Sheet**
- Click the name of the style you want to copy then click **Duplicate**
    or click in an element that uses the style, open the context menu ▶ in the **CSS Styles** palette and choose **Duplicate**.
- Rename the new style.
- Make the necessary changes.
- Click **OK**.

Deleting a style

When you delete a style, the elements which use the style lose the corresponding formatting.

- **Text - CSS Styles - Edit Style Sheet**

    Select the name of the style you want to delete then click **Remove**.

    or click in an element that uses the style then open the context menu on the **CSS Styles** palette and choose **Delete**.

    or click the **Delete Style** button in the **CSS Styles** palette.

Creating an external style sheet

Obviously, in order to save time and keep the same presentation, you are not going to recreate the same style sheet for each new document in your site. You can create a file for your site's style sheet, and all the pages will refer to this file, making it the only source of styles. The style file always has .css as its extension.

Creating a .css file

- Create a new document.
- **Text - CSS Styles - Edit Style Sheet**
- Click the **Link** button.
- Type the name of your style sheet in the **File/URL** text box, and do not forget the .css extension.
- Leave the **Link** option selected under **Add As**.

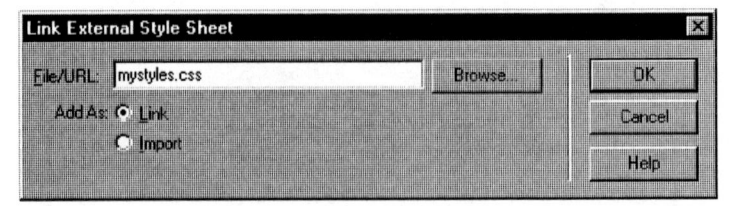

- Click **OK**.

    The style sheet is created and linked to the active document.

- To edit the style sheet, select the **mystyles.css (link)** sheet then click **Edit**.
- Click the **New** button in the **mystyles.css** dialog box and create styles as shown previously.

Style sheets

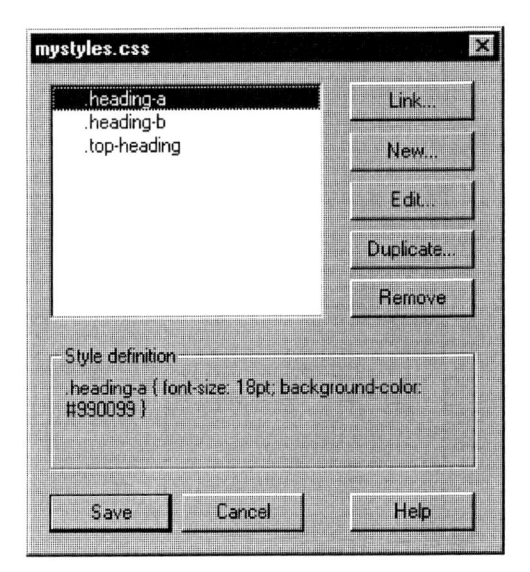

*This window's title bar indicates that you are creating styles for the **mystyles.css** style sheet.*

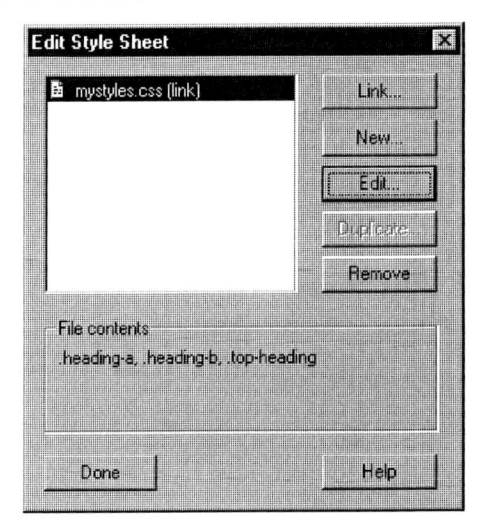

➥ Click **Save**.

*A list of the styles appears in the **File contents** frame.*

➥ Click **Done**.

©Editions ENI - All rights reserved

Dreamweaver 3
Style sheets

Your styles are created and can be used in the new document:

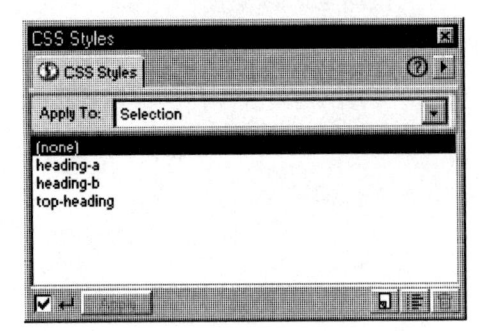

- In the HTML code, Dreamweaver makes a link to the styles file:

```
<link rel="stylesheet" href="mystyles.css">
```

- In your site folder, Dreamweaver has created a mystyles.css document. Press F5 to see the files in your site.

You can see the file in its folder.

Linking a .css file

Now you can create a new document and link it to the mystyles.css style sheet.

- Create a new document.
- **Text - CSS Styles - Edit Style Sheet**
- Click the **Link** button.
- Type the name of your style sheet in the **File/URL** box, or click **Browse** to select it.
- Leave the **Link** option active under **Add As** to create a dynamic link with the source.

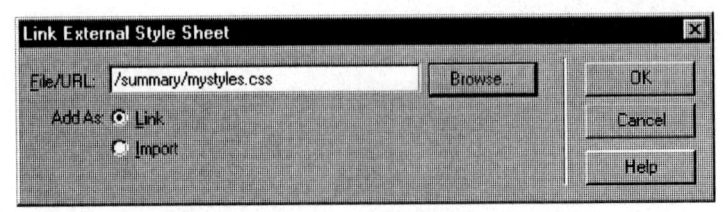

The **Import** option enables you to incorporate the mystyles.css sheet in the document's style declaration (@import "mystyles.css"). This option is not often used.

- Click **OK** then **Done**.

Style sheets

The style sheet is now linked and available.

- Make the same link for all the pages in your site. By doing this, you will have a single source for styles in your site. Furthermore, there is nothing to prevent you from creating styles specifically for certain pages in addition to the styles in the sheet.

Editing an external .css file

Now that you have created the mystyles.css style sheet, if you edit this source, all elements that use its styles in your site will be updated automatically.

- Go to an open document which is linked to the mystyles.css style sheet.
- **Text - CSS Styles - Edit Style Sheet**

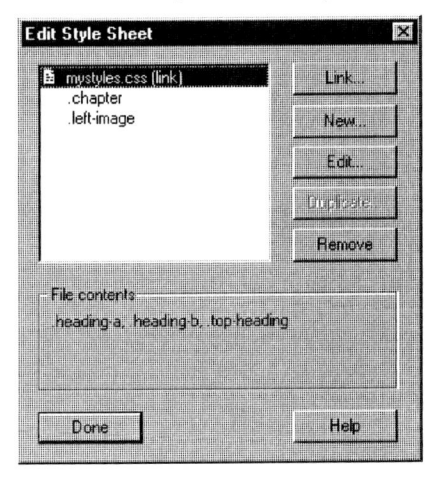

In this example you can see two extra styles that have been created in this page, alongside the styles from the linked sheet, mystyles.css.

- Select the linked sheet and click **Edit**.
- Select the style you want to change and click **Edit**.
- Make the necessary changes.
- Save the style sheet.
- Click **Done**.

All elements that use the style are updated.

You can also show the files in your site by pressing [F5] then double-clicking the .css file's icon to open the style sheet.

©Editions ENI - All rights reserved

Defining preferences for CSS styles

In the preferences, you can define the syntax of the code that Dreamweaver generates.

⊡ **Edit - Preferences - CSS Styles** category

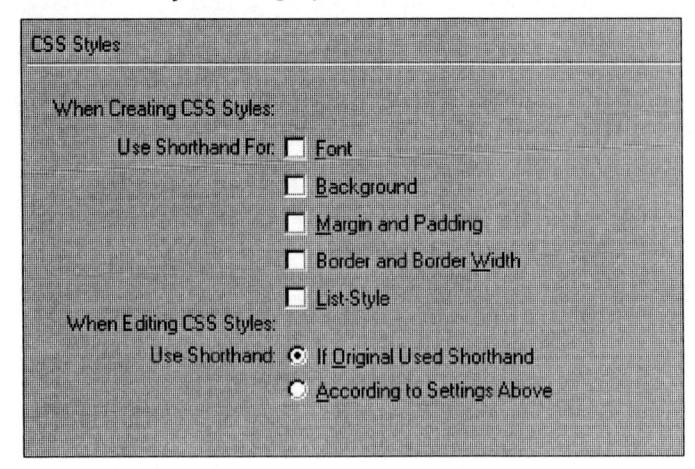

The **Shorthand** can be used to write css code more concisely, making it easier to use for programmers.

⊡ You can use **Shorthand** for the different styles indicated **When Creating CSS Styles** and/or **When Editing CSS Styles**.

This is the code of a style written in longhand. All the attributes that describe the `font` are given one after the other:

```
.header1 { font-family: Verdana, Arial, Helvetica, sans-serif;
font-size: 10pt; font-style: italic; font-weight: bold}
```

This is the same style, using the **Shorthand** option. All the `font` attributes are nested:

```
header1 { font: italic bold 10pt Verdana, Arial, Helvetica, sans-serif;}
```

Converting styles

As you have seen, only version 4.0 or later browsers can interpret CSS-1 styles. If you want your pages to be visible and formatted in older browsers, you need to transform the style sheets into standard HTML formatting elements.

⊡ **File - Convert - 3.0 Browser Compatible**

Style sheets

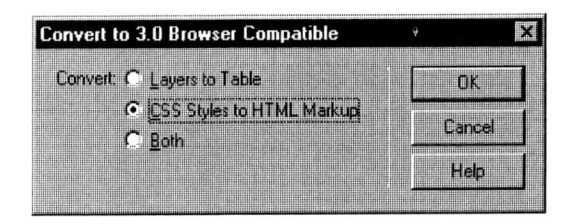

➡ Activate the **CSS Styles to HTML Markup** option or **Both** if you want to convert layers (CSS-P) and style sheets (CSS-1).

➡ Click **OK**.

Evidently, some CSS formatting elements do not have an equivalent in HTML.

Conversion table:

CSS Attribute	HTML element
color	FONT COLOR
font-family	FONT FACE
font-size	FONT SIZE="[1-7]"
font-style: oblique	I
font-style: italic	I
font-weight	B
list-style-type: square	UL TYPE="square"
list-style-type: circle	UL TYPE="circle"
list-style-type: disc	UL TYPE="disc"
list-style-type: upper-roman	OL TYPE="I"
list-style-type: lower-roman	OL TYPE="i"
list-style-type: upper-alpha	OL TYPE="A"
list-style-type: lower-alpha	OL TYPE="a"
list-style	UL or OL with appropriate TYPE
text-align	P ALIGN or DIV ALIGN as appropriate
text-decoration: underline	U
text-decoration: line-through	STRIKE

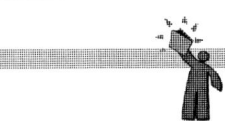

© Editions ENI - All rights reserved

Dreamweaver 3
Links

Different types of link

Hyperlinks are a fundamental part of a Web site. They make links between pages, so that users can browse from one page to another. They determine the structure and navigation of your site.

Internal hyperlinks enable users to move around in the same page and to go from page to page within your site. You can also create external links, which link to other Web sites, e-mail addresses or FTP addresses.

Links can be textual, consisting of a word or several words on which users can click. They can also be images, consisting of a button to click, an image map, which is a large image on which you can define hotspots for the links, or of rollover images.

An example of text links: *An example of image links:*

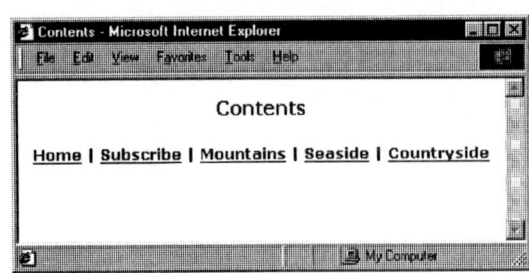

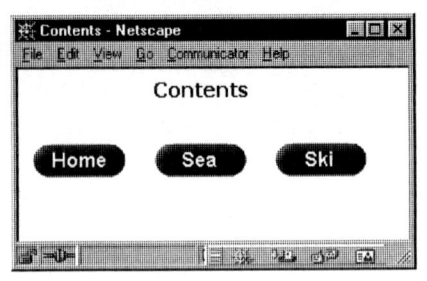

Formatting text links

In Dreamweaver

In each page you create you can change the colour of the links.

🖅 **Modify - Page Properties**

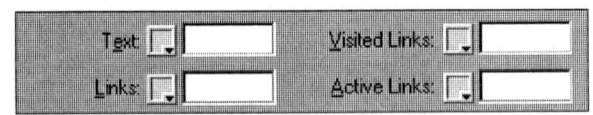

🖅 Choose the colours of the following:

Links	colour of unvisited links.
Visited Links	colour of links the user has already used.
Active Links	colour of links when the user clicks them.

©Editions ENI - All rights reserved

Links

In browsers

If you do not specify any particular colours for your links, the colours defined in the browser will be used. Generally, unvisited links are blue and underlined, and visited links are shown in purple, and are also underlined. However, if you specify colours in Dreamweaver, they will be used by browsers (though Netscape Navigator has an option which overrides the colours specified, if it is set).

- In Microsoft Internet Explorer 5: **Tools - Internet Options - Colors** button.

    You can change the colour of **Visited** *and* **Unvisited** *and* **Hover** *links in the* **Links** *frame.*

- In Netscape Navigator 4: **Edit - Preferences - Appearance** category - **Colors**.

    Under **Links** you can choose the colour of **Unvisited Links** and **Visited Links** and, if necessary, activate the **Underline links** option.

    If you activate the **Always use my colors, overriding document** option, the link colours specified in Dreamweaver will not be used, but those of Netscape Navigator will be applied.

Creating links in the same page

In order to create links in a page, you first need to insert a "marker" at the destination in the page. These markers are called anchors.

Displaying the anchors

- First make sure that the anchors are active as invisible elements:

    Edit - Preferences - Invisible Elements category

- The **Named Anchors** option should be active.

- Now display the invisible elements: **View - Invisible Elements**.

Positioning anchors

- In an open document which contains structured text, click before the text you want to mark with an anchor.

- **Insert - Named Anchor**

    or, choose the **Invisibles** panel in the **Objects** palette and click the **Insert Named Anchor** button.

© Editions ENI - All rights reserved

Dreamweaver 3
Links

→ Type the **Anchor Name** in the dialog box and click **OK**.

The invisible element (the anchor) appears.

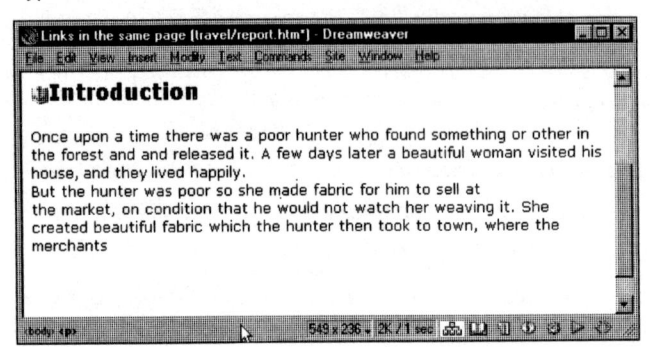

→ You can change the anchor's name by clicking its icon and using the Property inspector:

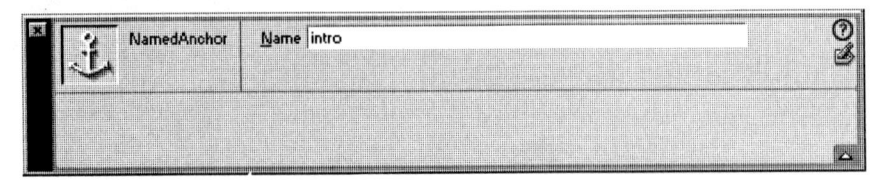

Creating links

→ Type the text of the links in your document then select the first one. In the Property inspector, go to the **Link** text box, type # then, immediately afterwards (do not type a space), the name of the named anchor.

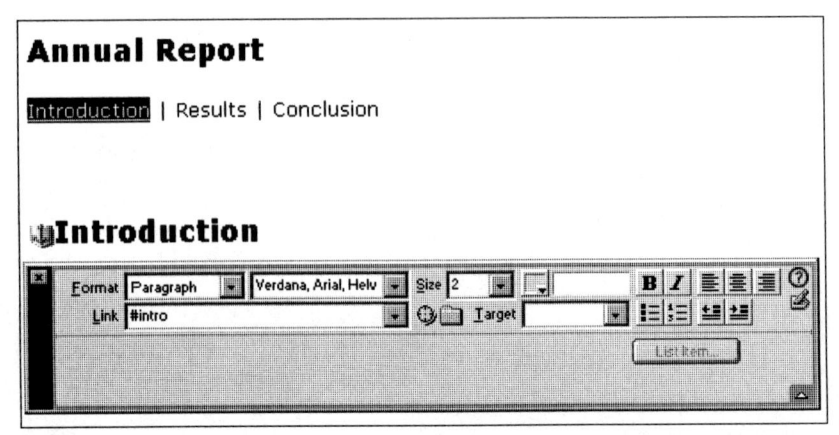

©Editions ENI - All rights reserved

Links

- You can also drag the **Point to File** button from the Property inspector to the named anchor.

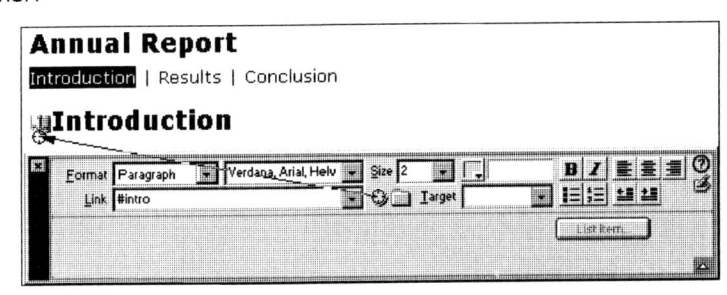

*The link appears in the **Link** text box: #intro.*

Creating page to page links

Defining the document file paths

- Use exactly the same principle as you do for images. You should look at the **Image file paths** paragraph in the **Images** chapter.

Creating links to a page

- In an open document, select the text of the link.
- **Modify - Make Link**

    or go to the **Link** box in the Property inspector and click the **Browse for File** button.

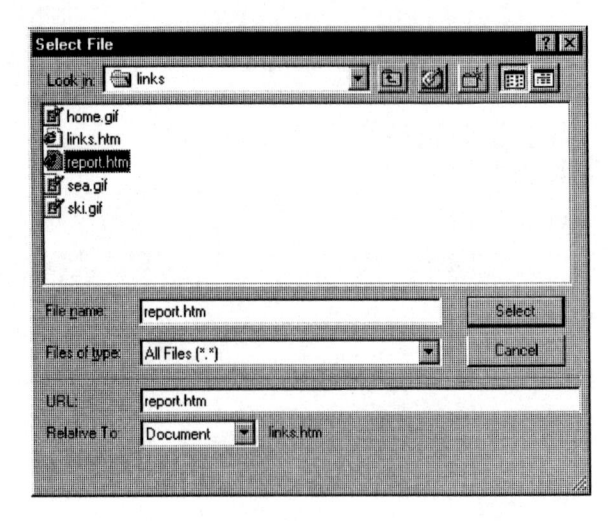

Dreamweaver 3
Links

- Select the file that is the target of the link in the **Select File** dialog box.
- Choose **Document** or **Site Root** in the **Relative To** pop-up menu.
- Click the **Select** button.

    *The link appears in the **Link** box in the **Property** inspector:*

Creating a link to an open document

*You can use the **Point to File** icon in the same way as for named anchors.*

- Open the document that is the target of the link.
- Open the document that contains the link text.
- Resize the windows so that they are both visible at once.
- Select the link text.
- Click the **Point to File** icon in the Property inspector and drag it to the window of the target document (it does not matter where you point to in the document).
    You can also shift-click the selection to drag the pointer to the target document.
    The **Point to File** icon becomes active automatically.

    The link is made.

Links

Creating a link to a closed document

*You can use the **Point to File** icon here too.*

- Open the document that contains the link text.
- Press F5 to see the site map.
- Resize the windows so that you can see both of them at once.
- Drag the **Point to File** icon from the Property inspector to the site window and point to the icon of the target file, or shift-click the selection then point to the target file's icon.

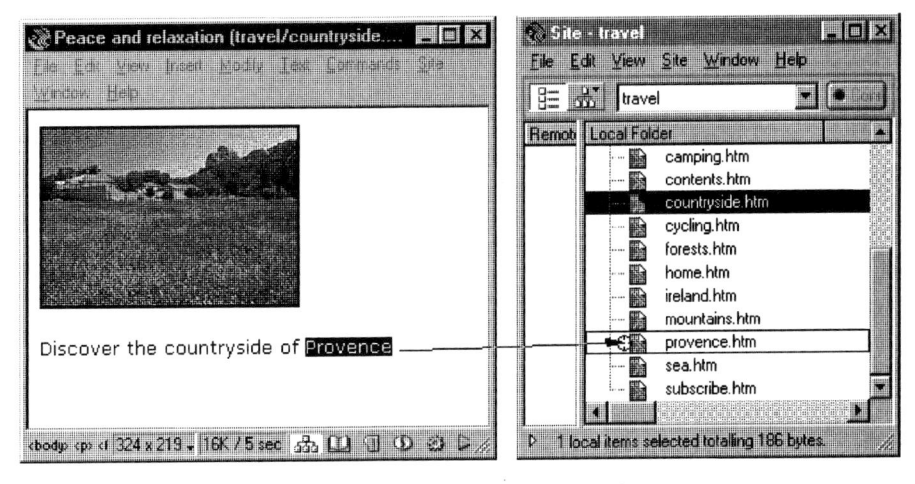

This example shows a link being made using the "shift-click" technique.

If you know the exact name of the target file then you can type its full path in the **Link** text box in the Property inspector.

Creating a link to an anchor in a page

You can create a hyperlink to an anchor in a page so that your link goes to a precise location in the page.

- Select the link text.
- In the **Property** inspector, in the **Link** box, type a link like this: pagex.htm#name (with no spaces), which will link to the anchor called **name** in the **pagex** document.

©Editions ENI - All rights reserved

Dreamweaver 3
Links

🏛 You can also drag the **Point to File** icon ⊕ to an anchor in an open page.

Creating links in the site map (1st method)

Another way to create links is in the site map. This map shows the structure of your site.

- Display the site map using **Window - Site Map**.
- In the map of your site (and not the file structure), select the file that is to contain the link.
- Drag the **Point to File** icon ⊕ (which appears next to the selected file) to the target of the link.

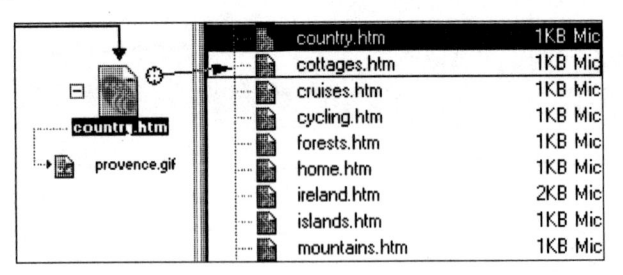

	country.htm	1KB Mic
cottages.htm		1KB Mic
cruises.htm		1KB Mic
country.htm	cycling.htm	1KB Mic
	forests.htm	1KB Mic
provence.gif	home.htm	1KB Mic
	ireland.htm	2KB Mic
	islands.htm	1KB Mic
	mountains.htm	1KB Mic

The link is made and the text of the hyperlink takes the name of the linked file, which is cottages in this example. The link is always placed at the end of the document.

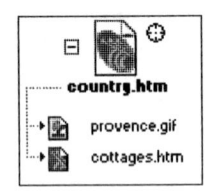

```
country.htm
   provence.gif
   cottages.htm
```

Creating links in the site map (2nd method)

- In the site map, select the file that is to contain the link.
- In Windows use **Site - Link to Existing File** or **Link to New File**.

  In Macintosh use **Site - Site Map View - Link to Existing File** or **Link to New File**.

- If you are linking to an existing file, select this file, and if you are creating a new file, this dialog box appears:

©Editions ENI - All rights reserved

Links

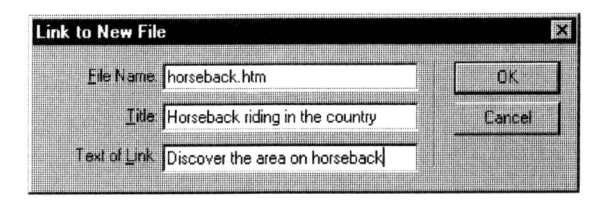

⇨ Type the name of the new file you want to create in the **File Name** box, and do not forget the .htm extension.

⇨ Type the page's title (<title> tag) in the **Title** box.

⇨ Enter the text of the hyperlink in the **Text of Link** box.

Jump menus

A jump menu is a pop-up menu whose options lead to a file. Dreamweaver uses JavaScript to detect which menu option has been chosen and to create a link to the corresponding file.

Creating the menu

⇨ Place the insertion point where you want to create the menu.

⇨ **Insert - Form Object - Jump Menu**

or click the **Insert Jump Menu** button from the **Forms** panel in the **Objects** palette.

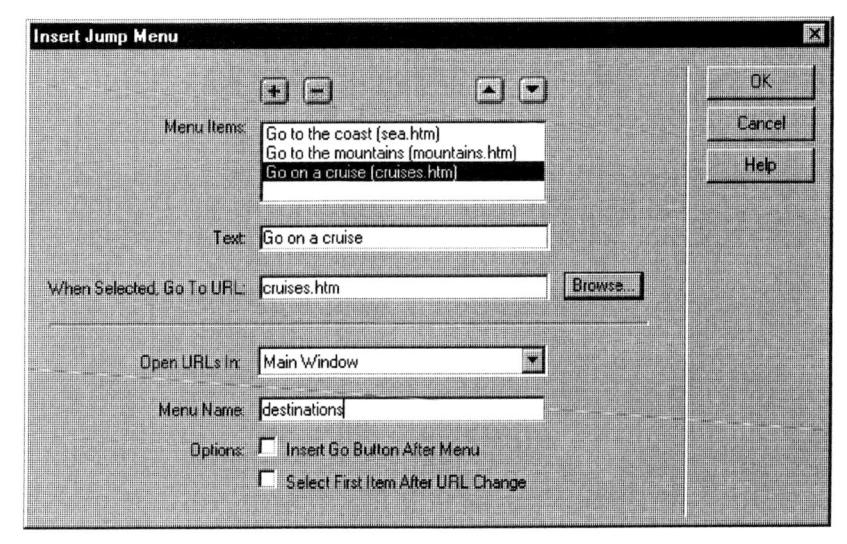

Dreamweaver 3
Links

- Type the text that will appear in the pop-up menu in the **Text** box.
- In the **When Selected, Go To URL** box, enter the path to the appropriate file or click **Browse**.
- Click the ⊕ button to add another option. Enter the **Text** and **URL** information.
- You can change one of the items by selecting it from **Menu Items**, then making the relevant changes in the **Text** and **URL** boxes.
- Delete an item by selecting it and clicking the ⊖ button.
- To change the order in which the items appear, select the item you want to move and use the ▲ and ▼ buttons.
- Use the **Open URLs In** pop-up menu if you are using a frameset, if you are not the target always opens in the **Main Window**.
- Under **Options** you can tick the **Insert Go Button After Menu** check box if you want a button next to the pop-up menu that users can click to activate the link to the file they have chosen in the jump menu.
- Activate the **Select First Item After URL Change** option if you want to define a default option in the menu after the user has chosen a link.

Editing the menu

- To edit a jump menu, first select it in your page.
- Use the Property inspector.

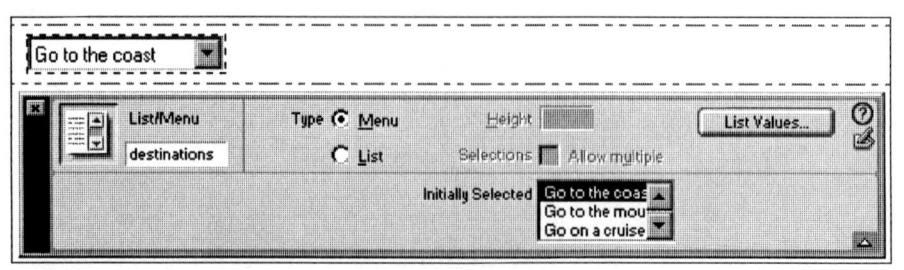

You can see the standard parameters for a menu in a form.

- Click the **List Values** button to change the text of the items.

Links

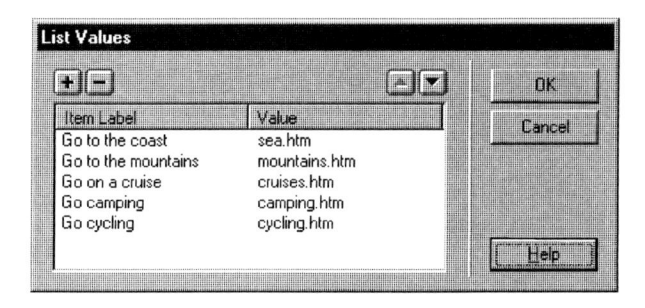

*The **Item Label** column contains the text that appears in the menu. In the **Value** column you can see the names of the linked files.*

⇨ Use the **Initially Selected** list to choose the item that will be selected in the menu by default.

*You can also re-open the jump menu creation dialog box from the **Behaviors** palette.*

⇨ Select the jump menu then use **Windows - Behaviors**.

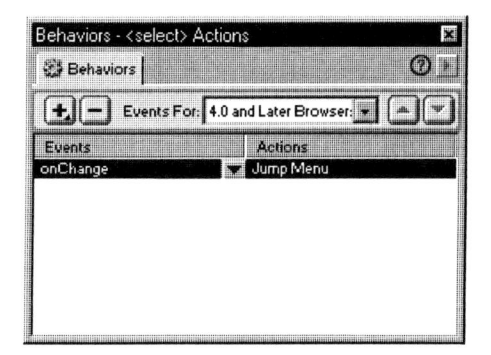

Double-click the **Jump Menu** action.

A jump menu looks like this is in a browser:

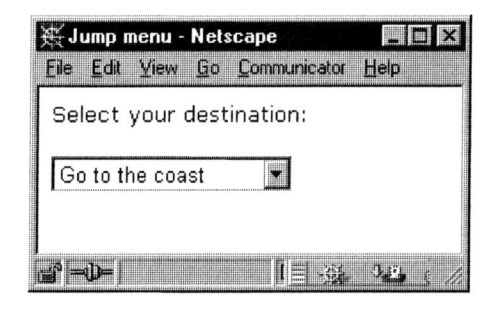

©Editions ENI - All rights reserved

Creating external links

To another site

You can create links to another site in the same way as you can create them in your own site.

- Select the link text.
- In the **Link** box in the Property inspector, type the full URL of the target page:

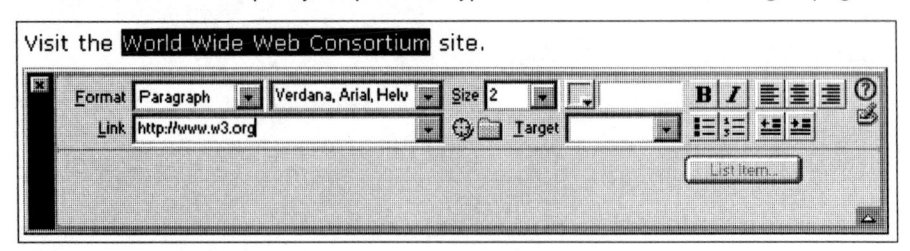

If you want to link to an anchor situated in a page in a folder of a site, the URL will be: http://www.site.org/folder/document.htm/#anchor.

By default, the target page will open in the browser window, but if you want to keep your page open you can choose to have the target page open in a new window.

- Choose **_blank** in the **Target** pop-up menu.

To an e-mail address

You can create hyperlinks that lead to e-mail addresses in your documents. When a user clicks the link, his or her e-mail application (such as Eudora or Outlook) will open automatically and the recipient's e-mail address will be entered.

- Place the insertion point where you want to insert the link.
- **Insert - E-Mail Link**

or click the **Insert E-Mail Link** button in the **Common** panel of the **Objects** palette.

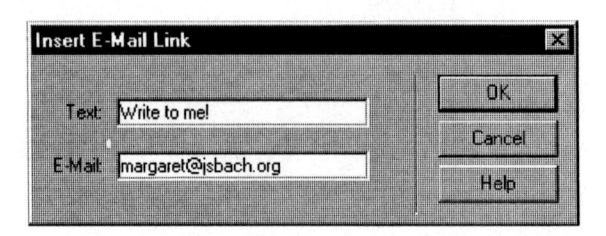

Links

- Type the link text in the **Text** box.
- Enter the e-mail address in the **E-Mail** text box.

    *The text appears in the document window and, in the **Link** box in the Property inspector, the e-mail address is shown:*

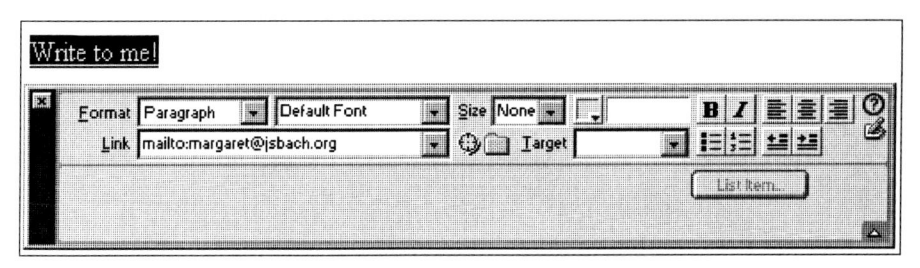

    You can also type the e-mail address directly in the Property inspector.

- Type the link text. Type a **mailto:blah@blah.net** type link in the **Link** box in the Property inspector.

To an FTP server

If your site contains files that can be downloaded you can insert a hyperlink to the FTP server.

- Select the link text.
- In the **Link** box in the Property inspector, type an **ftp://ftp.blah.net** link.

Creating links on images

There are many possibilities: from a simple button on which users can click to rollover images, image maps and navigation bars. To use all these elements, you need to have created the different images which act as links.

Buttons

First you should create an image that will work as a button for your hyperlink.

- Place the insertion point where you want to insert the button.
- Insert the image and select it.
- In the **Link** box in the Property inspector, create the link as shown previously.

©Editions ENI - All rights reserved

Dreamweaver 3
Links

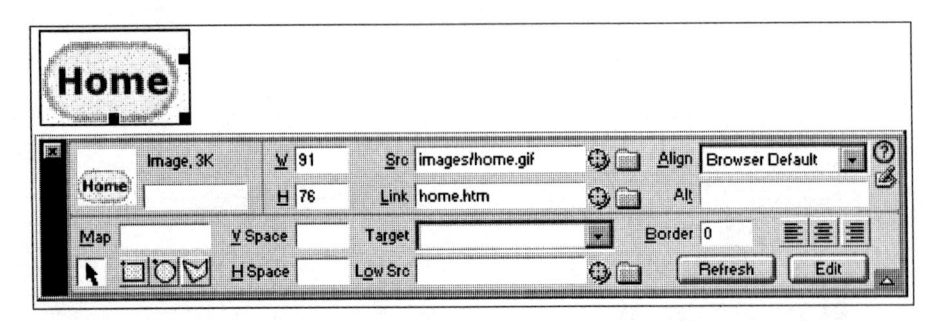

Notice that, by default, Dreamweaver sets the image's **Border** to 0, which prevents the appearance of a blue border around this hyperlink image.

Image maps

Image maps are images on which you can define hotspots (rectangles, circles or polygons), which are hyperlinks.

- First make sure that the hotspots on image maps are visible: **View - Image Maps**.
- Place the insertion point where you want to insert the image in your document.
- Insert the image then select it.
- Go to the Property inspector.

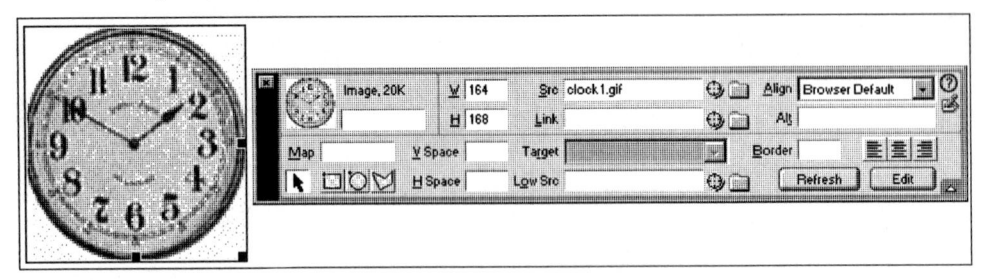

- Give the map a name in the **Map** text box. This is compulsory.
- Choose a shape for your hotspot.
- Draw the shape in the appropriate place on the image.

©Editions ENI - All rights reserved

Links

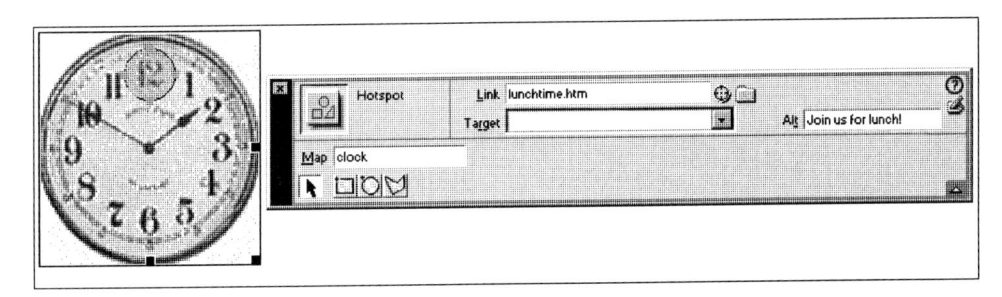

In this example, the hotspot is over the number 12.

- You can change or move the hotspot using the **Pointer Hotspot** tool.

- Type the URL in the **Link** box or use the **Point to File** button to select the open document window or the file icon in the site map. You can also click the **Browse for File** button to select the file in your site.

- In the **Target** pop-up menu, choose the frame you want to use if you are working with framesets.

- Type the screen tip text in the **Alt** box. This text will appear in a yellow screen tip when a user points at the hotspot.

You can select hotspots on an image and align them in relation to each other, and make the width and/or height of all the hotspots the same. Use the options in the **Modify - Layers and Hotspots** menu. The last hotspot you select is the reference hotspot.

Rollover images

Rollover images can give your page a little dynamism. The principle is very simple: create an image for a button in its inactive state (when the pointer is not over it, the onMouseOut *state in JavaScript), and an image for the button in its active state (when the pointer is over it, the* onMouseOver *state in JavaScript).*

- In an open document, place the insertion point where the button is to appear:

  Insert - Rollover Image

  or click the **Insert Rollover Image** button on the **Common** panel of the **Objects** palette.

©Editions ENI - All rights reserved

Dreamweaver 3
Links

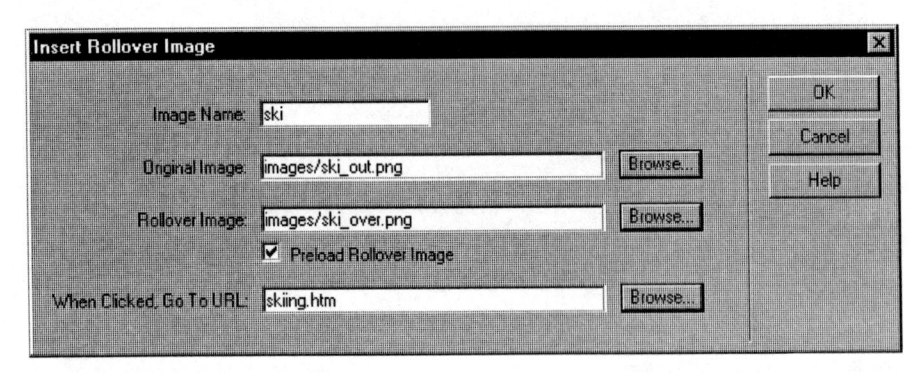

- Enter the name of the image in the **Image Name**, or leave the name that Dreamweaver suggests.
- Type the name of the inactive state (onMouseOut) image in the **Original Image** box, or click **Browse** to select the file.
- Type the name of the active state (onMouseOver) image in the **Rollover Image** box, or click **Browse** to select the file.
- Leave the **Preload Rollover Image** option active so that there is no delay when the rollover image is used.
- Type the path to the target file in the **When Click Go To URL** box, or click **Browse** to select the file.

  In a browser, move the mouse pointer over the image: it should change:

Links

Navigation bars

Navigation bars enable you to create a series of hyperlinks using buttons that have different JavaScript states: inactive (onMouseOut), active (onMouseOver), activated (onClick) and during dragging (onMouseMove: when a user clicks the button, then moves the mouse over it). You will need to prepare all the images you want to use for the links first. You can have only one navigation bar in a page.

- Place the insertion point where you want to insert your navigation bar.
- **Insert - Navigation Bar**

    or click the **Insert Navigation Bar** button on the **Common** panel of the **Objects** palette.

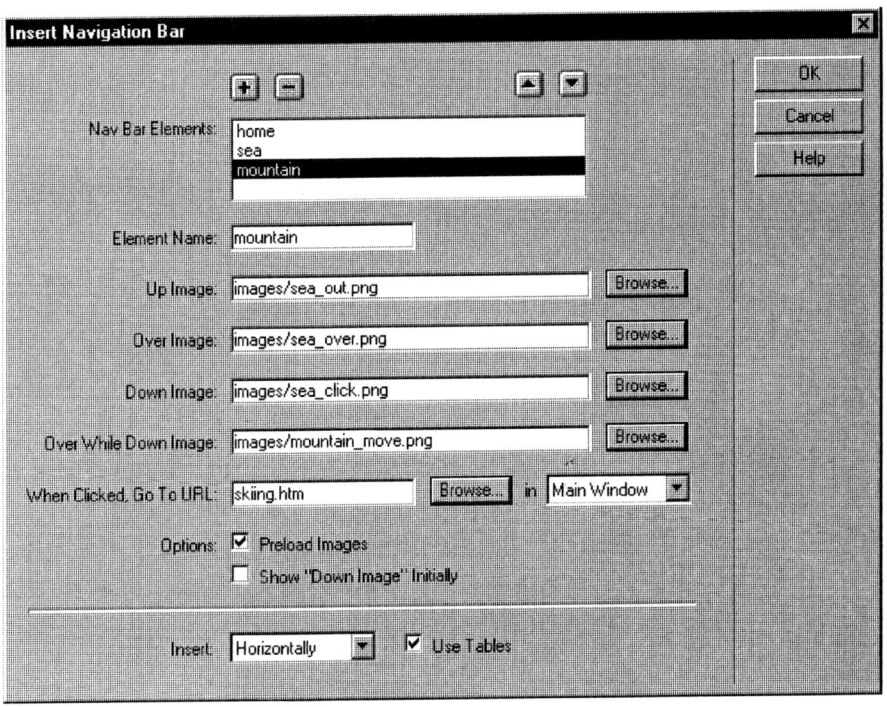

- Type the name of the group of images in the **Element Name** box.
- Type the image for the onMouseOut state in the **Up Image** box or click **Browse** to select the file.
- Type the image for the onMouseOver state in the **Over Image** box or click **Browse** to select the file.

©Editions ENI - All rights reserved

Dreamweaver 3
Links

- Type the image for the onMouseDown state in the **Down Image** box or click **Browse** to select the file.
- In the **Over While Down Image** box, type the name of the image for the onMouseMove state or click **Browse** to select the file.
- Type the path for the target file in **When Clicked, Go To URL**, or click **Browse** to select the file.
- If you are using framesets, select the frame in which the target page should open in the **in** pop-up menu.
- Under **Options**, leave the **Preload Images** check box ticked to avoid any downloading time when the user points to the button. The image that represents the onMouseOver state will already be loaded, as will that for the onClick state.
- Activate the **Show "Down Image" Initially** option if the button should appear in its clicked state (onClick) when the page that contains these buttons opens and the button targets itself.
- Add a new link by clicking ⊞ button. Specify the same information for this group of images and URL.

  Delete a link by selecting it and clicking the ⊟ button.
  You can change the order in which the links appear by selecting one and moving it using the ▲ and ▼ buttons.
- Choose the bar's orientation in the **Insert** pop-up menu: **Horizontally** or **Vertically**.
- Leave the **Use Tables** option active if you want the bar to be inserted in a table.
- If you want to see the behaviors associated with the images, select one of the images in the bar then **Window - Behaviors**.

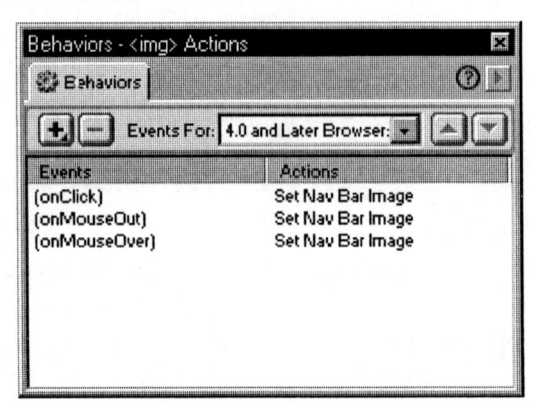

Links

You can see the JavaScript events in the **Events** column.

- Edit a behavior by double-clicking it in the **Actions** column.

*In the **Basic** tab you can see the settings defined previously.*

*You can use the **Advanced** tab to define more specifically the way in which the images should swap. You will need to insert and name at least one more image in order to understand these functions better.*

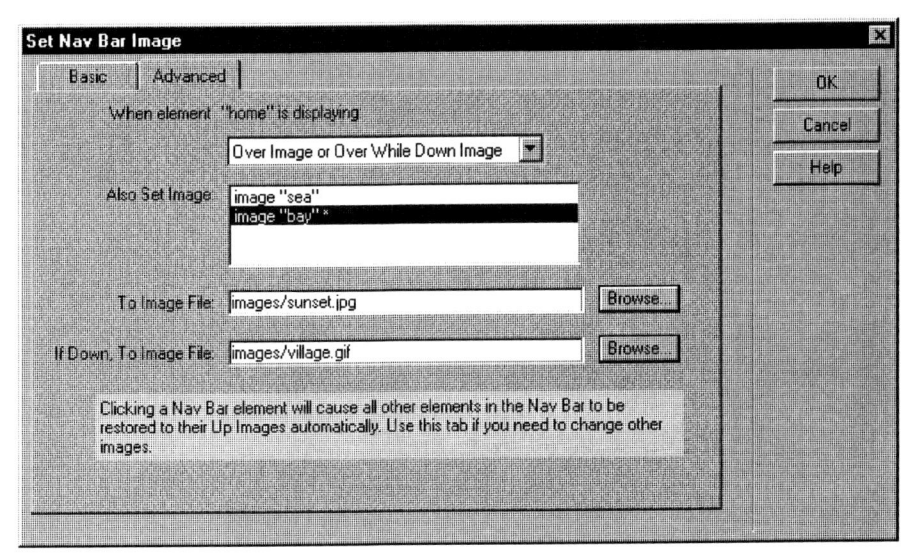

- In the **When element "element_name" is displaying** pop-up menu, choose a mouse event: **Over Image or Over While Down Image** or **Down Image** (here, the one you inserted specifically for this example).
- Select the image you inserted and named previously from the **Also Set Image** list.
- In the **To Image File** box, type the name of the image file, or click **Browse** to find the file, that should appear in place of the image indicated previously, when the pointer moves over the button.
- Preview the navigation bar by saving the page and opening it in a browser.

Dreamweaver 3
Links

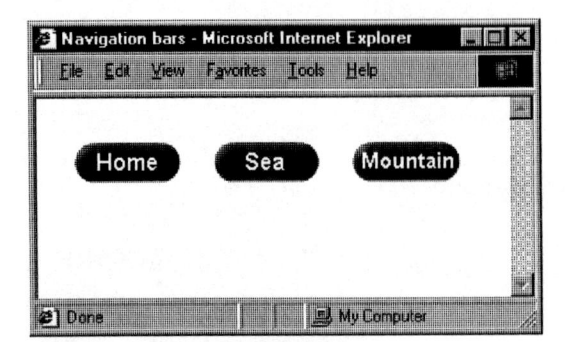

This is a simple navigation bar: you can move the pointer over the different buttons, click them, and so on, to see the changes in the buttons' appearance.

This navigation bar is more complicated: the **Sea** button is shown with its "down" appearance (on-Click) because this is the target page of the button and the **Show "Down Image" Initially** option has been activated.

Here the pointer is over the **Home** button: the button's image has changed, and the bay has been replaced by a picture of a tropical sunset. This is a result of the settings in the **Advanced** tab of the behaviors: when the pointer leaves the **Home** button, the image below will return to the original bay.

©Editions ENI - All rights reserved

Links

Managing your site's structure

Displaying the site map

You can use the site map to see the structure of your site and the links between different files.

- Display the site map by activating the **Site Map** option in the **Window** menu.

- Click the **Site Map** button in the site map window to see the structure of the files.

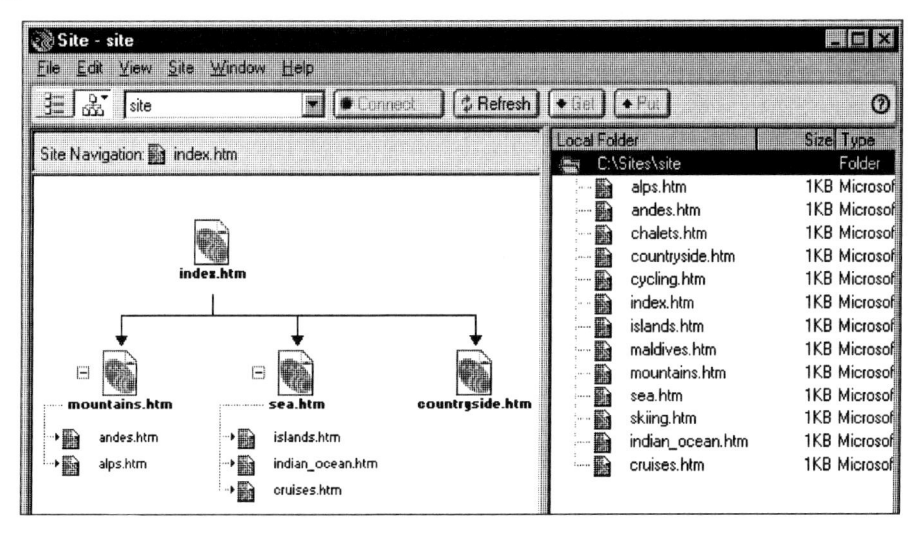

*In the left of the window the **Site Navigation** from the home page (index.htm in this screen) is shown. All the files in your **Local Folder** are shown on the right.*

- To see the site map and/or the structure, click the arrow on the button, but do not release the mouse button, and then choose **Map Only** or **Map and Files**.

Defining the appearance of the map

- In order to format your site map, access its parameters using **Site - Define Sites**.

    or select **Define Sites** from the pop-up menu situated in the top of the window.

- Select the current site and click the **Edit** button. You can also use the **View - Layout** command in the site window.

Dreamweaver 3
Links

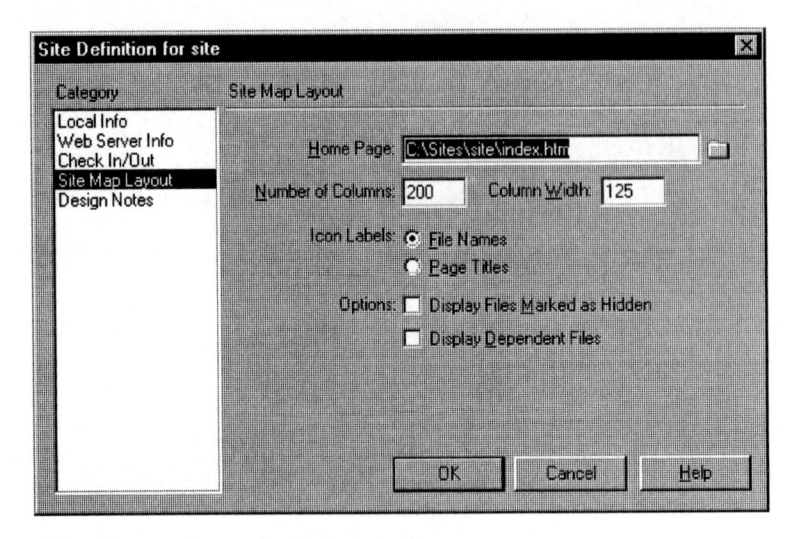

- Select **Site Map Layout** from the **Category** list.

- Make sure that the correct page is defined as the **Home Page**. A home page is generally called index.htm, or default.htm. If you need to, click the ▢ button to select the home page.

- Indicate how many files should be visible on each row of the site map in the **Number of Columns** text box.

- Use the **Column Width** text box to specify the width of each column, in pixels.

- Choose the **File Names** option under **Icon Labels** if you want to use the name as saved on the hard disk, or **Page Titles** to use the titles entered in the **Page Properties** (`<title>` tag).

- Under **Options**, activate the **Display Files Marked as Hidden** if you want to be able to see pages that are marked as hidden. These files appear in italics.

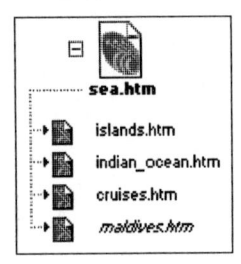

In this example the maldives.htm file is marked as hidden, but the others are not.

©Editions ENI - All rights reserved

⊟ Tick the **Display Dependent Files** check box if you want to see non-HTML files in the site structure, such as images, templates, Shockwave and Flash files.

In this example the country.htm file contains the image village.gif.

Changing the home page

As you have seen, a Web site home page is usually called index.htm or default.htm.

⊟ If you want to change the home page, select the new home page file in the **Local Folder** file list, then open the context menu and choose **Set as Home Page**.

The site map is updated immediately.

Expanding and collapsing a branch

⊟ In the site map, you can expand and collapse the branches of files linked to a page using the ⊞ and ⊟ buttons (in Windows; in Macintosh, click the expander arrows):

The sea.htm file with its branch collapsed:

The sea.htm file with its branch open:

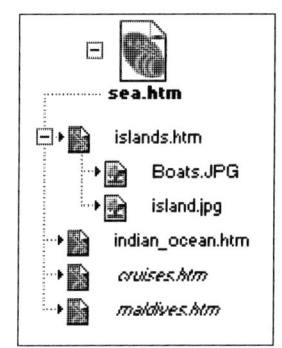

©Editions ENI - All rights reserved

Showing page titles

You can choose to show the page titles (`<title>` tag) rather than the file names:
- in Windows, use: **View - Show Page Titles**.
- in Macintosh, use: **Site - Site Map View - Show Page Titles**.

Site map with the file names:

Site map showing the page titles:

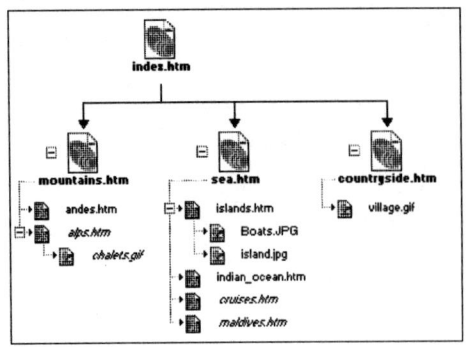

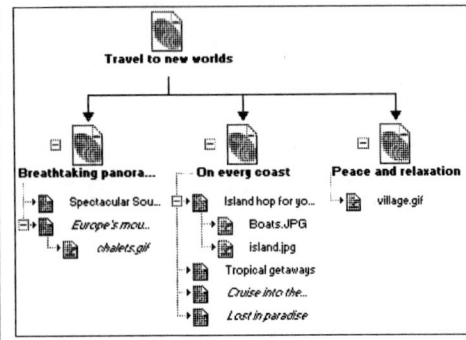

Showing/hiding hidden files

If you have a complicated site which contains a high number of files, you might find it useful to hide some pages on the site map in order to see the main pages better.

To mark a file as hidden, select the file(s) concerned then:
- in Windows use **View - Show/Hide Link**.
- in Macintosh use **Site - Site Map View - Show/Hide Link**.

Those files marked as hidden appear in italics in the site map.

To show or hide files marked as hidden:
- in Windows use **View - Show Files Marked as Hidden**.
- in Macintosh use **Site - Site Map View - Show Files Marked as Hidden**.

The files appear in or disappear from the site map.

Showing/hiding dependent files

You can choose to show or hide the images, animations, etc... contained within pages.

In Windows use **View - Show Dependent Files**.

In Macintosh use **Site - Site Map View - Show Dependent Files**.

©Editions ENI - All rights reserved

Links

Viewing a branch of the site

If you are working with a complicated structure you might find it useful to choose to view only one branch of the site, starting from a selected file.

- Select the file whose branch you want to see:
  - in Windows use **View - View as Root**.
  - In Macintosh use **Site - Site Map View - View as Root**.

Dreamweaver indicates this change under **Site Navigation**:

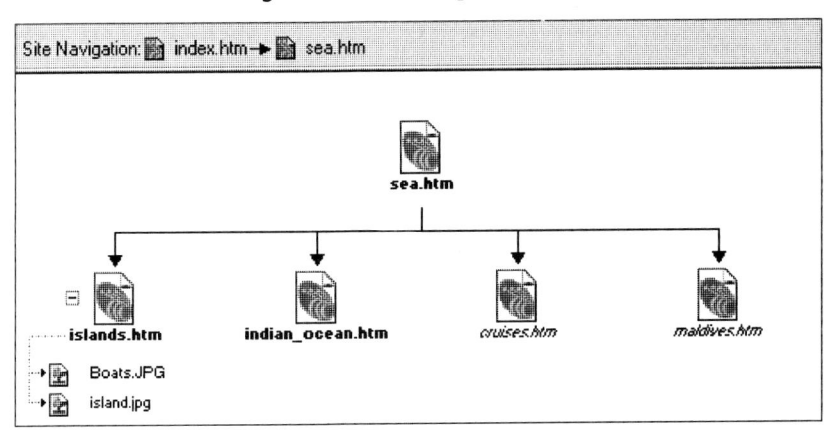

- Return to the full structure starting from the home page by clicking the home page icon (which is index.htm in this example) under **Site Navigation**.

Refreshing the view

After making changes to your site map you can update the view.

- In Windows use **View - Refresh Local**.

  In Macintosh use **Site - Site Map View - Refresh Local**.

Managing links

Updating links

You can ask Dreamweaver to verify the links systematically when you move or rename a document which is linked in the site map.

- **Edit - Preferences - General** category

©Editions ENI - All rights reserved

Dreamweaver 3
Links

- In the **Update Links** pop-up menu choose:

  Prompt   if you want Dreamweaver to display a dialog box containing the names of the files which are linked to the renamed/moved document, and so need to be updated.

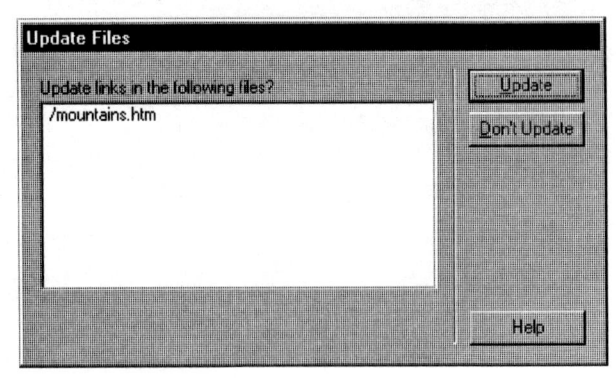

  Always   if Dreamweaver should update the links without displaying the dialog box.

  Never   if you do not want Dreamweaver to update the linked files.

Updating the site cache

Dreamweaver uses a cache in which it saves your site's structure and all the links, which it uses to manage your site. When you define the site parameters, it is a good idea to choose to create a cache.

- **Site - Define Sites**
- Select the site in question and click **Edit**.
- Activate the **Use Cache to Speed Link Updates** option in the **Local Info** frame.
- If you have made many changes to your site it is a good idea to recreate the site cache using **Site - Recreate Site Cache**.

Changing a file's link

- Select the linked file then:
  - in Windows use **Site - Change Link**.
  - in Macintosh use **Site - Site Map View - Change Link**.
- Select the file which is to be linked in place of the current one.
- Update any files that have links to this new file.

©Editions ENI - All rights reserved

Changing all the links

If your site includes a lot of links it can be extremely useful to change all the links in the site that target a particular file. For example, imagine you are managing a site which offers travel information, and you have a promotion page which changes every week. At a given moment, a number of pages will target the page for the 12th week, called 12w.htm. The following week, you create a page called 13w.htm and you can change all the links so that they target the 13w.htm page.

⊡ **Site - Change Link Sitewide**

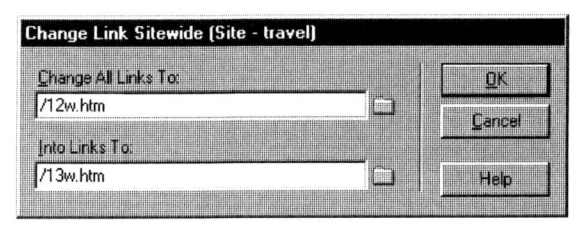

⊡ Type the name of the current target file in the **Change All Links To** text box, or click to select the file.

⊡ Type the name of the new target file in the **Into Links To** box, or click to select it.

⊡ Click **OK**.

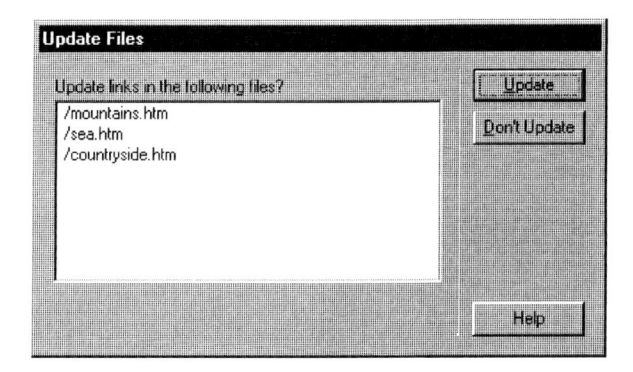

*Dreamweaver indicates all the files concerned in the **Update Files** window.*

⊡ Click **Update**.

You can do the same thing if you want to change an e-mail address link in the entire site.

Opening the source of a link

You can open the file that contains a link to a linked page.

- Select the linked page in the site structure.
- In Windows use **Site - Open Source of Link**.

    In Macintosh use **Site - Site Map View - Open Source of Link**.

Removing a link

If you have made a mistake, you can delete a link to a file.

- Select the linked page in the site structure.
- In Windows use **Site - Remove Link**.

    In Macintosh use **Site - Site Map View - Remove Link**.

Checking links

Checking a link in a page

All the links you create in a page are not active, but you can still open the linked page to make sure that the link is correct.

- Select the link you want to check.
- **Modify - Open Linked Page**

    or hold the ⌘ (Macintosh) or Ctrl (Windows) key down and double-click the link.

©Editions ENI - All rights reserved

Checking all the links in a page

You can check that all the links in a page (internal and external links, e-mail links, etc) are correct.

⮡ **File - Check Links**

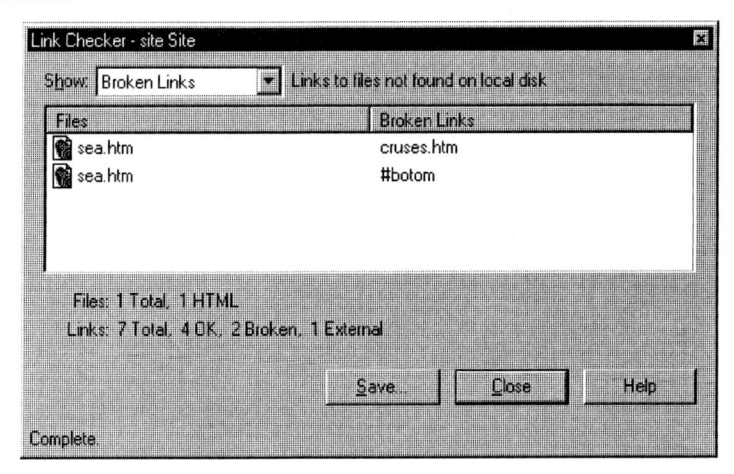

⮡ Make sure **Broken Links** is selected in the **Show** pop-up menu.

In this example there are two broken links: the link to the cruises.htm page and the link in the page to the #bottom anchor.

⮡ To correct a broken link, double-click the link's icon in the **Files** column on the left in the **Link Checker** window (Dreamweaver selects the link in the page and in the **Link** box in the Property inspector) and make the necessary corrections.

or, if you know the correction, make it in the **Link Checker** window: click in the **Broken Links** column and change the name of the linked file or click the 📁 button to select the file in the site:

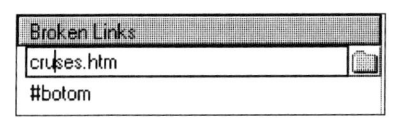

©Editions ENI - All rights reserved

Dreamweaver 3
Links

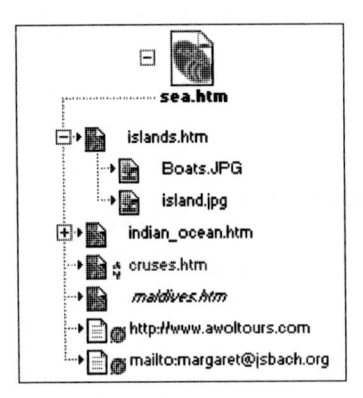

As soon as there is a problem with a link, Dreamweaver displays it in the site map. Linked files whose link is broken are shown with a picture of a broken chain.

Looking at external links

- To see links in the current page that lead outside your Web site use **File - Check Links**.
- Choose **External Links** in the **Show** pop-up menu.

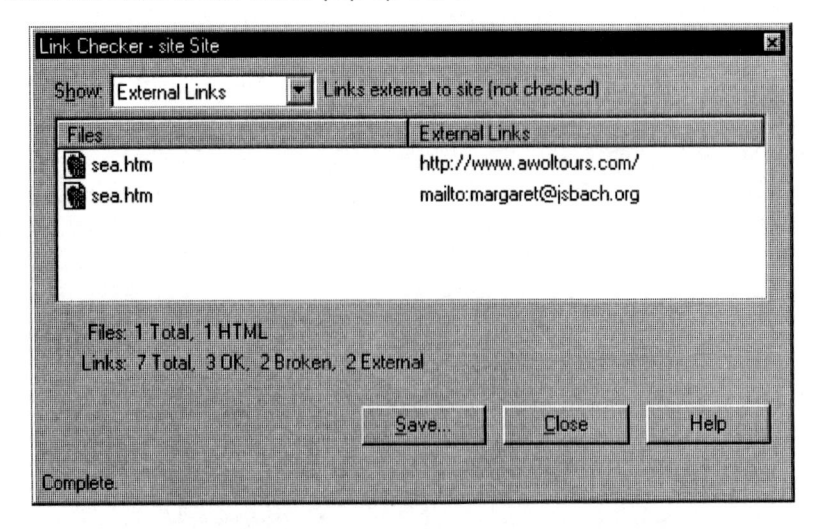

In this example you can see a link to another site and one to an e-mail address. In the site map, external links have a particular symbol:

Links

Checking links in certain files

- In your site's file list, select all the files whose links you want to check (using the `Shift`, `Ctrl` keys in Windows, and the ⌘ key in Macintosh).
- **File - Check Links**

Checking all the links in the site

Rather than checking links page by page, you can check the whole site at the same time.

- In the file list use **Site - Check Links Sitewide**.

  In the **Show** pop-up menu you can find the **Broken Links** and **External Links**, which you can use as explained above.
  You will also find **Orphaned Files**, which shows a list of all the files (html, images, etc) that are not linked and thus not used in the site:

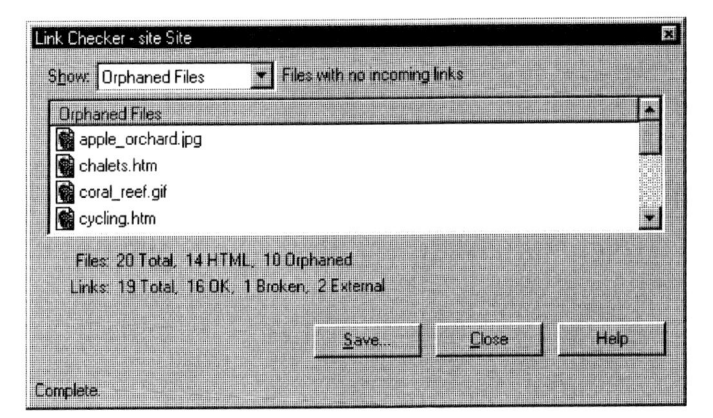

In this example you can see two HTML pages, a .gif image and a .jpg image. This feature helps you to "tidy up" your site before publishing it on a server.

Checking links in a browser

Another way to check the links (and the rest, such as movies and scripts) of your site is simply to test it in a browser.

- Open your home page.
- **File - Preview in Browser**

© Editions ENI - All rights reserved

Dreamweaver 3
Frame sets

Principle

Framesets allow you to split the browser window into several sections - frames - which each contain an HTML file. A frameset is an HTML file that contains all the information necessary for the construction of the frames.

Framesets make it easier to browse a Web site. You can create a fixed frame on the left of the screen that contains hyperlinks for displaying different linked pages in another frame on the right. In this way, users can simply click these links to browse the pages of your site.

In this example, the page on the left is fixed and it contains links to pages that will appear in the frame on the right:

This example requires at least three files: the file that contains the frameset information, the file that contains the links down the left of the screen, and the page presented on the right.

Naturally, the window can contain several frames. If this is the case, the frame that contains other frames is declared as the parent frame, and the frames it contains are child frames.

©Editions ENI - All rights reserved

Frame sets

Creating a frameset

You can use several methods to create a frameset: create it yourself or use preset framesets.

Showing the frame borders

- You need to make sure that the frame borders are visible on the screen in order to be able to see them properly: **View - Frame Borders**.

    A grey border appears to indicate the frame borders. However, this does not indicate the physical thickness of the frame borders (you define the thickness yourself).

- You should also make sure that the **Frames** palette is visible: **Window - Frames**.

Creating your own frameset

- In a new, empty document, split the window in order to define the frameset. You can make a simple separation by splitting the window either horizontally or vertically:

    Modify - Frameset - Split Frame Left, **Split Frame Right**, **Split Frame Up** or **Split Frame Down**.

    Vertical separation: *Horizontal separation:*

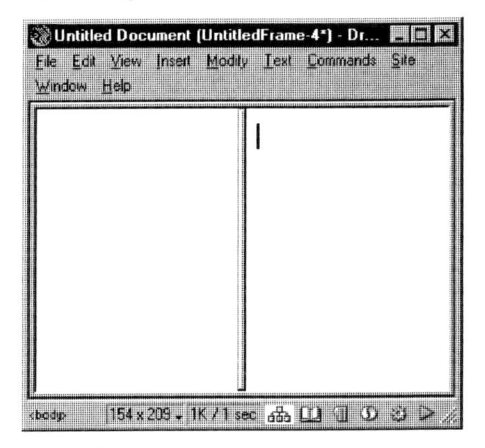

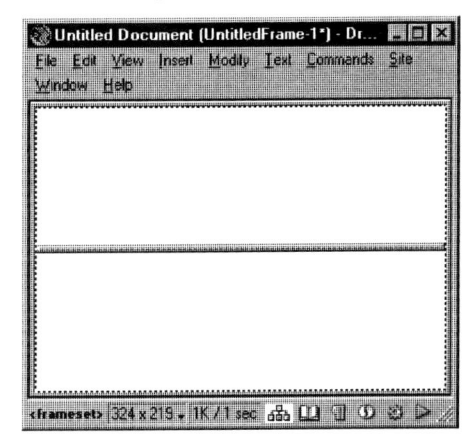

The difference between **Split Frame Left** and **Split Frame Right** or **Split Frame Up** and **Split Frame Down** is of no importance at the moment. You can choose either option.

Dreamweaver 3
Frame sets

For a more complicated separation of the window, you need to start by splitting the whole window in two. If you want to split the window in the same way as the example below, start by splitting horizontally then split vertically:

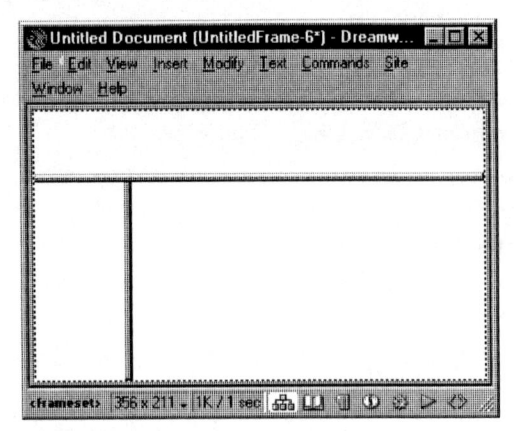

- **Modify - Frameset - Split Frame Down** or **Split Frame Up.**
- Click in the frame in the bottom of the document window, and you can see the insertion point there.
- **Modify - Frameset - Split Frame Left** or **Split Frame Right.**

   You can also create your own frameset using the mouse. Again, for a more complicated presentation, you must always start by splitting the window in two.

- Make sure you can see the frame borders: **View - Frame Borders**.
- Hold down the ⌘ (Macintosh) or Alt (Windows) key.
- Drag the top border to make a horizontal split, or the left border for a vertical split.

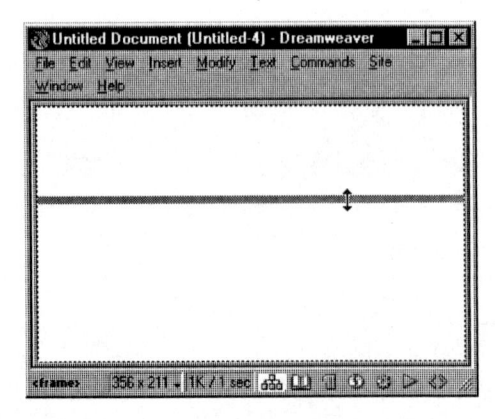

©Editions ENI - All rights reserved

Frame sets

⇨ Select the frame you want to split next in the **Frames** palette.

⇨ Hold the [⌘] (Macintosh) or [Alt] (Windows) key.

⇨ Drag the left border to split the window vertically:

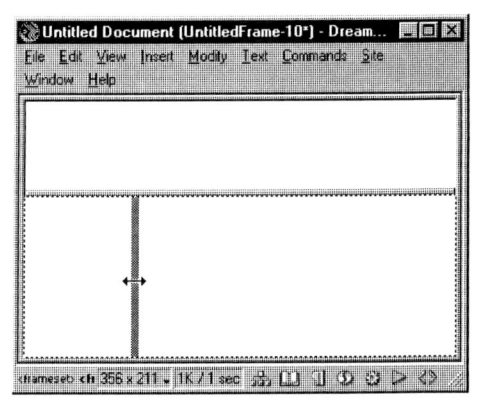

The frame you selected appears with a dashed border in the document window.

⇨ Delete a frame by dragging its border to the parent frame.

In the example, you would drag the vertical border to the right of left border of the window.

©Editions ENI - All rights reserved

Dreamweaver 3
Frame sets

Using a preset frameset

You can also use predefined framesets, which means you can construct your page more rapidly.

- Create a new document.
- Choose the **Frames** panel in the **Objects** palette.

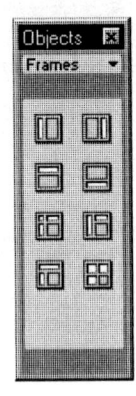

- Click the frameset you want to use

    or **Insert - Frames - Left**, **Right** or **Top**.

    *To split the window in a more complicated way you can use the last four framesets in the **Frames** panel of the **Objects** palette.*

- You can also use the **Frames** palette to split a window that is already split. In the document window, click in the frame you want to split again or select the frame in the **Frames** palette by clicking it.
- Click a new predefined frameset. And so on...

Saving a frameset

Now that you have created your frameset, you need to save it.

- **File - Save Frameset**

Do not confuse saving a frameset, which is saving the file that stores the window splitting information, with saving the pages which are displayed in each of the frames.

©Editions ENI - All rights reserved

Frame sets

Formatting a frameset

Selecting a frameset

You can use the **Frames** palette to select framesets in order to define their settings. In the example shown below a three-frame frameset is used: the top frame splits the whole window horizontally, and the other two split the lower part of the window vertically.

- If necessary, show the **Frames** palette: **Window - Frames**.
- To select the parent frameset, click the outline of the frameset, which appears in relief in the **Frames** palette:

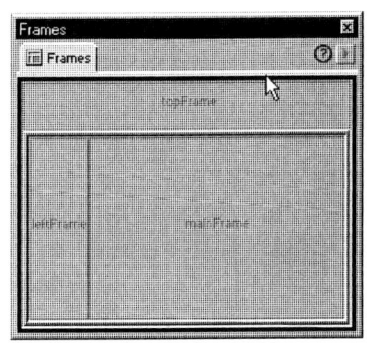

In a frameset that uses three frames, as shown in this example, there are two framesets. The first, which is uppermost in the hierarchy, separates the window horizontally into two parts.

- To select the nested (lower down the hierarchy) frameset, which splits the lower part of the window into two vertically, click its outline:

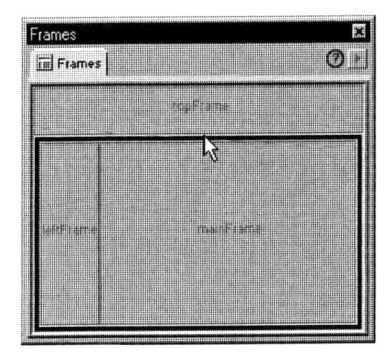

Formatting the frameset

In a complicated presentation, each frameset needs to be formatted. In the previous example, you would need to format both framesets.

- Select the first frameset, the parent.

©Editions ENI - All rights reserved

Frame sets

- Go to the Property inspector:

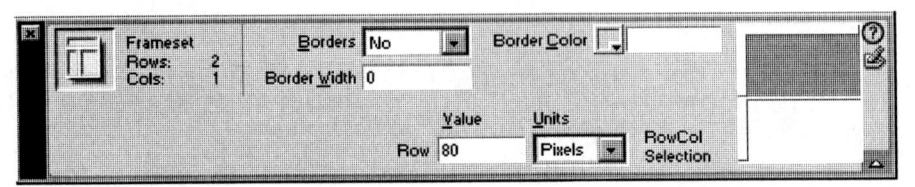

  [Property inspector showing: Frameset Rows: 2, Cols: 1; Borders: No; Border Width: 0; Border Color; Row: 80; Units: Pixels; RowCol Selection]

  *Dreamweaver gives the structure of the frameset in the **Frameset** box: in this example, there are 2 rows and 1 column.*

- Use the **Borders** pop-up menu to indicate whether you want borders to separate the frames in the browser:

Yes	there will always be borders.
No	there will never be borders.
Default	the appearance, or not, of borders will depend on the browser's default settings.

- If you have chosen to have borders, use the **Border Width** box to enter their width and, in the **Border Color** box, choose the colour (using either the color picker or by typing the colour's name or hexadecimal code).

- To define the height of the frame rows, select the row concerned by clicking it in the right of the Property inspector (the top row is selected in the example) then type the height in the **Row** text box and choose a unit from the **Units** pop-up menu:

  Pixels to indicate an absolute value. If you choose **150 Pixels**, for example, the height of the row will always be 150 pixels, no matter what the height of the browser window.

  Percentage you can indicate a value in relation to the size of the browser window. If you choose **25%**, the row will always be a quarter of the height of the browser window, even if the user resizes the window.

  Relative to indicate a value which is relative to the amount of space left after the other frames have been allocated their space. For example, for a window split in two, if the first row uses 150 pixels, and you indicate 1 as a relative height, the second row will use all of the rest of the screen. Another example: for a window that is split in three, if the first row uses 150 pixels, the second has 1 as a relative height and the third has 2 as a relative height, the last two rows will use the rest of the screen space together, with the third row taking twice as much space as the second.

Frame sets

- Select the second row by clicking it in the Property inspector and define its height, following the same principle.
- Now select the second frameset, the nested one, and format it in the Property inspector:

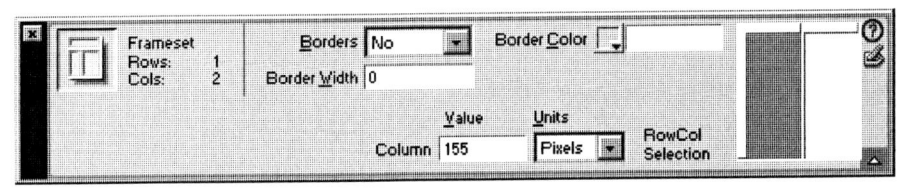

*Under **Frameset** Dreamweaver indicates the structure of the selected frameset: here there is 1 row and 2 columns. Do not forget to select the column concerned in the right of the window before you define its width.*

Formatting frames

You also need to format each frame in the frameset.

Selecting a frame

- First open the **Frames** palette using **Window - Frames** then click in the appropriate frame.

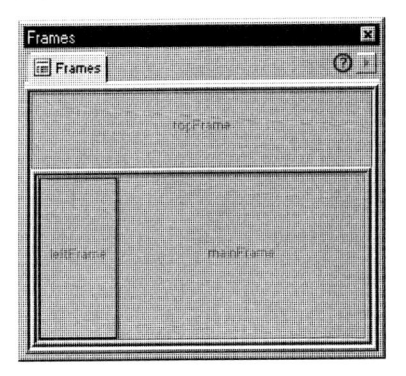

*The selected frame is outlined in grey in the **Frames** palette and is surrounded by a dashed border in the document window.*

Formatting a frame

You need to format all the frames in each frameset, one after the other, in the Property inspector.

- Select the frame you want to format.

©Editions ENI - All rights reserved

Dreamweaver 3
2-1-6 Frame sets

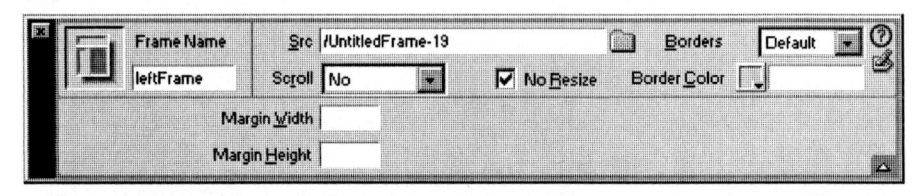

→ Give the frame a name in the **Frame Name** box.

You absolutely must name your frames in order to refer to them in framesets and to create links.

→ Type the name of the page that should appear in the frame in the **Src** box, or click to select it in your site folder.

Dreamweaver uses the "virtual" file called UntitledFrame by default.

→ Use the **Borders** pop-up menu to indicate whether the frame should have borders:

Yes	always to have borders.
No	never to have borders.
Default	the default browser settings will determine whether you have borders or not.

*Choosing borders around the frames will override the **No** choice for borders in the framesets.*

→ If you have chosen to use borders, use the **Border Color** box to choose the colour of the borders (using the color picker, or typing the colour's name or code).

The colour of the frame borders overrides that of the frameset borders.

→ Use the **Scroll** pop-up menu to choose whether or not you want scroll bars:

Yes	you will always have scroll bars.
No	there will never be scroll bars, even if the frame contents are too big in relation to the window.
Auto	scroll bars will be displayed only if they are necessary. If the frame contents are entirely visible, the browser will not show scroll bars. If the frame contents are very large, or if the browser window has been resized, scroll bars will appear.
Default	uses the default settings of the browser, which generally display scroll bars only when necessary.

→ Activate the **No Resize** option if you do not want users to be able to resize your frames.

→ Use the **Margin Width** and **Margin Height** boxes to define the horizontal and vertical distance from the frame border and the border of the page it contains.

©Editions ENI - All rights reserved

Frame sets

Formatting pages in a frameset

- Each page contained in a frameset can be exploited in the same way as a normal page.
- When you want to define the title that will appear on the browser's title bar, you need to do so for the frameset which is uppermost in the hierarchy, and use **Modify - Page Properties**.

    Type the appropriate text in the **Title** text box.

- Save each page using **File - Save**.

    To save the pages and the frameset, use **File - Save All**.

Construction strategy for framesets

When you are constructing a frameset, you can create all the documents in advance, or as and when you need them.

Preparing your documents in advance

- The first option is to create and save all the documents you will use to create the frameset in advance.
- Create the frameset in a new document and define its settings.

    For the parameters of each frame, indicate the page, which you have already prepared, that should appear in the **Src** box in the **Property** inspector.

    Src left.htm

Creating documents as you go

This second option can be used when you do not have the documents that will appear in the different frames.

- Create a frameset, define its parameters, and save it. Now click in the first frame in the document window: insert all the elements you want, then save the document. Do this for each frame.

Preparing and creating the documents

There is nothing to stop you from combining both these methods: you can create some documents in advance, construct your frames in an existing document and create new documents.

- To insert a frameset into an existing document, with the existing document in the top frame and a new one in the bottom frame use **Modify - Frameset - Split Frame Up**

  or click the **Insert Bottom Frame** button from the **Frames** panel in the **Objects** palette.

  The blue part of the button represents the existing document and indicates that it will be placed in the top frame. The white part is the document to be created, which will be placed in the bottom frame. This principle applies to the other buttons.

Defining links in a frameset

Traditional targets

As you have seen previously, it is very important to name your frames if you want to be able to refer to them in hyperlinks. When you create a hyperlink in a frameset you indicate the target page in the traditional way, but it is also imperative that you define the frame in which the page is to open.

- Select the link text or image.
- Use the **Link** box in the Property inspector to indicate which page is to be loaded.
- Select the name of the target frame from the **Target** pop-up menu:

  Link offers.htm   Target main

  *In this example the **offers.htm** page will be opened in the frame called **main**.*

Special targets

- Along with traditional links, there are also links to reserved targets:

  _blank   to open the page in a new browser window. Thus the user will see a window containing the target page, but will keep the window containing the source page. This is very useful if you do not want your site to be "lost" when a link leads to another site.

  _parent   to open the linked page in the link's parent frameset.

Frame sets

In the example below you can see a frameset with two frames. The top frame contains the links which open other pages, themselves made up of framesets, in the bottom frame. In the screen on the left the **Contents** link has been activated: the new page appears in the frame below.

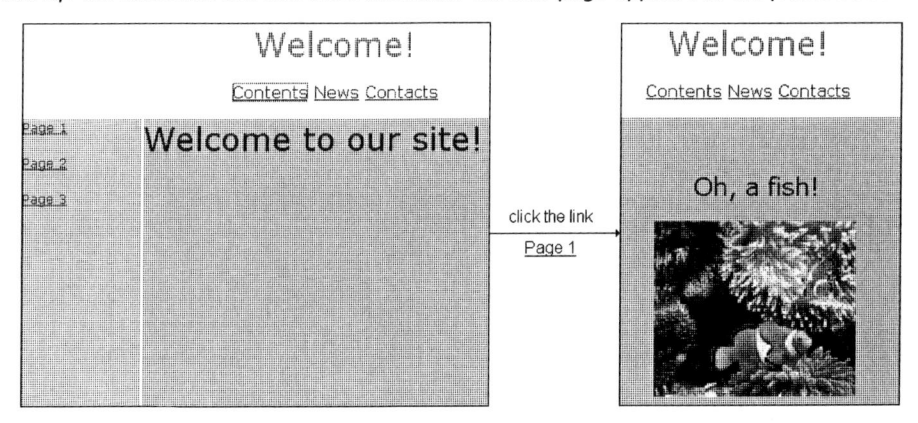

The "Page" links in the left frame have the target `_parent`, which means that the linked page will appear in the parent frame, meaning the frame in which the page containing the links appears. In this case it is the bottom frame. The screen shown on the right appears when the **Page 1** link is clicked.

_self   the linked page will open in the same frame as the link, replacing the contents. This is the default target, used if you do not specify one.

_top   if you want to open the linked page in the frame which is highest in the hierarchy, which is the browser window. In this case your frameset will no longer appear on the screen. This target is used to "delete" framesets.

Defining the frameset-free content

Some computers may still have browsers that do not support frames. You can specify what these browsers should display.

- Open a document from the frameset then select the highest level frameset in the **Frames** palette.
- **Modify - Frameset - Edit NoFrames Content**

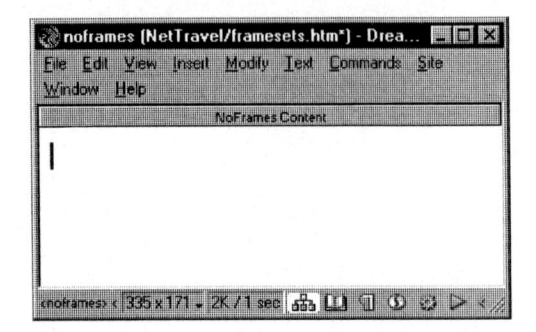

Dreamweaver 3
Frame sets

- Enter the content that should appear if the browser does not support framesets.
- To return to a view with frames use **Modify - Frameset - Edit NoFrames Content**.

Defining behaviors linked to framesets

Principle

The behaviors supplied with Dreamweaver allow users to interact with your pages. A behavior is the association of an event (such as a mouse click, or the loading of a page) and a JavaScript action. To learn more about behaviors, see the chapter about them.

Accessing several frames

The **Go To URL** action enables you to open a page in a frame. What is interesting about this action is that it can be used to open several pages in several different frames, all with one mouse click.

In the example below a frameset containing three frames is used: one on the left for links, and a top and bottom one.

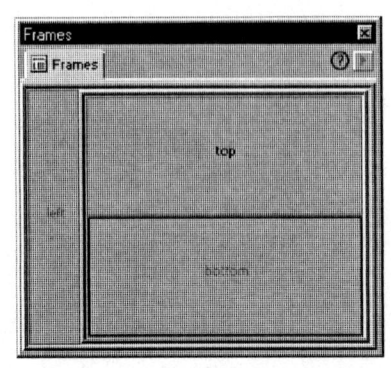

Frame sets

In the page contained in the frame called "left" a button image has been inserted in order to trigger the event.

- Show the **Behaviors** palette: **Window - Behaviors**.
- Choose the browser version from the **Events For** pop-up menu.
- Select the image button then click the ⊕ button to add a behavior and choose **Go To URL**.

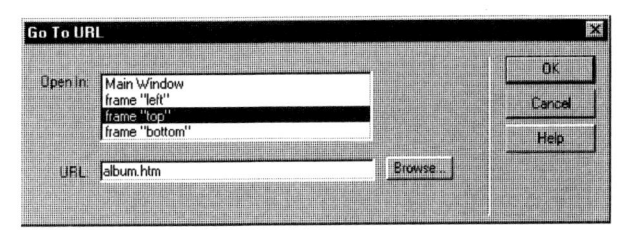

- Choose the frame in which the page should appear from the **Open In** list.
- Indicate the HTML page you want to open in the **URL** text box.
- Do the same if you want to open a second page in another frame, making sure you select the second frame before specifying the second page.
- Click **OK**.

    *In the **Behaviors** palette you can see the two events that will open the pages in the frames:*

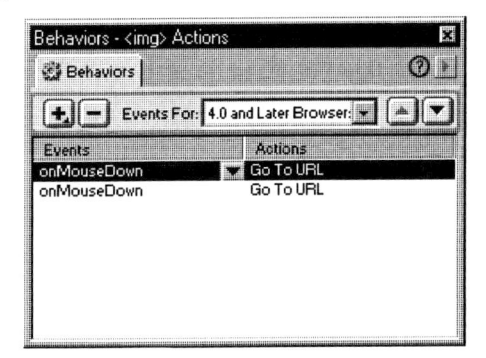

- To test these behaviors, save your document then preview the page in a browser.

©Editions ENI - All rights reserved

Dreamweaver 3
Frame sets

In this example the frame on the left contains a button which triggers the action. The two other frames contain the initial pages (**Top1** and **Bottom1**).

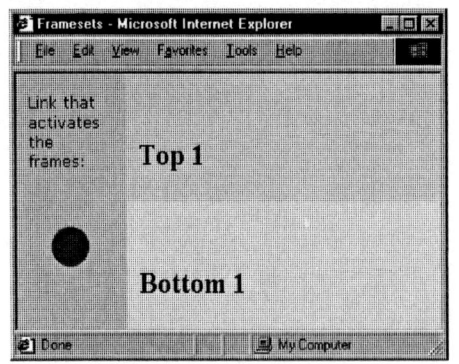

After the user clicks the button, the **Top2** and **Bottom2** pages are loaded in the frames:

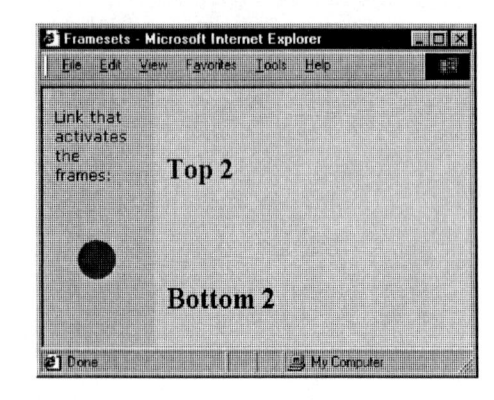

Changing the contents of a frame

You can use a button image and an event (such as `onClick` or `onMouseOver`) to delete the entire contents of a frame and replace it with text or HTML formatting elements of your choice (such as formatted text or an image). You could also make use of JavaScript functions.

- Insert a button image into one of the frames in your frameset using **Insert - Image**.
- Make sure the image is selected then choose a browser version in the **Behaviors** palette.
- Click the button to add a behavior and choose **Set Text - Set Text of Frame**.

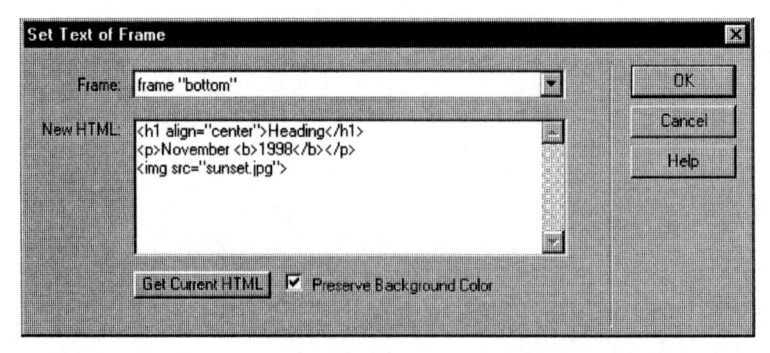

- Choose the target frame, whose contents will be deleted, from the **Frame** pop-up menu.

©Editions ENI - All rights reserved

Frame sets

- Type the replacement text in the **New HTML** text box, or type the HTML code (as shown in the example).

    The **Get Current HTML** button allows you to copy the contents and formatting of the frame which contains the action.

- If you want to keep the background and text colours of the target frame, activate the **Preserve Background Color** option.
- Click **OK**.
- Choose an event, such as `onClick` or `onMouseOver`.
- Test the behavior by saving your page then previewing it in a browser.

    In this example, the top frame contains the trigger button: when a user clicks it the contents of the lower frame are deleted and replaced by new text and the cbsnbc.jpg picture:

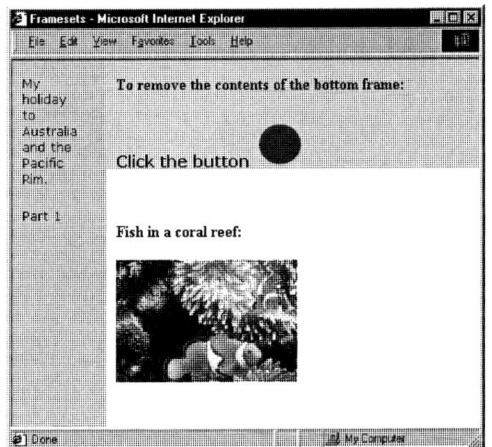

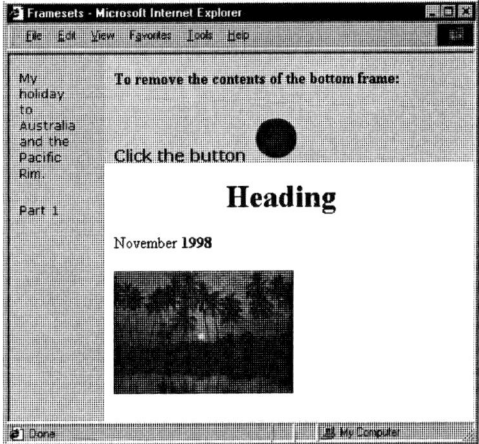

©Editions ENI - All rights reserved

Principles

Libraries

Web sites often contain recurring items: addresses, headers, contact references (such as names and telephone and fax numbers) and such like. You can lose a lot of time in typing and retyping these items, and while the Copy/Paste function is useful, it is not dynamic! If one of these items changes, you will need to change it throughout the site.

Using libraries means that you can place recurring items into a library then insert them into your pages by simply clicking the mouse. If you change something in one of these items, all you need to do is update the original in the library and the same change will be made to all the instances of the item.

Templates

Page templates work under the same principle but, this time, you can save a complete page template and use it to create new pages.

In this template you can define editable zones (areas you can edit when you use the template to create a new page) and non-editable zones (the parts of the page you do not want to edit because, for example, you need to respect a particular graphic layout, applied to all the pages).

If you change something in a template, all the pages in the site that use the template will also be changed. This technique is perfect if you want to present pages of a catalogue or magazine, for example.

Using a library

Creating an item in a library

Create library items in a normal page.

- Type and insert all the necessary objects, such as text and images, in your document.
- Open the **Library** palette using **Window - Library**.
- Select the objects you want to store in the library.
- **Modify - Library - Add Object to Library**

    or click the **New Library item** button in the **Library** palette.

    or use the **Library** palette context menu and choose **New Library Item**.

Libraries and templates

The item is added to the library.

- Type the item's name.
- Confirm with ⏎.

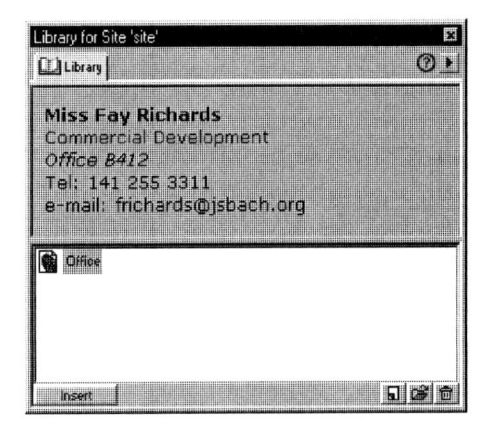

Once the item has been added to the library, an instance of the item is immediately used in the current page.

- Click the item in your page.
- You can see information about it in the Property inspector:

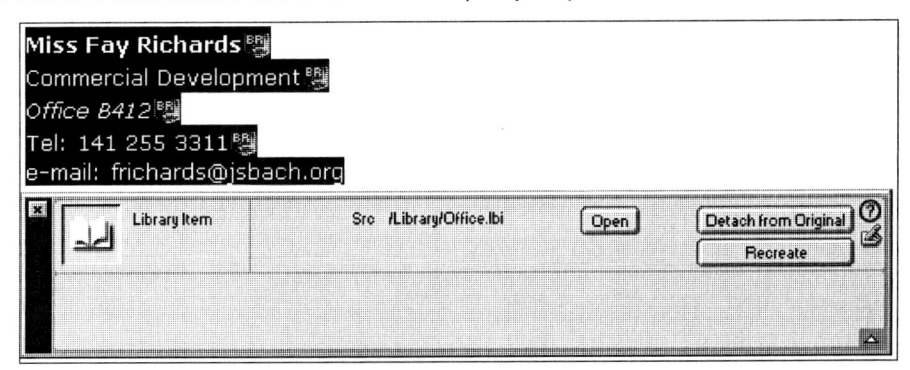

Src *indicates the library item's path and name.*

Dreamweaver 3
Libraries and templates

Be careful, because when you create an instance of a library item you cannot edit the instance in the document. You can make changes only to the item, not its instances.

Highlighting the library items in use

Each library item you use appears with yellow highlighting, which you can change if you wish:

- **Edit - Preferences - Highlighting** category

  Library Items: #FFFFCC ✓

- Make sure that the highlighting is active (the checkbox should be ticked).

  You can change the colour if you wish.

- Check that the invisible elements can be seen: **View - Invisible Elements**.

Looking at the library

When you add an item to the library, Dreamweaver creates a folder in your site folder and calls it Library. This folder contains a file with the same name as your library item, with the extension .lbi. The Library folder should always be at the root of your local folder.

- Press `F5` to see the site map.

  Library
      Office.lbi

  All the items you add to the library are placed in the Library folder, so there should be as many files as there are items.

Inserting a library item

You can insert an item from the library into your document whenever you wish.

- Place the insertion point in the document where you want to insert the item.
- Select the name of the item you want to add in the **Library** palette.
- Click the **Insert** button

  or drag the item's icon into your document

  or open the **Library** context menu ▶ and click **Add To Page**.

  If you need to, you can insert an instance of a library item without linking it to the item. However, if you do this the instance will not be updated automatically if you make any changes to the item in the library.

- To insert an instance without linking it to the item, hold down `⌥ ⌘` (Macintosh) or `Ctrl` (Windows) and drag the library item into the page.

©Editions ENI - All rights reserved

Libraries and templates

If you select the inserted text, no yellow highlighting appears: it is "normal" text.

Editing a library item

The usefulness of library items is their dynamism when you edit them: if you change a library item, all the instances of the item in your site are updated.

There are several ways to open a library item.

- Press [F5] to show the site map.
- Open the Library folder if you need to.

> Library
>   Office.lbi

- Double-click the library item you want to edit

    or select it in the **Library** palette and click the **Open Library Item** button

    or open the **Library** context menu and click **Open**.

    or select an instance of the item in the document then click the **Open** button on the Property inspector.

    The item's window opens. Look at the Dreamweaver window's title bar:

    > <<Library Item>> (Office.lbi) - Dreamweaver

    The title bar indicates that you have opened a library item: **<<Library Item>>** *and its name:* **(Office.lbi)**.

- Make the necessary changes.
- **File - Save**

    Dreamweaver asks you if you want to update the files that use the item:

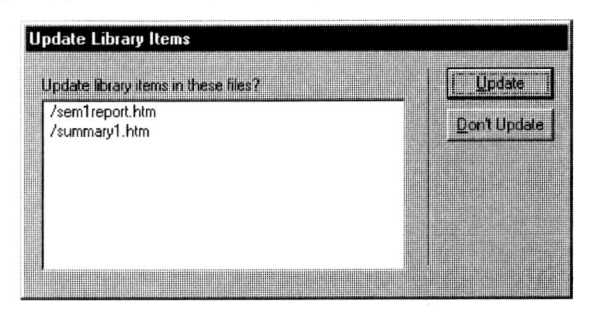

    > **Update Library Items**
    > Update library items in these files?
    > /sem1report.htm
    > /summary1.htm
    > [Update] [Don't Update]

©Editions ENI - All rights reserved

Dreamweaver 3
Libraries and templates

⏏ Click **Update**.

Dreamweaver shows a summary of the update:

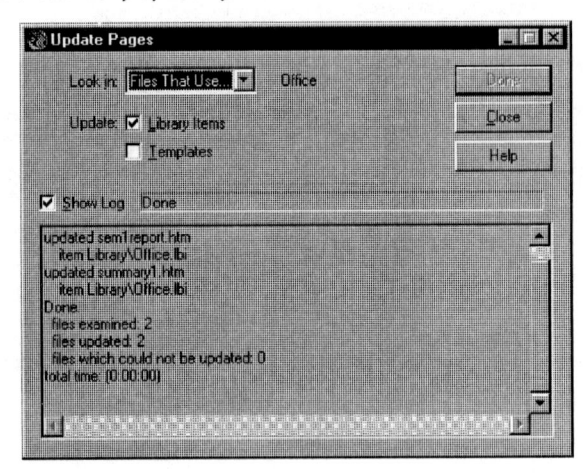

Updating pages that use library items

*There is nothing to stop you editing a library item (the office.lbi item in the example) without updating the documents that use this library item. Simply click **Don't Update** when you save the changes. If you do this, you will need to update the pages that use instances of the library item yourself.*

⏏ Open a page that uses an instance of the edited library item.

⏏ **Modify - Library - Update Current Page** or **Update Pages**

©Editions ENI - All rights reserved

Libraries and templates

Dreamweaver updates instances of the library item in the current page or throughout the site. This dialog box appears:

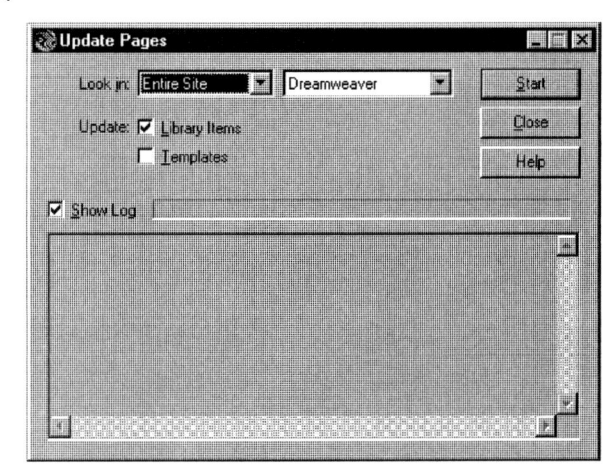

- From the **Look in** pop-up menu, choose:

  Entire Site   to update all the pages in the site and all the library items.

  Files That Use   if you want to update only those pages that use the library item that you can choose from the menu on the right.

- Leave the **Library Items** check box ticked.
- Leave **Show Log** active if you want to see a summary of the update.
- Click **Start**.

  Dreamweaver displays a summary after the update.

Renaming a library item

- Select the item you want to rename in the **Library** palette.
- Open the context menu and choose **Rename**

  or right-click the item to see its context menu and choose **Rename**.

  or select the item in the **Library** palette and click its name: the name is selected.
- Enter the item's new name and confirm with .

  Dreamweaver asks you if you want to update pages that use this item.
- Click **Update** or **Don't Update**, depending on your wishes.

©Editions ENI - All rights reserved

Dreamweaver 3
Libraries and templates

Removing the link with the library item

As you have just seen, when you insert an instance of a library item in a document, a dynamic link is created to the source file. You may want to break this link for any number of reasons.

🖅 Click in the item in your page.

Information about it appears in the Property inspector:

```
Miss Fay Richards
Commercial Development
Office B412
Tel: 141 255 3311
e-mail: frichards@jsbach.org
```

Library Item   Src /Library/Office.lbi   [Open]   [Detach from Original] [Recreate]

🖅 Click the **Detach from Original** button.

Dreamweaver alerts you that, if you break this link and make the instance editable, it will no longer be updated automatically.

🖅 Click **OK**.

Now the instance has become standard, editable text.

Deleting an item from the library

When you delete an item from the library, you delete the corresponding file in the Library folder, but the code that inserts the items into pages remains. You need to tidy up your pages to remove this now useless code (see the chapter about optimising code).

🖅 Select the item you want to delete in the **Library** palette.

🖅 Open the context menu ▶ and choose **Delete**.

or click the **Delete Library Item** button 🗑

or right-click the item and choose **Delete**.

🖅 Click **Yes** to confirm the deletion.

©Editions ENI - All rights reserved

Libraries and templates

Recreating a library item

If you have deleted a library item by accident you can always recreate it. As you have seen, when you delete a library item, the relevant code is not deleted in your page. You can use this instance to recreate the item.

- Select an instance of a deleted library item in one of your documents.
- Click the **Recreate** button in the Property inspector.

The item takes the name it had before it was deleted and is placed in the **Library** palette.

Using templates

Creating a template

Templates are created using normal pages in which you can insert text, tables, images, scripts and so on, all with the appropriate formatting.

As for the document header, you can create all the formatting elements you want, but when you create a document using the template, only the title (HTML element `<title>`) will be editable, and the other heading settings will not. This means that you cannot create elements which place HTML code in the header (`<head>`), such as style sheets, timelines and behaviors.

- Insert all the appropriate elements into a new page or open an existing page you want to use as a template.
- **File - Save as Template**

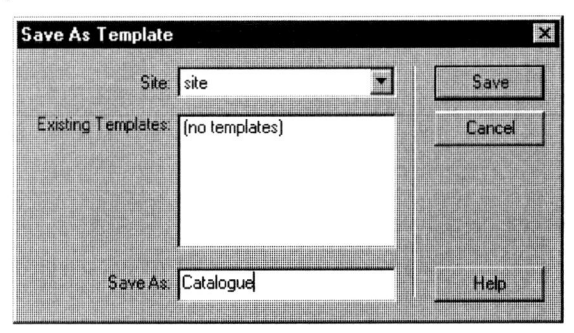

- Select the site in which you want to save the template from the **Site** pop-up menu.

    The **Existing Templates** box shows any templates you have already created.

- Type the template's name in the **Save As** text box.

©Editions ENI - All rights reserved

Dreamweaver 3
2-3-2 Libraries and templates

- Click **Save**.
- Show the **Templates** palette using **Window - Templates**.

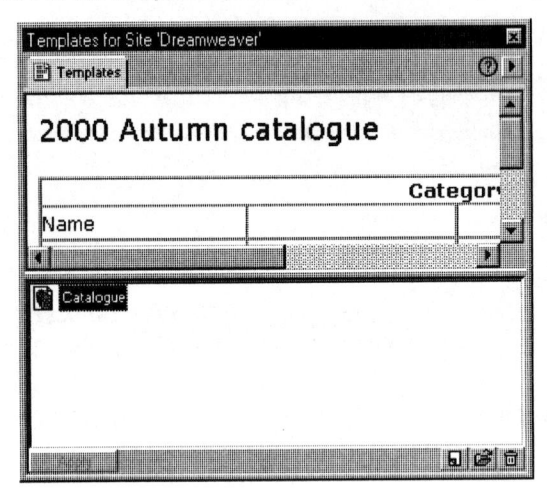

    The template file appears in the Templates palette, with a preview of the page:

    The window's title bar reminds you that the active document is a template:

<<Template>>	tells you that you are in a template.
(Catalogue.dwt)	tells you the name of the template, with the extension .dwt, for "Dreamweaver template".

- To create a template in the **Templates** palette, open the context menu and choose **New Template** or click the **New Template** button. Give the template a name, insert all the necessary elements, and save it.

Looking at the templates folder

When you create templates, Dreamweaver creates a new folder at the root of your local folder, and calls it Templates. Each template is shown in the folder with the extension .dwt.

- Press [F5] to see your site map.

Libraries and templates

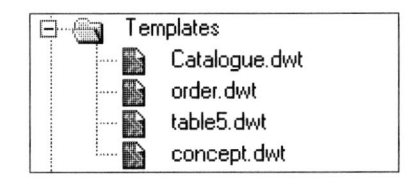

Creating editable regions

When you create a template, everything in it is locked and cannot be edited. You need to create editable regions that can be changed when you create a new document using the template. When you create editable and locked regions, they are highlighted in the page. The highlighting colours are specified in the preferences:

- **Edit - Preferences - Highlighting** category

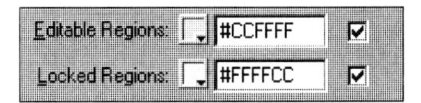

- If you want to, change the colours and leave the checkboxes ticked.
- In the page, make sure you can see the invisible elements: **View - Invisible Elements**.
- To mark a region as editable, first select it.
- **Modify - Templates - Mark Selection as Editable**

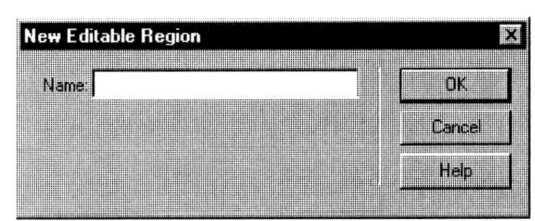

- Type the editable selection's name in the **Name** text box.
- Click **OK**.

  The selected editable area is highlighted in cyan.

- To make a part of the document editable, click in the appropriate place.
- **Modify - Templates - New Editable Region**
- Type the name of the editable region in the **Name** text box.
- Click **OK**.

©Editions ENI - All rights reserved

Dreamweaver 3
Libraries and templates

The editable region is highlighted in cyan and its name appears between braces.

In this example, the **Category** text is an editable selection, and the regions {n1}, {n2}, {p1}, {p2}, {a1} and {a2} editable regions.

Category		
Name	{n1}	{n2}
Price	{p1}	{p2}
Availability	{a1}	{a2}

Going to an editable region

In complicated templates, you can go directly to a specific editable region.

▸ **Modify - Templates**

At the end of the **Templates** submenu is a list of all the regions.

▸ Click the one you want.

Making regions non-editable

If you have marked a region as editable by mistake you can undo this.

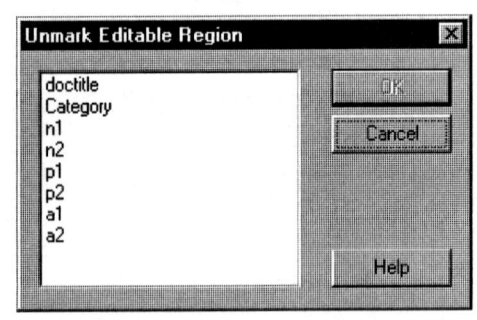

▸ **Modify - Templates - Unmark Editable Region**

▸ Select the name of the appropriate region.

▸ Click **OK**.

Creating a document using a template

Now that you have created your template you can use it to create a new document.

▸ **File - New from Template**

©Editions ENI - All rights reserved

Libraries and templates

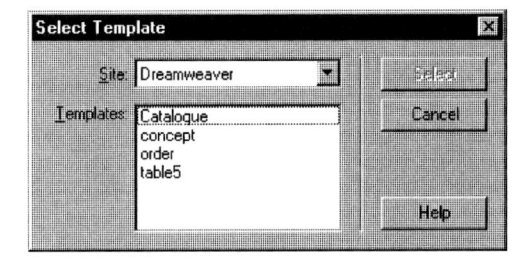

- Choose the site that contains the template you want to use in the **Site** pop-up menu.
- Select the template you want to use from the **Templates** list.
- Click **Select**.

    Dreamweaver creates a new document based on this template. The editable regions appear as normal, and locked regions are shown with yellow highlighting.

    In this example the regions 2000 Autumn Catalogue, Name, Price and Availability are locked (yellow highlighting). The {n1}, {n2}, {p1}, {p2}, {a1} and {a2} regions are editable:

2000 Autumn catalogue

	Category	
Name	{n1}	{n2}
Price	{p1}	{p2}
Availability	{a1}	{a2}

Entering information in editable regions

There are two methods for entering data in editable regions.

- Select or click the editable region then type the text

    or click the name of the editable region in the **Modify - Templates** menu then type your text.

- Use the key to go to the next region.

    If you try to type text in a locked region (highlighted in yellow) your computer will beep to tell you that you cannot.

- When you have finished, save your document as you would normally.

Applying a template to a document

You can also apply a template to a document that is already open. This can be a completely empty document, or it might contain text or images that must be placed in an editable region.

©Editions ENI - All rights reserved

Dreamweaver 3
Libraries and templates

- Open the **Templates** palette using **Window - Templates**.

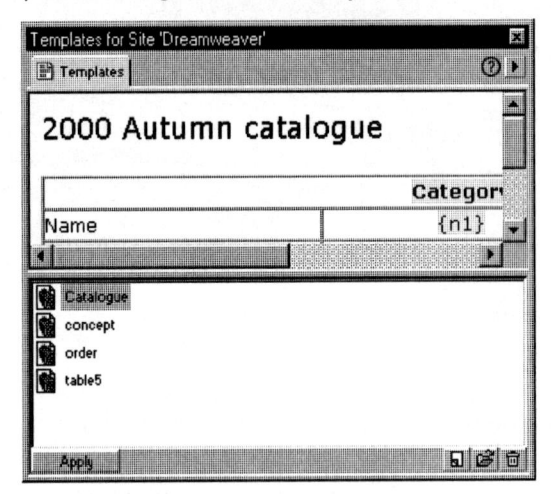

- Select the template you want to use from the list and click the **Apply** button

    or open the context menu ▶ and choose **Apply To Page**.

    or drag the template's icon to the page.

    If the document is not empty, Dreamweaver asks you where you want to place the elements:

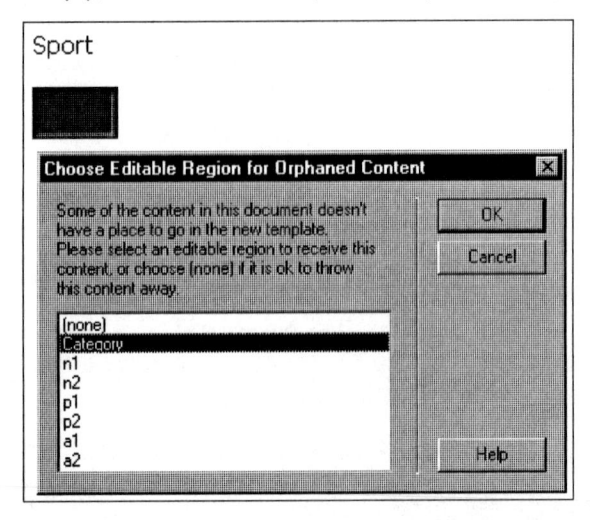

©Editions ENI - All rights reserved

Libraries and templates

- Select the editable region that is to contain the elements already present in your page from the list and click OK.

☞ You can choose only one!

2000 Autumn catalogue		
Sport		
Name	{n1}	{n2}
Price	{p1}	{p2}
Availability	{a1}	{a2}

- Type your text in the editable regions as shown previously.

Editing a template

As with library items, when you edit a template, Dreamweaver asks you if you want to update all the documents created using the template.

- Select the template you want to edit in the **Templates** palette.
- Click the **Open Template** icon

    or open the context menu and choose **Open**.

    or double-click the icon of the template you want to edit

    or use **Window - Site Files** to see your site files, open the Templates folder and double-click the file you want to open.

    Notice the template window's title bar:

    <<Template>> (Catalogue.dwt) - Dreamweaver

    <<Template>> *reminds you that you are in a template, and* **(Catalogue.dwt)** *is the name of the template.*

- Make all the necessary changes.
- Save the file using **File - Save**.

©Editions ENI - All rights reserved

Dreamweaver asks you if you want to update all the documents created using the template:

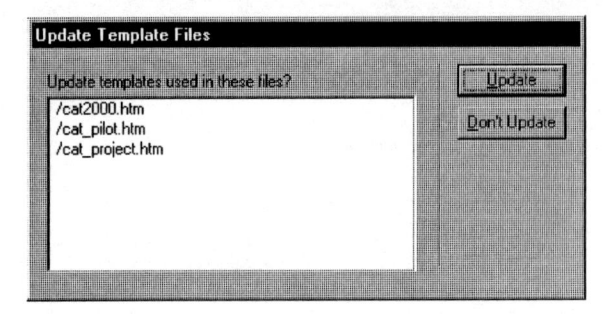

→ Click **Update**.

Dreamweaver shows a summary:

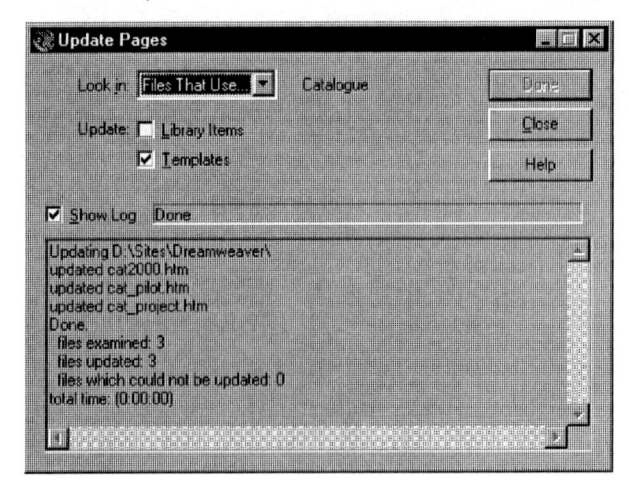

Updating a document

You can make changes to your templates without necessarily updating all the documents that were created using the template. If you do this, you will need to update the documents one by one, or update the whole site.

→ Open a template and edit it as shown previously.

Dreamweaver asks you if you want to update your files based on this template.

→ Click **Don't Update**.

→ Open a document that uses the template.

→ **Modify - Templates - Update Current Page** or **Update Pages**

Libraries and templates

If you take the first choice, the page is updated and you can see the changes made to the template. Take the second choice, and a dialog box appears.

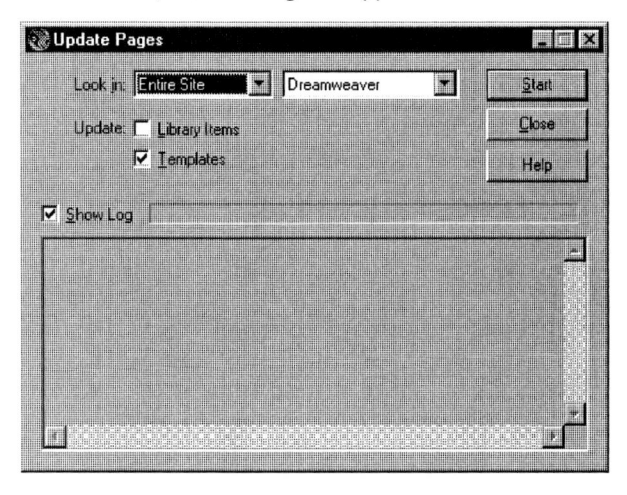

- Choose **Entire Site** from the **Look in** pop-up menu if you want to check the whole site.
- In the pop-up menu on the right, select the name of the site that is to searched and updated.
- Leave the **Templates** option active under **Update**.
- Leave the **Show Log** check box ticked if you want to see the summary.
- Click **Start**.

Renaming a template

You can rename a template whenever you like.

- Select the template you want to rename from the **Templates** palette.
- Open the context menu and click **Rename**.

    or right-click the template and choose **Rename**.

- Type the new name and confirm with .

    Dreamweaver asks you if you want to update all the documents that use the template.

- Click **Update**.

©Editions ENI - All rights reserved

Removing the link to a template

You can break the link between a template and the document(s) created using it. Of course, if you do this, your documents will no longer be updated with changes to the template.

- Open a document created using the template.
- **Modify - Templates - Detach from Template**

  The link is broken. You are free to make changes.
- Make any required changes.
- Save the document.

Deleting a template

When you delete a template you are deleting the file from the Templates folder, but not the links with the documents that are based on the template. These documents will thus be linked to "ghosts"! You also need to break the link with the deleted template, as shown previously.

- Select the template you want to delete in the **Templates** palette.
- Click the **Delete Template** icon 🗑

  or open the context menu ▶ and choose **Delete**

  or right-click the template and choose **Delete**.
- Click **Yes** in reply to the warning message.

Exporting data in XML format

Knowing XML

HTML is the language currently used to create Internet pages. However, it does have many drawbacks:

- it is purely descriptive: HTML elements can be used to apply formatting, but no more.
- it is limited and cannot be extended: you can use only existing HTML elements, you cannot create your own elements.
- it does not have any semantic content: when you want to indicate the address of someone in your page, you use the `<p>` or `<h3>` elements without knowing the real contents. The person's name, surname, address, town and postal code information are lost in the description elements.
- it is not structured: you cannot exchange information with databases.

Libraries and templates

However, to be fair, HTML was not designed to do this. In order to compensate for these limitations, the W3C created a new language called XML: eXtensible Markup Language (http://www.w.org/XML)

You can create your own tags using this language, which means you can extend it ad infinitum: the tags have a semantic content (the tag `<town>Chester</town>` certainly indicates that the tag content is the name of a town!) and it is a perfectly structured language. It is impossible to predict the future, but XML may very well be the future standard for the exchange of structured data over the Internet.

So how does this apply to Dreamweaver and its templates? In a template each editable region is perfectly named and unique, which means that you can use these names to create XML tags in order to exchange structured data.

Example

This example is based on the creation of a template for typing a simple address book.

- Create a new document.
- Insert a table of 4 rows and 6 columns.

  The first row contains only the "field" names: Title, Name, Surname, Address, Town/City and Postal Code.

- Save the document as a template called Addresses.
- Create editable regions with the names given below:

  `t` for `title`, `n` for `name`, `s` for `surname`, `a` for `address`, `tc` for `town/city` and `pc` for `postal code`.

  Each row is a record, identified by its number: from 1 to 3.
  `s2` is thus the surname of the second person in the address book.

Title	Name	Surname	Address	Town/City	Postal Code
{t1}	{n1}	{s1}	{a1}	{tc1}	{pc1}
{t2}	{n2}	{s2}	{a2}	{tc2}	{pc2}
{t3}	{n3}	{s3}	{a3}	{tc3}	{pc3}

- Save the template.

Dreamweaver 3
Libraries and templates

- Create a new document based on the template then enter the following data:

Title	Name	Surname	Address	Town/City	Postal Code
Mr	Tim	Watson	55 Station Road	Carlisle	CA6 1BN
Mrs	Kim	Bright	20 Wesley Court	Coventry	CV5 2PP
Mr	Mike	Pringle	13 Dean Avenue	Gorebridge	EH22 9LK

- Save this document and call it myaddresses.

Exporting in XML format

Now that you have created your document and entered the data you need to export it in XML format.

- **File - Export - Export Editable Regions as XML**

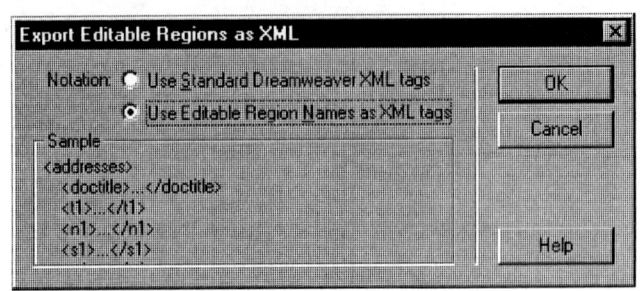

- Choose a format under **Notation**:

    Use Standard Dreamweaver XML tags to write tags like: `<item name="t1">_</item>`.

    Use Editable Region Names as XML tags to write tags like: `<t1>_</t1>`.

    Choose the second option, which is the simplest.

- Click **OK**.

- Give the XML document the name **myaddresses** then open the **myaddresses.xml** document.

- Press F10 to see the source code.

©Editions ENI - All rights reserved

Libraries and templates

```
<?xml version="1.0"?>
<addresses template="/Templates/addresses.dwt">
    <doctitle><![CDATA[<title>Untitled Document</title>]]></doctitle>
    <t1><![CDATA[Mr]]></t1>
    <n1><![CDATA[Tim]]></n1>
    <s1><![CDATA[Watson]]></s1>
    <a1><![CDATA[55 Station Road]]></a1>
    <tc1><![CDATA[Carlisle]]></tc1>
    <pc1><![CDATA[CA6 1BN ]]></pc1>
    <t2><![CDATA[Mrs]]></t2>
    <n2><![CDATA[Kim]]></n2>
    <s2><![CDATA[Bright]]></s2>
    <a2><![CDATA[20 Wesley Court]]></a2>
    <tc2><![CDATA[Coventry]]></tc2>
    <pc2><![CDATA[CV5 2PP ]]></pc2>
    <t3><![CDATA[Mr]]></t3>
    <n3><![CDATA[Mike]]></n3>
    <s3><![CDATA[Pringle]]></s3>
    <a3><![CDATA[13 Dean Avenue]]></a3>
    <tc3><![CDATA[Gorebridge]]></tc3>
    <pc3><![CDATA[EH22 9LK ]]></pc3>
</addresses>
```

You can see the structure XML document: the document's root tag is `<addresses>` *...*`</addresses>`*. Each "field" is named and has a semantic content:* `<n1><![CDATA[Tim]]></n1>` *is the first person's name.*

This document can be exchanged with a database that uses the same structure, providing the database recognises XML.

Importing an XML document

You can also import an XML document into a template, providing, naturally, that the XML document and the template have the same structure. The names of the XML tags and the number of records must match up exactly! This does somewhat restrict imports.

- Create a new empty document.
- **File - Import - Import XML into Template**
- Select the xml file you want to import.

Dreamweaver 3
Libraries and templates

If the file does not indicate which Dreamweaver template is to be used, you should specify which template you want:

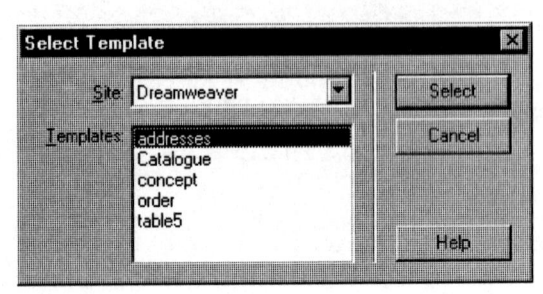

→ Select the appropriate template and click **Select**.

Dreamweaver creates a document based on the template you choose, and each XML tag is placed in the editable region with the same name.

Behaviors

Principles

Actions and events

Inserting a behavior allows you to increase interactivity with users and to add dynamism to your pages. A behavior is a combination of an event and an action. An **event** is generally something the user does with the mouse (pointing to an object, clicking a button or submitting a form, for example), or the loading of a page, closing of a page, etc. An **action** is generated by JavaScript and allows a change in the page (such as an image being replaced by another or the playing of a movie) or a programmed action (such as the verification or calculation of a form field or search for a particular browser version).

Events and browsers

Some events are not recognised by different versions of the main browsers. You should be careful in your choice of events, depending on the version of browsers you are targeting.

→ Open the **Behaviors** palette with **Window - Behaviors**.

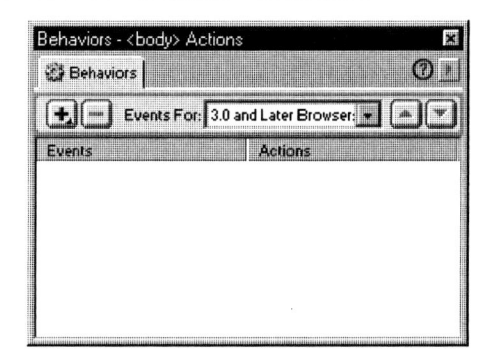

→ Choose the browser developer and version you want from the **Events For** pop-up menu.

→ Browser abbreviations:
   - NS3: Netscape Navigator 3
   - NS4: Netscape Navigator 4
   - IE3: Microsoft Internet Explorer 3
   - IE4: Microsoft Internet Explorer 4
   - IE5: Microsoft Internet Explorer 5

©Editions ENI - All rights reserved

Dreamweaver 3
Behaviors

Page events

onAbort (NS3, NS4, IE4) is generated when the user stops the loading of an image by clicking the **Stop** button.

onLoad (NS3, NS4, IE3, IE4) is generated when an image or the page has finished loading.

onUnload (NS3, NS4, IE3, IE4) is generated when the user closes the page.

onResize (NS4, IE4) is generated when the user resizes the window or a frame.

onError (NS3, NS4, IE4) is generated when an error occurs while the page is loading.

Form field events

onBlur (NS3, NS4, IE3, IE4) is generated when the insertion point is no longer in the field, or when the focus is removed from it (when it no longer contains the insertion point).

onChange (NS3, NS4, IE3, IE4) is generated when the user changes the value in the field.

onFocus (NS3, NS4, IE3, IE4) is generated when the insertion point appears in the field, or when it becomes the focus of user interaction.

onSelect (NS3, NS4, IE3, IE4) is generated when the user selects text in the field.

onSubmit (NS3, NS4, IE3, IE4) is generated when the user clicks the button that submits the form.

onReset (NS3, NS4, IE3, IE4) is generated when the user clicks the button that resets the form.

Mouse events

onClick (NS3, NS4, IE3, IE4) is generated when the user clicks an object.

onDblClick (NS4, IE4) is generated when the user double-clicks an object.

onMouseDown (NS4, IE4) is generated at the moment when the user clicks an object and before he/she releases the mouse button.

onMouseMove (IE3, IE4) is generated when the user moves the mouse while pointing to an object.

onMouseOut (NS3, NS4, IE4) is generated when the user moves the mouse pointer away from the object's surface.

©Editions ENI - All rights reserved

Behaviors

onMouseOver (NS3, NS4, IE3, IE4) is generated when the user places the mouse pointer over an object.

onMouseUp (NS4, IE4) is generated at the moment when the user releases the mouse button after having clicked an object.

Keyboard events

onKeyDown (NS4, IE4) is generated when the user presses a key on the keyboard, and before he/she releases the key.

onKeyPress (NS4, IE4) is generated when the user presses a key on the keyboard and releases it.

onKeyUp (NS4, IE4) is generated when the user releases a key on the keyboard after having pressed it.

Microsoft Internet Explorer events

onAfterUpdate is generated when the active page is updated.

onBeforeUpdate is generated when an item of data in the active page is about to be updated.

onBounce is generated when a marquee has reached the end of its area.

onFinish is generated when a marquee has finished its loop.

onHelp is generated when a user clicks the help button.

onReadyStateChange is generated when an object's state changes.

onRowEnter is generated when the record pointer of the bound data source has changed.

onRowExit is generated when the record pointer of the bound data source is going to change.

onScroll is generated when the user scrolls the page using scroll bars.

onStart is generated when a marquee starts its loop.

Netscape Navigator events

onMove is generated when a window or frame is moved.

©Editions ENI - All rights reserved

Managing behaviors

Several behaviors for the same object

When you want to create complex pages that contain a lot of user interactivity, you can apply several actions, via several events, to the same object (such as an image button, or the `<body>` tag for the loading of the page).

Changing behaviors

- To change an event, select the behavior concerned from the **Behaviors** palette. Open the **Events** context menu and choose a new event.

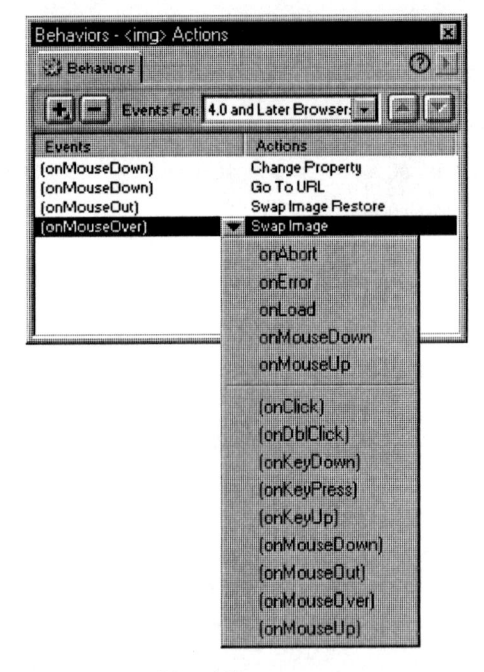

This image has four behaviors triggered by different events.

Do not forget that the events available to you depend on the browser chosen in the **Events For** pop-up menu.

- To change an action's settings you can select the appropriate behavior then double-click the action concerned in the **Actions** column.

Behaviors

- Click the ⊕ button to add a behavior.
- Click the ⊖ button to delete the selected behavior.

    In the **Behaviors** palette, behaviors are listed in alphabetical order depending on the event. If one event triggers several actions, the actions are listed in chronological order.

- You can change the order of the behaviors by clicking the ▲ and ▼ buttons to move them.

Using a JavaScript

This behavior is very straightforward, and allows you to run a script from an event. Firstly, you will need to create a script then call this script by using its function name.

Example: creating a form

In this example you will see how to create a small form to calculate the square root of a value entered by the user. First you need to create the form.

- Insert a form and call it **kalculate**.
- Insert a text field and call it **number**. This is the field in which the user will enter a value.
- Insert another text field and call it **result**. This is the field in which the square root will appear.

    At the end, insert a button, but do not give it an action.

    Number: [   ]
    Square root: [   ]
    [Calculate]

    Now you need to create the script that will calculate the square root of the entered value.

- Press F10 to open the source code.

©Editions ENI - All rights reserved

Dreamweaver 3
Behaviors

- Type this script in the `<head>` element:

```
<script language="JavaScript">
<!--
function calculation() {
a=document.kalculate.number.value
document.kalculate.result.value=Math.sqrt(a)
}
//-->
</script>
```

In the script you have defined a function (`function`) called `calculation()`.
The variable `a` allows you to recover the value `value` in the `number` field of the `kalculate` form in the `document`.
You have applied the mathematic square root function `Math.sqrt()` of the variable `a` as the value `value` to the `result` field in the `kalculate` form in the `document`.

Now you need to assign this script to the button.

- Select the **Calculate** button in the form.
- Choose the browser version from the **Events For** pop-up menu in the **Behaviors** palette.
- Click the [+] to add a behavior and choose **Call JavaScript**.

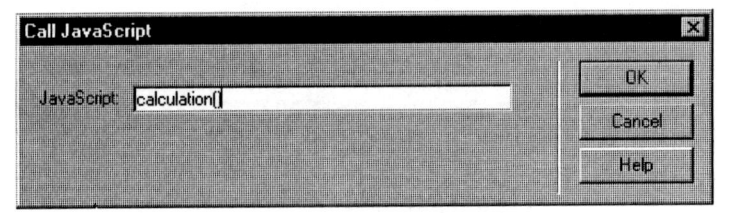

- Type the function's name in the text box and click **OK**.
- Choose an event in the **Behaviors** palette: `onClick`, `onMouseDown`, and so on.
- Test the behavior by saving your document and previewing it in a browser.
- Type a number in the **Number** field then click the **Calculate** button.

©Editions ENI - All rights reserved

Behaviors

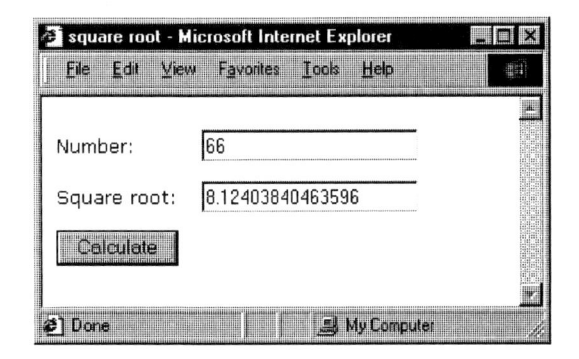

Changing an object's properties

This behavior enables you to change certain properties for some objects, such as changing a layer's background colour, replacing an image with another, or changing the character size of text in a layer.

Creation: first example

In this example you will see how to change the background colour of a layer.

- Insert an image that will work as a button to trigger the action.
- Draw the layer.
- You must give the layer a name in the Property inspector in order to select it later.
- Type some text in the layer.
- To create the behavior, go to the **Behaviors** palette and choose a browser version.
- Click the button to add a behavior and choose **Change Property**,

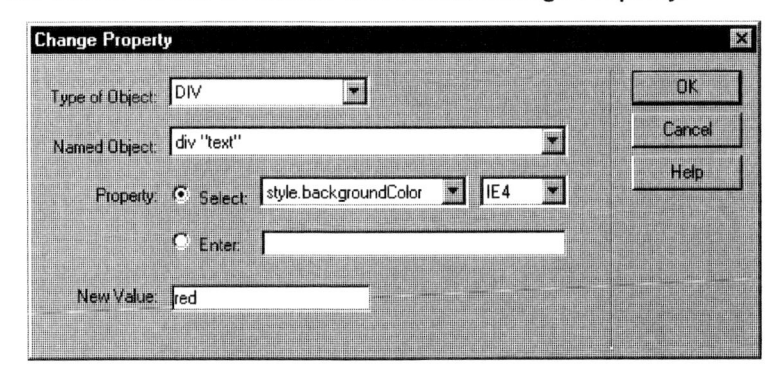

©Editions ENI - All rights reserved

Dreamweaver 3
Behaviors

- In the **Type of Object** pop-up menu choose the one you want: division elements (`<div>` or `<span>`), image (`<img>`), or form elements (`<form>`, `<input>`, `<textarea>` and `<select>`).

  *In the example a layer has been chosen (`<div>`). In the **Named Object** pop-up menu Dreamweaver gives a list of the layers and their names. The one used here is called "text".*

- Choose a property under **Property** (here **style.backgroundColor** has been chosen), that is recognised by a browser, **IE4** in the example.
- Indicate the new value for the chosen property in the **New Value** text box. Here it is **red**.
- Click **OK**.
- Choose an event in the **Behaviors** palette: `onClick`, `onMouseOver`, etc.
- Test the behavior by saving your document then previewing it in your browser. Activate the button to trigger the event.

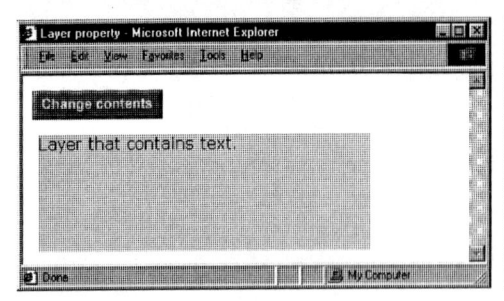

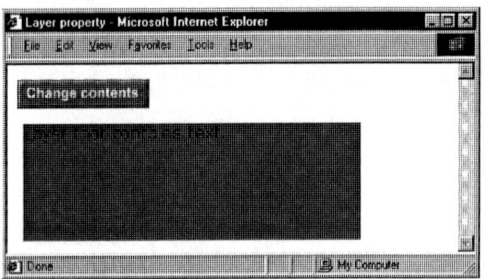

Creation: second example

Below you will see how to swap two images with a simple click of the mouse.

- Import two images of the same size into your site folder.
- Insert a button image to trigger the action into your document.
- Insert the first image and name it in the Property inspector.
- Select your button image.
- Choose a browser version in the **Behaviors** palette.
- Click the button to add a behavior and choose **Change Property**.

©Editions ENI - All rights reserved

Behaviors

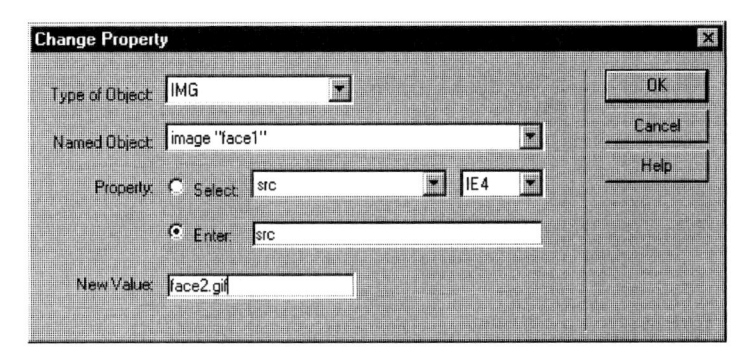

- Select **IMG** from the **Type of Object** pop-up menu to change an image.
- Select the name of the image that you have just inserted from the **Named Object** pop-up menu.
- Under **Property** indicate the parameter you want to change in the **Select** pop-up menu. Choose **src** to change the image source and choose a compatible browser. Here **IE4** has been chosen.
- In the **New Value** text box, type the file name of the second image.
- Click **OK**.
- Choose an event in the **Behaviors** palette: onClick, onMouseOver, etc.
- Test the behavior by saving your document then previewing it in a browser:

©Editions ENI - All rights reserved

Dreamweaver 3
Behaviors

Opening a browser window

This behavior enables you to use an event (such as a mouse click or the loading of a page) to open a page in a new window of the browser, for which you can specify the size and properties. This behavior is perfect for advertising or online help.

- Prepare the page that is to open in a new page.
- Create a standard page with text and images if necessary, then save it.
- To open the new window when the page loads, assign the behavior to the `<body>` element: select the `<body>` tag **<body>** in the status bar of the active window.
- Click the button in the **Behaviors** palette to add a behavior and choose **Open Browser Window**.

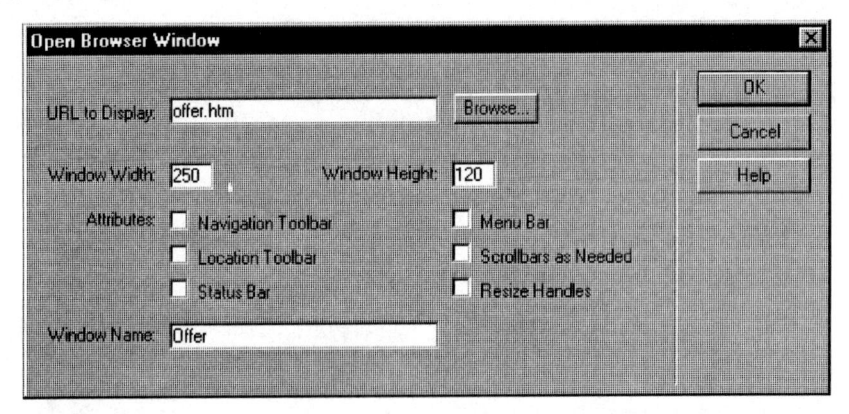

- Click the **Browse** button in the **URL to Display** box to select the page to be shown in the new browser window.
- Indicate the size of this window in the **Window Width** and **Window Height** boxes.
- Choose the window options you want under **Attributes**. If you do not specify any attributes, the new window will have the same characteristics as the window that carries out the action.
- Type the new window's name in the **Window Name** box (you must not use any spaces).

©Editions ENI - All rights reserved

Behaviors

You can see this behavior in the **Behaviors** palette:

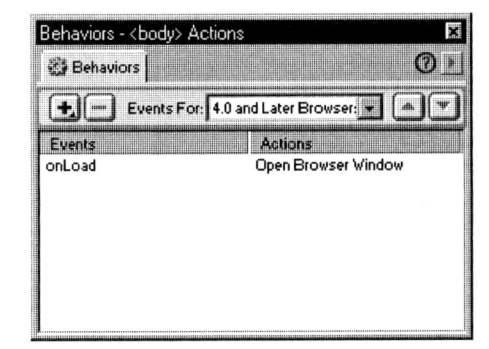

The **onLoad** event occurs when the page is loaded.
The action is **Open Browser Window**.

⇥ Test the behavior by saving your page and previewing it in your browser.

As soon as the page loads, the new window opens. In this example, the little **Special offer** window opened as soon as the **African vacation** window had loaded:

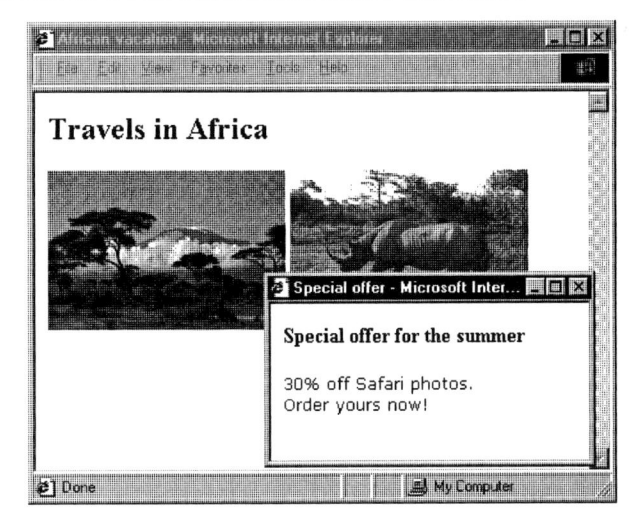

Dreamweaver 3
Behaviors

Displaying a message

With this behavior you can make a message box appear after an action. This box has only one button, OK, and is generally used to inform users.

The event can be a mouse action or the loading of the page (onLoad). Depending on the event you choose, insert a button image or select the <body> tag in the status bar as shown previously.

- Choose the browser version in the **Behaviors** palette.
- Click ⊞ button to add a behavior and choose **Popup Message**.

- Type the appropriate text in the **Message** box, using ⏎ to insert line breaks.
- Choose an event:
    - onClick, onMouseOver, etc if you have chosen a mouse action.
    - onLoad if you want the message to appear when the page loads.
- Test the behavior by saving your page then previewing it in a browser.

If you have chosen the onLoad event, the message appears as soon as the page has loaded.

©Editions ENI - All rights reserved

Changing the text in a form field

You can choose the text you want to display in a text field of a form. In this example, imagine that the user has entered some information and that you want to thank them for their visit and the time they have taken to fill out the form.

- Insert a form into your document.
- Insert text fields for the user.
- Insert a multi-line text field and call it **comments**. This is where your text will appear.
- Insert submit and reset buttons in the form.
- To associate the submit button with a behavior, start by selecting the button.
- Choose a browser version in the **Behaviors** palette.
- Click the button to add a behavior and choose **Set Text - Set Text of Text Field**.
- Choose the named field that will contain your text from the **Text Field** pop-up menu.
- Type the text in the **New Text** box.
- Click **OK**.
- Choose an event, **onMouseDown** if the text is to appear before the form is sent, which happens **onClick**.

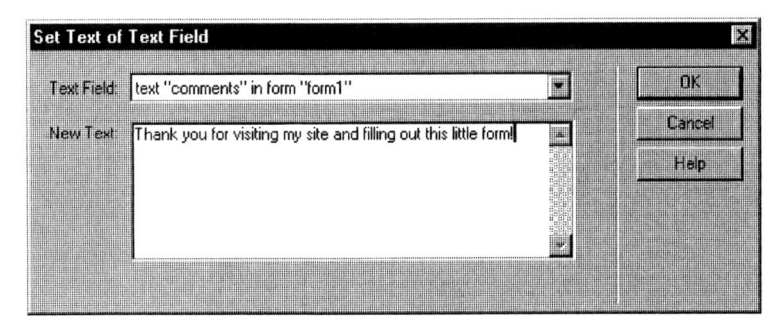

The user must not be able to enter anything in the comments field, so you need to deactivate it.

- To deactivate the comments field, select it, press F10 to see the source code, and add the disabled attribute:

```
<textarea name="comments" cols="40" rows="3" disabled></textarea>
```

©Editions ENI - All rights reserved

- Test the behavior by saving the document then previewing it in a browser.

    *In this example the user enters information into the form, and when he/she clicks the **Submit** button, without releasing the mouse button, the comment appears (in grey because the text box is disabled). As soon as the user releases the mouse button the form is subject to the script that manages it.*

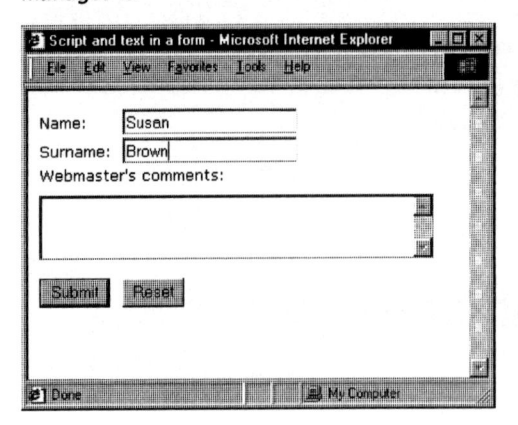

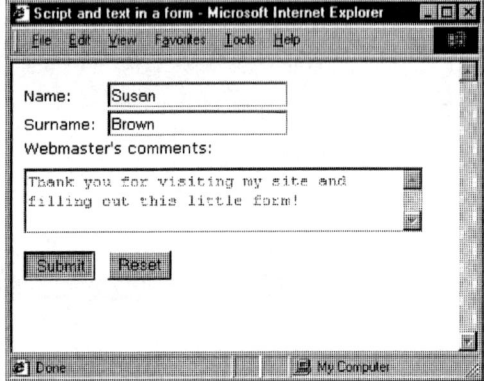

Placing text on the status bar

You can choose to display a message on the status bar, perhaps in order to give more information about a link. You can also include JavaScript functions.

- Select a hyperlink.
- Choose a browser version in the **Behaviors** palette.
- Click the [+] button to add a behavior and choose **Set Text - Set Text of Status Bar**. 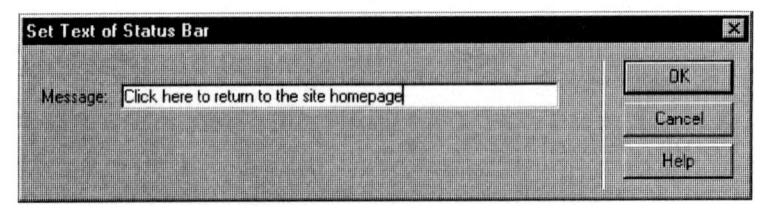
- Type the appropriate text in the **Message** text box.
- Click **OK**.
- Leave **onMouseOver** as the event.

⊡ Test this behavior by saving your page then previewing it in a browser.

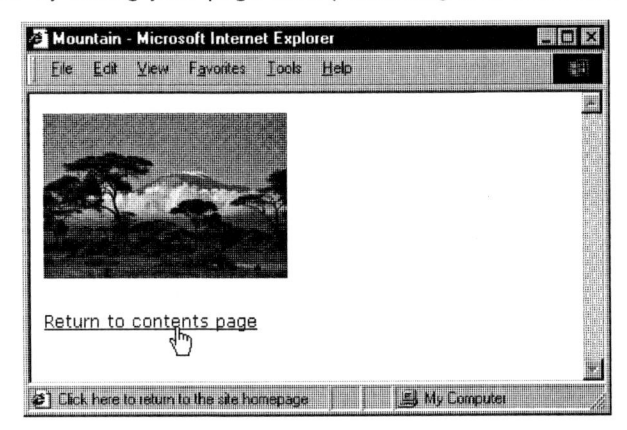

The text appears on the status bar.

Checking plugins

When you create a standard Web page you use HTML and Script. These are the standard elements that browsers should recognise and interpret. However, if you insert movies, sounds, animations etc you will need to add a plugin to the browser so that it can interpret these elements.

Not all Internet users have all the existing plugins. You will need to remember to place some script in your page that will check whether the user has the plugin required to see your page.

This script should ideally run when the page is loaded.

⊡ Select the `<body>` tag on the status bar.

⊡ Choose the relevant browser version in the **Behaviors** palette.

⊡ Click the ⊞ button to add a behavior and choose **Check Plugin**.

©Editions ENI - All rights reserved

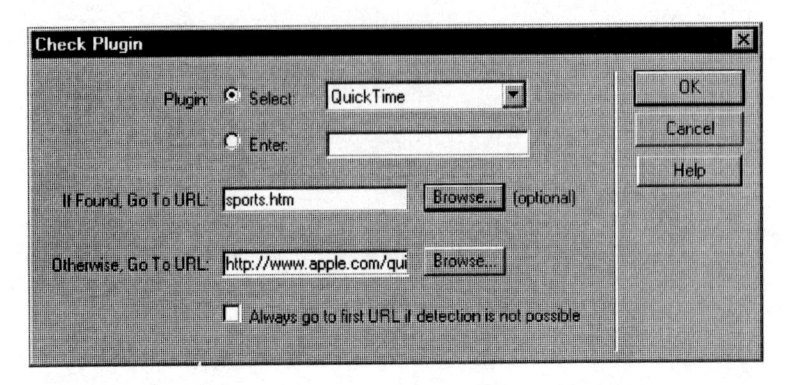

Dreamweaver 3
Behaviors

- Under **Plugin** choose the plugin you want to check for in the pop-up menu. If you do not find it, type its name in the **Enter** text box.
- In the **If Found, Go To URL** box, indicate the page that should be loaded if the user has the plugin, or click **Browse** to select the file in your site folder.
- In the **Otherwise, Go To URL** box, indicate the page that is to be loaded if the user does not have the relevant plugin, or click the **Browse** button to select the page.

    If you want to use a page from another site, you should give the full URL: http://www.whatever.org/folder.

- The **Always go to first URL if detection is not possible** option tells the browser what to do if it cannot check for the plugin. The user is generally sent to the home page of the plugin developer so that they can download it.

    The **onLoad** event is selected in the **Behaviors** palette:

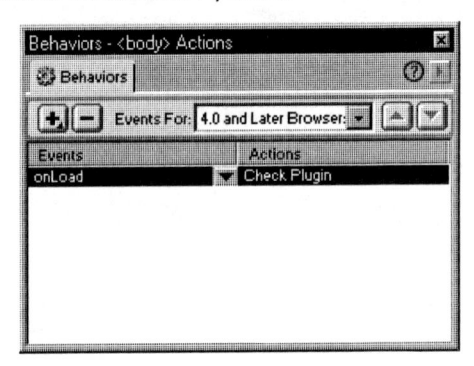

©Editions ENI - All rights reserved

Behaviors

- Test the behavior by saving the document then previewing it in a browser.

Checking the browser

When you want to use recent technology in your pages such as CSS-1, CSS-P, DHMTL, Script, etc, you should always remember that not all users have the latest version of browsers. It may be useful (though incredibly time-consuming) to create pages that are optimised for different browser versions.

If you choose to do this, you can insert a behavior to detect which browser a user has. Following the result, the page optimised for the user's browser will be loaded.

This behavior is best used if it runs when the page is loaded.

- Select the <body> tag on the status bar.
- Choose the correct browser version in the **Behaviors** palette.
- Click the ⊕ button to add a behavior and choose **Check Browser**.

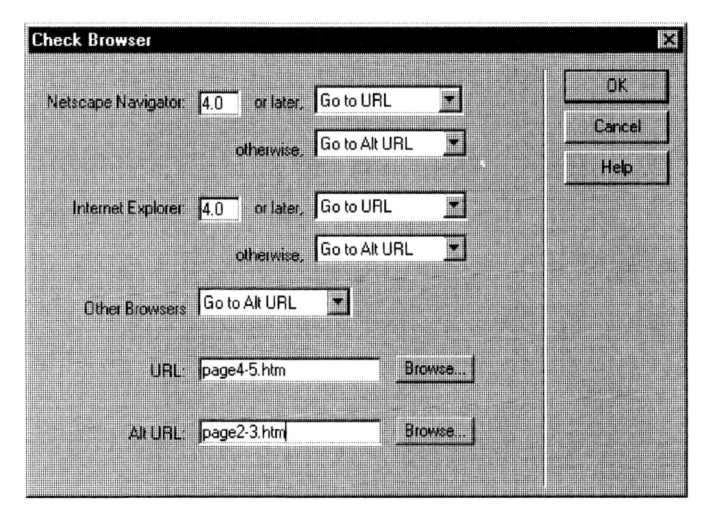

- Under **Netscape Navigator: or later**, indicate the version you want to check for.
- Use the pop-up menu on the right to indicate which page is to be loaded if the specified version is detected or not:

   Go to URL   opens the page indicated in the **URL** box.
   Stay on this Page leaves the current page open.
   Go to Alt URL   opens the page indicated in the **Alt URL** box.

©Editions ENI - All rights reserved

Dreamweaver 3
Behaviors

- Do the same for Microsoft **Internet Explorer**.
- For other browsers, use the **Other Browsers** pop-up menu.
- Click **OK**.

The **onLoad** event is selected in the **Behaviors** palette:

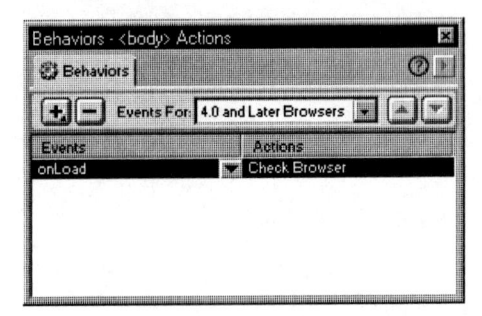

- Test the behavior by saving your document and previewing it in a browser.

Other behaviors

Other behaviors are explained in the chapters that correspond to the elements to which they are linked:

Behavior	See chapter
Going to several frames	Framesets
Loading frame contents	Framesets
Loading layer contents	Layers
Swapping images	Images
Preloading images	Images
Playing a sound	Inserting objects
Controlling Flash or Shockwave movies	Inserting objects
Showing and hiding layers	Layers
Moving layers	Layers
Managing timelines	Layers

©Editions ENI - All rights reserved

Behaviors

Downloading more behaviors

You can also go to the Macromedia® site to download more behaviors, most of which are free.

- Click the [+] button in the **Behaviors** palette to add a behavior and choose to **Get More Behaviors**.

    URL: http://dynamic.macromedia.com/bin/MM/exchange/dreamweaver/main.jsp

- Once you have downloaded the behaviors, install them to make them available in the **Behaviors** palette.

Dreamweaver 3
Optimising HTML code

Why optimise code?

Macromedia® Dreamweaver is a visual Web site creation application, which means that you do not need to know HTML to be able to create pages in a Web site. However, it is sometimes necessary to change the source code in order to optimise the page, such as: adding an HTML element rapidly, changing an attribute, finding an HTML element with a particular attribute in order to replace it with another in a page or throughout the whole site, deleting needless or redundant HTML elements, or adding standard HTML elements that are not available in Dreamweaver.

Furthermore, you might need to manage data from other applications, in which case you will need to choose how Dreamweaver should behave when you open these documents.

Setting HTML code parameters

Customising the HTML code font

You can change the font and size of the characters used in the HTML source code inspector window.

- **Edit - Preferences - Fonts/Encoding** category
- Choose the character font and size you want to use when you look at the HTML source code in the **HTML Inspector** and **Size** pop-up menus.

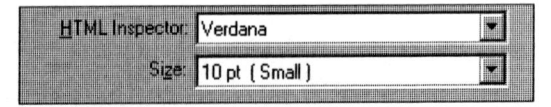

Customising the HTML code colours

You can change the colours of the HTML source code in order to group similar HTML elements by colour.

- **Edit - Preferences - HTML Colors** category

© Editions ENI - All rights reserved

Optimising HTML code

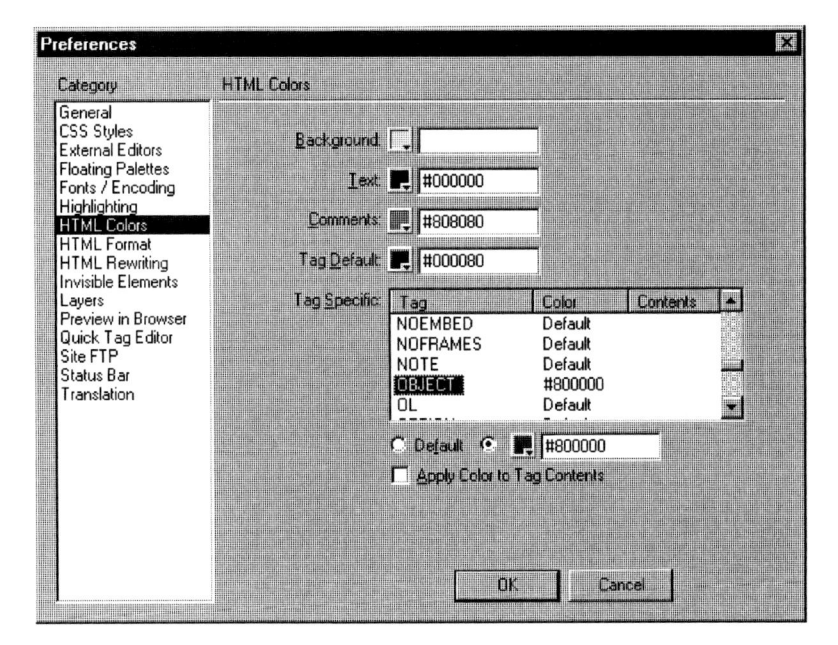

- The **Background** option is for changing the background colour of the window when you are entering code.
- The **Text** option specifies the colour of the text between tags.

    Example:

    ```
    <td>My text</td>
    ```

    Only the words "My text" will be in the chosen colour, not the `<td>` *and* `</td>` *tags.*

- The **Tag Default** option defines the default colour of all HTML elements visible in the source code, except comments and specific tags.
- The **Comments** option defines the colour of comments tags and their content.

    Example of a comment:

    ```
    <!This is the beginning of my report-->
    ```

- The **Tag Specific** options are for customising the colour of some HTML elements such as: open and close tag (not the contents). Select one or more tags (using the ⌘ (Macintosh) or Ctrl (Windows) key), activate the option in front of the color picker and choose a colour. If you want the contents of the HTML element to be the same colour, activate the **Apply Color to Tag Contents** option.

©Editions ENI - All rights reserved

Dreamweaver 3
2-6-6 Optimising HTML code

Customising the HTML code format

You can change the appearance of the HTML source code so that the lines of code are better structured.

◘ **Edit - Preferences - HTML Format** category

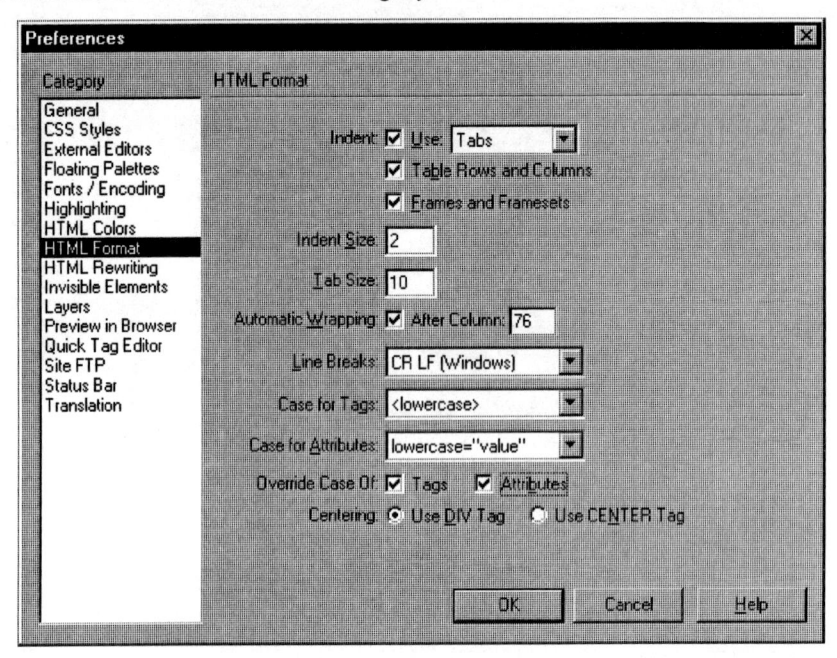

◘ Activate the **Indent** option to activate the indentation of the INDENT tags in the SourceFormat.txt file in the Configuration folder of the Dreamweaver folder.

Extract of this file:

```
<address break="1,0,0,1">
<applet break="0,1,1,0" indent>
<base break="1,0,0,1">
<blockquote break="1,0,0,1" indent>
<body break="1,1,1,1">
<br break="0,0,0,1">
```

The `<applet>` and `<blockquote>` elements are indented in the source code inspector window.

◘ The **Use** option indicates the sort of indent you want to use: **Tabs** or **Spaces**.

©Editions ENI - All rights reserved

Optimising HTML code

- Activate the **Table Rows and Columns** option to apply this indentation to the `<tr>` and `<td>` elements in tables and the **Frames and Framesets** option to apply it to nested `<frame>` and `<frameset>` elements.
- Use the **Indent Size** text box to indicate the size of the indent chosen in **Indent**. If the value is **4** and the indents are **Tabs**, the indent will be 4 tabs. Indicate the size of the tabs in the **Tab Size** text box.

   *The **Tab Size** must be a multiple of the **Indent Size**.*
- The **Automatic Wrapping After Column** option inserts a carriage return when the line gets to the specified number of characters, but only if this has no bearing on the appearance of the document.

   This is not the same thing as the **Wrap** option in the HTML Source inspector window, which simply places the code on the next line without inserting a carriage return character.
- Use the **Line Breaks** pop-up menu to tell the FTP server on which your site is stored which character is used for line breaks.
- The **Case for Tags** menu indicates whether you want the names of tags to be in `<UPPERCASE>` or `<lowercase>`
- In the **Case for Attributes** menu you can indicate whether the names of attributes should be in **UPPERCASE="value"** or **lowercase="value"**.
- The **Override Case Of Tags** and **Attributes** options automatically convert the case of tags and attributes in HTML documents that you open to the preferences you have specified.

   Examples:

   ```
   <p align="center">paragraph text</p>
   ```

   or

   ```
   <P ALIGN="CENTER">paragraph text</P>
   ```
- The **Centering** options are for indicating which HTML element you want to use to centre text or an image that is not included in a paragraph `<p>`: the `<DIV>` element or `<CENTER>` (which has been declared obsolete by W3C).

   Examples:

   ```
   <div align="center">my text</div>
   ```

© Editions ENI - All rights reserved

Dreamweaver 3
Optimising HTML code

or

```
<center>my text</center>
```

> These preferences, which are stored in the SourceFormat.txt file, are applied only to the documents created after you define them. To apply the new settings to existing documents, you need to open the document and use **Commands - Apply Source Formatting**.

Visualising code in the page

Using the status bar

You can use the status bar to see and control the HTML elements used for the formatting of your page. In the left of the status bar the HTML code for the element selected in the page is always visible.

- First make sure that you can see the status bar: **View - Status Bar**.
- Select an element in your page.

    Example of an image in a table:

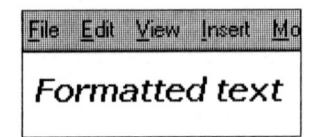

    `<body> <table> <tr> <td> <img>`

    The selected image is `<img>`.
    It is in a cell: `<td>`
    In a row: `<tr>`
    In a table: `<table>`.

Selecting tags

To select the tag of the selected element or formatting in your page you can use the status bar, which contains all the tags in use. Below is an example of formatted text:

Formatted text

- And its appearance on the status bar:

    `<body> <p> <font> <b> <i>`

©Editions ENI - All rights reserved

Optimising HTML code

The text is in italics: `<i>`
It is in bold: `<b>`
In a paragraph: `<p>`
The paragraph is in the body of the page: `<body>`.

- Select the paragraph by clicking the `<p>` tag.

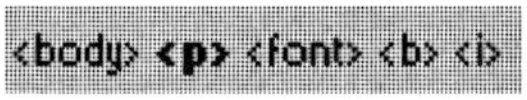

`<body> <p> <font> <b> <i>`

- You can also follow the nesting of the tags: select the parent or child tag. To select the lowest level tag when the insertion point is in the text use **Edit - Select Parent Tag**.

    Dreamweaver selects the most nested tag, which is the italics here. The text is selected too:

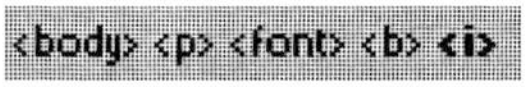

    `<body> <p> <font> <b> <i>`

- If you want to move up in the nesting use **Edit - Select Parent Tag**.

    Dreamweaver selects the next tag up in the nesting, the bold tag:

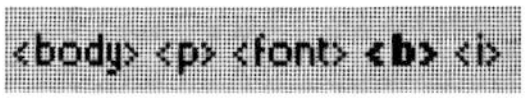

    `<body> <p> <font> <b> <i>`

    And so on...

- If you are in the paragraph level `<p>` and you want to go down the tag nesting, use **Edit - Select Child**.

    Dreamweaver selects the next tag down the nesting:

    `<body> <p> <font> <b> <i>`

    *This selection technique is linked to the **Quick Tag Editor** (see the paragraph below), and is an extremely efficient way of editing the HTML code directly in the page.*

Changing the source code

Using the HTML source inspector

You can look at and change the source code of your page whenever you want.

- **Window - HTML Source**   F10

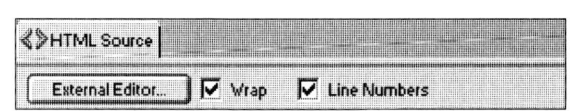

©Editions ENI - All rights reserved

Optimising HTML code

- The **Wrap** option will send the source code to the next line if the window is not wide enough to see all the code on one line.
- The **Line Numbers** option shows the number of each line of source code.
- Make the necessary changes to the HTML code.
- Press F10 to return to the document.

Using the Quick Tag Editor

If you are keen on code, you can use the **Quick Tag Editor** *to check, add, edit and delete HTML elements quickly, all in the page creation window.*

This is a very useful tool for those who have a good knowledge of HTML and want to change the code quickly, without having to open the source code inspector window and find the element to be changed.

- To insert an HTML element, place the insertion point in the appropriate place.
- Click the **Quick Tag Editor** button on the Property inspector or press ⌘ T (Macintosh) or Ctrl T (Windows).

  The **Quick Tag Editor** window opens and contains the text **Insert HTML**.

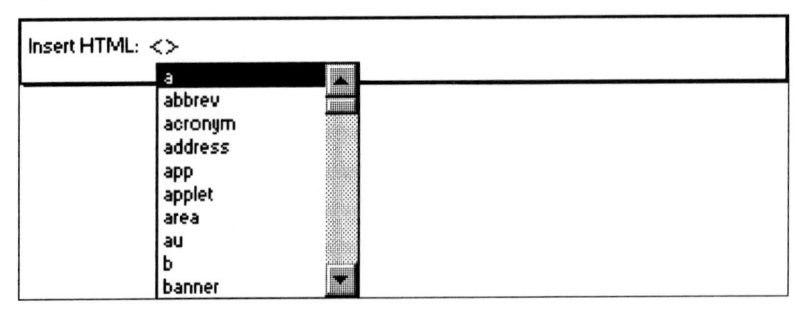

  ```
  Insert HTML: < >
              a
              abbrev
              acronym
              address
              app
              applet
              area
              au
              b
              banner
  ```

- Select the element you want to insert by scrolling down or type the first letter of the element.

  The **Quick Tag Editor** *selects the first element in the list that starts with that letter.*

- Press ↵ to accept the HTML element and press ↵ again to confirm.

© Editions ENI - All rights reserved

Optimising HTML code

*For example: Dreamweaver does not have the element <sup>, which formats a character in superscript, in any of its menus. If you want to type text such as 10m2 you can use the **Quick Tag Editor**.*

- Type 10m2.
  Select only the number 2.
  Click the **Quick Tag Editor** icon to activate it, or use the keyboard shortcut.
  When the list of tags appears, type s on the keyboard. The **Quick Tag Editor** selects the first tag that starts with "s" (or you can type su). Now press the ↓ key to scroll down the list until the <sup> tag is selected.

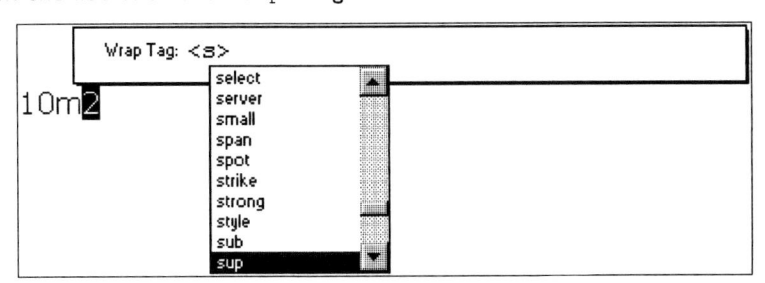

  Press ↵ to confirm the choice of tag.
  Press ↵ to apply the element.
  Preview the page in a browser because this W3C standard element is not displayed in Dreamweaver.

- To edit an HTML element, select the object in question (such as text, an image or a table).

- Click the **Quick Tag Editor** button on the Property inspector.

  or press ⌘ T (Macintosh) or Ctrl T (Windows).

  or use the context menu and choose **Edit Tag**.

  *The **Quick Tag Editor** window opens with the words **Edit Tag**.*

- Change the element's attributes.

  Use the ↹ key to select attributes and values one after the other.

- Press ↵ to confirm the changes.

  For example: you have created a table with simple attributes and you want to change the formatting quickly but the Property inspector is not open.

- Select your table.

  Activate the **Quick Tag Editor**.

©Editions ENI - All rights reserved

Dreamweaver 3
2-7-2 Optimising HTML code

```
Edit Tag: <table width="240" border="1"
          cellspacing="0" cellpadding="0">
```

South	West	East
54	87	65
32	54	21

The value 240 *of the attribute* width *(the first one) is selected.*

If you want to change the thickness of the table's border, press ⏎ twice to select the value of the **border** attribute.
Type the new value and confirm with ⏎.

Adding an extra HTML attribute

You can use the same principle to add an extra HTML attribute.

For example: using the previous example, you can centre the table in the page by using the align="center" *attribute.*

→ Select the table.

Activate the **Quick Tag Editor**.

Use the ⇥ key to move to the end of the opening tag and type a space then the letter a just before the > symbol.

The list of attributes appears, and the align *attribute is selected (as it is the first in the list).*

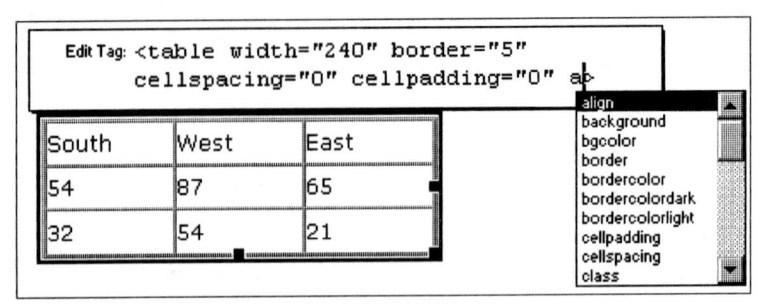

```
Edit Tag: <table width="240" border="5"
          cellspacing="0" cellpadding="0" a>
```

South	West	East
54	87	65
32	54	21

```
align
background
bgcolor
border
bordercolor
bordercolordark
bordercolorlight
cellpadding
cellspacing
class
```

Press ⏎ to confirm.

A list of attributes for this attribute appears immediately. In this case left, center *or* right.

©Editions ENI - All rights reserved

Optimising HTML code

Type the letter **c** for center or use the ⬇ key.

Confirm by pressing ⏎ twice.

⇨ If you want to add an extra HTML element, select the object you want to change (such as text, an image or a table) and click the **Quick Tag Editor** button in the Property inspector

or press ⌘ **T** (Macintosh) or Ctrl **T** (Windows).

*The **Quick Tag Editor** window opens with the words **Wrap Tag**.*

Add any extra HTML elements.

Press ⏎ to confirm the change.

Example:

⇨ Select a word that is already formatted, for example the word "text" in italics.

Activate the **Quick Tag Editor**.

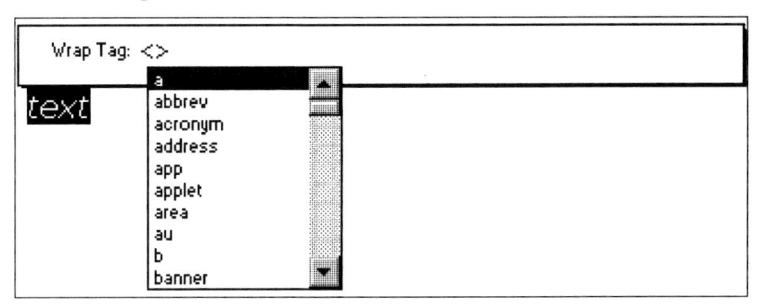

Type the letter **u** to add the element <u>, which will underline the text.

Press ⏎ twice to confirm.

⇨ To go from one mode (**Insert HTML, Edit Tag** and **Wrap Tag**) to another while the **Quick Tag Editor** is active press ⌘ **T** (Macintosh) or Ctrl **T** (Windows) once.

©Editions ENI - All rights reserved

Optimising HTML code

- To delete an HTML element select the object you want to edit (such as text, an image or a table).
- Activate the HTML element's context menu in the status bar and choose **Remove Tag**.

    For example: take the text from the previous example, which is in italics and underlined, and delete one of the attributes rapidly.

- Click in the word.

    Activate the context menu on the status bar for the <u> tag: `<body> <p> <i> <u>`.

    Choose **Remove Tag** in the context menu.

- You can set the preferences in **Edit - Preferences - Quick Tag Editor** category.

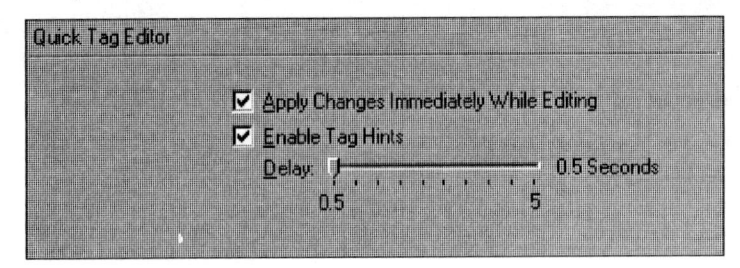

- Use the **Apply Changes Immediately While Editing** option if you want to see the changes in the document immediately.
- The **Enable Tag Hints** option is for displaying (or not) a list of HTML elements when you type code.
- Drag the **Delay** cursor to define the time (in seconds) before the list of HTML elements should appear.

Using a different application

You can also read and edit your source code in an external HTML editor. Macromedia Dreamweaver is supplied with Allaire HomeSite (Windows) and BareBones BBEdit (Macintosh).

- After you have installed the application on your computer:
- **Edit - Preferences - External Editors** category

Optimising HTML code

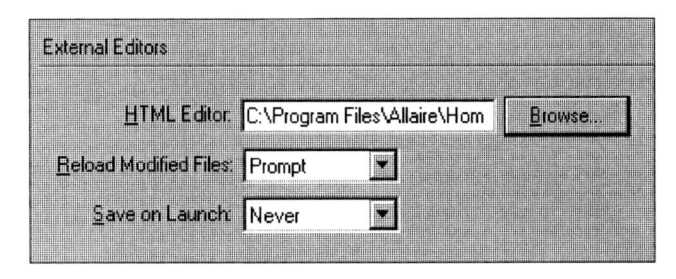

- Click the **Browse** button under **HTML Editor** to choose the software you want to use.

  When you want to use both applications you need to tell Dreamweaver whether to save the document when the external editor is opened.

- Use the **Reload Modified Files** pop-up menu to indicate what should happen when the source code of a page open in Dreamweaver has been modified outside of Dreamweaver, in an external editor:

Always	Dreamweaver will save the changes made in the external editor immediately.
Never	the changes made in the external editor will not be taken into account in the document.
Prompt	you can choose (**Yes** or **No**) whether to reload the document that has been edited in an external editor.

- Use the **Save on Launch** pop-up menu to choose what Dreamweaver should do when you want to open an external editor without having saved the current document:

Always	the document edited in Dreamweaver will be saved immediately.
Never	the document edited in Dreamweaver will not be saved.
Prompt	you can choose (**Yes** or **No**) whether you want to save the document edited in Dreamweaver.

- To start the external HTML editor use **Edit - Launch External Editor**.

Visualising errors

If you make an invalid change to the HTML code, Dreamweaver will highlight the incorrect code in yellow. For example, here the closing tag </i> has been added to the source code inspector, but without the opening tag <i>. When you return to the page, the error is detected.

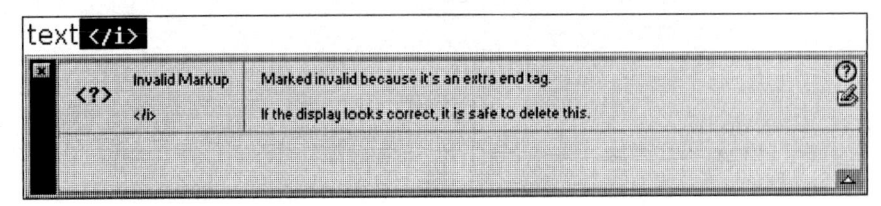

Finding and replacing HTML

You can look for a sequence of HTML code and replace it with another in the active document, in a folder, or in the whole site.

Finding HTML code

Here you need to use a broad definition of the term "HTML code". It may be an element of the language HTML or text you have typed, which is the content of an HTML element.

- **Edit - Find**

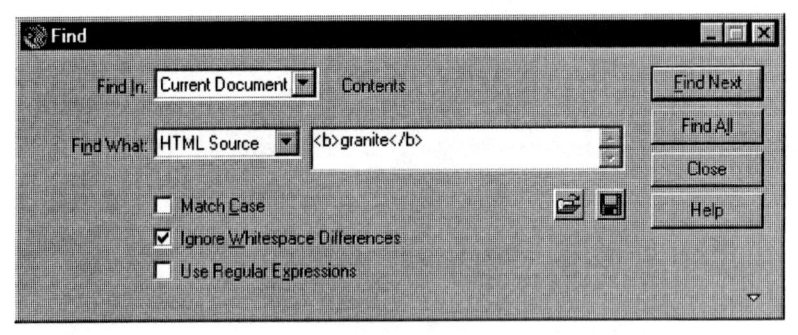

- Choose where you want to search for the element in the **Find In** pop-up menu:

    Current Document: if you want to search only the active document.

    Current Site: to search all the files in the site.

    Folder: to search in a folder, which you can select on the right.

- Choose **HTML Source** in the **Find What** pop-up menu and, to the right, type the code you are looking for. This can be HTML code or everyday text (thus the content of an HTML element).

©Editions ENI - All rights reserved

Optimising HTML code

- Define the search options:

    Match Case: if you want to distinguish between upper and lowercase characters in the text you have typed and the text in the document.

    Ignore Whitespace Differences: to ignore any extra whitespaces typed in the text box.

    Use Regular Expressions: if you want to use wildcard characters when searching for unknown characters in a word, or if you want to find the beginning of a word, for example (see Dreamweaver help for all the wildcard characters).

- Click the ![] button if you want to save the search in a .dwq file that will be stored in the Queries folder of the Dreamweaver folder.

    Use the ![] button to open a search saved previously.

- Click **Find Next** to find the occurrences, one after the other.

    Each occurrence is selected in the HTML source code window.

- Click the **Find All** button to find all the occurrences at once: the result will appear in the lower part of the search window.

    In this example, all the occurrences of the word "granite", in bold (<b> element) have been searched for:

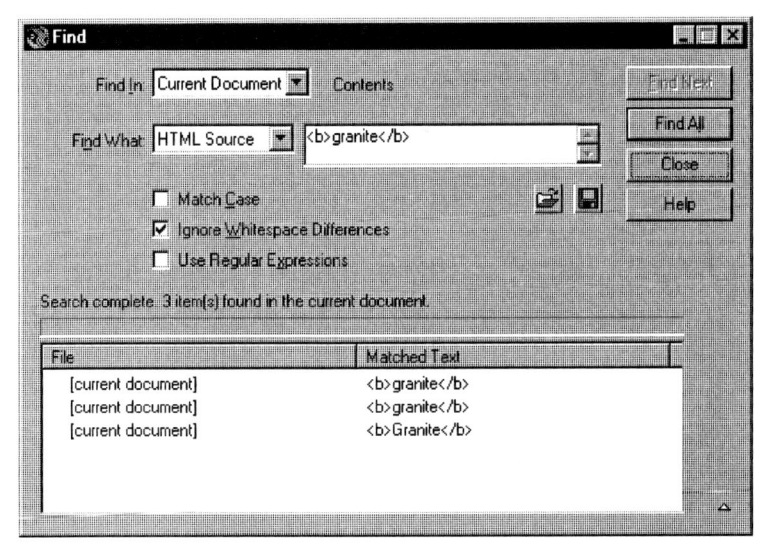

©Editions ENI - All rights reserved

Dreamweaver 3
Optimising HTML code

⇨ To go to an occurrence double-click it in the **Find** window, and it is selected in the source code of the document.

Finding an HTML tag

Searching for a tag allows you to make a more precise search.

⇨ **Edit - Find**

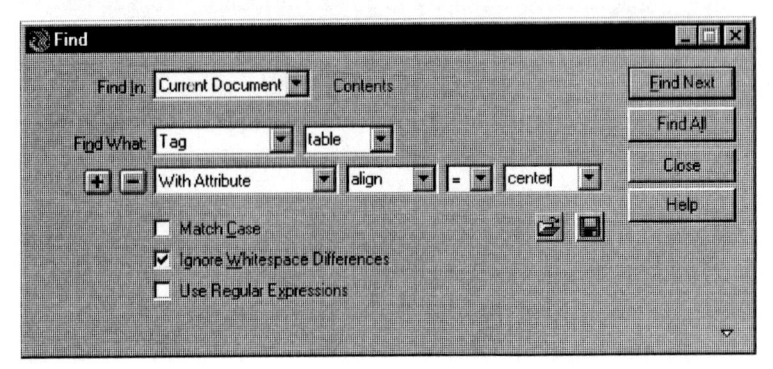

⇨ Choose where you want to search in the **Find In** pop-up menu:

Current Document: to search only in the open document.

Current Site: to search all the files in the site.

Folder: to search the folder you can select on the right.

⇨ Select **Tag** in the **Find What** pop-up menu. Use the pop-up menu on the right to select or type the tag you want to find.

⇨ Choose an attribute option:

With Attribute: to specify the attribute you want find with the tag. On the right you can select the type of attribute you want to find (the list is updated according to the choice of tag), and the comparison criterion (=, <, > or !=) then the value of the attribute you want to find.

Without Attribute: you can specify the attribute that should not be present in the code you are finding. Select the attribute that is not to be present on the right.

Containing: indicates that the text or tag you want to find is included in another tag. Type the text you want to find or choose the included tag on the right.

Example:

```
<i><font color="red">text</font></i>
```

The `<font>` *tag is included in* `<i>`.

©Editions ENI - All rights reserved

Optimising HTML code

Not Containing: uses the same principle, but excludes tags or text.

Inside Tag: to indicate inside which tag the tag you want to find should be. Select the tag that includes the searched tag from the menus on the right.

Not Inside Tag: indicates the tag inside which the one you want to find will not be. Select the tag that does not include the searched tag on the right.

- Click the ➕ and ➖ buttons to add or remove search options.
- Start searching by clicking the **Find Next** or **Find All** buttons, as shown previously.

Replacing HTML code

You can use the same principle to find HTML code and replace it with some different HTML code.

- **Edit - Replace**
- Choose the search area in the **Find In** pop-up menu.
- Choose **HTML Source** in the **Find What** pop-up menu and type the code you want to find in the box on the right.
- Type the replacement code in the **Replace With** text box.

The other options are the same as those examined above.

- Click the **Find Next** button to find the first occurrence of the code you are looking for.

The code is selected in the HTML source inspector.

- Click:

Replace	to replace the code found with the specified code.
Find All	to find all the occurrences of the code you are looking for.
Replace All	to replace all the occurrences of the code with the specified replacement code.

For example, you might have created a button called green.gif in your Web site. Unfortunately it is not appropriate and you need to replace it with a different button called blue.gif. You can find all the occurrences of the green button and replace them with the blue button.

- **Edit - Replace**

© Editions ENI - All rights reserved

Dreamweaver 3
Optimising HTML code

Indicate the different parameters:

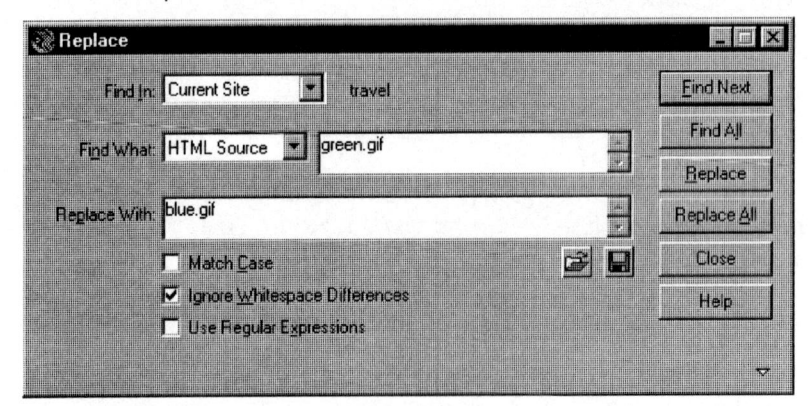

Click **Replace All** (as you are 100% sure that is what you want to do).

Dreamweaver tells you that you cannot undo this action in those documents that are not open, then shows the result of the operation.

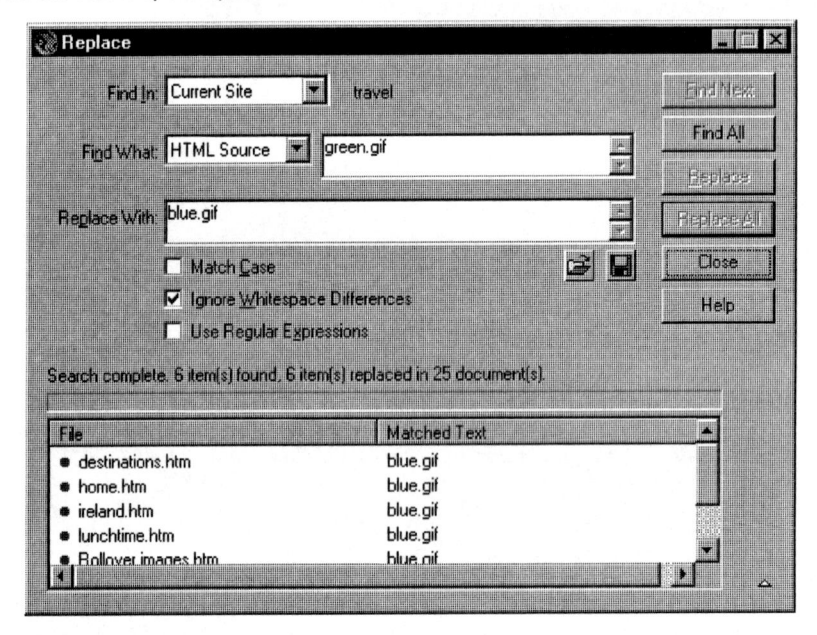

Optimising HTML code 2-8-1

Replacing an HTML tag

In this type of search you are working with the opening tag of an HTML element. This means that your searches and replacements can be very precise.

- **Edit - Replace**
- Specify the search area in the **Find In** pop-up menu.
- Choose **Tag** in the **Find What** menu and select or type the name of the tag on the right. Next choose the tag's attributes.
- Under **Action**, choose the action to be assigned from the pop-up menu.

Example: you have aligned the paragraphs on the left in a document:

```
<p align="left">...</p>
```

and you want to apply a justified alignment:

```
<p align="justify">...</p>
```

All you need to do is search for all the paragraphs in the current document that contain the attribute `align` with the value `left` and replace this with `justify`.

- **Edit - Replace**

Indicate the different search criteria:

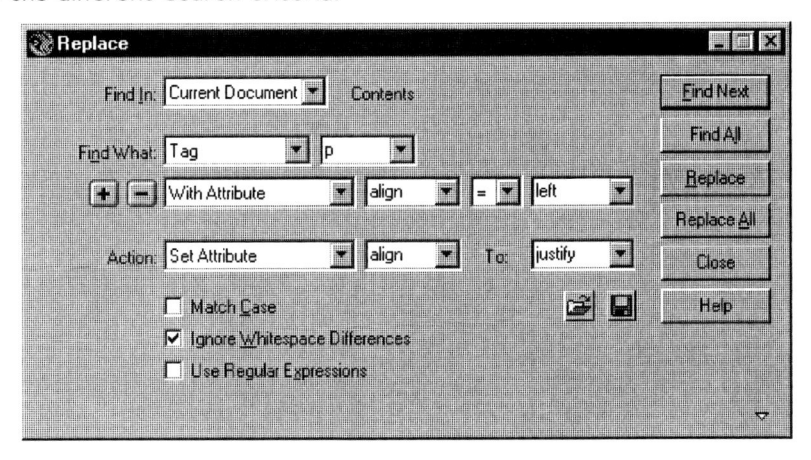

- Click **Replace All**.

Dreamweaver tells you how many occurrences have been replaced.

©Editions ENI - All rights reserved

Dreamweaver 3
Optimising HTML code

Cleaning up HTML source code

After having done a lot of work in a page, you might find that some of the changes made (such as additions or deletions) have generated unnecessary code, which increases the size of the page, and thus its download time in a browser. Equally, when you insert elements from other applications some comments from these programs might be inserted too.

- **Commands - Clean Up HTML**

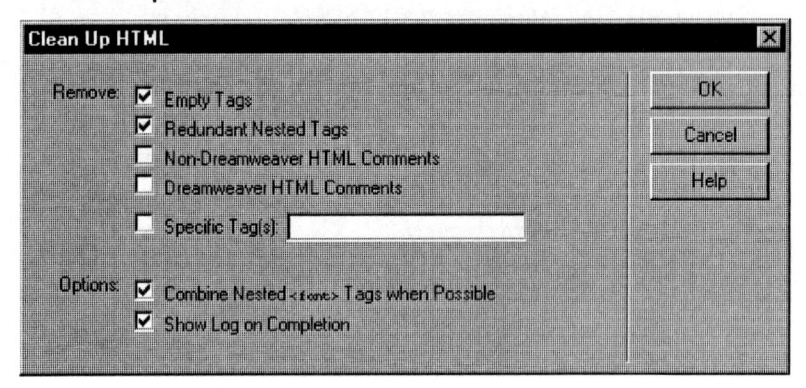

- The **Empty Tags** option will remove elements with no content.

    Example:

    ```
    <i></i>
    ```

    or

    ```
    <font size="3"></font>.
    ```

- The **Redundant Nested Tags** option will remove nested elements, which appear when they do not need to.

    Example:

    ```
    <i>This is an <i>example</i> of redundant elements.</i>
    ```

- The **Non-Dreamweaver HTML Comments** option will remove any comments inserted when you imported HTML code from another application.

©Editions ENI - All rights reserved

Optimising HTML code

This example is from the insertion of an image cut from Macromedia Fireworks:

```
<!-- Fireworks 3.0 Dreamweaver 3.0 target. Created Tue Mar 07 22:11:41 GMT+0100 (Paris, Madrid) 2000 -->.
```

Comments inserted by the Web site creator will not be deleted.

Example of a standard comment:

```
<!--Start of interactive section -->
```

⇨ Activate the **Dreamweaver HTML Comments** option if you want to delete comments inserted by Dreamweaver for the management of libraries, templates and tracing images. Be careful: in this case you will delete the dynamism of the updates of these libraries and templates.

Example of a comment inserted by Dreamweaver:

```
<!-- #BeginLibraryItem "/Library/Office.lbi" --> ...<!-- #EndLibraryItem -->
```

Comments inserted by the Web site creator will not be deleted.

⇨ Use the **Specific Tag(s)** option to delete the HTML elements specified in the text box. Separate the different opening tags with a comma.

Example: `blink,pre`.

⇨ The **Combine Nested <font> Tags when Possible** option will reduce text formatted using several `<font>` elements to just one `<font>` element.

Example:

```
<font color="#FF0000"><font size="2"></font></font>
```

The two <font> tags will be combined to achieve:

```
<font color="#FF0000" size="2">the text</font>
```

⇨ The **Show Log on Completion** option will display a dialog box that tells you the results of the operation.

⇨ Click **OK**.

Dreamweaver tells you about the changes made in the log.

Cleaning up HTML code from Microsoft Word

You can save Microsoft® Word documents in HTML format. However, the code generated by this often contains unnecessary elements, or elements that are specific to Microsoft®.

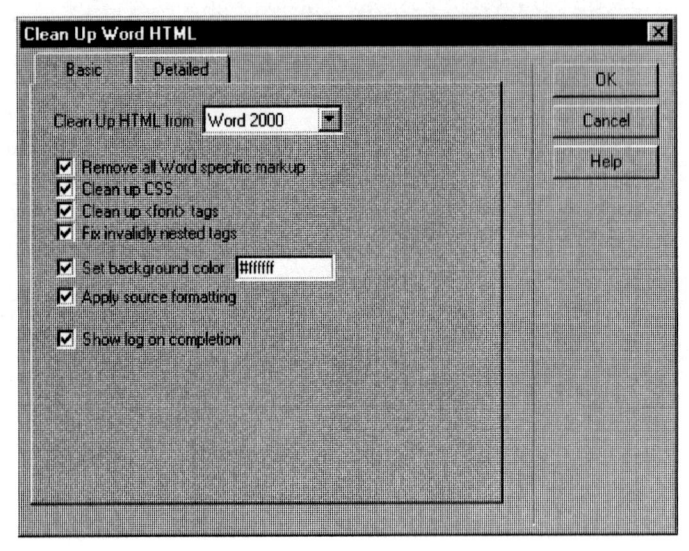

🡆 **Commands - Clean Up Word HTML**

🡆 Use the **Remove all Word specific markup** option to delete all the HTML and XML elements that are specific to Word.

🡆 The **Clean up CSS** option will delete all the Word specific style sheets from the header.

🡆 The **Clean up <font> tags** option will convert the default character size of the text to size 2.

🡆 Activate the **Fix invalidly nested tags** option to delete any `<font>` tags that are situated outside of paragraphs `<p>`.

🡆 Use the **Set background color** option to choose the colour you want (type the hexadecimal code) for the page background.

🡆 The **Apply source formatting** option is for applying the HTML code formatting preferences (**Preferences** dialog box, **HTML Format** category).

🡆 In the **Detailed** tab you can choose more detailed settings for cleaning, according to the version of Word in use: Word 2000 or Word 97/98.

Optimising HTML code

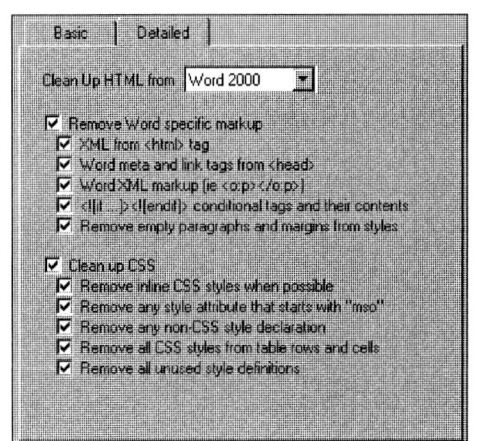

With Word 2000: *With Word 97/98:*

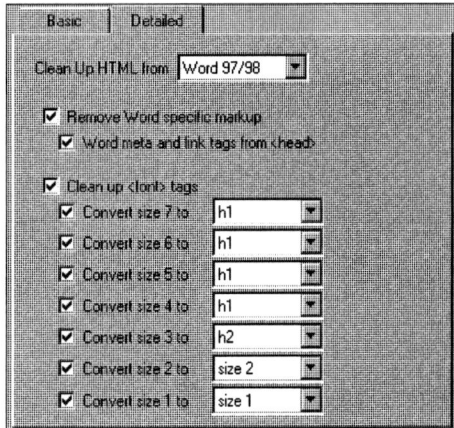

⇨ Click **OK**.

Setting the corrections

You can define what Dreamweaver should do when correcting the source code in an imported HTML page, when the page is opened.

⇨ **Edit - Preferences - HTML Rewriting** category

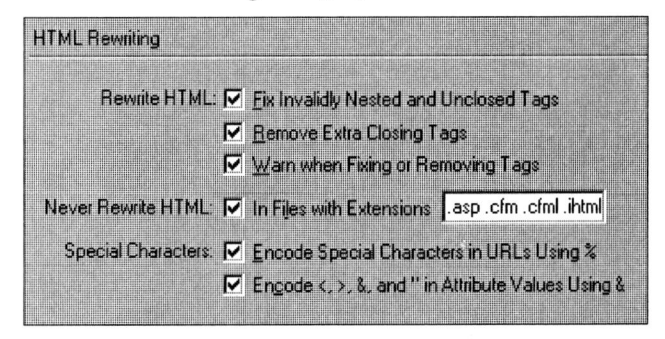

⇨ The **Fix Invalidly Nested and Unclosed Tags** option will correct any errors in the placing of HTML elements.

Example:

```
<p>  <b><u>word</b></u>  </p>
```

©Editions ENI - All rights reserved

Dreamweaver 3
Optimising HTML code

Will be changed to:

```
<p> <b><u>word</u></b> </p>
```

This option will also close any HTML elements with only an opening tag.

For example:

```
<p><b>word</p>
```

Will be changed to:

```
<p><b>word</b></p>
```

- The **Remove Extra Closing Tags** will delete any closing tags that do not have an opening tag.

    Example:

    ```
    <p>word</u></p>
    ```

    Will be changed to:

    ```
    <p>word</p>
    ```

- Use the **Warn when Fixing or Removing Tags** option if you want to see a dialog box containing the result of the corrections.
- The **Never Rewrite HTML: In Files with Extensions** option will prevent modification to the source code of files that carry the extension specified in the associated text box.
- The **Special Characters** options are for encoding certain characters that might be entered in the Property inspector in a particular way.

    Examples: in the URL box in your browser, for links between files, the space character is coded with the symbol %20. This makes it very easy to find your way around the source code if you are working on a project that contains several complicated pages.

©Editions ENI - All rights reserved

Optimising HTML code

Showing comments

You can use comments to insert a descriptive text into your HTML code that will not be visible in the browser window. This can be very useful for finding your way around the code when several people are working on a project that involves complex pages.

Making the comments visible

First make sure that comments are activated as invisible elements, and that you can see invisible elements in your page:

- **Edit - Preferences - Invisible Elements** category
- Activate the **Comments** option.
- Display invisible elements in your page: **View - Invisible Elements**.

Inserting a comment

- Click in the appropriate place.
- **Insert - Comment**

    or click the **Insert Comment** button from the **Invisibles** panel in the **Objects** palette.
- Type the text of your comment in the window.

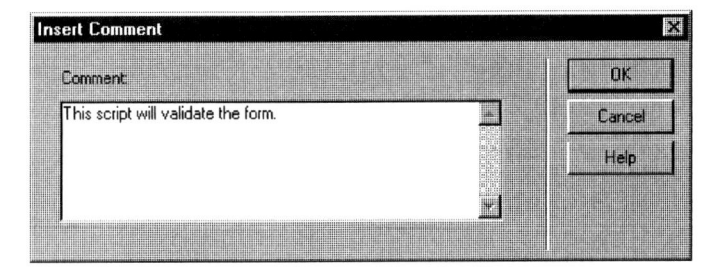

- Click **OK**.

    Your comment appears as the invisible element.

Editing a comment

- Select the comment's invisible element.

©Editions ENI - All rights reserved

Dreamweaver 3
2-8-8 Optimising HTML code

The comment text appears in the Property inspector:

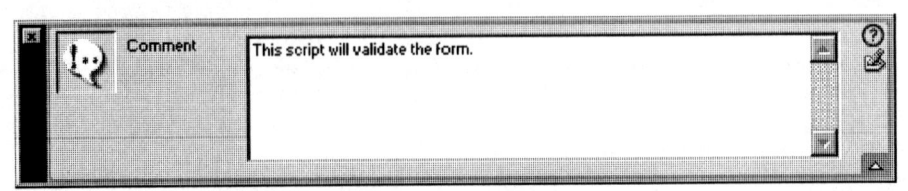

→ Make the necessary changes to the text.

Validating code for browsers

Principle

If you create a page or a site that uses recent developments (such as DHTML, CSS and multimedia), older generation browsers will not be able to display these elements correctly. It is thus necessary to check which elements are not recognised by which versions of the browsers.

Dreamweaver stores the compatibility information in .txt files situated in the BrowserProfiles subfolder of the Configuration folder in Dreamweaver. You can visit Macromedia's site to download browser profiles.

Converting style sheets

If you have used style sheets (CSS-1) for formatting and positioning sheets (CSS-P, layers in Dreamweaver) in your site these elements will be recognised only by version 4 or later browsers. If you want your pages to be visible in version 3 browsers you need to convert all the elements in your pages that use style sheets into HTML elements that are recognised by these browsers. Dreamweaver will transform layers into tables and formatting style sheets into simple HTML elements, wherever possible. You may find that some of your formatting is lost if there is no equivalent between the CSS-1 and HTML.

→ To convert a document use **File - Convert - 3.0 Browser Compatible**.

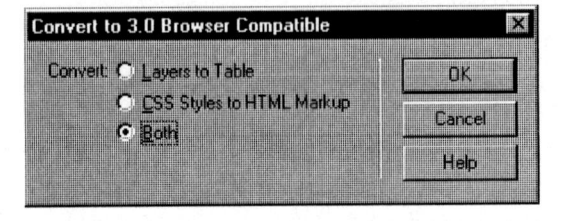

→ Choose the conversion option you want.

→ Click **OK**.

©Editions ENI - All rights reserved

Optimising HTML code

Checking compatibility

▭ In an open document or in the folder of the selected site use:
File - Check Target Browsers

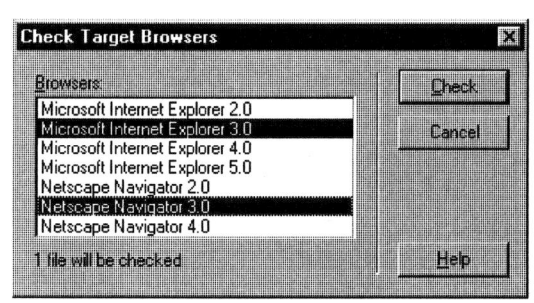

▭ Choose one or more browser profiles using the ⌘ (Macintosh) or Ctrl (Windows) key.

▭ Click **Check**.

A report is created in HTML format and opened in your browser:

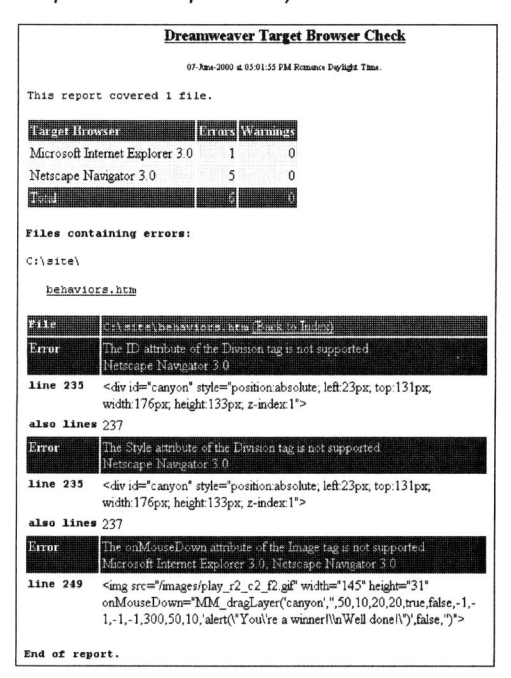

Make yourself known

Referencing a site

You can create a wonderful Web site, but this does not mean that anyone will know about it. When you publish a site you need to reference it so that people know about it. You have two possibilities for doing this: directories and search engines.

Directories are like Yellow Pages in the Web. The method they use for referencing and searching is based on filing sites according to their themes. Each topic contains sub-topics, which themselves contain sub-topics. When you reference your site, you will file it under the relevant sub-topics in this thematic filing system.

Search engines work slightly differently: you submit your site by giving its URL and the e-mail address of the Webmaster. When the search engine treats your submission, a "robot" accesses your site's server and will index a series of keywords in an enormous database. These databases link the indexed keywords with the sites that contain them.

The keywords that are indexed are often the page titles (`<title>` element), the most frequently used words in your site and those in the `<Meta>` tags, which are placed in the document header (`<head>` tag). These tags contain what is called meta-information.

Principle of `<meta>` tags

The `<meta>` tags in keywords (`keywords` attribute) enable you to insert a series of keywords into each page in your site in order to give an idea of the page contents, and so the site contents. These keywords are compared with the keywords typed by users of search engines when they carry out a search.

Description `<meta>` tags (`description` attribute) enable you to insert a brief description into each page in your site, which is often used as a summary in the search result pages of a search engine.

Furthermore, `<meta>` tags are "open", which means that you can create your own tags for use in very precise searches on an intranet, such as a search for authors' names or publication dates.

Publishing a site

Inserting meta-information

Inserting keywords

You can insert a different series of keywords in each page. If you do so, you will have a higher chance of discovery by Web users.

⊡ **Insert - Head - Keywords**

or click the **Insert Keywords** button on the **Head** panel of the **Objects** palette.

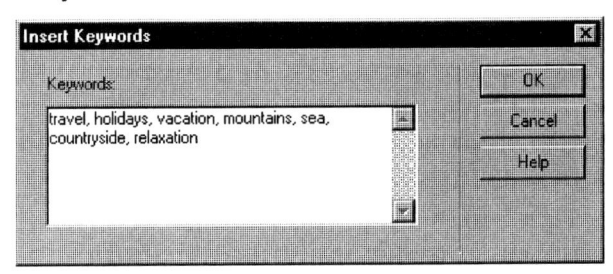

⊡ Type a dozen or so keywords in the **Keywords** text box, separating them with a comma.

⊡ To see and edit your keywords, show the header icon bar:

View - Head Content

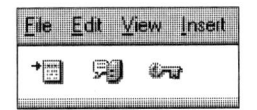

⊡ Click the keyword icon in this bar and use the Property inspector:

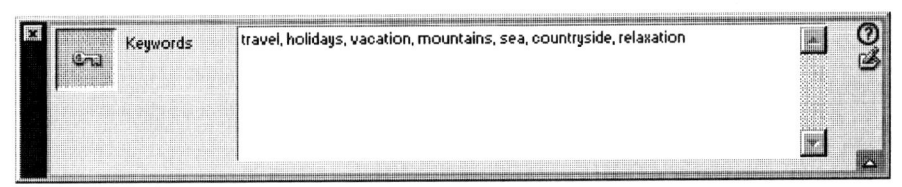

© Editions ENI - All rights reserved

Dreamweaver 3
2-9-2 Publishing a site

Inserting a description

- Insert a description in each page, as for keywords:

    Insert - Head - Description

    or click the **Insert Description** button on the **Head** panel of the **Objects** palette.

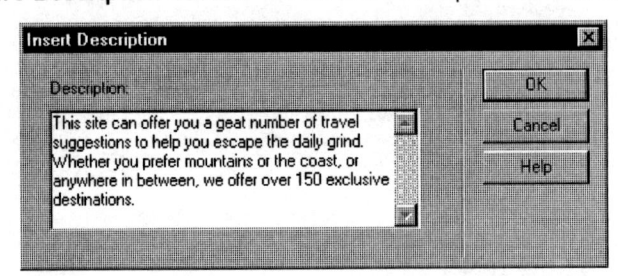

- Type a brief description of your page in the **Description** text box.

- To see and edit the description, click the icon on the header icon bar (use **View - Head Content** to see it) and use the Property inspector:

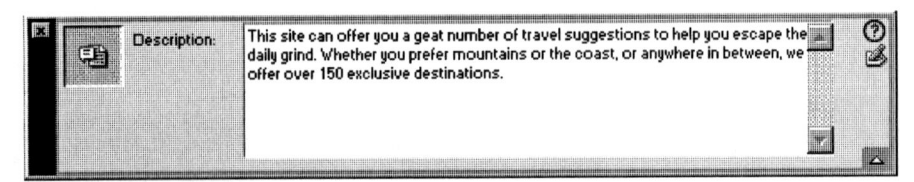

Inserting <meta> tags

Imagine that you work in a company that publishes all its internal documents on its intranet. Users can make use of a search engine to look for the authors of publications, the publication dates of documents, documents with a specific theme and so on.

- To create `<meta>` tags in a document: **Insert - Head - Meta**.

    or click the **Insert Meta** button in the **Head** panel of the **Objects** palette.

©Editions ENI - All rights reserved

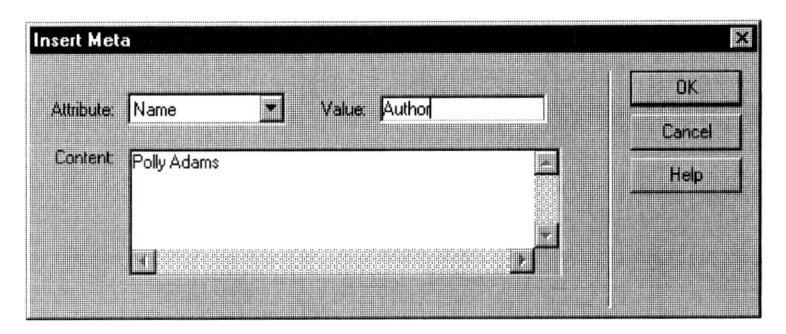

Publishing a site

- Choose **Name** in the **Attribute** pop-up menu.
- Type, for example, **Author** in the **Value** text box.
- Give the person's name in the **Content** text box.
- To see and edit your `<meta>` tag, click the icon on the header contents icon bar (**View - Head Content**) and use the Property inspector:

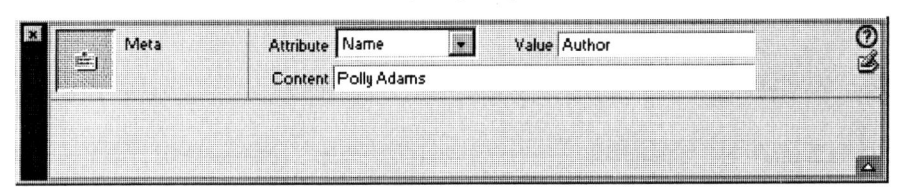

- Create a `<meta>` tag with the **Attribute** Name, Publication as the **Value** and July as the **Content**, which will allow users to search for publications according to their publication date.

In the header icon bar you will see as many icons as you have created Meta tags.

Inserting a refresh facility

If your site changes server, for any number of reasons, you can choose to send users from the old address to the new one automatically. Create a simple homepage on your old server, which contains a short introductory text. Add a refresh that transfers users to your new server after a few moments.

- In the homepage use **Insert - Head - Refresh**.

  or click the **Insert Refresh** button on the **Head** panel of the **Objects** palette.

©Editions ENI - All rights reserved

Dreamweaver 3
Publishing a site

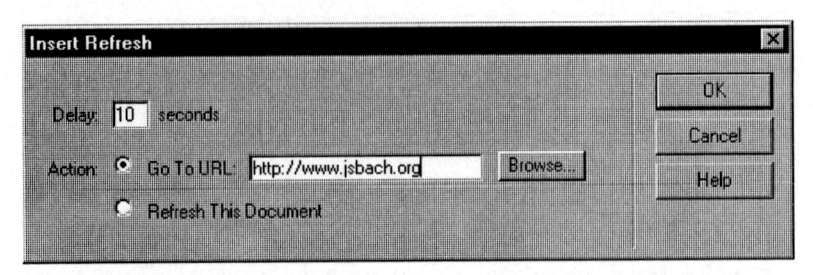

- Indicate the time that should pass before the page changes in the **Delay** text box.
- Choose an **Action**:

    Go To URL: to indicate the new address.

    Refresh This Document: simply reload the page.

- To see and edit the refresh, click the icon on the head content icon bar (**View - Head Content**) and use the Property inspector:

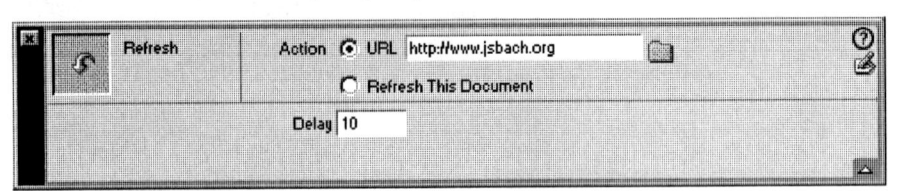

Inserting character encoding

By default, Dreamweaver inserts a `<meta>` *tag for information about the encoding used in a page, in each new document.*

- To see and edit this code, click the **Meta** tag icon on the head content icon bar (**View - Head Content**) and use the Property inspector:

- In the **Attribute** pop-up menu leave the **HTTP-equiv** choice, which allows information to be passed in HTTP response headers.
- In the **Value** text box indicate that you are giving information about the character set: **Content-Type**.

Publishing a site

- In the **Content** text box indicate the **text/HTML** style and the character encoding **charset=iso-8859-1**, for Latin type characters.

Information about links

Inserting a base for links

When you create links in your Web site, the browser can interpret them as absolute URLs by combining the relative URL given in the page and the indication in a reference base.

For example, you might indicate that the base's URL is http://www.site.org/folder. If the relative URL in a link is text.htm, the complete URL will be a concatenation of the two: http://www.site.org/folder/text.htm

- To insert a link base use **Insert - Head - Base**.

  or click the **Insert Base** button on the **Head** panel from the **Objects** palette.

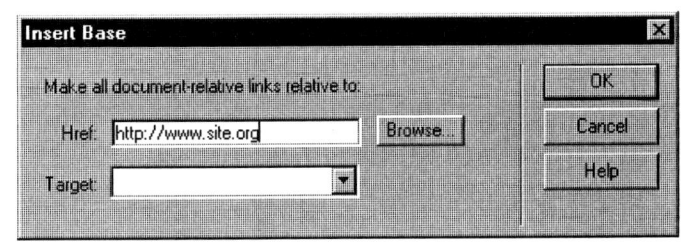

- Indicate the base's reference in the **Href** text box.
- If you are using a frameset indicate the target frame in the **Target** pop-up menu.
- To see and edit the base URL, click the **Base** icon on the header content bar (**View - Head Content**) and use the Property inspector:

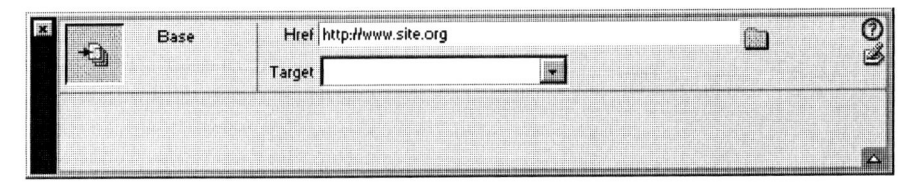

©Editions ENI - All rights reserved

Indicating relationships between documents

The W3C recommendations contain an HTML element which is hardly used by browsers: it is the `<link>` element. This element is placed in the document header and describes the relationships between the pages of a Web site. It was intended that browsers could use the `<link>` element to create contents pages and print a series of pages at once, rather than page by page.

- To insert link information use **Insert - Head - Link**.

  or click the **Insert Link** button on the **Head** panel of the **Objects** palette.

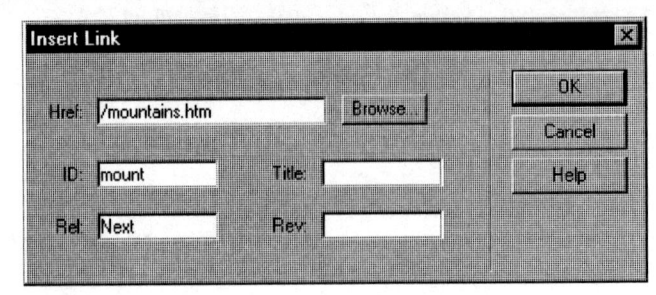

- Indicate the linked file in the **Href** text box.
- You can type a unique identifier for the link in the **ID** text box.
- The **Title** text box is for giving a descriptive title to the element.
- In the **Rel** text box, indicate the type of relationship between the current document and that specified in the **Href** box. You can enter:

Start	this refers to the first document in a series.
Next	refers to the next document in a series.
Prev	refers to the previous document of a series.
Contents	refers to the document containing the table of contents.
Index	refers to the document that gives an index of the current document.
Glossary	refers to a document that contains a glossary for the current document.
Stylesheet	refers to an external style sheet that is linked to the current document.

  You can give more types of relationship; visit the W3C site for more information (http://www.w3c.org).

- In the **Rev** text box enter the reverse relationship between the active document and the one given in the **Href** box.

Publishing a site

You can enter the same relationships as for the **Rel** text box.

- To see and edit this link information, click the **Link** icon in the header icon bar (**View - Head Content**) and use the Property inspector:

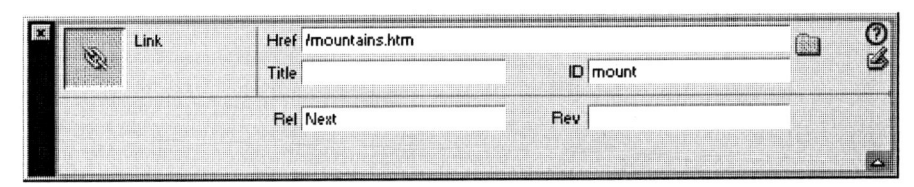

You will see a link icon in the icon bar for each link you insert. In the same document you can indicate links for the previous page, the following page, the contents page, the glossary, and so on.

Managing the site

Configuring the server

When you create a Web site you always begin by configuring your local site, which is the one on your computer. Once the site is ready, you need to publish it on a Web server. You will need to define the settings for the relationship with this server. If you are not connected to the server directly you can publish your site using FTP (File Transfer Protocol), and if you have a link over your company's network you will publish your site over your local network.

- To configure the server use **Site - Define Sites**.
- Select the site you want to publish from the list of sites.
- Click **Edit**.
- Choose the **Web Server Info** category.
- If you are using FTP to publish your site, choose **FTP** from the **Server Access** pop-up menu.

©Editions ENI - All rights reserved

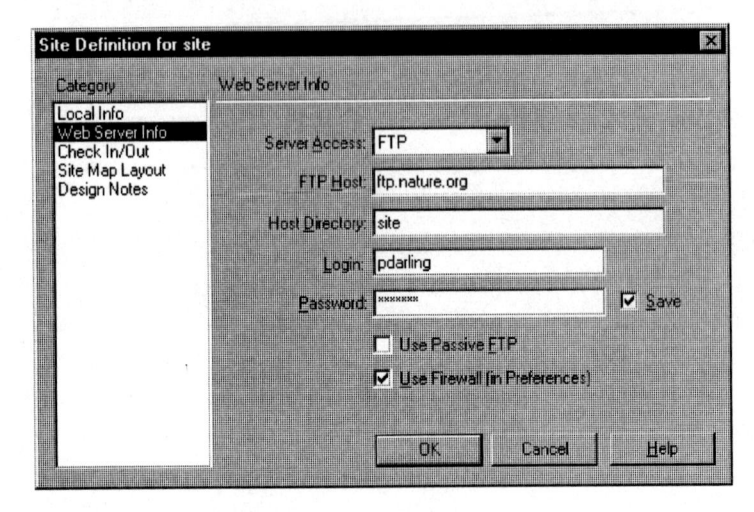

Dreamweaver 3
Publishing a site

- Give the server name in the **FTP Host** text box.
- Enter the name of your site's publication directory in the **Host Directory** text box. In general, this is the same name as the one used for your local site.
- In the **Login** text box enter the name of the person who has permission to publish on the server.
- Give the user's password in the **Password** text box.
- Activate the **Save** option if you do want to have to enter the password again.
- If the server is protected by a firewall, tick the **Use Firewall** check box.
- If the connection is established by your program and not the firewall, tick the **Use Passive FTP** option.
- If you are publishing on a local network choose **Local/Network** from the **Server Access** pop-up menu. 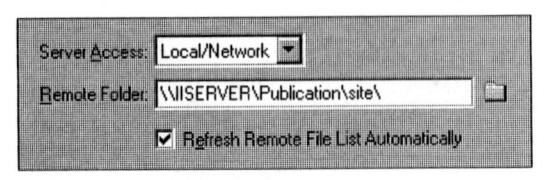
- Click the icon next to the **Remote Folder** text box to browse your local network and select the folder that is to contain the site.

© Editions ENI - All rights reserved

Publishing a site

◫ Tick the **Refresh Remote File List Automatically** option so that, whenever files are added or removed from the server, the file list in the **Remote Site** column in the Dreamweaver site files window is updated.

Managing the preferences

There are also some server management options accessible in the preferences.

◫ **Edit - Preferences - Site FTP**

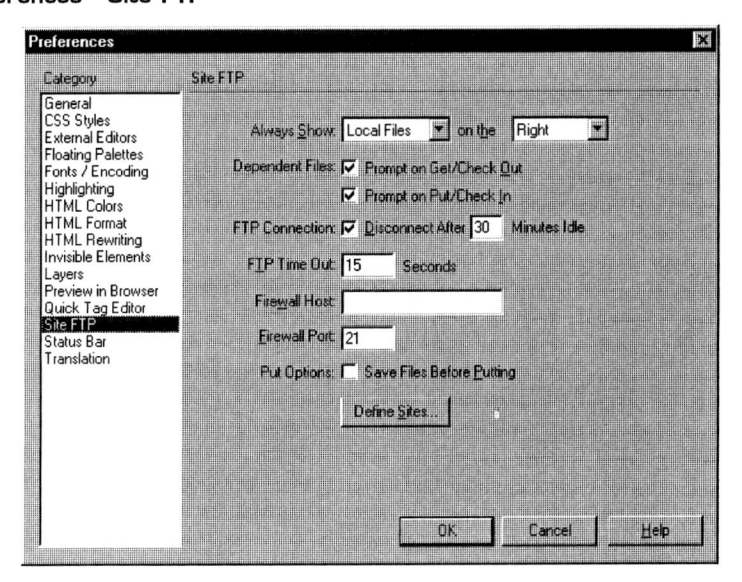

◫ In the **Always Show** pop-up menu you can choose to show **Local Files** or **Remote Files** on the **Right** or **Left**.

◫ If the two **Prompt** options in the **Dependent Files** (such as images, CSS-1 and movies) options are ticked then Dreamweaver will ask you if these files should also be published or got etc, when you publish or get HTML files that use them.

◫ Indicate the number of **Minutes Idle** under **FTP Connection** before you should **Disconnect**.

◫ Indicate the time delay after which up- or downloading should be cancelled if the FTP server does not answer in the **FTP Time Out** text box.

◫ In **Firewall Host** give the address of the proxy server used when you connect through a firewall.

©Editions ENI - All rights reserved

Dreamweaver 3
3.0.0 Publishing a site

- The **Firewall Port** text box gives the port used by the FTP server connection. This is usually port number **21**.

- In **Put Options**, tick the **Save Files Before Putting** check box so that unsaved documents will be saved before they are published, but no confirmation will be sought.

Using the site window

- Having configured the remote publication server, if you are in a document, go to the site window using **Site - Site Files** or press [F5].

    If you can see your site map then click the **Site Files** icon or use **Window - Site Files** to see the remote server section.

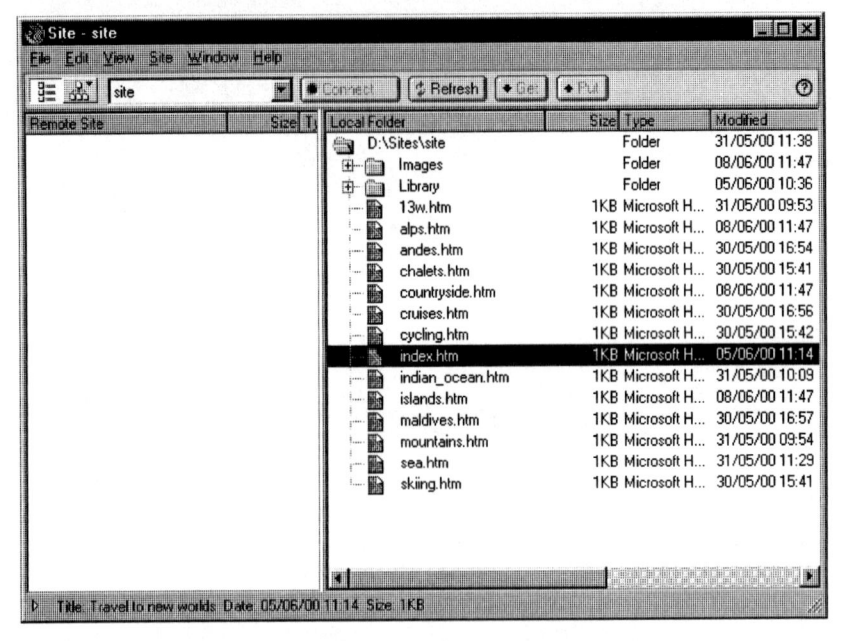

On the toolbar at the top of the window you can find a number of controls that can be used to manage your site: the **Connect**, **Refresh**, **Get** and **Put** buttons.

In the right of the window you can see a list of the files in your **Local Folder**, which is the folder on your computer.

In the left of the window is a list of the files in the **Remote Site**, which is on the Web server.

Publishing a site

Managing files

- If you are working on a site that contains a large number of files you would be well advised to arrange your files carefully so that they are easier to find. There are several solutions for doing this.

  The first solution is suited to sites that do not contain a vast number of files. You organise your site folder according to file types: one folder for images, one for movies, one for HTML pages and so on.

  The second solution is for files with lots of files. You can choose to organise your files according to topics, so you will create as many folders as there are topics in your site. In each folder you should place all the files that fall under that topic: HTML pages, images, style sheets, movies, etc.

  The third solution is for truly enormous sites, and involves a hybrid of the first two solutions in which you organise your files according to topic and type. If you have a subscription theme, you will thus have a subscription folder for images, a subscription folder for HTML pages, one for movies and so forth. Of course, you will need to name your folders carefully. For example, your subscription folder for images could be called subscription_img, and you could have subscription_HTML and subscription_mov folders.

- To create a folder in your local folder, in the **Local Folder** section use **File - New Folder**.

- To create an HTML file in your local folder, in the **Local Folder** section use **File - New File**. Name the file and do not forget the .htm extension.

- Move a file to a folder by dragging its icon onto the folder icon.

  If the file is referred to in another page, Dreamweaver will ask you if you want to update it:

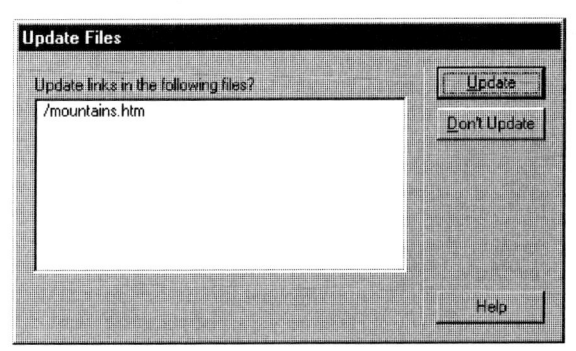

  According to your requirements click **Update** or **Don't Update**.

- To rename a file, click its icon and use **File - Rename**.

Dreamweaver 3
Publishing a site

If the file is referred to in another page, Dreamweaver asks you if you want to update it.

- To delete a file, click its icon and use **File - Delete**.

  If the file is referred to by another, Dreamweaver asks you to confirm the deletion:

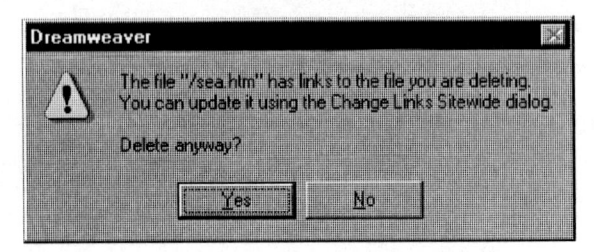

  > **Dreamweaver**
  > The file "/sea.htm" has links to the file you are deleting. You can update it using the Change Links Sitewide dialog.
  > Delete anyway?
  > [Yes] [No]

  If you are sure about the deletion click **Yes**, otherwise click **No**.

- To sort the files, either in the **Local Folder** or the **Remote Site**, click the header of the column you want to sort by:

  | Local Folder | Size | Type | Modified | Checked Out By |

  To sort in the inverse order, click the same column header again.

Publication

Accessing the server

If you are connecting to the server over your local network, access is immediate. If you are accessing via FTP, you need to connect to the server first.

- **Site - Connect**
- Click the [● Connect] button.

If you forget to do this, Dreamweaver will connect you automatically when you publish your site.

Publishing the site

- Select your site folder's icon in the **Local Folder** section.
- **Site - Put**

  or click the publication button [◆ Put].

  Dreamweaver asks you to confirm publication of the whole site.

- Click **OK**.

©Editions ENI - All rights reserved

Publishing a site

Dreamweaver asks you if you want to include dependent files (such as images, external CSS-1 and movies).

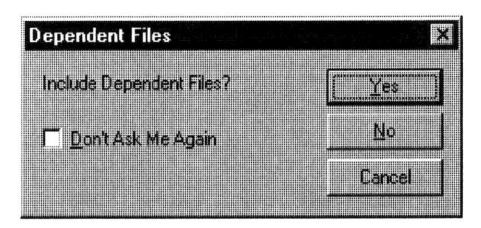

- When you publish the site for the first time click **Yes**.

    The whole site is published:

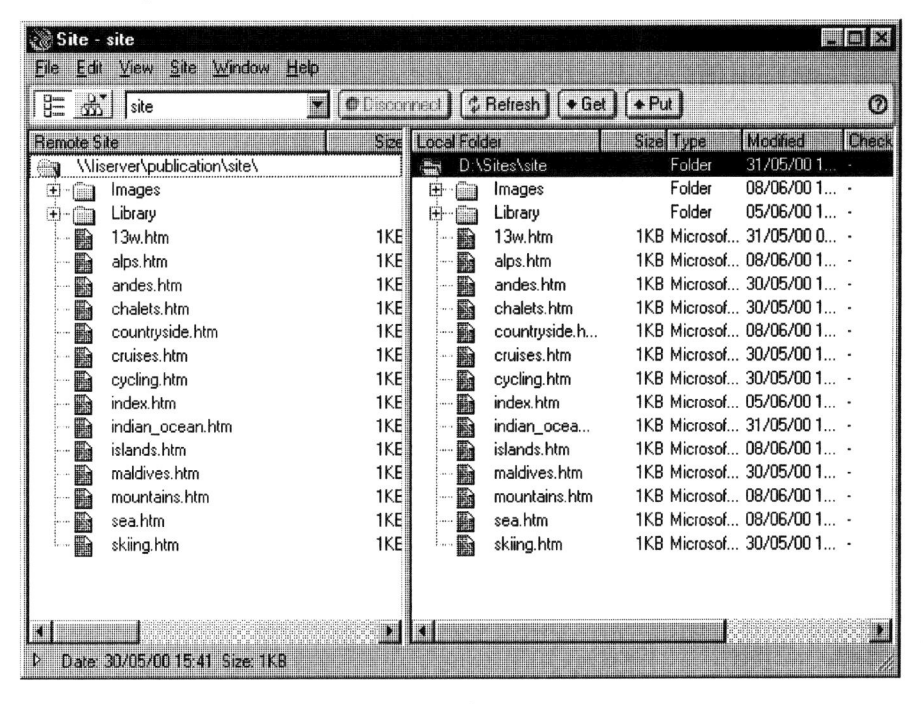

    *All the files are copied from the **Local Folder** to the **Remote Site**.*

- If you are working with an FTP connection, after you have disconnected, you can check the file transfer by looking at the log:

    - in Windows use **Window - Site FTP Log**.
    - in Macintosh use **Site - Site FTP Log**.

©Editions ENI - All rights reserved

Publishing files

After having published your site you might make changes to pages and add new ones, and so on. In this case you will need to update the files on the server.

- In the **Local Folder** file list, select the files that have been changed and any new files.
- Click the [Put] button.

Dreamweaver asks you if you want to include dependent files.

- If your new pages include images, click **Yes** and these images will be published with the HTML file automatically. If you have only changed the text in published pages, click **No**. Even if these pages contain images, they have not been edited and so it is unnecessary to include or update them on the server.

You can also publish files by dragging the files selected in the **Local Folder** to the **Remote Site** window.

Getting files

It is possible that some files might be edited on the server but not on your machine. If you are working in a workgroup, one of your colleagues may have updated a file on the server and you would like to recover this file on your machine.

- To get files via an FTP connection, establish the connection.
- In the **Remote Site** file list select the file(s) you want to recover.

You can check the publication dates.

- Click the [Get] button.

Dreamweaver asks you if you want to include the dependent files. Follow the same principle as before, depending on the case.
Dreamweaver asks you to confirm the replacement of the local file with the remote file.

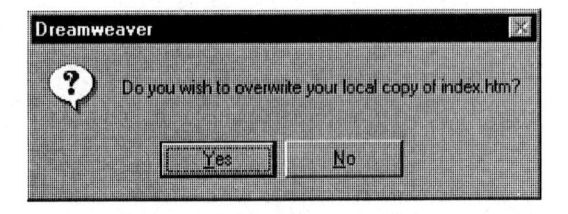

- Click **Yes**.

Publishing a site

As above, you can also get files by dragging the selected files in the **Remote Site** to the **Local Folder**.

Synchronising files

Having published your site on a remote server you can rapidly publish files, which have recently been edited in the local site on your machine, to the server. The synchronisation also works from the server to the local site.

*If you did not tick the **Refresh Local File List Automatically** check box in the **Local Info** category and the **Refresh Remote File List Automatically** check box in the **Web Server Info** category (only available for a local network), then it may sometimes be necessary to update the files in the local site and on the server manually.*

→ **View - Refresh Local** and **View - Refresh Remote**

or click the [Refresh] button to update both file sets (local and remote).

→ To start by checking the files you have modified locally, select your site folder in the **Local Folder** file list and use **Edit - Select Newer Local**.

Dreamweaver selects the files that have been modified most recently by comparing the dates of the files on the local machine and server.

→ Do the same thing in the opposite direction to see published files that are more recent than local files: select the site folder in the **Remote Site** file list and use **Edit - Select Newer Remote**.

→ Synchronise the sites with **Site - Synchronize**.

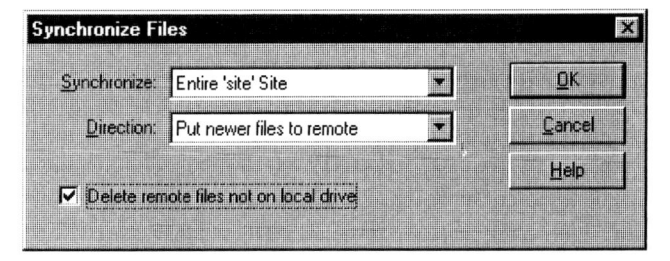

→ In the **Synchronize** pop-up menu choose:

Entire 'site_name' Site: to synchronise all the files in the site.

Selected Local Files Only: to synchronise only the files selected previously.

© Editions ENI - All rights reserved

Dreamweaver 3
3.06 Publishing a site

- In the **Direction** menu choose:

    Put newer files to remote: to publish files that have been edited locally on the server.

    Get newer files from remote: to recover files from the server that have recently been modified.

    Get and Put newer files: to update recently updated files on both the server and your computer.

- The **Delete remote files not on local drive** option is for deleting files published on the server that do not have an equivalent on the local machine.

    Dreamweaver makes the necessary comparison and shows the result:

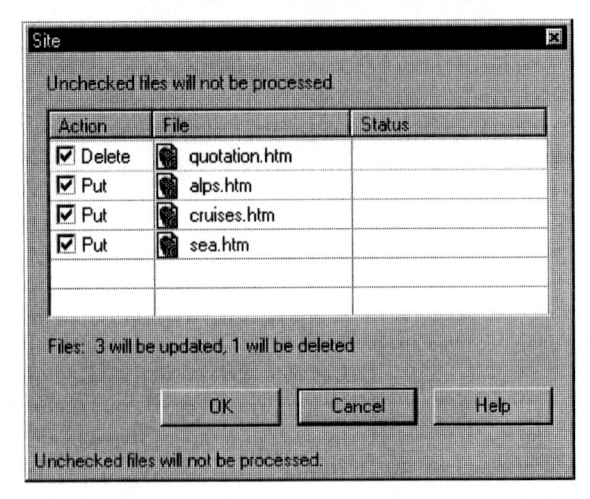

Action	File	Status
☑ Delete	quotation.htm	
☑ Put	alps.htm	
☑ Put	cruises.htm	
☑ Put	sea.htm	

    Files: 3 will be updated, 1 will be deleted

    Unchecked files will not be processed.

    In the **Action** column Dreamweaver indicates what will be done to the **File**. If you do not want Dreamweaver to carry out the action, deactivate the check box.

- Click **OK**.

Publishing a site

If you are deleting a file, Dreamweaver asks you to confirm.
*When the synchronisation is complete Dreamweaver, shows the results in the **Status** column:*

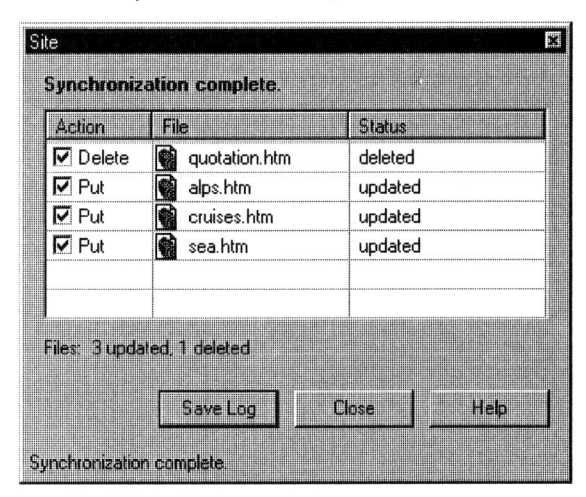

- If you want to save a trace of your updates click the **Save Log** button.

    Dreamweaver creates a .txt file in which these actions are noted.

Finding files

If the organisation of a site differs between the local folder and the remote folder published on the server it can be useful to be able to find the corresponding file in each folder.

- To find a file on the server, select the local file you want to find in the **Local Folder** file list and use **Edit - Locate in Remote Site**.
- To find a file in the local folder, select the published file in the **Remote Site** file list and use **Edit - Locate in Local Site**.

Dreamweaver 3
Publishing a site

Teamwork

Principle

When you are working on a big Web site project it is rare to be working alone. You will be working with a Web graphic designer, a programmer, an animation expert, and so on.

In addition to spoken communication, you can also pass information to your workgroup colleagues via notes that are associated with a page, or objects inserted into pages.

Any team member can work on the page, and when they publish it the other group members will be informed that it has been updated.

Design Notes

When several people are working on the same project it is useful to know things like where an image has come from, and whose responsibility specific changes to the script are, etc. You can make use of Design Notes to pass this information around. These working notes can be associated with documents or with objects included in a page, for example.

- To configure the Design Notes use **Site - Define Sites**.
- Select the current site and click the **Edit** button.
- Select the **Design Notes** category.

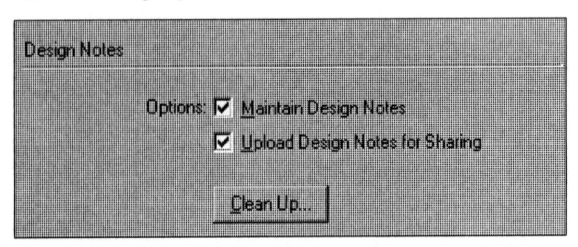

- Tick the **Maintain Design Notes** check box to activate the Design Notes.
- Activate the **Upload Design Notes for Sharing** option to share the Design Notes with your colleagues. When you put or get files, the Design Note is associated.

   The **Clean Up** button is for deleting orphan Design Notes that are not associated with any document.

- To add a Design Note to a document, open the file and use **File - Design Notes**.

© Editions ENI - All rights reserved

Publishing a site

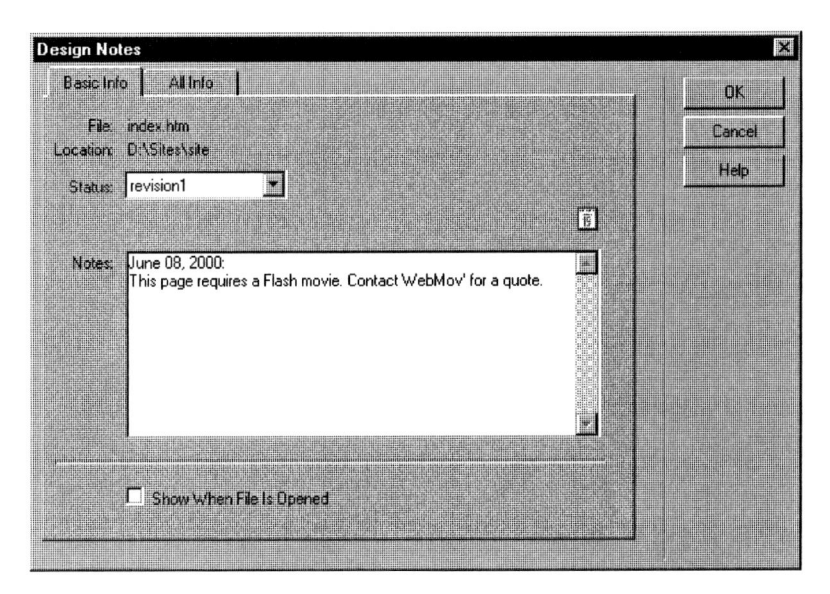

*In the **Basic Info** tab Dreamweaver gives the **File** name and its **Location**.*

- Choose a status in the **Status** pop-up menu (such as **revision** or **draft**).
- Click the **Date** icon to insert the note's date automatically.
- Type the necessary comments in the **Notes** text box.
- Activate the **Show When File Is Opened** option if the note is to open when the file is loaded.
- In the **All Info** tab, you can add extra information.

Dreamweaver 3
Publishing a site

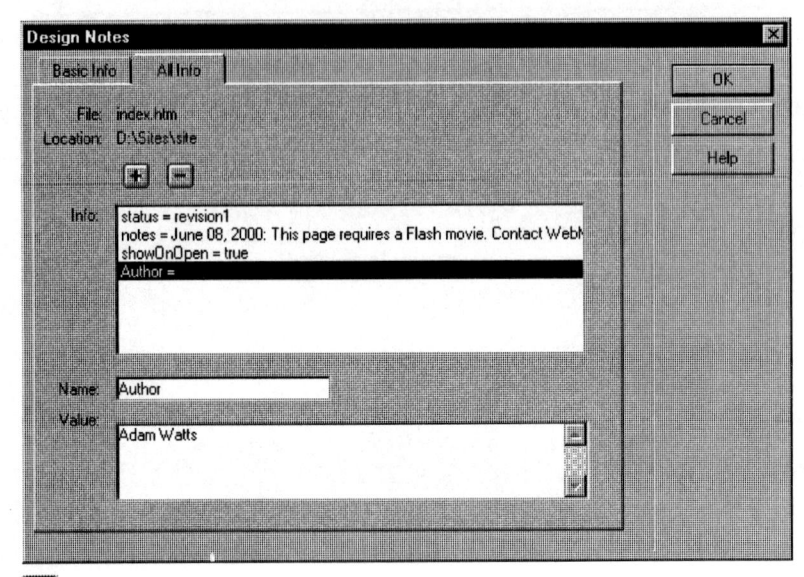

- Click the ⊞ button to add new information.
- In the **Name** box, type the name of the information, such as **Author**.
- Type the text of the information in the **Value** text box.

  All the notes are saved in a folder called _notes which can be found at the same level in the site as the file that contains them. The name of the notes file takes that of the file that contains it and has the extension .mno.

  For example, notes for the index.htm file: index.htm.mno.

- To add Design Notes to an object, select the object (such as an image).
- Use the context menu and choose **Design Notes**.
- Do the same as for a note added to a page.

  Notes associated with objects are stored in a _notes folder that can be found at the same level in the site folder as the object that contains them. The notes file name is that of the object's file name followed by the extension .mno:

  For example, this is the village.gif notes file: village.gif.mno.

- To delete a Design Note, open the file that contains the note. Open the **Design Notes** window via the **File** menu for documents, or the context menu for objects, then click the **All Info** tab and select the information and click the ⊟ button.

©Editions ENI - All rights reserved

Publishing a site

Working in a group

The check in and out facilities enable you to know who is working with each file and who has published files. It also gives you the possibility to lock sensitive files in read-only.

- To define the check in and out settings use **Site - Define Sites**.
- Select the current site in the list and click **Edit**.
- Select the **Check In/Out** category.

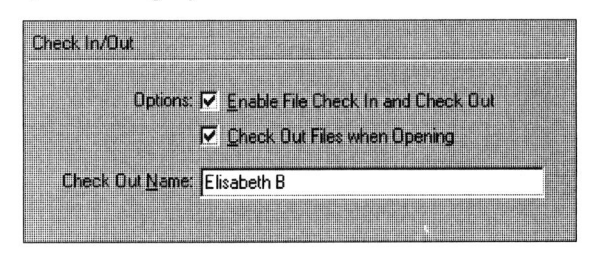

- Activate the **Enable File Check In and Check Out** option to enable group working.
- Tick the **Check Out Files when Opening** option if read-only files should be unlocked automatically when you double-click them to open them in the site map.
- Type the name that should appear next to the checked out file in the **Check Out Name** text box.

  *In the site window toolbar two new buttons appear: **Check Out** and **Check In**.*

- Put the files on the server.

  In the examples that will follow, two people will be working on the same site: Elisabeth and Peter.

© Editions ENI - All rights reserved

Dreamweaver 3
3.1.2 Publishing a site

First we will look at Elisabeth's work: she is looking at the files in her site. In the **Local Folder** list, there is no name under the **Checked Out By** column.

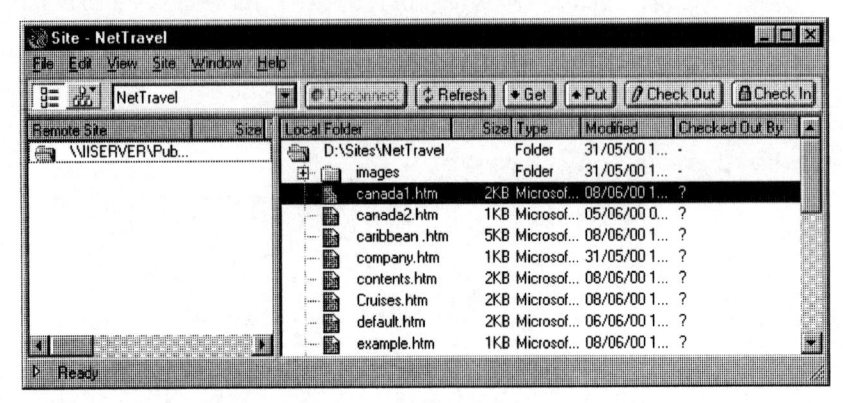

Elisabeth selects the local site folder and clicks the **Put** button.

The site is published on the server.

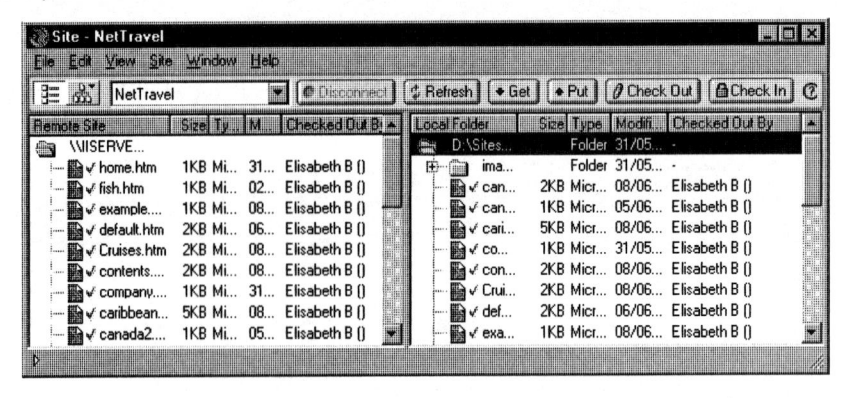

On the server and the local computer you can see the name **Elisabeth B** in the **Checked Out By** column, as she was the person who published these pages. The files are accompanied by a green tick.

©Editions ENI - All rights reserved

Publishing a site

Now we are going to look at another team member's computer, that of Peter A, who is working on the same site and has just created the file called australia.htm on Elisabeth's computer, where the site is managed:

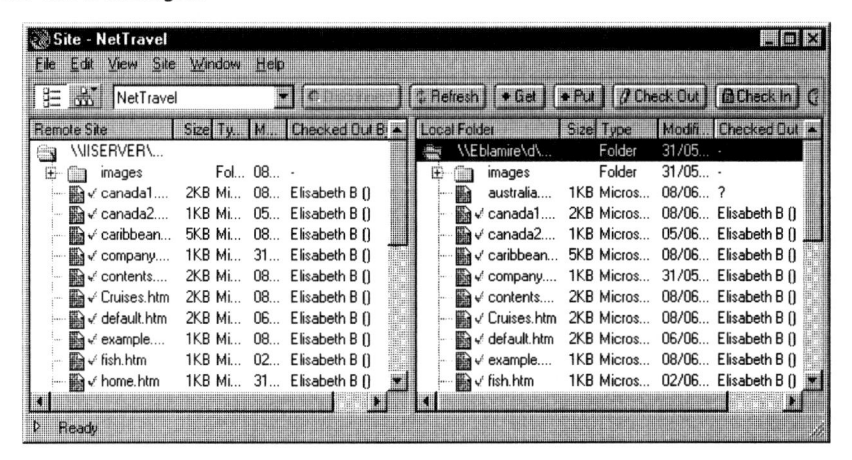

Peter sees the other files with a red tick because he did not create them. These files were created by Elisabeth, and her name is shown in the **Checked Out By** column. The author of the australia.htm file is not marked because it has not been published.

Now, Peter publishes the australia.htm file on the server:

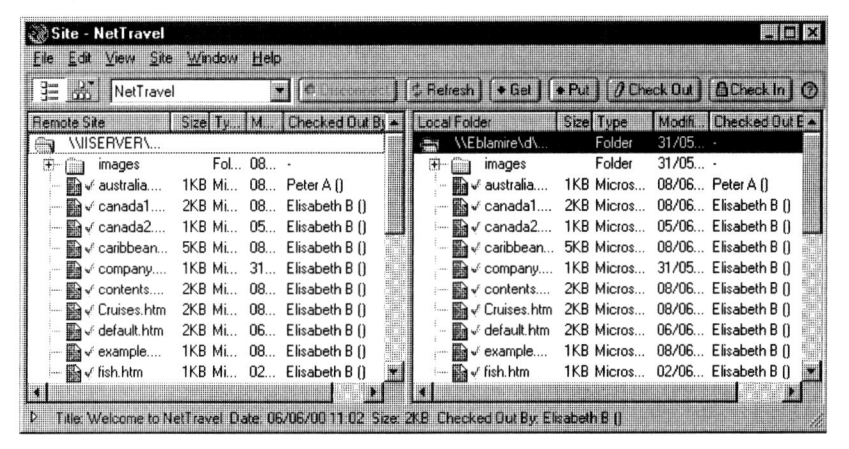

Dreamweaver 3
Publishing a site

On Peter's machine, the file he has created has a green tick and his name appears in the **Checked Out By** column. The opposite is true on Elisabeth's computer:

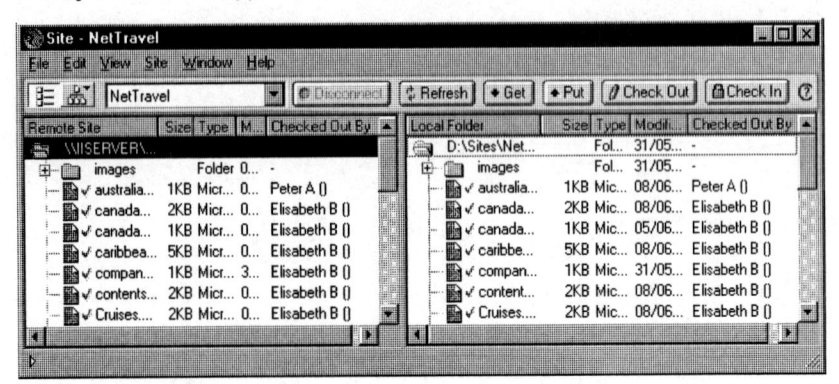

Now Elisabeth creates a new document called andorra.htm and publishes it. She also wants to signal that the file is "engaged" and that, because she is working on it, nobody should edit it. To do this she will check it in.

In the **Local Folder** pane she selects the file and clicks the [Check In] button.

The file is published on the server and a padlock symbol appears to the left of the file's name. In the local folder the file is automatically saved as read-only, but not on the server because Elisabeth created the document.

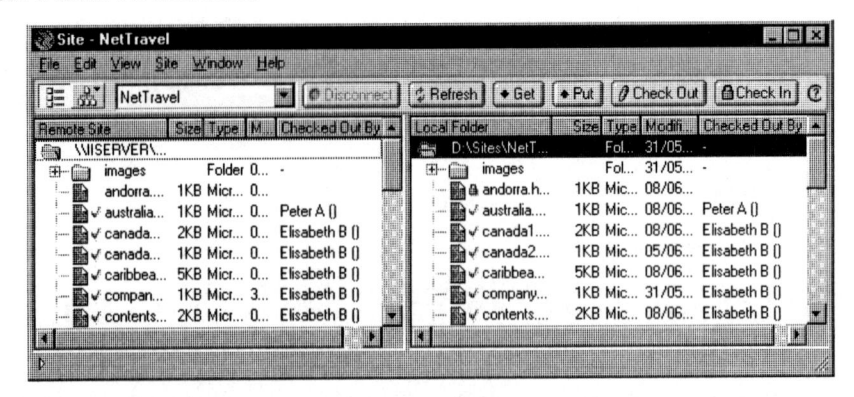

©Editions ENI - All rights reserved

Publishing a site

Peter's screen shows a similar scenario:

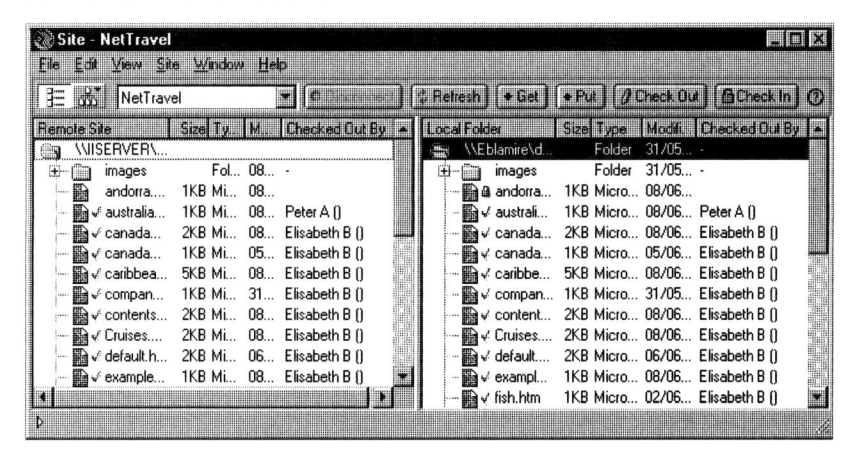

When Elisabeth double-clicks the file that is checked out, the read-only is deactivated so that she can edit the file. Once the file is saved it is no longer in read-only, and the padlock disappears.

The same goes for Peter: when he double-clicks the file it opens and the read-only is deactivated. As soon as he saves the document, the file is no longer in read-only.

In each case, the **Check Out Files when Opening** option is coming into play. This option is defined when the site is configured, in the **Check In/Out** category.

If this option is not ticked then, when a user wants to open a file that is checked in, and thus locked, a message appears:

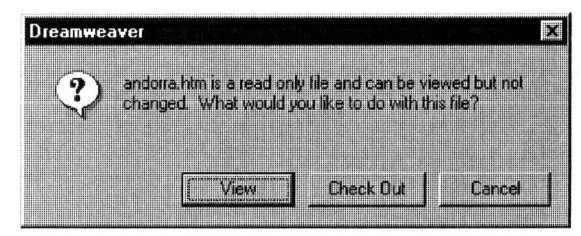

If the user clicks **View**, he or she can open the file and save his or her changes using the **Save As** command. If he/she clicks the **Check Out** button, the file can be edited.

©Editions ENI - All rights reserved

3.1.6 Dreamweaver 3
Publishing a site

The read-only facility is overridden if a user passes by the **File - Open** command. Once Elisabeth has finished working on the andorra.htm file she can make it available to other people in the group. To deactivate the read-only she clicks the `Check Out` button.

The padlock symbol disappears and the tick is green as Elisabeth is the document author.

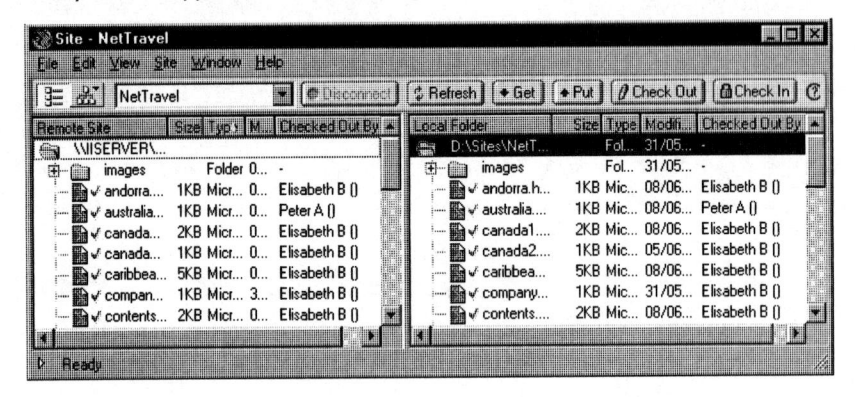

On Peter's machine the padlock has disappeared but the tick is red as he is not the document author:

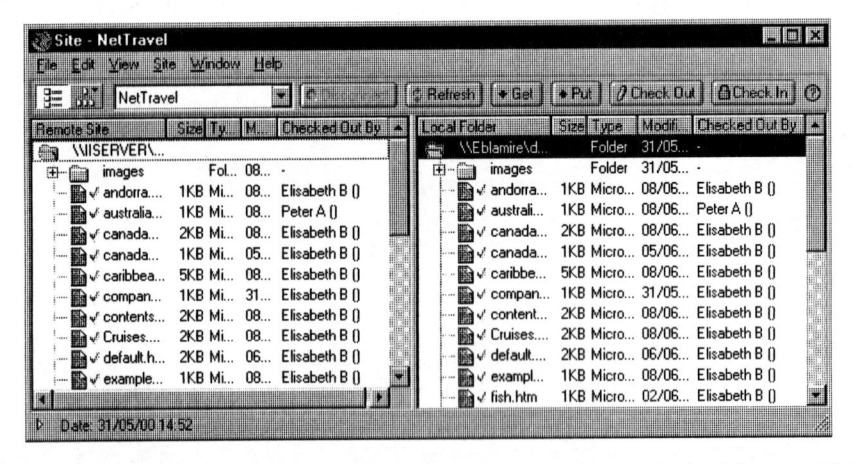

Imagine that Peter now creates a document and he checks it in (thus publishes it too): this file is read-only. However, Elisabeth can check it out and make it available to everybody. In this case the file is marked **Checked Out By** Elisabeth B.

©Editions ENI - All rights reserved

Publishing a site

If Peter now creates a file called kenya.htm and publishes it, without checking it in and Elisabeth wants to check it in, a message appears:

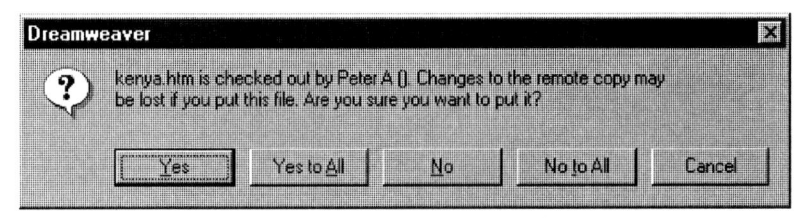

Dreamweaver asks if Elisabeth is sure that she wants to erase the version of the file that was placed on the server by Peter.

If Peter's Kenya.htm file is simply published (checked out) but not checked in and Elisabeth wants to check it out, a message appears:

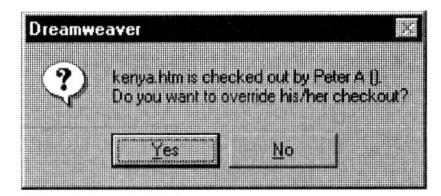

Dreamweaver asks Elisabeth if she wants to replace Peter's checkout with her own.

Customising Dreamweaver

The Objects palette

Principle

When you create sites in which the same elements are used again and again (such as the company's address, telephone and fax numbers, e-mail addresses, employees names etc), it quickly becomes irritating to type them out time after time. While the Copy/Paste function can be used it is not ideal. You can customise your **Objects** palette to add a button you can use to insert your formatted text by simply clicking the button.

Organising the Objects palette

All the items on the **Objects** palette are stored in the Dreamweaver/Configuration/Objects folder. This folder contains subfolders, which are in fact the different panels from the **Objects** palette: Frames, Characters, Common and so on.

Each button is associated with an HTML file, and possibly a JavaScript. The button itself is a `.gif` image, 18 pixels by 18. The button and the HTML file absolutely must have the same name.

You can create your own category by creating a subfolder in the Objects folder.

Creating an object

Below you can see how to create a button that will enable you to insert the address of a company.

- Create your personal category in the **Objects** palette by creating a folder called Custom, for example, in the Objects folder.
- Use graphics software to create a button that is 18 pixels by 18 and save it under the name address.gif in the folder you have just created.
- To create the object, open an HTML editor (such as BBEdit or HomeSite) and type the HTML code that should be inserted when you click the button.

For example:

```
<p><font size="3" color="blue"><b>My Company</b></font><br>
15 Castle Street<br>
Edinburgh<br>
EH3 IJA</p>
```

- Save this file under the same name as the button in your custom folder.

Customising Dreamweaver

To see the object in the palette in Dreamweaver you will need to open Dreamweaver to reload <u>the</u> extensions. If Dreamweaver is already open, hold down ⌘ (Macintosh) or Ctrl (Windows) and open the **Objects** palette context menu and choose **Reload Extensions**.

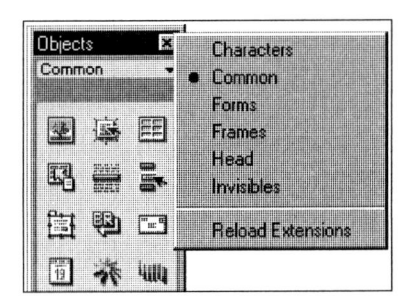

To use the object you created, choose your custom category in the **Objects** palette context menu (here it is called **Custom**).

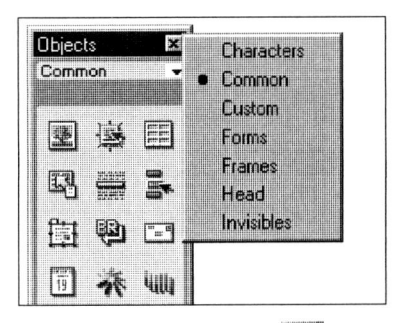

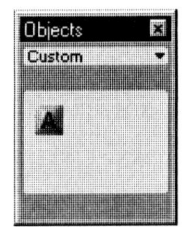

Click the button, here A.

The text is inserted automatically.

My Company
15 Castle Street
Edinburgh
EH3 IJA

The command associated with the new button can also be found at the end of the **Insert** menu.

©Editions ENI - All rights reserved

Dreamweaver 3
Customising Dreamweaver

Changing the Commands menu

Using the History palette

You have already seen that you can use the **History** palette to undo steps of your work. You can also use these steps to save sequences of work that you do frequently. These sequences are stored in JavaScript in the Commands folder in the Configuration folder, and are accessible via the **Commands** menu.

In the example below you will see how to create a new command from a custom format which you have created for a table.

- Open a new document.
- Show the **History** palette: **Window - History**.
- Insert a table and format it.
- In the **History** palette select the steps for the formatting by dragging:

- Click the **Save selected steps as a command** button on the **History** palette.

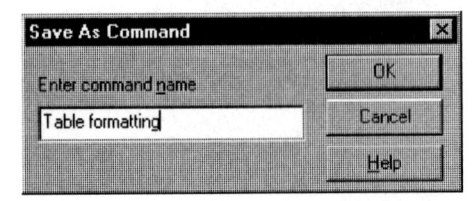

- Give the command a name.

©Editions ENI - All rights reserved

Customising Dreamweaver

*The command is saved and can be found at the end of the **Commands** menu:*

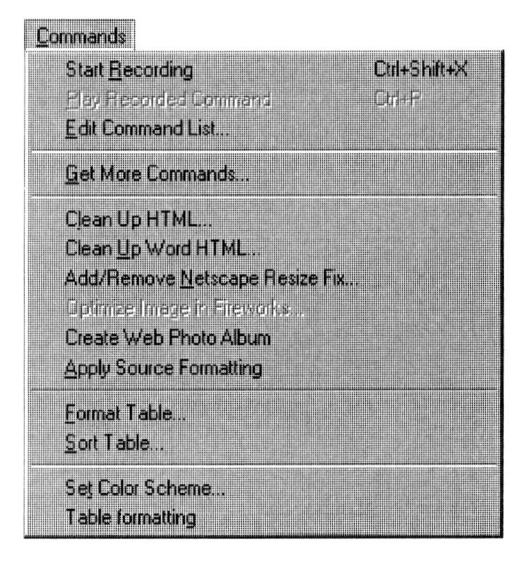

```
Commands
    Start Recording              Ctrl+Shift+X
    Play Recorded Command        Ctrl+P
    Edit Command List...

    Get More Commands...

    Clean Up HTML...
    Clean Up Word HTML...
    Add/Remove Netscape Resize Fix...
    Optimize Image in Fireworks...
    Create Web Photo Album
    Apply Source Formatting

    Format Table...
    Sort Table...

    Set Color Scheme...
    Table formatting
```

▭ To use the command, simply click the option after having selected a new table.
The formatting will be applied to this table.

▭ Open the **Table formatting.htm** document in the **Commands** folder:

```
<HTML>
<HEAD>
<!-- Portions Copyright 1999 Macromedia, Inc. All rights reserved. -->
<TITLE>Table formatting</TITLE>
<SCRIPT LANGUAGE="Javascript">
<!--
    // This command was recorded by Dreamweaver 3.0

    function runCommand()
    {
        // Set Attribute: cellpadding, 5
    dw.getDocumentDOM().setAttributeWithErrorChecking('cellpadding', '5');

        // Set Alignment: CENTER
    dw.getDocumentDOM().setAttributeWithErrorChecking('align', 'CENTER');
                                                                      .../...
```

© Editions ENI - All rights reserved

Dreamweaver 3
Customising Dreamweaver

```
.../...
            // Set Bg Color: #ccccff
    dw.getDocumentDOM().setAttributeWithErrorChecking('bgcolor', '#ccccff');

            // Set Attribute: bordercolor, #CC0000
    dw.getDocumentDOM().setAttributeWithErrorChecking('bordercolor', '#CC0000'

            // Set Border: 4
    dw.getDocumentDOM().setAttributeWithErrorChecking('border', '4');


    }
// -->
</SCRIPT>
</HEAD>
<BODY onLoad="runCommand()" >
</BODY>
</HTML>
```

You can change some of the parameters in this document.

Downloading commands

You can also download commands from the Macromedia® site. These will be placed in the **Commands** *menu.*

 Commands - Get More Commands

Or you can type the following URL: http://www.macromedia.com/software/dreamweaver/download/extensions/.

Customising Dreamweaver

Customising dialog boxes

You can change the appearance of dialog boxes for objects, commands and behaviors. These dialog boxes are created using an HTML form and JavaScript.

*To be on the safe side you should work in a copy of the file. In the example below you will see how to customise the **Insert Comment** dialog box. This is its standard appearance:*

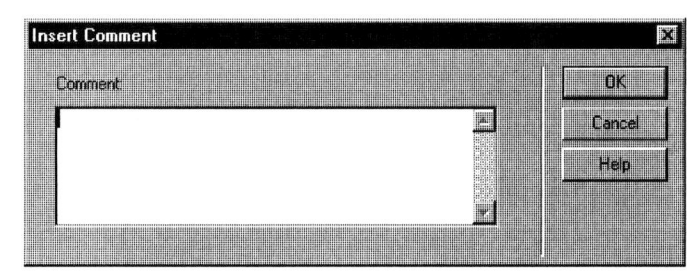

*The word **Comment** will be placed in bold and a short explanatory text will be added underneath the text box.*

- In an HTML editor (such as BBEdit or HomeSite) open the file that corresponds to the dialog box you want to customise. Here, open Dreamweaver/Configuration/Objects /Invisibles/Comment.htm.

Part of the code:

```
<script language="javascript"
src="Comment.js"></script>
<body>
<form name="theform">
   <table border=0>
      <tr>
         <td nowrap>  Comment:<br>
            <textarea name="comment" cols="60" rows="4" wrap="virtual">
            </textarea>
         </td>
      </tr>
   </table>
</form>
```

*You can see that the code refers to a script called **Comment.js**. The form called **theform** is made of a table with one row containing one cell.*

©Editions ENI - All rights reserved

Dreamweaver 3
Customising Dreamweaver

- To apply bold to the word **Comment** and add a new line, add this code:

```
<form name="theform">
   <table border=0>
      <tr>
         <td nowrap><b>  Comment:</b><br>
            <textarea name="comment" cols="60" rows="4" wrap="virtual">
            </textarea>
         </td>
      </tr>
      <tr>
         <td>
            <font size="2" color="red"><i>This comment will be visible only
            in the source code<br>
            and not in the browser.</i></font>
         </td>
      </tr>
   </table>
</form>
```

- Save the document.
- Open Dreamweaver and insert a comment in your custom dialog box:

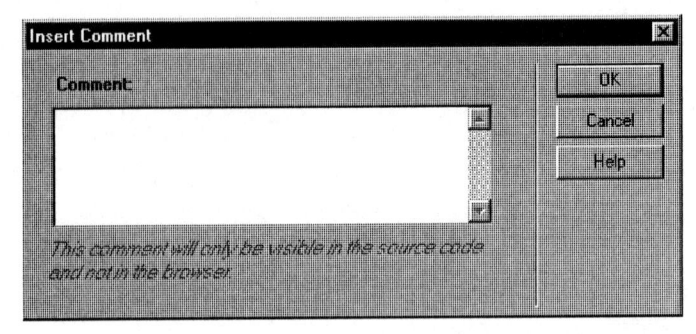

©Editions ENI - All rights reserved

Customising Dreamweaver

Customising the menus

Organisation of the menus

All the menus in Dreamweaver are defined in the menus.xml file in the Configuration/Menus folder. You can edit this file in order to add or remove commands from menus, change the names of the menus and commands, change keyboard shortcuts and so forth.

Be careful - you absolutely must try some tests in a copy of the file. Dreamweaver does have a backup of the original file called menus.bak. If you need to (having made an error) you can rename the menus.bak file as menus.xml.

Macromedia® recommends that you do not open the menus.xml file in Dreamweaver but in an editor (such as BBEdit in Macintosh or HomeSite in Windows).

In order to be able to edit the menus easily, it is necessary to know some XML. For more information about this language visit these essential sites:

- http://www.w3c.org/xml, the official site of the World Wide Web Consortium, and their pages about extensible Markup Language.
- http://www.xml.org, which is the principal portal for XML.

Menu syntax

There are several menu bars in Dreamweaver: one for open documents, one for the site window (only in Windows), and one for the context menus.

- Each menu bar is delimited by the `<menubar...>` and `</menubar>` tags.
- Each menu bar contains menus that are delimited by the `<menu...>` and `</menu>` tags.
- Each menu contains commands indicated with the `<menuitem.../>` tag.
- Each menu can also contain a separator, indicated by the tag `<separator/>`.

Customising Dreamweaver

Example:

```
<menubar...>
    <menu...>
        <menuitem.../>
        <menuitem.../>
        <separator/>
        <menuitem.../>
        <menuitem.../>
    </menu>
    <menu...>
        <menuitem.../>
        <menuitem.../>
    </menu>
<menubar/>
```

This example shows a menu bar that contains two menus. The first contains two items then a separator followed by two more items. The second menu contains two items.

Menu item syntax

Each menu item `<menuitem>` can have the following attributes:

name: this is the menu's name. This attribute is compulsory. The underscore character (_) precedes the letter that is underlined in the menu (the keyboard shortcut, which is only available in Windows).

id: is Dreamweaver's menu identification number. It too is compulsory and must be unique in the entire menu structure.

key: is the shortcut key. You can use:

Cmd	for the ⌘ (Macintosh) and Ctrl (Windows) keys.
Opt	for the ⌥ key (Macintosh).
Alt	for the Alt key (Windows).
Shift	for the Shift key for both platforms.
Ctrl	for the Ctrl key on both platforms.
+	is used to combine keys when a shortcut uses more than one, such as: cmd+shift+5. Special keys are named: from F1 to F12, and the arrow keys (→, ← etc), and so on.

Platform: indicates the command is for a specific platform: mac signifies Macintosh only, and win is for Windows only.

Customising Dreamweaver

If you do not specify a platform the command is active for both operating systems.

Enabled: is the name of a JavaScript function that indicates whether the item is currently active. If the function returns the value false the item is not accessible and is greyed out in the menu.

Command: is the JavaScript expression that runs when a user chooses this menu item.

File: the name of the HTML file that contains the JavaScript code that runs when the user chooses this menu item. For a complicated command you should use a `file` file rather than a `command` command. The `file` attribute has priority over `command`, `enabled` and `checked`.

Checked: is a JavaScript expression that indicates if a tick should appear in front of the item's name. If the expression returns `true`, the tick appears.

Dynamic: is the same as `file`. If it is present it indicates that a menu item should be created dynamically from an HTML file that contains JavaScript. This file will define the text and status of the item.

Example of adding a menu

In this simple example you will see how you add a new menu to the main menu bar (in the document window), which will contain two items.

The first item will add preset text to the document, and is a `command` type item.

The second item will open a dialog box in which the user can enter data, which will be formatted and entered in the document. This is a `file` type item.

Do not forget that you should be working on a copy of the menus.xml file!

Creating a command item

- For the first item, open the menus.xml file in BBEdit or HomeSite.
- The new menu is to be added to the main menu bar.
  First you need to find the appropriate character string:

```
<menubar name="Main Window" id="DWMainWindow">
```

- This is the main menu bar. The new menu is intended to appear in between the second last menu (`Window`) and the last (`Help`). You need to find this character string:

```
<menu name="_Window" id="DWMenu_Window">
```

Dreamweaver 3
3|2|8 Customising Dreamweaver

⇥ Now descend to the code that closes this menu:

```
</menu>
```

⇥ After the closing tag of the **Window** menu create your new menu, which you could call "Plus". Type this code:

```
<menu name="_Plus" id="ENI">
```

The menu here is called `Plus`. Its shortcut key under Windows is the letter P: `_Plus`. Its unique identifier is `ENI`.

⇥ Now you need to type this code to create the first item:

```
<menuitem name="JS _Bach" id="Plus-jsb"
command="dw.getDocumentDOM().setTextFormat('h3');
dw.getDocumentDOM().insertText('The life of Johann Sebastian Bach')"/>
</menu>
```

The item is called JS Bach: `<menuitem name="JS _Bach"`.
Its Windows shortcut key is the letter B: `_Bach`.
Its unique identifier is Plus-jsb: `id="Plus-jsb"`.
It is a JavaScript command type item: `command="_"`
The syntax inserts a level 3 heading:
`(dw.getDocumentDOM().setTextFormat('h3'))`, and the text:
`dw.getDocumentDOM().insertText('The life of Johann Sebastian Bach')`.
The `/>` symbolises the end of the menu item and `</menu>` is the menu's closing tag.

⇥ Save the menus.xml file.

⇥ Open Dreamweaver to see the result.

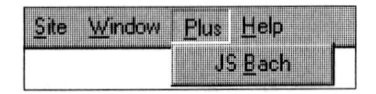

Site	Window	Plus	Help
		JS Bach	

⇥ Click the item you have created:

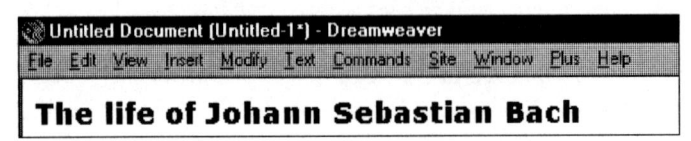

Untitled Document (Untitled-1*) - Dreamweaver
File Edit View Insert Modify Text Commands Site Window Plus Help

The life of Johann Sebastian Bach

©Editions ENI - All rights reserved

Customising Dreamweaver

Creating a file type item

*This item will run a script that is stored in a specific file. To keep the different menus separate, you should create a subfolder in the **Configuration** folder and save the script in it.*

- Open the **Configuration** folder in the Dreamweaver folder.
- Create a new folder. You could call it menuseni.
- To create the script, open an HTML editor (such as BBEdit or HomeSite) and type this code:

```
<html><head><title>Age script</title>
<script language="javascript">function age(){
var info=""info=prompt("How old are you?","")
dw.getDocumentDOM().applyFontMarkup('color', '#FF0000');
dw.getDocumentDOM().applyFontMarkup('face', 'Verdana, Arial, Helvetica, sans serif')
dw.getDocumentDOM().insertText('I am '+info+' years old')
}
</script>
</head>
<body onLoad="age()">
</body>
</html>
```

Explanation of the script:

You have created a function called age: `function age()`.

You have declared a variable called info, which is empty to begin with: `var info=""`.

A dialog box is opened in which the user must enter their age: `prompt("How old are you?","")`.

The user's answer is applied to the info variable: `info=prompt("How old are you?","")`.

You choose a Dreamweaver defined formatting of the colour red: `dw.getDocumentDOM().applyFontMarkup('color', '#FF0000')`.

You apply a Dreamweaver defined character format: `get.DocumentDOM().applyFontMarkup('face', 'Verdana, Arial, Helvetica, sans-serif')`.

The age given is inserted with another text, combined in a pre-programmed Dreamweaver function: `dw.getDocumentDOM().insertText("I am '+info+' years old')`.

You ask for this function to be loaded at the same time as the page, which is when the menu loads: `<body onLoad="age()">`.

Dreamweaver 3
Customising Dreamweaver

- Save this file in the **menuseni** folder and call it **howold.htm**.
- To place this item after the first one in the new menu, open the **menus.xml** file, find the item you just created, and add this code:

```
<menuitem name="Your _age" id="Plus-age"
file="menuseni/howold.htm"/>
```

The item is called **Your age**: `<menuitem name="Your _age"`
Its Windows shortcut key is A: `_age`
Its unique identifier is Plus-age: `id="Plus-age"`
It is a file type item: `file`
The howold.htm file is in the menuseni folder: `file="menuseni/howold.htm"`.

- Save the **menus.xml**.
- To see the result you need to open Dreamweaver.

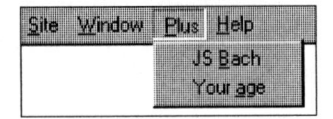

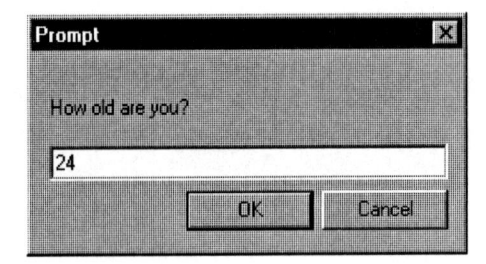

- Use the item you created: **Plus - Your age**.

- Enter a value and click **OK**.

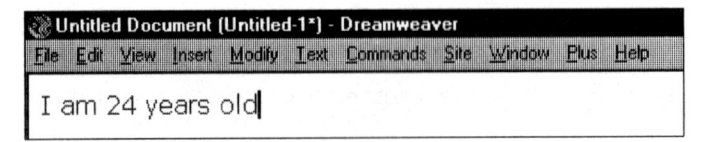

Customising Dreamweaver

Changing the menus

You can also change Dreamweaver's menus using a similar principle. You can create new menus with new items, remove items from menus, remove menus, change menu and item names, change the order in which menus and items appear, change the keyboard shortcuts, and so on.

All this can help you to create a Dreamweaver that is better adapted to the way you work, or the needs of a group of users.

Customising file types

Principle

When you use **File - Open** to open a file, Dreamweaver shows the **Files of type** pop-up menu. These extensions are stored in the **Extensions.txt** file in the Configuration folder of Dreamweaver.

You can customise this file to add extensions that you need in your work.

In the **Extensions.txt** file you should first indicate the different forms the extensions for a file type can take, separating them with a comma, then type a colon (:) and give a brief description.

Remember to work in a copy of the **Extensions.txt** file.

Adding an extension

🡒 Open the **Extensions.txt** file with a text editor (SimpleText or Notepad).

```
HTM,HTML,ASP,CFM,CFML,TXT,SHTM,SHTML,STM,LASSO,XML:All Documents
HTM,HTML:HTML Documents
SHTM,SHTML,STM:Server-Side Includes
XML:XML Files
LBI:Library Files
DWT:Template Files
CSS:Style Sheets
ASP:Active Server Pages
CFM,CFML:Cold Fusion Templates
TXT:Text Files
PHP:PHP Files
LASSO:Lasso Files
```

Dreamweaver 3
3-3-2 Customising Dreamweaver

- You could, for example, add this line of code at the end of the list to recognise files in the PERL language:

```
PL:PERL Files
```

- Save this file.
- Open Dreamweaver then use **File - Open**:

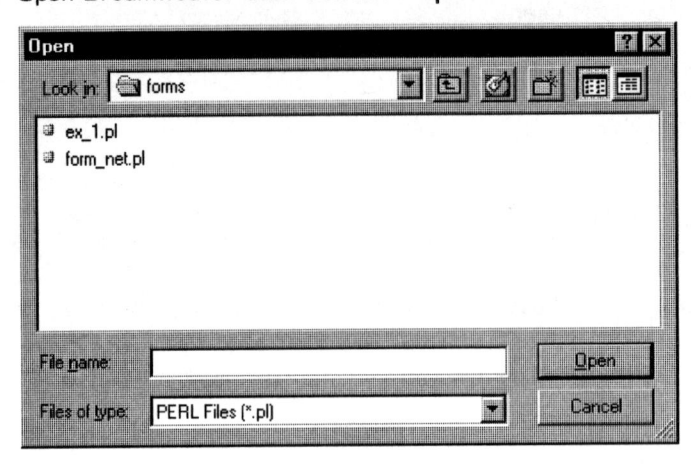

*The **PERL Files** type is available in the **Files of Type** list.*

Customising markup tags

When you want to create a complicated site that uses server-side data processing, you need to use a specific language: ASP (Microsoft® Active Server Page), PHP (Personal Home Page), ColdFusion (Allaire®) are some examples.

Dreamweaver needs to be able to see these markup tags in order to display them properly. These settings are stored in XML files in the Configuration/ThirdPartyTags/_.xml folder.

Example of an ASP.xml file:

```
<tagspec tag_name="asp"
  start_string="<%" end_string="%>"
  detect_in_attribute="true"
icon="ASP.gif" icon_width="17" icon_height="15">
</tabspec>
```

- When Dreamweaver comes across one of these tags, an invisible element is shown:

  Edit - Preferences - Invisible Elements category

©Editions ENI - All rights reserved

Customising Dreamweaver

- Tick the **Server Markup Tags** option.
- Make sure you can see the invisible elements: **View - Invisible Elements**.

    The ASP and PHP invisible elements are shown as: ▮ *and* ▮. *These icons are stored in the ThirdPartyTags folder.*

- You can use this principle to create your own server-side code profiles in an .xml file. Save this .xml file and its associated .gif file in the ThirdPartyTags folder.

Customising the source code format

Principle

In the chapter about optimising the HTML code you saw how to change the formatting of the HTML code that appears in the HTML Source inspector. These modifications are specified in the preferences, **Edit - Preferences - HTML Format** category, and are stored in the SourceFormat.txt file at the root of the Configuration folder. They are applied only once Dreamweaver has been restarted, and only to new documents. To apply the new source code formatting parameters to an existing document, you can use **Commands - Apply Source Formatting**.

You can choose the preferences or change the appearance of elements in the HTML source code by making changes directly in the SourceFormat.txt file. As always, remember to work in a copy of this file.

Customising the source code

- Open the SourceFormat.txt file with an HTML editor.

    The first section indicates the formatting specified in the preferences:

```
<?options>
<indention enable indent="2" tabs="4" use="spaces" active="1,2">
<lines autowrap column="76" break="CRLF">
<omit options="0">
<element case="lower">
<attribute case="lower">
<colors text="0x00000000" tag="0x00000000" unknowntag="0x00000000"
comment="0x00000000" invalid="0x00000000" object="0x00000000">
```

©Editions ENI - All rights reserved

Dreamweaver 3
3-3-4 Customising Dreamweaver

The second section shows the HTML element formatting:

```
<h3 break="1,0,0,1" indent>
```

This example shows that the h3 heading element has a line break `break`:
1: before its opening tag
0: not after the opening tag, the contents are just after
0: not before the closing tag
1: after the closing tag.

Example:

```
<p>Preceding text</p>
<h3>Text in the heading</h3>
<p>Following text</p>
```

→ Make the following changes:

```
<h3 break="1,1,1,1" indent>
```

You have inserted a line break after the opening tag and before the closing tag.

→ Save the SourceFormat.txt file, open Dreamweaver and create a new document with the same text as before, then open the source code:

```
<p>Preceding text</p>
<h3>
   Text in the heading
</h3>
<p>Following text</p>
```

©Editions ENI - All rights reserved

Customising Dreamweaver

Extending Dreamweaver's functions

Dreamweaver is an open application, which means that you can create your own commands, dialog boxes, property inspectors, floating palettes, and so on. In order to do this Dreamweaver has a JavaScript interpreter, an application programming interface (API) and a document object model (DOM). If you have a sound enough knowledge of these three fundamental elements you can extend Dreamweaver's functions using JavaScript or C.

To learn more about this programming, read the online documentation, which can be accessed via **Help - Extending Dreamweaver**.

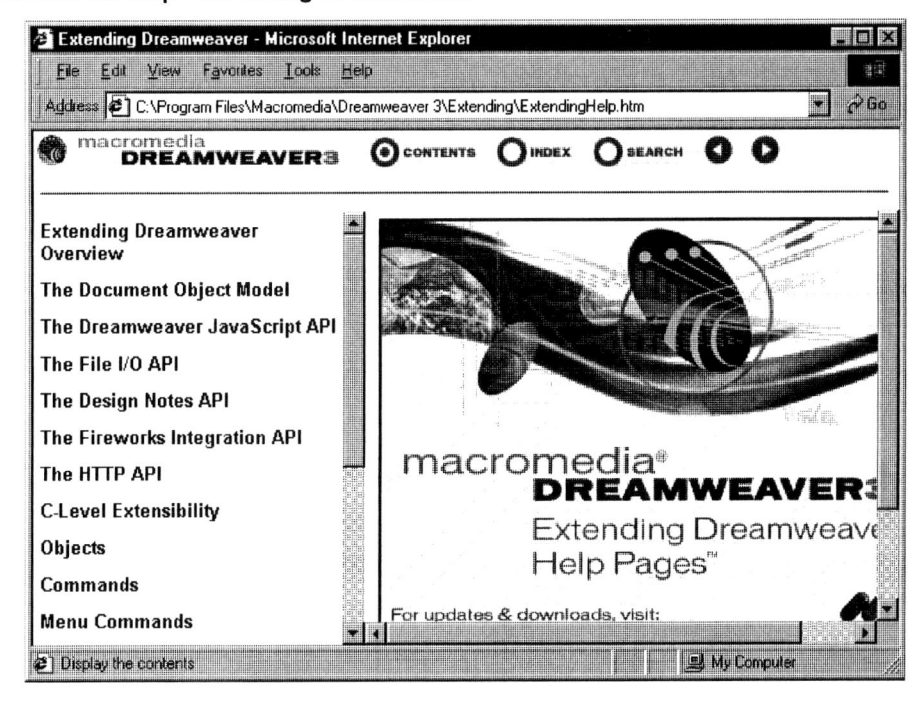

Glossary

ActiveX — component technology that runs on the client machine or the server. Microsoft® technology.

Applet — short application created using the Java language, which is linked to an HTML page. The Java applet is stored on the server and downloaded to the client machine at the moment when it is used.

ASP — Microsoft technology that can be used to create dynamic pages. For example, you can generate HTML pages using fixed text and variable data that come from a database search. The ASP code is inserted into the HTML file.

CGI — Common Gateway Interface. Switch between server applications and HTML pages (database access, form management, hit counters, etc). You can write CGI scripts in several languages.

CSS — Cascading Style Sheet. Defined by the W3C as a tool that formats HTML pages rapidly by separating the content from the formatting. CSS-1 generate page formatting for Web publication, CSS-2 are more complete and enable you to format HTML documents for a wider publication (on the Web, printing, vocal synthesis etc).

DHTML — Dynamic HTML. This is an association of scripts, HTML code and CSS that makes Web pages dynamic. You can create object movement, and change elements in the HTML page without having to reload it.

FTP — File Transfer Protocol. Used for downloading and uploading files between a server and a client machine (for updating a Web site).

Firewall — a security installation that allows users on a company's intranet to access the Internet, but blocks access to the intranet from outside.

GIF — image compression format, ideal for vector-based images, which flattens out the colours. The number of colours is limited to 256.

HTML — HyperText Markup Language. Programming language used to create Web pages that are interpreted by browsers: it is decreed by the W3C.

HTTP — HyperText Transfer Protocol. Communication protocol used for transferring Web pages from the server to the client machine.

Java — object-oriented programming language created by Sun. Java is used to create applets that can run on most computers.

Glossary

JavaScript	script language created by Netscape that can be used to make Web pages more interactive. The JavaScript is integrated into the HTML page.
JPG	image compression format ideal for use with photographs. The number of colours can go into millions (24 bits) and the creator of the image determines the compression rate.
Perl	Practical Extraction Report Language. Modular programming language used for manipulating files and exploiting data. Mostly used on servers.
PHP	script language inserted into HTML pages that enables the creation of pages dynamically.
Plugin	an application add-in which extends the functions of browsers that interpret only HTML and scripts. Plugins enable you to play videos, listen to sounds, and so on.
PNG	24-bit image compression format that enables you to access the more advanced aspects (gamma, alpha layer, etc). Current browsers do not recognise the format fully in its advanced form. See the W3C site: http://www.w3c.org/graphics/png.
Proxy	security element that isolates an intranet from the Internet using a by-user, by-content filter.
Referencing	using search engines and directories to promote a Web site.
Web server	a computer that manages HTTP, amongst other things, and that stores Web sites. Web users can consult these sites by connecting to the server using Web addresses (URLs).
SGML	computing norm for the creation of markup languages. HTML and XML are SGML applications.
Shockwave	Macromedia Flash and Macromedia Director exportation format for Web publishing.
URL	Universal Resource Locators. Addressing system for files on the Internet. URLs are what you use to connect to Web sites and the pages that constitute them.
W3C	World Wide Web Consortium. Group of the main players (researchers, industry representatives, software companies, etc) in the Internet, which decrees the different languages that can be used on the Internet (such as HTML, SML, CSS, and XSL).
XML	eXtensible Markup Language. Markup language used to exchanged structured data over networks.

Index

A

ACTIONS
Automating	13
Memorising temporarily	14
Undoing	12
See also EVENTS	

ACTIVEX
Inserting a control	113

ADDRESS
Automatic address refreshment	293
See also LINKS, PUBLISHING	

ALIGNMENT
Alignment for styles	165
Cells (tables)	82 - 83
Hotspots	191
Images	65
Layers	134
Paragraphs	28

ANCHORS
Displaying	179
Inserting	179
Naming	179
See also LINKS	

ANIMATIONS
Adding	147
Adding an object to a channel	147
Adding timelines	149
Behaviors	151
Copying	148
Creating	143
Deleting	149
Editing	145
Layer properties	146
Playing using behaviors	149
Previewing in a browser	144
Watching in the page	144
See also MOVIES, OBJECTS, TIMELINES, TIMELINE INSPECTOR	

APPLETS
See JAVA

B

BBEDIT
External HTML editor	274

BEHAVIORS
Accessing several frames	220
Animations	149, 151
Changing	248
Changing an object's properties	251
Changing the contents of a frame	222
Changing the text in a form field	257
Checking plugins	259
Checking the browser	261
Displaying a message	256
Displaying text on the status bar	258
Downloading	263
Example: a calculation form	249
Example: changing the background	251
Example: swapping images	252
Forms (inserting in)	102
Forms (validating)	102
Images (preloading)	73
Images (swapping)	71
Layers (changing the contents)	152
Layers (moving)	156
Layers (showing/hiding)	153
Linked to objects	122
Movies (controlling)	123
Opening a browser window	254
Principles	245
Several for the same object	248
Sounds (playing)	122
Using JavaScript	249
See also EVENTS	

BORDERS
Around an image	67
Colour of table border	80
Frame border colours	216
Frame borders (showing)	209
Tables	80

BRANCH
See also SITE MAP

BREAK
Creating a line break   28

BROWSERS
Checking (behaviors)   261
Checking compatibility with the code   289
Colour of text links   179
Defining the browsers   11
Layer compatibility   138
Selecting (events)   245
Setting the default character size   53
Setting the default font   50

BUTTONS
Links (creating)   189
Submit/reset buttons in forms   101

C

CELLS
Alignment (horizontal)   82
Alignment (vertical)   83
Background image/colour   84
Formatting   82
Formatting contents   86
Merging   87
Selecting   81
Splitting   88
Width/height (deleting)   81

CHARACTER SIZES
Absolute   51
Browser default size (setting)   53
Relative   52

CHARACTERS
Colour (default)   54
Colour (standard)   53
Encoding   23, 57
Font (applying)   48
Inserting special characters   27
Locution elements   46
Superscript/subscript   45
Traditional styles   45
See also CHARACTER SIZES, FONTS, STYLES

CHECK BOX
Initial state (setting)   95
Inserting (forms)   95

COLOUR
Cell background   84
Cell borders   84
Characters (standard)   53
Default page colours (defining)   22
Frame border colours   216
HTML code   264
In page background   21
Layer background   129
Of editable and locked regions (templates)   233
Of text links (in browsers)   179
Of text links (in Dreamweaver)   178
Style background   163
Table background   80
Table border   80
Text colour for styles   163

COLUMNS
See TABLES

COMMANDS
Changing the menu   320
Creating a command item   327
Downloading   322
See also HISTORY

COMMENTS
Displaying   287
Editing   287
Inserting   287

CONTEXT MENUS
Using   16

COPYING
Animations   148
CSS Styles   171
HTML styles   57
Sites   19
Text   26

CSS
See STYLE SHEETS

Index

D

DATE
- Inserting — 108

DELETING
- Animations — 149
- CSS Styles — 172
- Files — 302
- HTML styles — 57
- Library items — 230
- Link between a file and template — 240
- Links — 204
- Removing link with a library item — 230
- Rows/columns (tables) — 87
- Templates — 240

DESIGN NOTES
- Using — 308

DIALOG BOXES
- Customising — 323

DICTIONARY
- Editing — 37

DIRECTOR
- Inserting a Shockwave movie — 110

DIVISIONS
- Defining — 31

DOCUMENTS
- Applying a template — 235
- Creating from a template — 234
- File extensions — 15
- Opening — 15
- Opening locked files — 16
- Preparing for framesets — 218
- Restoring previous version — 12
- Saving — 12, 19
- Size and download time — 10
- *See also FILES*

DREAMWEAVER
- Description — 2
- Extending — 335
- Workgroups — 308, 311

E

E-MAIL
- Links to e-mail addresses — 188

EDITABLE REGIONS
- Creating — 233
- Entering information — 235
- Going to — 234
- Making non-editable — 234

EDITORS
- Images — 68
- Object editors — 107

ENCODING
- Characters — 23

ENVIRONMENT
- Description — 3

EVENTS
- Definition — 245
- Form field events — 246
- Keyboard events — 247
- Microsoft Internet Explorer events — 247
- Mouse events — 246
- Netscape Navigator events — 247
- Page events — 246
- Select the browser — 245
- *See also BEHAVIORS*

EXPORTING
- In XML format — 242
- Tables — 90

EXTENSIONS
- Adding — 331
- Extensions.txt file — 331

F

FIELDS
- Events — 246
- File fields — 98
- Hidden fields — 99

Index

Password fields 94
Validating in forms 103
See also FORMS

FILES
Checking in 311
Checking out 311
Creating HTML files 301
CSS 172
Deleting 302
Extensions 331
Extensions for saving Dreamweaver documents 15
Finding in the local folder or remote site 307
Getting 304
Inserting file fields into forms 98
Links (changing) 202
Moving 301
Playing plugin files 116
Publishing 304
Removing the link to a template 240
Renaming 301
Saving 19
Synchronising 305
Updating after editing the template 238
See also EXPORTING, EXTENSIONS, IMPORTING, LINKS, SITE MAP, TEMPLATES

FINDING
Formatted text 34
HTML code 276
HTML tags 278
Simple text 32
Tags 34

FIREWORKS
Creating a photo album 69
Inserting a Fireworks object 111
Using 69

FLASH
Inserting a Flash movie 109

FOLDERS
Creating 301

FONTS
Applying 48
Browser's default font (setting) 50
Character groups (creating) 49
Choosing for a style 162
HTML code 264
Owned 47
Substitutes 48
See also CHARACTERS

FORMAT
Image file formats 60

FORMATTING
Cell contents 86
Cells (tables) 82
Characters 45
Horizontal rules 58
Images 64
Layers 127
List bullets 39
List numbers 40
Pages in a frameset 217
Paragraphs 28
Saving as a style 54
Tables 79
Text links (in browsers) 179
Text links (in Dreamweaver) 178

FORMS
Check boxes (inserting) 95
Creating 92
Customising messages (validating) 104
File fields (inserting) 98
Hidden fields (inserting) 99
Hidden fields script 100
Password fields 94
Pop-up menus (inserting) 96
Principle 91
Radio buttons (inserting) 95
Scrolling lists (inserting) 97
Submit/reset buttons 101
Text fields (multi line) 94
Text fields (simple) 93
Validating 102
Validating at submission 102
Validating field by field 103

©Editions ENI - All rights reserved

Index

See also BEHAVIORS

FRAMES
Formatting	215
Selecting	215
Showing the borders	209

See also BEHAVIORS, FRAMESETS

FRAMESETS
Behaviors	220
Construction strategy	217
Creating	209
Formatting	213
Formatting the pages	217
Frameset-free content (defining)	219
Links	218
Predefined	212
Principle	208
Saving	212
Selecting	213

FTP
Links to an FTP server	189

G

GENERATOR
Inserting Generator objects	110

H

HEAD
<Meta> tags	292
Automatic address refreshment	293
Description	292
Keywords	291
Links base	295
Links between pages in the site	296

HEADINGS
Defining	30

HISTORY
Automating actions	13
Memorising actions temporarily	14
Principles	12

Using	320

HOME PAGE
Changing	199

HOMESITE
External HTML editor	274

HORIZONTAL RULE
Formatting	58
Inserting	58

HOTSPOTS
Aligning	191
Creating	190
Width/height (changing)	191

HTML
Description	1

See also HTML CODE

HTML CODE
Cleaning up	282
Cleaning up code from Microsoft Word	284
Customising	333
Editing	269
Errors (visualising)	276
External editor (defining)	274
Finding	276
Preferences	264
Replacing	279
SourceFormat.txt	333
Validating for browsers	288
Visualising	268
Why optimise the code?	264

See also TAGS

HTML SOURCE INSPECTOR
Customising	264
Using	269

HTML STYLES
See STYLES

HYPERLINKS
See LINKS

© Editions ENI - All rights reserved

Index

I

IMAGE MAPS
Creating	190

IMAGES
Absolute paths	61
Aligning horizontally	65
Behaviors	71
Border	67
Cell background	84
Creating a rollover	191
Document-relative paths	61
Editing externally	69
Editing in Fireworks	69
External editor	68
File formats	60
File paths	60
Formatting	64
In page background	21
Inserting	62
Layer background	128
Links (creating)	189
Low-definition	67
Photo album	69
Preloading	73
Properties	63
Root-relative paths	62
Spacing between image and text	67
Style background	164
Swapping (behaviors)	252
Table background	80
Title	64
Vertical alignment	65
Width/height (changing)	63
Wrapping	66

See also TRACING IMAGES

IMPORTING
Tabular data	78
XML	243

INSPECTORS
See HTML SOURCE INSPECTOR, PROPERTY INSPECTOR, TIMELINE INSPECTOR

ITEMS
Customising menus	326
File type items (creating)	329
Menu command items (creating)	327
Menu item syntax	326

See also LIBRARIES, MENUS

J

JAVA
Inserting applets	111
JavaScript (using)	249

JAVASCRIPT
See BEHAVIORS, JAVA

JUMP MENUS
Creating	185
Editing	186

K

KEYWORDS
Inserting	291

L

LAUNCHER
Display preferences	6
Mini-Launcher (showing on the status bar)	6
Using	5

LAYERS
Aligning	134
Attributes	131
Behaviors	152
Browser compatibility	138
Creating	126
Formatting	127
HTML element	125
Moving	133
Name	131
Nested	132

344 Index

Positioning	124
Preferences	133
Principle	124
Properties	146
Resizing	134
Ruler and snap feature	135
Selecting	130
Showing/hiding	131
Stacking order	128, 132
Style sheets	124
Timelines	142
Tracing images	140
Transforming into a table	136

LIBRARIES

Creating an item	224
Deleting an item	230
Editing items	227
Highlighting elements	226
Inserting a library item	226
Principle	224
Recreating an item	231
Removing a link with an item	230
Renaming items	229
Updating pages that contain library items	228
Using	224
Visualising	226

LINKS

Base	295
Changing all the links	203
Checking	204 - 205
Checking (in a browser)	207
Checking (in certain files)	207
Checking (throughout the site)	207
Colour of text links (in browsers)	179
Colour of text links (in Dreamweaver)	178
Creating in the site map	184
Default colour	22
Deleting	204
External links (creating)	188
External links (visualising)	206
In a frameset	218
In the same page	179
Internal links (creating)	180
Links between pages in the site	296

On images	189
Opening the source	204
Page to page links	181
Removing between a file and template	240
Removing link with a library item	230
Seeing broken links	205
To a closed document	183
To an anchor	183
To an open document	182
Types	178
Updating	201

See also ANCHORS, HOTSPOTS, IMAGE MAPS, NAVIGATION BARS

LISTS

Bulleted lists (creating)	38
Changing the type	43
Definition	38
Definition list (creating)	43
Formatting the bullets	39
Formatting the numbers	40
Identifying elements	44
Nested lists (creating)	42
Numbered lists (creating)	40

See also SCROLLING LIST

LOCAL FOLDER

See SITE

M

MARGINS

Creating in a page	23
For styles	165

MENUS

Changing	331
Changing the Commands menu	320
Customising	325
Example of an addition	327
Item syntax	326
Organisation	325
Syntax	325

See also CONTEXT MENUS, JUMP MENUS, POP-UP MENUS

Index

META
See HEAD, TAGS

MINI-LAUNCHER
See LAUNCHER, STATUS BAR

MOVIES
Controlling	123
Inserting	115
Inserting a Flash movie	109
Inserting a Shockwave movie	110

See also ANIMATIONS

NAVIGATION BARS
Creating	193

NESTING
Layers	132
Lists	42
Tables	89

OBJECTS
ActiveX control	113
Behaviors	122
Creating in the Objects palette	318
Date	108
Description	107
External editor	107
Fireworks object	111
Flash movie	109
Generator objects	110
Java applet	111
Movie	115
Netscape plugin	114
Objects palette	7
Playing plugin files	116
Script	117
Shockwave movie	110
Sounds	114

OPTIMISING
Images in Fireworks	69

PAGES
Background colour	21
Background image	21
Default colours (defining)	22
Encoding	23
Events	246
Formatting in a frameset	217
Margins	23
Properties	20
Templates	24
Title	21
Updating after editing the template	238
Updating pages that contain library items	228

PALETTES
Behaviors palette (using)	245
CSS Styles palette (using)	160
Customising	15
Display preferences	4
Frames palette (using)	209
History palette (using)	13, 320
HTML styles palette (using)	55
Layers palette (using)	127
Library palette (using)	224
Objects palette (customising)	318
Objects palette (organising)	318
Objects palette (using)	7
Templates palettes (using)	232
Using palettes in general	5

See also LAUNCHER, OBJECTS

PARAGRAPHS
Alignment	28
Creating	25
Definition	25
Indents	29
Spacing	28

See also LISTS

346 Index

PASSWORD
Inserting password fields (forms)   94

PATHS
Absolute paths   61
Document file paths   181
Document-relative paths   61
Root-relative paths   62

PHOTO ALBUM
Creating with Fireworks   69

PICTURES
See IMAGES

PLUGINS
Checking (behaviors)   259
Inserting plugin content   114
Playing files   116

POP-UP MENUS
Inserting (forms)   96

PREFERENCES
Choosing the language (spelling)   36
CSS Styles   176
Customising palettes   15
Default encoding   24
Defining the preview browsers   11
Editable and locked regions (templates)   233
Encoding   57
External editor (images)   68
File extensions for saving documents   15
FTP   299
HTML code colour   264
HTML code font   264
HTML corrections   285
HTML editor   274
HTML format   266
Launcher palette   6
Layers   125, 133
Library items   226
Number of actions memorised in the history   12
Object editors   107
Objects palette   7
Opening documents   15
Opening locked files   16
Setting the connection speed   10
SSI   121
Startup screen   15
Tables   77
Window sizes   9

PREVIEW
Animations in a browser   144
Previewing pages in a browser   11

PROPERTIES
Pages   20

PROPERTY INSPECTOR
Showing   8

PUBLISHING
Configuring the server   297
Files   304
Referencing your site   290
Site   302
Synchronising files   305

Q

QUICK TAG EDITOR
Using   270, 272

R

RADIO BUTTONS
Inserting (forms)   95

RECORDING
Commands   14

REPLACING
HTML code   279
HTML tags   281
Text   35

ROLLOVER IMAGES
See IMAGES, LINKS

ROOT
Site map	201

S

SAVING
Documents	12
Files as templates	231
Formatting as a style	54
Framesets	212

SCREEN
At startup	15
Description of the Document window	3
Size of the window	9

SCRIPT
Concatenation script	100
Custom messages (forms)	104
Inserting	117

See also JAVA

SCROLLING LIST
Inserting (forms)	97

SELECTING
A site	20
Cells/rows/columns (tables)	81
Frames	215
Framesets	213
Layers	130
Tables	79
Tags	268

SERVER
Accessing	302
Configuring	297

See also FTP

SHARING
HTML styles	57

SHORTCUT KEYS
Main shortcut keys	17

SITE
Cache (updating)	202
Change of address	293
Changing the home page	199
Changing the parameters	19
Copying	19
Creating a local site	18
Local folder	300
Principles	18
Publishing	302
Referencing	290
Remote site	300
Selecting	20

See also ROOT

SITE MAP
Branches	199
Creating links	184
Defining appearance	197
Dependent files	200
Displaying	197
Hidden files	200
Page titles (showing)	200
Refreshing	201
Viewing a branch	201

SIZES
See CHARACTER SIZES, DOCUMENTS

SOUNDS
Inserting	114
Playing	122

SPACING
Around a table	80
Between image and text	67
Between table cells	80
Paragraphs	28
Word/letter spacing in styles	164

See also WHITESPACE

SPELLING
Checking	36
Dictionary	37
Language	36

SSI
Creating	120
Editing	122
Inserting	120

Index

Principle	120
Showing (in a page)	121

STATUS BAR

Displaying text on the status bar (behaviors)	258
Document size and download time	10
Showing	9
Showing the Mini-Launcher	9
Size of the window	9
Tag selector	9
Visualising HTML code	268

STYLE SHEETS

Converting	288
Creating	160
Creating .css files	172
CSS preferences	176
Editing an external sheet	175
External	172
Internal	160
Layers	124
Linking .css files	174
Principle	160

STYLES

Applying	169
Converting	176
Copying	171
Custom Style (creating)	161
Defining	162
Deleting	172
Editing	171
HTML styles (copying)	57
HTML styles (creating)	55
HTML styles (managing)	57
HTML styles (sharing)	57
HTML tags (redefining)	161
Predefined HTML (applying)	55
Principle	54
Removing	171

See also STYLE SHEETS

T

TABLES

Background image/colour	80
Converting the units	81
Creating	75
Exporting	90
Formatting	79
Importing data	78
Name	80
Nesting	89
Preferences	77
Principles	74
Rows/columns (adding)	86
Rows/columns (deleting)	87
Selecting	79
Sorting	89
Structure	86
Templates	84
Transforming into layers	139
Width/height (changing)	81
Width/height (deleting)	81

See also CELLS

TAG SELECTOR

Description	9

TAGS

<Meta>	290
Character encoding	294
Customising markup tags	332
Finding	34, 278
For list elements	44
Redefining HTML tags	161
Replacing	281
Selecting	268

See also HEAD, HTML CODE, KEYWORDS, QUICK TAG EDITOR

TEMPLATES

Applying to a document	235
Applying to a table	84
Creating	231
Deleting	240
Editing	237
Example of XML template	241
Folder	232

Importing in XML	243		Page titles in the site map	200
Principle	224		**TRACING IMAGES**	
Renaming	239		Concept	24
Using	24		Inserting	140
See also EDITABLE REGIONS, TRACING IMAGES			Principle	140
			Using layers	141

TEXT

Copying/pasting	26		**V**	
Creating a line break	28		**VIEW**	
Default colour	22		*See ENVIRONMENT, PREFERENCES, SCREEN*	
Entering	25			
Entering in editable regions	235			
Finding	32		**W**	
Inserting special characters	27		**W3C**	
Preformatted (inserting)	32		Description	1
Preformatted (principle)	31		**WEB SITE**	
Spacing between image and text	67		Creation software	1
Whitespace: definition	25		Links to Web sites	188
Wrapping around an image	66		*See also SITE*	

TEXT FIELDS

Inserting (forms)	93 - 94		**WHITESPACE**	
			Definition	25
			Whitespaces in styles	165

TIMELINE INSPECTOR

Description	142		**X**	

TIMELINES

Adding	149		**XML**	
Description of the inspector	142		Description	240
Name	149		Exporting in XML format	242
Principle	142		Importing	243
See also ANIMATIONS, TIMELINE INSPECTOR				

TITLE

Defining the page titles	21
Image	64

▲ **Quick Reference Guide** ▲ **Practical Guide** ▲ **Microsoft® Approved**
▲ **User Manual** ▲ **Training CD-ROM** Publication

VISIT OUR WEB SITE http://www.eni-publishing.com

Ask for
our free brochure

For more information on our new titles please complete this card and return

Name: ....
....
Company: ....
Address: ....
....
Postcode: ....
Town: ....
Phone: ....
E-mail: ....

Please affix stamp here

ENI Publishing LTD

500 Chiswick High Road

London W4 5RG